WOMEN AND POPULATION DYNAMICS

WOMEN AND POPULATION DYNAMICS

Perspectives from Asian Countries

Edited by
K. MAHADEVAN

SAGE PUBLICATIONS
New Delhi/Newbury Park/London

First published in 1989 by
Sage Publications India Pvt Ltd
M-32 Greater Kailash Market I
New Delhi 110 048

Sage Publications Inc
2111 West Hillcrest Drive
Newbury Park, California 91320

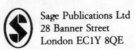

Sage Publications Ltd
28 Banner Street
London EC1Y 8QE

Published by Tejeshwar Singh for Sage Publications India Pvt Ltd, phototypeset by Aurelec Data Processing Systems, Pondicherry, printed at Chaman Offset Printers, Delhi.

Library of Congress Cataloging in Publication Data

Women and population dynamics: perspectives from Asia/edited by K. Mahadevan.
p. cm.
1. Women—Asia—Social conditions. 2. Fertility, Human—Asia. 3. Women—India—Social conditions. 4. Fertility, Human—India. I. Mahadevan. K., 1940-

HQ1726.W64   1989   305.42'095—dc20   89-34757

ISBN 0-8039-9615-2 (US)
81-7036-157-5 (India)

Dedicated to
Smt. Indira Gandhi

Contents

Acknowledgements

I have great pleasure in acknowledging the direct and indirect co-operation and assistance rendered by several persons from India and other Asian countries. Though it is difficult to mention everybody by name, I thank specially all the contributors to this volume. I also thank all the office-bearers of AFDAPS for their enthusiasm and cooperation in making this venture a reality. Dr (Ms) R. Jayasree and Mr Dominic E. Azuh rendered valuable and continuous assistance in processing the manuscript, Dr (Ms) M. Radhamani and Dr (Ms) Latha Thampi rendered editorial assistance and Mr N. Lokanadhan and Mr D.V. Chalapathi efficiently typed the manuscript.

K. Mahadevan

Preface

The proposal for this book, the second in a series, was conceived in 1985, when a few of us established an Asian Organization on Development and Population Studies (AODAPS). The need for a book on this theme was felt due to the paucity of literature in this field. Rapid control of high fertility and mortality and the speedy promotion of family planning programmes can make an important contribution to stimulating and strengthening all-round socio-economic development. For, improvement in the all-round status of women creates scope for speedy socio-economic development, better control of fertility and mortality leading to large-scale acceptance of family planning and, ultimately, a general improvement in the quality of life. Such sequential changes and improvement of the people and society at large can be more easily achieved by sharing the successful experiences of the people from the same continent, and the developing countries in particular.

A few countries in Asia have advanced considerably in the status of women and population control. The experience of China, Taiwan, Thailand and the state of Kerala in India offer fascinating insights and lessons for new models of development. Certain extremely under-developed societies in a few countries, and even in the developed regions of Asia can learn valuable lessons from such successful experiences to promote efforts to tackle this problem realistically and expeditiously. Certain experiences of the developed countries themselves are also bound to be valuable for Asians, though they cannot be fully adopted because of limitations of finance, cultural constraints, and the other factors of diversity among themselves. Therefore, though there is ample literature on the status of women in developed countries, its paucity regarding Asian countries hampers our efforts at sharing and pooling our own experiences that indeed are more relevant and feasible for the future development of women and of population control programmes. These compelling considerations explain the motivation for this book.

The concept of status of women came to international prominence after the United Nations organized a year-long and subsequently a decade of celebration to draw attention to the importance of women during the 1970s through the 1980s. However, the genesis of women's liberation movements date back to 1870, when the Married Women's Property Act was introduced in the British House of Commons by Russel Gurney. The issue gained more importance in developed countries only during 1900, when women got voting rights in Europe, though still not on par with men. Since then, progressive reforms were introduced in several European countries through the efforts of enlightened writers, social reformers, and politicians. Henrick Ibsen (1828–1909), the Norwegian dramatist who championed the cause of women focused attention on the political, social, moral and domestic suppression of women through his plays, *A Doll's House* (1879) and *Ghosts* (1881). Such candid expositions shocked the smugly complacent late nineteenth century society and awakened them to the imperative need to concede several legitimate demands of women.

Despite all intellectual endeavours, women have achieved only limited rights in several fields of life even today both in the developed and the developing countries. They do not enjoy equal rights of inheriting property or of voting. They are rarely allowed to take independent decisions on many issues, or to have higher education, to choose their life partners, to participate in several social, cultural, political and developmental activities and so on. These discriminations and the differential status of women depend on a country's level of development, religious composition and political ideology. Such factors differ among the developing countries themselves. In the light of these complexities, it was decided to consolidate at least the existing fragmentary and isolated literature on this neglected area of knowledge from as many Asian countries/regions as possible into a book.

Another compelling reason for bringing out this book was the growing realization that the status of women is a major determinant in socio-economic advance and control of population growth, particularly in the developing countries. Several empirical studies confirmed that improvement in several dimensions of the status of women reduces fertility, maternal mortality and childhood mortality, and promotes rapid implementation of family planning programmes. These demographic changes are linked to changes at many levels on the concept of status of women. Even today we are not fully aware of the many dimensions of this concept, how they influence it directly and indirectly, the order of importance of such dimensions and their type of relationship with the major parameters of population. This is, therefore, a pioneering effort to document the available literature on various dimensions of the status of women and to relate them with several vital events, including family planning, in order to get a country-wide and holistic picture of these factors from accessible parts of Asia.

Scholars who have defined the concept of status of women have done it differently giving differing emphasis to its specific dimensions. The term 'status' is used, first, to denote the access to resources such as economic, gainful employment and health services and, second, the position (power, prestige, authority) that a woman has in various situations. The term 'role' refers to the various activities that a woman performs in relation to her status in a given situation (Oppong 1980; Dixon 1978). Safilios-Rothschild (1982) defines the status of women in terms of the power they wield in the family and society. 'Thus, female power can be defined as women's ability to control or change other women's or men's behaviour and the ability to determine important events in their lives, even when men and older women are opposed to them.' But the overall status of women in different contexts may add several other dimensions to the meaning of this concept. This multi-dimensional and dynamic concept must be considered on a relative basis. It comprises dimensions like the importance of one's own legacy and achievements including money, property, materials, merits, privileges, access to resources, benefits, comforts, power and decision-making autonomy. Along with such roles and opportunities, progressive characteristics and achievements also indicate female status. All these may lead to efficiency and better quality of life of women in many spheres of society.

Most papers in this book commence with a historical account of the status of women, meaning of the concept of status in different situations, certain dimensions of status of women, its diversity and change over the years and the influence of status on various vital events and family planning. While certain papers are somewhat lengthy because of the complexity of this concept in certain cultures, countries/regions and availability of data, others are slightly shorter due to many inadequacies existing in several areas. However, the content more or less focuses on certain common features because of the identical guidelines given to the contributors by the chief editor. Many papers cover women's status in political, economic, educational, occupational and other social fields, and their influence on marriage, fertility and mortality. Certain papers could not cover all the aspects because of the paucity of data available in their respective countries/regions. Further, several salient aspects of the status of women as outlined in the conceptual model (Part III) could not be included, because it was evolved as an offshoot of the first two parts at a later stage. Part III is also based on the other existing literature. Therefore, it may guide future research and development of more comprehensive literature, policies, etc., in the years to come.

There is considerable difference among the Asian countries them selves with respect to the status of women and the levels of fertility, mortality and family planning performance. While the status of women is relatively better among most of the ethnic groups of Mongoloid population spread over several countries, it is by and large, much lower elsewhere. However, in many Muslim-dominated countries, the status of women is relatively low and their vital events—fertility and mortality—very high, and their performance in family planning programme poor.

The differentials in the status of women and demographic profile are highly conspicuous among several states within the union of India itself. While Kerala, Maharashtra and Punjab manifest better status among their women along with rapid decline and low level of vital events, eastern and central India including the south-central plateau (Madhya Pradesh) and Andhra Pradesh (South Central India) lag a great deal behind in all these areas. These differences are also noticed among different communities and between rural and urban areas. However, the existing literature is not sufficient to give any conclusive evidence on a cross-cultural basis from the Indian subcontinent or from other Asian countries. The papers presented here, therefore, highlight the urgent need for strengthening the data base, expanding the scope of investigation and interventions to improve the existing poor status of women in general.

The papers included in this volume provide much valuable information on the role of women, particularly on certain changing activities among the traditional groups and their relationship with a few population parameters. Major gaps still exist in the understanding of the diverse facets of the status of women itself and their relationship with several vital events and family planning behaviour. Since this is a pioneering venture on Asia and all Asian countries could not be covered in a single volume, certain limitations might exist in the present form. But it will stimulate further research in this field and may enable comprehensive consolidation in the years to come. When such efforts are made in future the people of diverse ethnic, cultural and religious groups of this continent can develop better understanding among themselves. It may also help in promoting an Asian identity with fewer crises, prejudices and conflicts, leading to the consolidation of a Pan-Asian solidarity.

This book is divided into three parts. Part I consists of eight chapters representing eight Asian countries: China, Thailand, Taiwan, Malaysia, Bangladesh, Pakistan, Iran and Kuwait. The selection has been narrowed down to eight from a dozen countries originally proposed, for want of suitable experts, or their poor enthusiasm from Indonesia, Korea, Sri Lanka and the Philippines. However, their exclusion does not affect the coverage of a major segment of population and their diversity from Asian nations. Ethnically, the Asian continent is inhabited by the Mongoloid, Australoid and Caucasoid population.

The countries represented in the eight chapters cover two or more samples of nations representing each of these major ethnic groups. Further, the larger and more populous countries with great diversity in culture, differences in fertility, mortality and different levels of development and acceptance of family planning have been included. These range from the most populous countries of China and India and the smallest ones like Kuwait, relatively developed countries in certain aspects like China, Kuwait, Iran and Taiwan, moderately developed ones like Thailand and Malaysia and the least developed ones like Bangladesh and Pakistan.

The differential demographic scenario also merges more or less with the differential development of the countries as classified above. While China and Taiwan have the lowest fertility, Pakistan and Bangladesh have very high birth rates and the other countries fall between these two extremes. They also represent diverse religious and political ideologies, namely Buddhist, Muslim and Hindu and communist, socialist and capitalist. Diversity can be observed in the status of women also. While the Chinese, Taiwanese and Thai women enjoy relatively better status on several dimensions, their sisters in other Asian countries have relatively low status, with the exception of certain isolated regions/small countries here and there, namely, Kerala in India, Sri Lanka and Singapore.

Part II covers the major regions/states in India representing the diversity in culture, differences in development, and demographic scenario. They are the most socially developed, modernized and demographically fascinating state of Kerala, followed by regions of western India like Maharashtra, Punjab and Haryana and the southern state of Tamil Nadu, which are industrially most advanced but not equally developed socially and progressive demographically. In addition, we have the culturally complex but economically backward region represented by West Bengal in eastern India.

The moderately developed southern region is represented by Andhra Pradesh, and the most economically backward region and demographically falling at the early phase of transition represented by Madhya Pradesh. In view of the tremendous diversity demonstrated in different regions of India, Part II allots greater coverage to this single major and diverse country. By and large the most extreme and moderate regions/states of this country have been presented in seven chapters. A summary picture of the country as a whole is given in the opening chapter.

Part III focuses attention on theoretical and methodological issues which are mostly intended for a sound understanding of this problem, both for the present and for the future. The incorporation of this part became inevitable because of the negligible consolidated and holistic theoretical-cum-methodological ideas now existing on the status of women in relation to population dynamics. Social science research in this field will not grow in the absence of such theoretical and methodological literature. All the research in this field has chosen factors randomly for study depending upon the background of the researcher and the availability of data.

Part III provides a comprehensive list of probably important factors that directly and/or indirectly affect the status of women in society, and also the population parameters. Depending upon the feasibility, appropriate factors from the list of analytical framework can now be chosen for sound studies in this field in future. The conceptual model additionally provides insights into the position of macro and micro variables, and their types of causal relationship, besides the broad holistic understanding of this problem. Specific studies may choose appropriate and relevant group of variables from the framework and conceptual model depending upon the ingenuity of the researcher and the characteristics of the population concerned.

The book, on the whole, will be valuable for getting a comprehensive picture of the differential development of women, and their changing demographic profile in most major countries/regions of Asia. It may provide much beneficial knowledge and information for these and several other countries in the developing world, to avoid the limitations of future planning and development of the status of women and population control programmes. This volume will serve as a source of reference and a textbook for scholars in Sociology, Population Studies, Home Science, Anthropology, Management, Social Obstetrics and Gynaecology, Paediatrics and Preventive Medicine. As the body of knowledge develops in this field, a subsidiary discipline on the status of women under Sociology, Home Science and Population Studies may emerge. And in the long run, an independent interdisciplinary subject on Women's Studies may evolve. A beginning in this direction has, in fact, already been made in many countries. The spread of this literature in course of time may also bring the Asian peoples closer to each other.

K. Mahadevan

I

WOMEN IN ASIAN COUNTRIES

Women in China Today

CHI-HSIEN TUAN

Of the many changes in a short span since the founding of the People's Republic of China in 1949, nothing parallels the profound progress in the general status of the Chinese women. Numbering 507 million at the end of 1985, Chinese women have been eulogized as 'half of the sky.' While their conditions have definitely improved, any suggestion that equality between the two sexes has been achieved would be misleading. To clarify the situation and present the real picture, a recollection of history is necessary.

The most conspicuous liberation of women is undoubtedly manifested in the bare fact that most women born after, say, 1950, have natural feet in contrast with women born earlier. The physical molestation and deliberate handicap of women is supposed to have started in the royal palaces over a thousand years back. Apparently it gave pleasure to the emperors and princes to see women with bound feet, for they felt women's beauty was enhanced if their figure was as fragile as a willow when walking and replicated the attractiveness of a new moon. But its widespread practice among the peasantry reflected the extent of insensitivity and tyranny built on patriarchy and male chauvinism, which had trodden on the 'half' of the sky' for thousands of years. Chairman Mao, in his revolutionary papers, exclaimed in exasperation that the feudal women bore one misery more than those they shared with their husbands—their complete subjugation to masculine authority.[1]

The feudal ethical code specified the qualities a woman must strive to have, and her mode of conduct. The basics include: 'The virtue of women is in them without intelligence,' and 'three obediences and four principles of ethics (three obediences: obedience to father before marriage, to husband after marriage and to son after husband's death; four principles of ethics: women's ethical quality, way of speech, appearance and skill.)' Chastity and loyalty were absolute essentials of a fine woman. The Chinese male ego had gone as far as to prompt the emperors to honour the virtues of chastity and loyalty in women even to the extent of bestowing a memorial archway to widows who un-disputedly demonstrated the virtues, and there was no lack of women who merited that honour. Such practices of encouraging widows to stay single had also the consequence of controlling the population which might well have been the underlying reason for its advocacy. In days when mortality was as high as 35 per 1000 population, only half of the people of an original cohort could survive to age 15, and 40 per cent to age 30. If young widows did not remarry, the birth rate could fall significantly, which might suit an unconscious demand of the society to check population growth.

The ethical code modelled the traditional woman to suit several important functions necessary for the sustenance and continuation of society. She was a domestic creature entirely responsible for house-keeping. But her labour had no economic value, and rarely any explicit socio-politico merit. She performed the role of a household manager, whereas all the responsibilities that the man handled had full recogni-tion for their politico-socio-economic significance.

This was the soil upon which woman's degrading status was nurtured. And it could only bear her a detestable destiny—a destiny women would rather shun. Thus a mother in old Hunan province, for example, while mourning her dead daughter offers her the following advice should she be reincarnated: 'Don't be reborn a chick or duck. Even a waterfowl is better off because it has fishes to eat.'

The ethical code not only confined her to domestic labour, but also defined her as a sex object and a reproductive machine. The sex role was intertwined with the virtue of chastity which fostered man's sense of possessiveness over woman and subjugated her to him. Chastity has been taken for granted for so long that it has lost its lustre. But for a woman to be without this virtue would not only be a great misfortune but also cause her husband's insanity, for this would drive him to do dreadful things. Traditional culture rendered the plight of a husband whose wife has had an affair most odious and a sobriquet was invented for such a man. He was referred to as wearing a 'green hat'. This was considered the worst disgrace a man could be subjected to. The shame of it could drive him to slaughter the 'lascivious' woman or the adulterous man, or both. History is full of such instances. Wu Song, the hero of a famous novel *Shui Hu Chuan* (*The Adventures on the Waterfront*), well exemplifies it. He avenged his brother's death on his sister-in-law who had been unfaithful to her husband. Not long ago, in Guangdong, the established punishment for an adulteress was to confine her in a bamboo pigcage. Masculine possessiveness has been so strong that to this day, it affects the sex relation of the men and women, and mating and marriage behaviour and is at the root of much social trouble and sex-related crime.

In the male-dominated feudal society, a woman was expected to bear sons. She was blamed if she failed to bear male offspring. Female infanticide became quite common.

A woman was expected to abide by the traditional ethical code and conform to the norm of a virtuous wife and a fine mother. Her identity and independence hardly merited attention. She was a commodity that was even transferable. The restrictions imposed on women were severe, and greatly affected their development. Even Confucius, the most famous Chinese Philosopher was biased against women: 'Villains and women can hardly be cultivated.'

However, social prejudice against women did not, and indeed could not, keep women's development strictly within the bounds of custom, and Chinese history has repeatedly produced, under such severe conditions, famous women of various types. In politics, generally regarded as out of bounds for women, Chinese women have always wielded considerable influence. The most successful woman was per-haps Wuzhetian (624–705 A.D) who usurped the throne of the Tang dynasty and became the first and the only powerful empress in China. Others were less luminous, but some were more admirable. In times of crisis, there usually emerged important female figures who rendered important services, which men found incapable of rendering. But the major reason for their success was almost invariably their sex. Thus, Xishi, whose name is now a byword for beauty, was presented to the King of Wu by the King of Yue in fifth century B.C. to undermine the former's strength. She succeeded, trapping him with her incontestable beauty, she misled him on the way to destruction.

Sex traps have often been successfully used to ensnare an enemy. The success of a sex trap depends, first, on the woman's grasp of the significance of the cause, her willingness and courage to make the sacrifice and skill to accomplish the mission. But the Chinese male tends to think that every woman poses a trap. Even the Chinese communists, who claim to be liberated from all the traditional pre-judice and are for the equality of the sexes, are indeed not so. Back in the Yenan days when Madam Jiang Qing applied to the Communist Party Central Committee for permission to marry Mao Zedong, her request was turned down by a few top leaders for fear that she might be a sex trap set up by the Kuomintang. When permission was finally granted, it was tagged with a condition that she should not meddle in Mao's political activities. The ambitious Jiang was kept in oblivion for many years until the late 1960s when she indignantly exploded the Party. No wonder that Jiang Qing, as soon as she had access to power in the years of the Cultural Revolution, acted very tough with those leaders who she said had oppressed her.

Sex traps were directly opposed to the moral code of chastity. But male dominance decided when and how the moral code could be waived and superseded for other considerations. Emperor Tang Ming Huang forced his son out of the marriage with Yang Yuhuan, and made her his Yang Guifei, the Noble Imperial Concubine. The Chinese have a horror of incest. If nobody at that time dared to criticize Emperor Tang, that is understandable. But it is extraordinary that in the 1200 years since his death, the Emperor's crime of incest has seldom been mentioned; in fact, it is probably known only to a handful of historians, though most Chinese can recount one or two events of this spicy romance.   Chastity, nevertheless, is to this day the major yardstick of a woman's respectability. To be called a loose woman is the worst abuse for a woman (and to a lesser degree for a man as well). A married woman who has strayed from marital fidelity even once is cast into an abyss of disgrace. In the past, a licentious woman was a disgraced outcaste, while a wayward male was treated much more leniently. In the novel *Jin Pin Mei*, Ximen Qing, the adulterer, is only occasionally pulled up for his evil waywardness, but Pan Jinlian, the adulteress, is all the time hauled over the coals. But things have changed a little today. A cadre usually would not be accused openly of adultery or other sex offences; but if he is convicted on some other account, adultery or even rape is only tagged on to the main crimes. The double standard remains to this day. Jiang Qing's conviction is evidence of this. She has been made a scapegoat for the ten years of turmoil from 1966–1976 in a clear instance of double standards.

Engels maintained that sex should be based on love,[2] but in the Chinese culture the traditional form of marriage precedes the personal experience of love. Any inclination to reverse this order had led to interference. During the transitional period, there were instances when an already married man or woman fell in love with someone else. Some cadres or partisans in a street committee or neighbourhood committee, who were essentially apologists, would break into a house suspected of illegal sex late in the night.

Official policy, nominally holding up the ethical code of virtue, intends to avoid confrontation with tradition. In cases of extra-marital sex, experience has taught the authority not to go against popular sentiment. Adultery with the wife of an army man is definitely a felony, and the adulterer is punished. This is for the protection of the servicemen. Things are well under control of the Party in time of peace, but during the early troubled years of the Cultural Revolution, factional struggle exposed a lot of sex scandals of some high ranking officials. One of them was Qui Huizuo, the commander-in-chief of the Logistics Department of the PLA, and a strong supporter of Marshal Lin Biao. Dazibao ('big-character wallpaper') listed many young women whom Qui Huizuo had exploited sexually. When once the mobs nearly killed him, his boss, Marshal Lin, sent his wife to rescue him in person. To save the reputation of the army, Lin set up the criteria of major and minor moral integrity for servicemen, sex being classified under the minor category. This classification saved a lot of high ranking officials and some cadres in higher positions. Although the Chinese Communist Party means to change everything, the ethical code of chastity overshadowed by male dominance basically remains intact. The public does not mention the romantic affairs of any cadres, who are thus protected while giving the appearance of maintaining the traditional code of sex virtue. Apparently the practice is more favourable to the male sex.

The result of this double standard has been to encourage adultery. And if it is felt that adultery may be more prevalent in urban areas than in the countryside where tradition has a stronger hold among the peasants, this is wrong. The author participated in a survey conducted in the early 1960s, when she found that in a village about eighty kilometres north of Beijing, instances of adultery had reached shocking levels. The weakening of the traditional code of sex ethics may not be the sole reason for this. The commune system had taken away all economic incentive and other interests from the peasants, turning life into a dull and dry mechanical routine. Sex seemed to be the only thing left with some flexibility. In the Cultural Revolution years 'the capitalist roaders' were thrown into the 'cow shed', that is, makeshift custody. When the enthusiasm of the Red Guards subsided in the later years of the Revolution, these people, many of them denounced by their spouses or despised by their children, were left to themselves in the 'cow shed', where many sought solace in the opposite sex.

Western influences have made the young question the value of arranged marriage with its emphasis on the parental command and the matchmaker to the total neglect of love and affection. Even if we accept that love could become an element of the arranged marriage, it is arranged in the wrong order, like putting the cart before the horse. With increase in social mobility and access to education, the interaction between the sexes has increased. The insistence of the youth on free choice and individual preference was a great challenge to parental authority and to patriarchy, and shook the feudal society to its base. Fifty years ago, many young educated men who joined the revolution and later became the ruling class, were more often than not driven to desperation by arranged marriage and went to Yenan to seek freedom of marriage.

Opposition to arranged marriage should in theory have been as beneficial to women as to men, but in actual fact the movement was dominated by men, and women had to bear the painful consequences. It was mostly the men's choice and preference which mattered. Being better educated and more mobile than women, men were emancipated first, while their wives were still left out in the old tradition. While men found new lovers and romance, the wives hardly knew what this was all about, and suffered in consequence. Chairman Mao was among the many revolutionary leaders who had such experience. Even after so many years, this painful transition has not ended. The experience is common today among rural peasants, who become mobile and get into better positions. Women are still not on an equal footing with men in the choice of marriage partners.

An analysis of the traditional status of Chinese women cannot be complete without a consideration of another important ethic—filial piety. The Chinese patriarchy subordinated women to men. But the filial ethic entitled the mothers as much as fathers to filial respect. The women's status in the family rose with age. This is typified in the Chinese classic *The Dream of the Red Chamber*, where Jai Mu, the grandmother of the family, represents the authority of the aristocratic family. If a woman could survive to the age of 40, her condition usually changed for the better and she could enjoy this change longer because of lower adult mortality of women. An old saying puts it: 'Many years' life of a daughter-in-law tortured her into grandmotherhood'.

Since 1949, many changes have come about in Chinese society, but the Chinese minds have not become broadened enough to accept equality of the sexes. There is a growing number of female intellectuals who want to emancipate themselves from the remnants of the traditional confines. The case of Liu Xiaoqing, a successful actress, is a typical example of the conflict between the archaic notions of man and the reasonable demands of a modern woman. Liu is a dedicated actress. Her role in the film *Yuan Ye* (The Open Country) required her to appear a little sexy. But being sexy runs against the feudal code of chastity, which hurt her husband's male ego. Like a traditional husband, he resorted to corporal punishment. This led to marriage breaking up. Before signing the divorce papers, her husband once again gave her a good beating to vent his spleen. A divorced Liu became the object of curiosity for many men and women and had to undergo their inquisitiveness and interference. In her autobiography, *Wo De Lu* (My Way), she observed: 'It is hard to be a human being, harder to be a woman, and the hardest to be a famous woman.' It was remarkable that a woman had the courage to title her book *My Way*, something unthinkable in a country where people were constantly being indoctrinated that their path was given by the Party, and that everybody should obey the Party and its leader. Of a billion Chinese, not one in the past thirty years had the courage to discard as junk the fallacies and declare that it is the people themselves who make their own way.

But Liu was not fighting for her sex as such, she was only fighting for herself. In fact, there is nobody who can make the claim of having fought for the entire womanhood in China.

Since 1949, everything has been under the control of a unified leadership. The Communist Party has incorporated the women's cause in its overall package of revolution. By law, women were supposed to have the same rights as men since 1949. The All China Association of Women, an official organization founded in 1949, is organized bureaucratically with branches all over the country. Being a part of the bureaucracy, it has never presented itself to the public with an independent platform, goals of long and short term, and means to achieve them. It subordinates itself to the overall political programmes and authority of the Party and the government. Although its existence is barely noticeable, its influence may sometimes be felt in the effort to protect the interests of women. It has succeeded in getting the legal age for marriage lowered, in blocking the passage of the proposed Planned Birth Law, which had been repeatedly debated since 1979 by the Standing Committee of the People's Congress with its demand for some flexibility in birth control laws, as well as others like marriage, divorce, complaints on ill treatment by husbands or in-laws, inheritance, etc. The Association reflects the personality of the Chinese woman. It works quietly and unobtrusively. Since the Party's priorities concern people as such, it does not mark the male out as the target for attack. On the whole, women work alongside men to improve their status and well-being.

Not all the Chinese women behave as gently and meekly as the majority appear to be, especially the post-revolution generations brought up in the urban areas. The Red Guards are loathed almost everywhere, but it is hardly known that the devastating movement of the Red Guards was started by young women. A high school girl, together with several schoolmates, wrote to Chairman Mao in 1966 asking if it was all right for her to organize the Red Guards to carry out the revolution. Encouraged by the man who was in supreme command, the Red Guards, like a spark in the prairie, set the whole country on fire. To many innocent people, the Red Guards were beasts and demons who gloated on bloodshed and torture. The worst of the lot often were a handful of women who outdid their male counterparts in cruelty. When a girl Red Guard, on behalf of all the Red Guards from all over country, honoured Mao with an armband on the rostrum of Tian An Men in 1966—he was reviewing them for the first time—Mao learned that her name meant 'gentle'. He then advised her not to be gentle but violent. This may have encouraged some women to demonstrate they could be more violent than men.

But it was also the femininity of women that touched the heart of the people to reflect on the insanity of the Cultural Revolution. This first came about in 1978 when a short story 'Shanghen' (The Scar), appeared on a wall paper at the campus of Fudan University in Shanghai. It told of a girl Red Guard who bitterly rejected her mother on reasons trumpeted up during the early period of the Cultural Revolution. When time sobered her down and age brought her maturity, she was remorseful. Now she yearned to meet her mother. She hurried home only to find her mother lying on her death bed. The story aroused great sympathy from the nation and set people reflecting on the course of the Cultural Revolution.[5]

Setting up offices of Women's Association everywhere is certainly a good thing, but its being an appendage of the Party deprives it of spontaneity and enthusiasm on the part of women to make efforts for the good of their own sex. Routine and a wariness about raising up controversy make the work proceed at snail's pace. The unbalanced conditions will therefore prevail for a long time to come. The conditions are generally better in the urban areas and educated women enjoy more freedom and equality than the less educated.

POLITICAL STATUS

Feudal China designated that women should look after internal affairs of the family while men took care of those outside it. Politics was out of their reach. Mao wanted this changed. He declared in 1939 that, 'The day women are aroused is the day when revolution wins its victory.'[4] Women were given suffrage and the right to be elected in 1949. On 6 March 1950 Mao said: 'The united front policy of suffrage should be that every Chinese who reaches the age of eighteen and is in favour of resistance and democracy should enjoy the right to elect and to be elected—irrespective of class, nationality, sex, creed, party affiliation or educational level.'[5] In the first election for the delegates to People's Congress held in 1954, among 1,226 delegates, 147 or 12 per cent were women. In the second People's Congress held in 1959, with the same number of delegates, the women's representation increased to 150. In 1964, when the third People's Congress met, 3040 delegates were elected; among them 542 or 18 per cent were women. The number of delegates for the fourth People's Congress declined to 2,885, but the number of women delegates rose to 653 or 23 per cent of the total. In 1978, the fifth People's Congress had, 3,497 delegates. Although the strength of the women delegates rose to 742, their percentage of the total declined slightly (21 per cent). In 1983 when the sixth People's Congress met, 2,978 delegates were present and 21 per cent of them were women.[6].

The proportion of women elected is by no means insignificant, but the impact of the People's Congress delegates is yet to be seen clearly. They mainly receive instructions from the central leadership rather than provide leadership to the central government. The people elected are mostly those who have kept themselves in line with the government's policies rather than be its critics. Being primarily workers, peasants and soldiers, it is doubtful if they possessed the ability to analyse the government's policies for constructive comments and suggestions. Even so, comparing with what women used to be before 1949, this change is of symbolic significance. The political status of women is now much better than before.

Real power rests with the Central Committee of the Communist Party. The twelfth Congress of the party, convened in September 1–11, 1982 in Beijing, elected 210 members for the Central Committee, of whom eleven were women, a bare 1 per cent of the total, and 138 alternate members, with twelve women or 9 per cent. Altogether, women accounted for 6.6 per cent of the full and alternate members.

The fact that the proportion of the alternate members was nine times as great as that of the full members demonstrates the Party's inclination to train more women for national leadership. The constituents of the Central Advisory ˈCommittee reflect the senior leaders of the years past. The twelfth Party Congress elected 172 members for the Committee. Among them only seven (or 4 per cent) were women. The Central Disciplinary Committee had 132 members, of whom thirteen were women. The most powerful organ of the Central Committee is the Central Political Bureau. The twelfth Central Committee elected twenty-five full members and three alternate members. Each had one female member.[7]

Regarding government functionaries, the situation of May 1982 may be taken to illustrate women's status in politics. There were ten members of the State Council, each with the status of vice-premier, and one of them was a woman. Among the 184 ministers and vice-ministers or their equivalents, six were women, which accounted for 3 per cent of the total.[8] The official policy is to recruit some women at all units and offices at every level. According to the 1982 census, 8 out of 16,206 leaders of the central government, 2,554 or 16 per cent were women. Of the 69,911 leaders at the level of government of provinces, 6,544 were women accounting for 9 per cent of the total. In governments at prefecture and county level, of the 808,793 persons who were in leading positions, only 5 per cent (41,844) were women. The proportion of women leaders was lower at the lower levels of government. This may have been because positions at higher levels of government require better qualifications, and fewer eligible candidates. Since better qualified women were relatively few, those who had the qualifications had better chances to fill the most important vacancies. So we find the proportion of women leaders at the central government level was 78 per cent higher than that at the provincial level, and 2.2 times more than at the prefecture and county level. The phenomenon was undoubtedly due to government policies of bringing up women cadres. And the influence of tradition that alienates women from politics was stronger at the lower rungs.

This is in a way true of urban and rural differentiations also because the influence of tradition is stronger in the villages. Women leaders in urban street committees numbered 6,131 or 22 per cent of the total. But at grassroot level of the urban areas, i.e., the residential committees, there were 83,831 women in leadership positions, accounting for 84 per cent of the total. But of 267,730 commune leaders (now Xiang heads) 4 per cent were women. Of the 1,720,639 brigade leaders (now village chiefs), only 2 per cent are women. Besides tradition, another factor is that in urban areas there is greater chance to absorb male labour forces, leaving the vacancies in street and residential committees more to women, who, not having many qualifications, are more readily available than men. Female leaders of enterprises and business units, which are mostly urban, totalled up to almost half a million, accounting for 9 per cent of the total.

In the communist party, women leaders at various levels numbered 67,224 or 7 per cent of·the total. Such mass organizations as the Communist Youth League, Workers Unions and Women's Association, had 127,300 women leaders, or 37 per cent of the total. As these organizations are closely related to the ruling party in order to implement party policies, the high proportion bears a clear mark that the ruling party instals more women in such positions so that they gain experience and training.[9]

All told, there were 844,223 women who headed an office or a unit at various levels, accounting for 10 per cent of the total. The conditions for women may not be ideal. But considering that this was incomprehensible only some thirty years back, the achievements are remarkable. The urban-rural differences also demonstrates that the best means to liquidate sex prejudice is development. Under a favourable and strong government policy of raising the status of women, development works to get rid of the sex prejudice left over by tradition, and provides opportunities to women to move up to positions of political significance.

Economic Status

Male dominance ensured that women were not qualified to be the head of the household. The most comprehensive work on the composition of family members for old China has been done by Professor Li Jinghan.[9] According to him, in Ding Xian, Hebei, in a sample of 5,255 rural families in 1930, there were only 211 female heads of families or 4 per cent of the total. None were married, and none of the males were spouses of the heads of families. This means that a married woman could not even nominally assume the title of head of the family. This may be due to the fact that she was originally from another family. In case there was no male in the family to be the nominal head, a young and unmarried daughter was named as the head even though the mother looked after the house.[10] Concubinage was negligible. Data from Ding Xian (1930) and South China (1930) show that in terms of number of persons per household head, there were 0.004 concubines in Ding Xian and 0.01 in South China. As the mean number of persons per family was 5.83 for Ding Xian and 5.03 for South China, the percentage of concubines in the total number of family was 0.1 for the former and 0.2 for the latter.[11]

Modern China, however, accepts the phenomenon of females as heads of households. According to the data of 1982 one per thousand fertility survey, in Hebei where Ding Xian is located, 15 per cent of the rural families and 28 per cent in the urban areas were headed by females.

The figures for Fujian, which may be considered part of South China, were 12 per cent and 35 per cent, respectively. In Liaoning in north-east China, the respective figures were 16 per cent and 23 per cent.[11] Data from the pilot census of 1980 for Wuxi City show that 44 per cent of the households were headed by women, and 28 per cent in Wuxi County.[12]

The Marriage Law, passed in 1980, allows children to take either their father's or mother's family name.[13] This had dealt a heavy blow to the system of patriarchy. The family name used to be something sacred in ancestor worshipping feudal China. Now many cadres have adopted this practice. Li Na, Chairman Mao's daughter from Jiang Qing, assumed her mother's original family name. Another daughter from his first wife, Ho Zizhen, also took Jiang's family name and bears the name Li Min.

The most sweeping change in the Chinese woman's status comes from the fact that almost all women of working age are employed. The census returns of 1982 (Table 1) reveal that 71 per cent of women in the age group of 15- plus or 231 million were economically active and 70 per cent were employed. Of the remaining 29 per cent, 21 per cent of the total were household workers, 3 per cent students, one per cent retired workers (this is because retirement plans have hardly reached women), and about 11.5 million or 4 per cent 'others', which may mean women who were either old and childless or handicapped. The Chinese female labour force, at 228 million, is the single largest army of working women in the world. Before 1949 rural women in the north seldom worked on the farm, and in 1949, female industrial workers accounted for only 7 per cent of the total workers.[14] But by 1983, they increased to 32 per cent of the state-employed workers.[15] The employment rate 70 per cent is the highest for women in the world,

TABLE 1
Percentage of Chinese Women by Age at Various Socio-Economic Status, 1982

Age (1)	Economically Active		Economically Inactive				
	Employment (2)	In Labour Force (3)	Total (4)	Student (5)	Household Worker (6)	Retirement (7)	Others (8)
15-19	0.78	0.80	20	16	4	—	—
20-24	0.90	0.91	9	1	8	—	—
25-29	0.89	0.89	11	—	11	—	—
30-34	0.89	0.89	11	—	11	—	—
35-39	0.88	0.88	11	—	11	—	—
40-44	0.83	0.83	17	—	14	1	2
45-49	0.71	0.71	29	—	24	1	4
50-54	0.51	0.51	49	—	40	2	7
55-59	0.33	0.33	67	—	55	3	9
60-64	0.17	0.17	83	—	68	4	12
65+	0.05	0.05	95	—	78	5	13
Total	0.70	0.71	29	3	21	1	4

Note: Col. 3 plus col. 4 should add to 100 and col. 4 should equal col. 5, 6, 7, and 8 combined. But figures do not add due to rounding off.
Source: 1982 Population Census of China (Beijing: China Statistical Press, 1985).

compared to 61.4 per cent for the United States and 55.9 per cent for Japan in the same year.[13]

Women start to work earlier than men.[16] The average age at employment in 1982 was 18 against 19 for men due primarily to differentiation of education. In the age group 15–19, 78 per cent of women were employed. The highest employment rate (90 per cent) was attained in the age group 20–24. Thereafter, the employment rate began to dip, slowly at first and more rapidly after age 40. In the age group of 65- plus there were only 5 percent women still in employment. Unlike men who stay employed as long as possible, women leave the ranks at the earliest possible age. The mean age at retirement for women was about 53 in 1982, against the official age of 55 for regular retirement. For men, the respective figures were 63 and 60. Twenty per cent of the men were still working in the age group 65-plus.

The rapid rise in female employment in China, unusual by world standards, was due primarily to the revolution which began in 1949 when land reform was extensively enforced. Land was distributed without compensation in the countryside, where 90 per cent of the people lived, on a per capita basis irrespective of age and sex. Women were suddenly found to have as much economic value as any man. This must have had a considerable impact on the peasant men as well as women. But if this had not been followed up by other effective measures, traditional inertia would have soon worn out the impressive effects of land distribution. In 1953, the agriculture cooperative movement was started in the countryside. Under this system, greater labour participation brought higher returns to the family. But the most powerful driving force that made rural women seek employment was the people's commune system which was started in 1958. Under this system income was distributed in terms of grain or cash entirely by the amount of work done. The more work points a family earned, the greater their income. Work points had a low value, and a single breadwinner's labour was hardly sufficient to feed the family. This made all possible labour forces, known in China as the whole and half labour forces including old folks and young children, take part in productive labour. Thus was established the government policy of universal employment, and women began to get used to working outside the family.

The outside employment however has not made the burden of domestic chores easier. To this day, the urban households have not basically become modernized. In 1983 only 29 out of 100 urban families had washing machines and 1.6 per cent had ice boxes.[17] In the countryside, such luxuries are virtually unheard of.

The taxing burden of housekeeping, which exhausts the energies of women, explains at least in part why a significant portion of them do not join the workforce. About 21 per cent of women were reported as housewives by the 1982 census (Table 1). The age-specific proportions of housewives started low in the very young age group of 15–19 (4 per cent), doubled at age 20–24, and remained stable for ages from 25 to 40 at 11 per cent. It was at age 40 that women began to leave employment and resumed their traditional role as houseworkers. This seems to suggest that the rapid rise in employment caused by external conditions (the revolution) rather than spontaneous desire (which usually evolves gradually) left a large amount of housework unattended, or not well attended. This tends to pull women away from employment to look after things which traditionally are their domain. By age 40, the children also would have become independent economic entities. That was why in the 45-plus age group, almost 80 per cent of women had left employment.

Applying the Life Table for 1981 to Table 1, which is for 1982, we can estimate the age-specific life expectancies for women at various socio-economic levels as shown in Table 2. The calculations show that a girl's life expectancy at birth is 32 years in employment and 37.5 years economically inactive. She would spend about eight years in childhood, and receive 7.3 years of education. On an average, a baby girl is expected to spend nineteen years in housework. Since retirement plans have not been extended to the countryside, a woman's expectancy in retirement is only one year. The rapidly rising age-specific proportion (see Table 1) seems to be consistent with this statement.

Although we adopt the term 'universal employment' to describe the economic status of the Chinese women, great geographic variations exist. Table 3 shows that the highest rate of provincial employment in 1982 (82.7 per cent for Xizan) is almost twice as high as the lowest level (43.8 per cent for Heilongjiang). The range of variation is 38.9 per cent. Dividing it by the national rate gives us a figure of 55 per cent as the index of variation. Lower indices indicate less variations. Generally speaking, the north-eastern provinces have the lowest female employment rate, which rises as one travels south-west. Geography, especially geomorphology and weather seem to account more for these differences than sub-cultural differentiations.[18]

TABLE 2
Mean Number of Years by Age Expected to be Spent in Various Socio-Economic Statuses for a Chinese Female, 1982

Age (1)	Activity				Inactivity				
	Employed (2)	In Labour Force (3)	Not in School (4)	In School (5)	Household Work (6)	Retired (7)	Others (8)	Inactivity (9)	Expectation of Life (10)
0	31.7	31.8	7.8	7.3	18.8	1.0	2.8	37.5	69.4
6	33.4	33.6	3.1	7.7	19.8	1.0	3.0	34.4	67.1
10	33.6	33.7	0.7	5.1	19.9	1.0	3.0	29.6	63.4
15	33.7	33.8	—	0.8	19.9	1.0	3.0	24.7	58.6
20	29.9	30.0	—	—	19.8	1.1	3.0	23.8	53.8
25	25.6	25.6	—	—	19.6	1.1	3.0	23.5	49.2
30	21.4	21.4	—	—	19.2	1.1	3.0	23.1	44.5
35	17.1	17.1	—	—	18.8	1.1	3.1	22.8	39.9
40	12.8	12.8	—	—	18.1	1.1	3.1	22.5	35.3
45	8.8	8.8	—	—	18.0	1.1	3.0	21.9	30.8
50	5.4	5.4	—	—	17.2	1.0	2.9	20.9	26.4
55	3.0	3.0	—	—	15.7	1.0	2.6	19.1	22.2
60	1.5	1.5	—	—	13.7	0.9	2.3	16.7	18.2
65+	0.7	0.7	—	—	11.4	0.7	1.9	13.9	14.6

Expectation of Life In: (years)

Note: Col. 4, 5, 6, 7 and 8 combined give col. 9. Col. 3 plus col. 9 should equal col. 10. This is not always so because of rounding off. Figures are calculated on the basis of 1981 mortality.

Source: Tuan, Chi-hsien, *China—Employment Status, Industrial Structure and Occupational Composition* (Beijing: New World Press, 1986).

TABLE 3

Women of Age 15 and over by Occupation as Per cent in Total Employment, Each Province or Municipality, 1982

Province or Municipality		Occupation							
	Total	I	II	III	IV	V	VI	VII	VIII
Total	100.0	4.4	0.4	0.7	1.9	2.4	77.1	13.0	0.1
Beijing	100.2	15.9	1.8	3.8	4.9	9.1	27.6	36.8	0.3
Tianjin	99.9	11.8	1.2	2.6	4.2	7.5	28.3	44.0	0.3
Hebei	100.0	4.3	0.3	0.7	1.6	1.6	81.1	10.3	0.1
Shanxi	100.0	5.7	0.3	0.9	1.9	1.9	78.8	10.4	0.1
Neimenggu	100.1	7.4	0.6	1.6	2.9	3.4	70.5	13.5	0.2
Liaoning	99.9	9.9	1.1	1.8	4.5	6.3	44.3	31.7	0.3
Jilin	100.0	10.7	1.1	1.7	5.3	6.6	48.4	26.0	0.2
Heilongjiang	100.1	12.5	1.1	1.9	5.8	8.7	40.1	29.8	0.2
Shanghai	100.0	10.4	1.2	2.3	3.8	8.5	30.0	43.7	0.1
Jiangsu	99.9	3.7	0.4	0.5	1.6	2.3	73.4	17.9	0.1
Zhejiang	99.9	4.7	0.4	0.5	2.3	2.8	56.8	32.3	0.1
Anhui	100.0	2.8	0.2	0.4	1.7	1.6	86.4	6.8	0.1
Fujian	100.0	5.0	0.3	0.8	2.3	2.2	74.3	15.0	0.1
Jiangxi	99.9	4.1	0.3	0.6	1.8	2.4	80.5	10.2	—
Shangdong	100.1	3.2	0.3	0.4	1.1	1.4	80.5	13.2	—
Henan	100.0	3.0	0.2	0.4	1.2	1.1	88.6	5.4	0.1
Hubei	99.9	4.2	0.4	0.6	1.8	2.5	79.3	11.0	0.1
Hunan	100.0	3.5	0.3	0.5	1.6	1.8	83.8	8.4	0.1
Guangdong	100.1	3.5	0.3	0.6	2.2	2.6	75.2	15.6	0.1
Guangxi	100.0	2.5	0.2	0.4	1.4	1.5	88.4	5.6	—
Sichuan	100.1	3.2	0.2	0.5	1.3	1.5	87.3	6.0	0.1
Guizhou	100.0	2.8	0.2	0.5	1.3	1.3	89.1	4.7	0.1
Yunnan	100.1	2.7	0.2	0.5	0.9	1.5	89.5	4.8	—
Xizan	100.1	3.1	0.5	0.7	0.5	1.3	89.1	4.9	—
Shaanxi	99.9	4.6	0.3	0.7	1.5	2.0	81.6	9.2	—
Gansu	100.0	3.1	0.2	0.6	1.2	1.6	86.7	6.5	0.1
Qinghai	100.1	5.9	0.3	1.0	1.7	2.8	75.9	12.3	0.2
Ningxia	100.1	4.9	0.3	0.9	1.6	2.5	80.5	9.3	0.1
Xinjiang	100.1	8.1	0.4	1.1	2.1	3.4	69.8	15.1	0.1

Note: Occupation I. Professionals and Technical Personnel; II. Heads of Organizations; III. Office Clerks and Related Staff; IV. Commerce and Sales Staff; V. Service Workers; VI. Agricultural Workers; VII. Industry, Transport and Related Workers; VIII. Other Unclassified Workers.

Source: *1982 Population Census of China* (Beijing: Statistical Press, 1985).

Since women's labour began to be recognized for its economic value only about thirty years ago, their lack of experience limits their present status. This can be seen from Tables 4 and 5 where the proportions of women's employment by industry and occupation respectively are given. Such historical heritage limits the women's role to primarily being a crude labour force employable at least at present, as supplementary to the male, whom history has deemed as the major productive force. Failure to recognize this fact cost China dearly during the years of the Great Leap Forward in 1958–1960. At that time, about 90 million labourers,[19] mostly young and able-bodied men, accounting for about half the male labour force, were removed from the agricultural sector. Ten million lives were lost on account of this administrative blunder. Improving women's employment status depends not only on government policy but especially on the progress of development. Failure of the Great Leap Forward movement may have adversely affected the cause of improvement of rural women's condition.

Tables 3 and 4 demonstrate that female employment is concentrated in agriculture. Since the Chinese economy is labour-intensive, the figures also reflect the level of development. To see how women are placed in industrial/occupational set-up, sex ratios of employment by industry and occupation must be considered (Tables 5 and 6). We find that sex ratios in agriculture by province are all lower than the sex ratio of the population. Agriculture being the parent source for labour for other industries, lower sex ratios in agriculture indicate that the male labour forces are more mobile. Therefore, sex ratios in other trades are usually higher. Exceptions are found in commerce, sales staff and service workers, where the skills required are simpler and the intensity of labour lower. Sex preference is manifest throughout the tables. The better jobs are more often held by men than women. This is most apparent in leadership and its related occupations (see Table 5, columns 5 and 6). The overall sex ratio for leadership jobs for the country as a whole is 860. This figure is apparently associated with the level of development. Metropolitans have much lower sex ratios than the less developed provinces. The highest is found in Ningxia, with a ratio of 1346 against 414 for Beijing. The range of variation for this occupation for the nation is 486 with an index of variation of 57 per cent. As the Chinese have been placing greater emphasis on bureaucracy than on the professionals, the sex ratios for the latter are much

Table 4
Employment by Industry of Women at Age 15 and Over, Each Province or Municipality, 1982

Province or Municipality	Total	Industry															First Industry (Industry I)	Second Industry (Industry II–VII)	Third Industry (Industry VIII–XV)
		I	II	III	IV	V	VI	VII	VIII	IX	X	XI	XII	XIII	XIV	XV			
Total	99.9	78.0	0.7	0.2	11.9	0.1	0.9	0.9	2.9	0.5	0.7	2.7	0.3	0.2	2.2	0.1	78.0	14.7	7.2
Beijing	100.1	29.3	0.4	0.4	36.2	0.1	3.4	2.7	8.5	2.2	1.3	4.9	4.4	0.3	5.8	0.2	29.3	43.2	27.5
Tianjin	100.0	29.3	0.3	0.4	45.3	0.2	2.6	2.5	7.6	1.5	1.0	3.7	1.0	0.3	3.6	0.1	29.3	51.3	19.4
Hebei	99.9	81.7	0.7	0.1	9.1	0.2	0.8	0.5	2.3	0.4	0.7	2.3	0.1	0.3	2.7	—	81.7	11.4	6.8
Shanxi	100.0	79.2	1.1	0.2	9.2	0.1	1.1	0.8	2.6	0.4	0.9	3.1	0.3	0.3	2.9	0.2	79.2	12.5	8.3
Neimenggu	99.9	70.7	1.6	0.3	11.1	0.2	2.0	1.4	4.5	0.8	0.9	3.8	0.3	0.4	3.7	0.1	70.7	16.6	12.7
Liaoning	99.9	44.9	2.3	0.5	31.2	0.1	2.7	2.1	7.3	1.2	0.9	2.9	0.5	0.3	2.7	0.1	44.9	38.9	16.2
Jilin	100.0	48.9	3.5	0.4	24.6	0.1	2.4	2.1	8.0	1.3	1.0	3.5	0.3	0.3	2.7	0.1	48.9	33.1	18.0
Heilongjiang	99.9	42.4	5.2	0.5	25.7	0.1	3.5	2.5	8.7	1.5	1.0	3.2	0.3	0.3	3.6	—	42.4	37.5	20.0
Shanghai	99.8	31.9	—	0.3	46.6	—	1.4	2.1	6.8	1.8	1.3	3.8	1.2	0.3	3.1	—	31.9	50.4	17.5
Jiangsu	99.9	74.5	0.4	0.1	17.9	—	0.5	0.9	2.4	0.4	0.6	2.6	0.2	0.2	1.6	—	74.5	19.8	5.6
Zhejiang	100.0	57.9	0.4	0.1	32.2	—	0.6	0.8	3.6	0.6	0.6	1.8	0.1	0.2	1.5	—	57.9	34.1	8.0
Anhui	99.9	86.4	0.5	0.1	6.3	0.1	0.6	0.7	2.5	0.3	0.8	2.6	0.1	0.1	1.5	0.1	86.4	8.2	5.3
Fujian	100.0	74.5	0.7	0.2	13.8	0.1	0.9	1.0	3.4	0.5	0.7	3.2	0.1	0.3	2.4	—	74.5	16.7	8.8
Jiangxi	100.0	81.5	1.0	0.2	9.0	0.1	0.6	0.9	2.8	0.4	0.7	2.7	0.2	0.2	2.1	—	81.5	11.8	6.7
Shangdong	100.0	84.8	0.5	0.1	9.1	—	0.5	0.4	1.7	0.2	0.7	2.6	0.1	0.2	1.6	0.1	84.8	10.6	4.6
Henan	100.2	88.7	0.4	0.1	5.3	0.1	0.4	0.5	1.8	0.3	0.7	2.8	0.1	0.2	1.5	—	88.7	6.8	4.7

Table 4 continued

Province or Municipality	Total	I	II	III	IV	V	VI	VII	VIII	IX	X	XI	XII	XIII	XIV	XV	First Industry (Industry I)	Second Industry (Industry II–VII)	Third Industry (Industry VIII–XV)
Hubei	100.0	80.2	0.3	0.2	10.5	0.1	0.9	1.0	2.9	0.4	0.6	3.1	0.2	0.3	2.1	—	80.2	13.0	6.8
Hunan	99.8	84.2	0.5	0.1	8.0	—	0.5	0.7	2.3	0.3	0.6	2.4	0.1	0.2	2.1	0.1	84.2	9.8	5.8
Guangdong	99.8	76.1	0.5	0.1	14.1	0.1	0.7	1.1	3.2	0.6	0.7	2.6	0.2	0.3	2.7	—	76.1	16.6	7.1
Guangxi	99.9	88.6	0.3	0.1	4.6	0.1	0.6	0.8	2.2	0.3	0.5	3.1	0.2	0.3	1.9	—	88.6	6.5	4.8
Sichuan	100.0	87.4	0.4	0.1	5.6	0.1	0.6	0.6	2.2	0.3	0.7	2.1	0.2	0.2	1.5	—	87.4	7.4	5.2
Guizhou	100.0	89.1	0.5	0.2	4.1	0.1	0.7	0.6	1.9	0.2	0.5	2.4	0.1	0.2	2.2	0.1	89.1	6.2	4.7
Yunnan	99.9	89.8	0.7	0.1	3.7	0.1	0.7	0.7	1.5	0.2	0.5	2.4	0.2	0.3	1.9	—	95.8	6.0	4.1
Xizang	100.0	91.9	0.1	0.1	2.1	—	0.8	0.8	1.2	0.3	0.7	2.1	0.2	0.3	4.6	—	95.8	3.9	4.2
Shanxi	100.1	82.2	0.3	0.2	8.5	0.1	0.9	0.6	2.4	0.6	0.9	3.5	0.5	0.3	2.3	0.1	82.2	10.6	7.3
Gansu	99.9	86.6	0.6	0.2	5.9	0.1	0.8	0.7	1.9	0.3	0.8	2.9	0.5	0.3	2.1	0.1	86.6	8.3	5.0
Qinghai	99.8	77.7	0.6	0.3	9.4	0.3	2.3	1.3	2.5	0.5	0.9	3.7	0.5	0.4	3.7	0.2	77.7	14.2	7.9
Ningxia	100.1	82.0	1.6	0.3	7.0	0.4	1.4	0.8	2.4	0.4	0.8	3.2	0.3	0.3	2.5	0.3	82.0	11.5	6.6
Xinjiang	99.9	75.8	1.4	0.3	8.2	0.2	3.0	1.8	3.3	0.4	0.7	2.6	0.3	0.4	3.1	0.2	75.8	14.9	9.2

Note: Industry I. Agriculture; II. Mining and logging; III. Electricity, Gas and Water; IV. Manufacturing; V. Geological Prospecting and Censuses; VI. Construction; VII. Transport, Posts, and Telecommunications; VIII. Commerce, Catering, Supply and Storage; IX. Housing, Public Utilities and Residential Services; X. Public Health, Sports and Social Welfare; XI. Education, Culture and Arts; XII. Scientific Research and Comprehensive Technical Services; XIII. Finance and Insurance; XIV. Government, Party and People's Organisations; XV. Others.

Source: Tuan, Chi-hsien, *China—Employment Status, Industrial Structure and Occupational Composition* (Beijing: New World Press, 1986).

TABLE 5

Sex Ratios of Employment by Occupation and for Populations at Age 15 and over, Each Province or Municipality, 1982

Province or Municipality	Pop. Age 15+	Total	I	II	III	IV	V	VI	VII	VIII
					Occupation (No. of Males per 100 Females)					
Total	105.0	128.8	161.9	860.1	309.3	117.0	108.5	113.7	182.2	140.1
Beijing	101.1	126.0	93.3	413.8	155.8	71.2	83.5	103.1	157.7	134.7
Tianjin	102.4	135.6	61.3	563.2	196.2	111.1	102.1	143.4	131.9	132.0
Hebei	104.3	148.5	151.5	1052.8	336.8	147.4	157.5	134.2	218.5	171.2
Shanxi	109.2	138.2	145.8	1329.5	320.5	114.7	150.9	109.4	304.5	190.9
Neimenggu	112.0	155.3	142.1	898.8	251.9	80.8	118.6	141.4	219.0	108.2
Liaoning	103.6	153.3	111.3	597.2	210.7	83.7	83.4	146.3	181.7	101.5
Jilin	105.3	187.3	118.1	672.2	297.0	73.4	89.1	219.9	175.5	94.9
Heilongjiang	105.3	194.4	115.9	824.9	275.5	66.8	95.0	241.6	191.6	100.5
Shanghai	98.7	112.7	117.1	494.0	195.4	120.3	85.7	68.5	131.9	161.2
Jiangsu	102.4	114.9	204.1	895.3	349.0	175.6	143.8	85.9	183.0	153.3
Zhejiang	107.4	157.2	146.6	825.1	320.3	156.1	103.6	174.1	122.3	155.4
Anhui	107.3	124.4	207.7	1114.0	359.8	105.5	128.8	109.4	235.8	138.5
Fujian	105.8	160.9	181.3	1066.8	427.5	162.1	120.2	143.8	211.7	147.3
Jiangxi	105.8	135.6	182.1	1063.4	339.5	101.4	101.6	115.2	253.9	125.9
Shandong	101.5	125.8	209.9	1039.5	422.1	192.9	165.7	113.4	146.7	133.0
Henan	102.5	119.3	191.6	1184.5	397.5	131.8	154.2	107.0	213.8	161.1
Hubei	104.9	122.1	176.4	805.3	296.8	120.3	101.8	105.9	187.2	133.7

Table 5 continued

Province or Municipality	Pop. Age 15+	Total	I	II	III	IV	V	VI	VII	VIII
					Occupation (No. of Males per 100 Females)					
Hunan	108.8	132.5	173.3	891.5	339.4	93.7	98.9	117.9	238.1	151.0
Guangdong	103.0	120.4	203.6	908.3	396.4	162.7	92.0	107.8	135.8	151.0
Guangxi	107.0	116.0	232.6	1043.3	460.6	116.4	82.1	105.1	188.7	145.7
Sichuan	107.2	117.8	158.5	866.0	309.4	94.7	112.5	105.7	233.4	143.1
Guizhou	104.5	110.5	169.1	901.3	263.3	86.4	69.6	101.8	195.6	157.5
Yunnan	101.7	110.0	189.2	1021.5	368.8	106.0	67.8	97.9	240.6	155.2
Xizan	93.3	101.0	196.3	703.1	458.1	106.1	83.6	88.5	234.3	240.0
Shanxi	107.2	149.0	186.5	1149.7	370.7	102.1	118.7	111.6	211.2	187.1
Gansu	108.0	118.7	211.4	1309.5	356.2	107.2	100.1	102.9	230.2	221.5
Qinghai	105.2	118.9	181.6	1261.2	334.1	95.9	105.4	98.4	180.3	100.0
Ningxia	106.1	121.3	170.1	1345.5	320.4	88.3	98.4	101.9	222.0	430.0
Xinjiang	106.2	127.7	130.4	1137.4	355.2	97.4	104.7	108.7	181.6	167.8

Note: Occupation I. Professional and Technical Personnel; II. Heads of Organisations; III. Office Clerks and Related Staff; IV. Commerce and Sales Staff; V. Service Workers; VI. Agricultural Workers; VII. Industry, Transport and Related Workers; VIII. Other Unclassified Workers.

Source: Same as Table 4.

TABLE 6

Sex Ratios of Employment by Industry, and for Populations at Age 15 and over, Each Province or Municipality, 1982

Industry
(No. of Males per 100 Females)

Province or Municipality	Total	I	II	III	IV	V	VI	VII	VIII	IX	X	XI	XII	XIII	XIV	XV
Total	128.8	116.2	416.4	281.8	127.0	331.0	433.6	339.1	130.9	123.3	107.9	182.9	179.6	212.5	384.4	174.8
Beijing	126.0	117.6	734.7	190.0	103.1	417.0	349.8	254.8	91.6	114.5	58.6	95.9	151.8	109.8	209.8	197.9
Tianjin	135.6	153.2	406.6	255.9	103.8	426.7	357.2	291.2	116.2	134.3	64.4	101.9	175.8	125.1	245.7	93.2
Hebei	148.5	135.5	612.4	268.6	148.6	249.4	460.9	485.4	153.4	137.3	133.4	166.8	188.6	208.1	397.7	81.1
Shanxi	138.2	114.4	864.1	232.9	169.4	400.9	338.3	391.3	138.8	101.9	113.9	155.7	158.9	209.0	451.9	374.9
Neimenggu	155.3	147.2	336.0	252.9	122.3	414.8	285.6	329.6	120.6	80.3	93.0	167.0	162.2	190.0	342.9	185.9
Liaoning	153.3	159.7	290.9	253.6	123.4	309.0	313.3	275.6	104.1	100.0	76.4	127.8	185.1	183.1	274.9	269.9
Jilin	187.3	226.5	271.7	264.5	116.4	440.0	277.6	276.7	104.3	94.1	92.5	143.8	200.2	175.1	350.4	153.3
Heilongjiang	194.4	252.0	264.9	259.0	121.1	391.3	236.1	273.0	95.0	86.3	81.5	132.2	172.1	233.5	308.2	167.8
Shanghai	112.7	70.5	234.8	294.1	109.7	418.4	562.9	386.7	125.9	127.5	59.2	106.3	213.5	146.3	231.6	120.9
Jiangsu	114.9	91.0	473.3	341.2	136.5	477.6	1308.5	372.2	163.0	174.4	113.5	184.9	166.2	206.2	437.2	123.4
Zhejiang	157.2	178.7	557.9	352.3	87.3	302.5	1148.9	475.4	131.0	141.6	109.5	131.8	208.7	158.0	422.2	204.0
Anhui	124.4	110.8	369.7	248.5	175.2	308.1	515.4	317.7	129.7	183.0	125.8	242.2	248.2	217.4	418.2	229.6
Fujian	160.9	144.2	574.8	404.5	134.0	455.8	727.2	489.9	170.7	174.5	122.1	191.0	263.8	260.8	465.2	301.5
Jiangxi	135.6	116.1	359.7	279.1	190.4	344.1	794.6	280.0	116.6	191.2	129.0	213.4	206.0	200.6	407.9	107.8
Shandong	125.8	113.2	614.9	298.6	129.3	304.7	563.2	473.2	181.5	162.0	127.8	239.1	175.4	238.1	528.2	421.2
Henan	119.3	108.0	549.3	324.1	150.9	308.8	419.3	402.4	156.4	118.3	148.8	218.5	235.5	232.0	551.8	120.4
Hubei	122.1	110.9	311.2	237.2	127.6	299.4	404.0	316.8	133.8	108.7	99.3	219.2	162.8	194.9	431.1	118.6

Table 6 continued

Industry
(No. of Males per 100 Females)

Province or Municipality	Total	I	II	III	IV	V	VI	VII	VIII	IX	X	XI	XII	XIII	XIV	XV
Hunan	132.5	120.3	575.5	305.6	152.8	349.9	599.3	350.0	105.7	130.1	109.4	193.9	186.9	198.2	397.4	159.4
Guangdong	120.4	110.2	316.4	411.0	89.4	295.7	503.5	344.1	167.3	130.4	107.3	226.5	208.6	272.4	374.8	110.9
Guangxi	116.0	106.0	436.4	387.2	134.0	278.4	279.7	272.3	132.8	112.9	112.3	304.9	227.5	304.7	510.6	84.6
Sichuan	117.8	106.6	568.1	260.8	158.0	317.9	387.4	335.1	122.5	119.4	132.8	172.0	161.9	197.2	431.5	134.7
Guizhou	110.5	102.6	308.3	257.1	142.6	186.5	222.1	256.7	100.6	82.1	105.5	220.5	154.4	231.2	330.4	137.5
Yunnan	110.0	99.9	251.6	262.0	145.4	328.4	323.2	302.5	127.2	77.1	108.0	230.8	212.2	324.1	422.8	207.9
Xizang	101.1	91.9	310.8	181.2	134.2	—	164.7	274.7	117.9	89.5	123.8	219.2	244.4	417.1	493.3	81.0
Shanxi	149.0	113.3	615.3	244.5	153.2	594.9	396.7	392.7	127.4	86.2	139.7	220.9	177.0	235.3	439.2	146.7
Gansu	118.7	104.7	446.7	220.6	143.8	331.9	335.3	334.3	143.2	77.8	150.1	297.8	214.0	271.0	443.8	142.8
Qinghai	118.9	103.9	386.9	300.8	108.2	418.7	224.2	273.0	117.2	68.3	96.9	213.7	189.6	208.7	371.5	232.6
Ningxia	121.3	103.2	374.2	256.1	127.6	342.9	354.3	352.4	110.7	83.0	122.2	212.4	171.3	222.1	458.5	612.7
Xinjiang	127.7	118.7	203.0	213.0	116.3	269.6	195.4	218.9	135.1	106.3	71.2	130.0	133.9	248.6	360.3	171.0

Note: Industry I. Agriculture; II. Mining and Logging; III. Electricity, Gas and Water; IV. Manufacturing; V. Geological Prospecting and Censuses; VI. Construction; VII. Transport, Post and Telecommunications; VIII. Commerce, Catering, Supply and Storage; IX. Housing, Public Utilities and Residential Services; X. Public Health, Sports and Social Welfare; XI. Education, Culture and Arts; XII. Scientific Research and Comprehensive Technical Services; XIII. Finance and Insurance; XIV. Government, Party and People's Organizations; XV. Others.
Source: Same as Table 4.

more balanced than for the former. The sex ratio of the professionals for the country is 162, less than 20 per cent of that of leadership jobs. Its range of variation is 49 with an index of variation at 30 per cent, which is a little over half of the level for leadership jobs. Geographically, the sex ratios of the professionals are also much more balanced than those of the bureaucracy.

The sex ratios by industry/occupation reflect the sex preference of society regarding a certain trade or job. Prejudice certainly is an important factor, as demonstrated above, as is history. A sex ratio for an industry/occupation that coincides with the sex ratio of the general population may not be economic because there are jobs and industries that fit one sex better than another. Generally, industries/jobs that are either risky or require greater physical strength would fit men better, whereas those needing greater patience and care are more suited to women. But conditions also change as technology advances. What is unsuitable for women today may become suitable at a later period, as technology gets refined. Conditions were more favourable to improve the economic status of women before the present economic reform with its stress on efficiency. The government pays great attention to the policy of equality between sexes, since instances of discrimination against women in job recruitment, student enrolment and retirement are often reported in newspapers.[20]

As labour is abundant and efficiency low and labour-saving machines for household work are few and expensive, it often happens that household work and children's education gets neglected. At the same time, factories and offices are overstaffed. Some have suggested doubling men's workload and wages so as to leave the wives free to attend to housework and thus improve the quality of life. Since there is work at home and somebody has got to do it, they argue, why not let the women do it?[21] But accepting the proposal would undermine the policy of universal employment for women. Economic independence is the only foundation upon which the eventual equality of women with men can be realized. Ruling women out of the labour market is certainly no answer to the efficiency problem. There are many men who are as inefficient as, if not more than, women. Why should they keep their job simply because they are men? Inefficiency originated in the continuous and rapid population growth, and aggravated by mismanagement. The ill-founded stress on heavy industry at the cost of consumption goods has kept housework at its old low status.

The principle of equal job for equal pay has been generally maintained in state-run businesses and offices. In the countryside, the commune system before 1980 usually accounted a woman's earning power at about 70 per cent that of an able-bodied man. Since the responsibility system started, lands were redistributed to individual families which then became the unit of account. But the recent economic reforms have aroused complaints regarding the promotion of women workers.[22]

EDUCATIONAL STATUS

Although the experience of the developed countries does not indicate that women's educational level rises proportionately with their general status and leads them towards real equality with the male, education is a prerequisite to a respectable and harmonious relation between men and women. Lack of sufficient progress does not refute the importance of education. But without a rise in the level of women's education, sexual equality is simply not possible. Education used to be the privilege of a few landowners and traditional China excluded women from it. It was only after 1949 that women began to be included in a programme of national education.

The 1982 census provides the first national assessment on the status of education.[23] In 1982 among the people of age 12 and over, 55 per cent of the females received elementary or higher education, against 81 per cent for the males. In other words, about 161 million females at age 12 or above were illiterate whereas 203 million were considered literate. Female literacy for the entire country as well as for each province/municipality is given in Table 8. Xizan has the lowest literacy rate at 16 per cent, while Beijing ranks the highest at 78 per cent. All other provinces have rates higher than 30 per cent, five of them between 30 and 40 per cent, and five provinces and municipalities between 70 and 80 per cent. The educational development, though geographically unbalanced, is not extremely so if Xizan is excluded. The range of national variation is 62 per cent with a variation index of 113 per cent. Excluding Xizan would reduce the range to 45 per cent with the variation index at 82 per cent.

Unlike politics and economics, where marks left by tradition cannot be easily erased, education must be taken as a basic right, and efforts to eliminate sex bias must start with education. For the ouster of sex prejudice in any sphere in the life of a society starts with equality of educational opportunity. The Revolution put all women on an equal footing and recruited them for economic activities, but it failed to be as successful in education as it had been in the economic sector. The sex ratio of literacy shows that women's chances of getting an education are almost half as that for men. The prejudice index, as defined in Table 7, is 148 per cent. It is interesting to note that the least prejudiced region is not Beijing City (119) but Liaoning and Xingjiang (both 117). On the whole, the north-east provinces have the lowest prejudice indices, which are only about 17–23 per cent higher than the idealized state. The prejudice index rises as one travels south-west, where the prejudice indices in Guizhou (216) and Xizan (246) are very high. This is very different from women's employment rates.

TABLE 7

Literacy and Illiteracy Rates of Women, Their Sex Ratios and Prejudice Index for Each Province/Municipality (For Women of Age 12+)

I. Whole Country

Province or Municipality	No. of People as % in Population of Age 12+		Sex Ratio (%)		Prejudice Index (5)/(4)
			Population of Age 12+	Literate	
	Literacy	Illiteracy			
(1)	(2)	(3)	(4)	(5)	(6)
Total	54.8	45.2	105	155	148
Beijing	77.7	22.3	102	121	119
Tianjin	73.8	26.2	102	127	125
Hebei	57.9	42.1	104	148	142
Shanxi	66.5	33.5	109	137	126
Neimenggu	58.5	41.5	111	148	133
Liaoning	76.6	23.4	104	122	117
Jilin	71.1	28.9	105	126	120
Heilongjiang	69.6	30.4	105	129	123
Shanghai	74.1	25.9	98	123	126
Jiangsu	49.6	50.4	103	167	162
Zhejiang	55.8	44.2	108	156	144
Anhui	35.9	64.1	107	211	197
Fujian	42.9	57.1	106	201	190
Jiangxi	51.6	48.4	106	171	161
Shandong	47.9	52.1	102	166	160
Henan	49.0	51.0	103	161	156
Hubei	54.8	45.2	105	158	150
Hunan	64.5	35.5	109	146	134
Guangdong	62.9	37.1	103	149	145
Guangxi	61.4	38.6	107	153	143
Sichuan	55.0	45.0	107	156	146

Table 7 *continued*

Province or Municipality	No. of People as % in Population of Age 12+		Sex Ratio (%)		Prejudice Index (5)/(4)
	Literacy	Illiteracy	Population of Age 12+	Literate	
(1)	(2)	(3)	(4)	(5)	(6)
Guizhou	32.6	67.4	105	227	216
Yunnan	35.6	64.4	102	188	184
Xizan	15.7	84.3	96	236	246
Shanxi	55.1	44.9	107	151	141
Gansu	35.4	64.6	108	206	191
Qinghai	37.2	62.8	107	195	182
Ningxia	42.4	57.6	107	178	166
Xingjiang	63.6	36.4	107	125	117
II. City					
Total	75.4	24.6	118	130	120
Beijing	83.1	16.9	103	119	116
Tianjin	79.4	20.6	103	123	119
Hebei	78.9	21.1	118	140	119
Shanxi	78.4	21.6	119	138	116
Neimenggu	78.3	21.7	107	123	115
Liaoning	83.4	16.6	103	116	113
Jilin	79.8	20.2	103	117	114
Heilongjiang	79.9	20.1	103	118	115
Shanghai	81.1	18.9	103	122	118
Jiangsu	75.2	24.8	109	134	123
Zhejiang	61.5	38.5	108	147	136
Anhui	66.4	33.6	115	149	130
Fujian	65.6	34.4	106	146	138
Jiangxi	74.4	25.6	109	134	123
Shandong	66.4	33.6	104	139	134
Henan	74.4	25.6	111	135	122
Hubei	78.0	22.0	109	131	120
Hunan	80.4	19.6	114	133	117
Guangdong	77.4	22.6	106	130	123
Guangxi	77.9	22.1	109	134	123
Sichuan	73.8	26.2	109	130	119
Guizhou	49.3	50.7	110	167	152
Yunnan	68.9	31.1	112	138	123
Xizan	62.8	37.2	117	151	129
Shanxi	77.8	22.2	112	132	118
Gansu	77.1	22.9	118	140	119
Qinghai	78.1	21.9	111	132	119
Ningxia	74.4	25.6	115	136	118
Xingjiang	77.1	22.9	106	120	113

Table 7 continued

Province or Municipality	No. of People as % in Population of Age 12+		Sex Ratio (%)		Prejudice Index (5)/(4)
	Literacy	Illiteracy	Population of Age 12+	Literate	
(1)	(2)	(3)	(4)	(5)	(6)

	III. County				
Total	51.0	49.0	105	162	154
Beijing	69.0	31.0	99	124	125
Tianjin	61.8	38.2	101	140	139
Hebei	55.2	44.8	102	150	147
Shanxi	64.1	35.9	107	137	128
Neimenggu	54.1	45.9	112	156	139
Liaoning	72.9	27.1	104	125	120
Jilin	68.0	32.0	106	129	122
Heilongjiang	65.4	34.6	106	135	127
Shanghai	65.9	34.1	93	124	133
Jiangsu	46.3	53.7	102	174	171
Zhejiang	54.5	45.5	108	159	147
Anhui	32.4	67.6	107	225	210
Fujian	39.2	60.8	106	216	204
Jiangxi	48.1	51.9	106	180	170
Shandong	45.4	54.6	101	172	170
Henan	46.2	53.8	102	165	162
Hubei	51.6	48.4	105	164	156
Hunan	62.8	37.2	108	148	137
Guangdong	60.7	39.3	103	153	149
Guangxi	60.1	39.9	107	155	145
Sichuan	52.8	47.2	107	160	150
Guizhou	29.8	70.2	104	245	236
Yunnan	32.7	67.3	101	197	195
Xizan	12.7	87.1	95	260	274
Shaanxi	51.2	48.8	107	157	147
Gansu	30.4	69.6	107	225	210
Qinghai	27.5	72.5	106	238	225
Ningxia	35.1	64.9	106	199	188
Xingjiang	59.9	40.1	107	127	119

Source: *Zhongguo Funu Bao* (Journal of Chinese Women), August 21 and October 11, 1985.

The variations of literacy rates shown above change with the level of development, the literacy rate for cities being 75 per cent and for the countryside 51 per cent. Among cities, the lowest rate is found in the cities of Guizhou (49 per cent) and the highest in Liaoning province

(83.4 per cent) and Beijing (83.1 per cent). The range of variation is 34 per cent and the index of variation is 45 per cent which is 40 per cent of the index for the city and rural areas combined. In the countryside, Xizan has the lowest rate (13 per cent) while Liaoning has the highest (73 per cent). The range of variation is 60 per cent and the index of variation is 118 per cent, which is 2.6 times the level of the city. Obviously, women's education in the city areas is much more balanced than in the countryside.

The prejudice index for city areas is 120, which means that women's opportunity of being educated is 20 per cent lower than that of men. City areas of sixteen provinces/municipalities out of a total of twenty-nine have a prejudice index below the national average. The highest index of prejudice is 152 (Guizhou) and the lowest is in Liaoning (113). The range of variation is 39 with an index of variation of 33 per cent. For the countryside, the national average of prejudice index is 154. The highest is found in Xizan (274) and lowest in Liaoning (120) which has a figure comparable to the city level. The range of variation is 154 and the index of variation is 100, which is 3.3 times the level for the cities. The sex prejudice against women's education is much stronger in the countryside than in the cities.

On the whole, the 1982 census shows that females have an average of 6.2 school years (as counted from educated females at age 6 and above, see Table 8) which does not differ much from that of the males (6.4). This shows that the majority of women are at the level of elementary education. Municipalities are a little better but their mean number of schooling years per female is at the most 7.8 years (Beijing). However, the range of variation is limited (2.2 years) and the index of variation is 35 per cent. Only six out of every thousand literate females at age 6 and above have attended college, less than 11 per cent have a high school education, 27 per cent junior middle school education and 62 per cent have an elementary education. If the entire female population is included, only four out of 1000 at age 6 and above have college education, 6 per cent high school, 15 per cent junior middle school and 35 per cent elementary level of education. Illiteracy is 44 per cent. On this basis, the mean number of schooling years per female would only be 4.2 years.

About half a century ago, less than 5 per cent of women had a chance to go to school (see Table 9). Since then, conditions have changed. There was a rapid improvement in the 1950s when women's literacy rate rose to about 50 per cent. More of the younger girls are

TABLE 8
*Level of Education for Chinese Females of Age 6 and over for
Each Province/Municipality, 1982*

Province or Municipality	Level of Education (No. of Women as % in Total Educated Women)				Mean No. of Schooling per Females of 6+
	College and Equivalent	High School	Junior/ Middle School	Primary	
Total	0.6	10.5	27.1	61.8	6.2
Beijing	4.9	25.4	36.3	33.5	7.8
Tianjin	2.3	19.2	36.4	42.1	7.2
Hebei	0.5	11.4	28.0	60.1	6.2
Shanxi	0.5	10.2	29.2	60.0	6.2
Neimenggu	0.6	12.1	29.6	57.6	6.4
Liaoning	0.8	12.0	36.7	50.5	6.6
Jilin	0.8	15.7	28.0	55.5	6.5
Heilongjiang	0.6	13.6	30.6	55.3	6.5
Shanghai	2.9	27.6	35.2	34.4	7.7
Jiangsu	0.6	10.6	31.2	57.5	6.3
Zhejiang	0.4	7.9	26.5	65.2	6.0
Anhui	0.6	7.5	26.1	65.8	6.0
Fujian	0.6	9.3	19.2	70.9	5.9
Jiangxi	0.4	7.9	18.8	72.8	5.7
Shangdong	0.4	8.8	27.6	63.2	6.1
Henan	0.3	10.0	30.3	59.3	6.2
Hubei	0.6	11.1	26.1	62.2	6.2
Hunan	0.4	8.7	23.2	67.7	5.9
Guangdong	0.4	9.6	22.5	67.5	6.0
Guangxi	0.3	9.5	23.1	67.0	6.0
Sichuan	0.5	6.5	23.4	69.6	5.8
Guizhou	0.7	7.5	23.7	68.0	5.9
Yunnan	0.6	6.9	22.5	70.0	5.8
Xizan	1.5	7.0	17.8	73.7	5.6
Shanxi	0.8	12.4	29.2	57.5	6.4
Gansu	0.8	13.3	24.6	61.3	6.3
Qinghai	1.3	13.0	31.0	54.7	6.5
Ningxia	1.0	11.0	32.3	55.8	6.4
Xingjiang	0.7	11.1	29.1	59.1	6.3

Source: Same as Table 7.

at school, and 86 per cent at age 12 have received some form of education. In 1983, 88.4 per cent of the girls at age 10 were at school (the highest age-specific group),[24] against 95.5 per cent boys in the same age group. In the city, 97 per cent of the females between 12 and

TABLE 9
Women's Age Specific Literacy and Illiteracy Rates and Sex Ratios by Urban and Rural Areas, 1982

Age	Whole China		City		County	
	Literacy	Illiteracy	Literacy	Illiteracy	Literacy	Illiteracy
	I. Literacy (No. of Women as % in the Age Totals)					
Total	0.548	0.452	0.754	0.246	0.510	0.490
12	0.859	0.141	0.967	0.033	0.845	0.155
13	0.853	0.147	0.966	0.034	0.838	0.162
14	0.851	0.149	0.965	0.035	0.836	0.164
15-19	0.853	0.147	0.968	0.032	0.835	0.165
20-24	0.767	0.233	0.950	0.050	0.726	0.274
25-29	0.639	0.361	0.904	0.096	0.584	0.416
30-34	0.597	0.403	0.873	0.127	0.545	0.455
35-39	0.566	0.434	0.847	0.153	0.514	0.486
40-44	0.426	0.574	0.757	0.243	0.354	0.646
45-49	0.256	0.744	0.576	0.424	0.186	0.814
50-54	0.148	0.852	0.406	0.594	0.098	0.902
55-59	0.103	0.897	0.310	0.690	0.067	0.933
60+	0.046	0.954	0.149	0.851	0.027	0.971
	II. Sex Ratio (No. of Males per 100 Females)					
Total	155	44	130	39	161	45
12	117	40	108	59	118	39
13	118	38	108	57	119	37
14	118	38	109	56	120	37
15-19	116	30	109	45	118	29
20-24	128	26	111	34	133	25
25-29	151	28	115	31	162	28
30-34	157	35	123	37	168	35
35-39	169	36	127	38	182	36
40-44	208	44	133	38	243	45
45-49	298	49	171	35	383	50
50-54	447	53	239	37	615	55
55-59	546	56	275	40	762	59
60+	742	55	363	42	1050	57

Note: City figures do not include those of townships.
Source: Same as Table 7

19 are literate, and in the countryside, 84 per cent. The highest school attending rate, at age 10, was 91 per cent for country girls as against the highest rate of 98 per cent for city boys.

Table 10 delineates the sex prejudice in matters of education. Women in the 60-plus age group have a prejudice index of 853. It

TABLE 10
Prejudice Index of Education Against Chinese Women by Urban and Rural Areas, 1982

Age	Sex Ratio for Total Population			Prejudice Index (%) (Sex Ratio for Literate/Sex Ratio for Total Population)		
	Whole Country	Urban	Rural	Whole Country	Urban	Rural
Total	105	108	105	148	120	153
12	106	107	106	110	101	111
13	106	106	106	111	102	112
14	106	107	106	111	102	113
15-19	104	107	103	112	102	115
20-24	104	107	103	123	104	129
25-29	107	107	106	141	107	153
30-34	108	112	108	145	114	156
35-39	111	113	111	152	112	164
40-44	114	110	115	182	121	211
45-49	112	113	112	266	151	342
50-54	112	119	110	399	201	559
55-59	107	113	106	510	243	719
60+	87	90	86	853	403	1221

Note: For the interpretation of the prejudice index, the unity figure shows that there is neither prejudice against females nor males. Any number above 100 indicates the degree of prejudice against females, and below it reveals the degree against males. Thus figure 152 means that the chances of women being educated are 53 per cent lower than those for men.
Source: Same as Table 7.

declines rapidly and at age 12, it is 110. In the cities, the prejudice indices for females in ages 12–19 are all 102, which is almost ideal. A rapid change in the rural conditions is also indicated by the fact that the prejudice index is 111 for females of age 12 against 1221 for women of age 60 and above.

Age specific rate for women by educational level is demonstrated in Table 11 and the corresponding prejudice indices are listed in Table 12. As the age range extends from age six onward, students as well as those who have left school are mixed. Care must be taken when one examines the figures as students' educational levels are associated with age. We find that the mode for the proportions of women with college education is within age 40–44 and their percentage is 1.2. They

Table 11
Educational Status of Chinese Women, 1982

	No. of women as % in Total Women for Each Age Group						
		Middle School				*Illiterate and*	*Mean No. of*
Age	*College and Equivalent*	*High School*	*Junior*	*Primary*	*Total Literate*	*Semi-literate*	*Schooling Years*
6-9	—	—	—	52.4	52.4	47.6	1.05
10-14	—	0.1	13.2	71.8	85.1	14.9	3.74
15-19	0.3	13.2	41.2	30.4	85.3	14.7	6.12
20-24	0.5	24.5	26.7	25.0	76.7	23.3	5.92
25-29	0.6	9.8	21.2	32.3	63.8	36.2	4.39
30-34	0.5	3.7	15.8	39.7	59.6	40.4	4.30
35-39	0.9	4.3	14.3	37.1	56.5	43.5	4.16
40-44	1.2	3.9	9.1	28.5	42.5	57.5	3.17
45-49	0.7	1.8	4.0	19.0	25.5	74.5	1.82
50-54	0.4	1.0	2.2	11.3	14.8	85.2	1.04
55-59	0.2	0.6	1.4	8.1	10.3	89.7	0.72
60+	0.1	0.3	0.5	3.7	4.5	95.5	0.32
Total	0.4	5.9	15.2	34.8	56.2	43.8	4.22

Source: Same as Table 7.

Table 12
Educational Status of Chinese Women in Comparison with that of Chinese Men, 1982

	No. of Men per 100 Women					
Age	*College*	*High School*	*Junior Middle School*	*Primary*	*Literate*	*Illiterate and Semi-literate*
6-9				120	120	91
10-14		147	128	116	118	41
15-19	279	136	131	87	116	30
20-24	249	135	156	88	128	26
25-29	202	180	192	143	151	28
30-34	249	206	206	132	157	36
35-39	254	188	218	146	169	36
40-44	302	236	244	189	208	45
45-49	369	324	402	270	298	49
50-54	431	426	656	410	448	53
55-59	536	498	774	512	547	56
60+	585	519	957	735	746	55
Total	290	160	170	136	148	49

Source: Same as Table 7.

received their college education mostly in years 1959–1964. The college education was interrupted by the Cultural Revolution. Therefore, we find the mode of proportions of women with high school education at the level of 24.5 per cent in the young age group 20–24. Junior high school was not quantitatively disturbed by the turmoils in the years from 1966–1976. Their age specific proportions appear smooth. The elementary education is the only case where two modes appear. The age distribution of the student population is one of the major reasons that causes such a phenomenon.

It is interesting to note that age-specific prejudice index for education does not always rise with the level of education. The indices for high school level are all lower than those for junior middle school level. This shows that more of the women who received junior middle education would go on to high school. Their parents must have been more motivated to support their daughters for higher education. But the prejudice indices rise again for college education, showing that more practical considerations prevented the females from having the precious and rare opportunities. On the whole, the prejudice index for college level is 290, 160 for high school, 170 for junior high and 136 for elementary education.

SOCIAL STATUS

For older Chinese women, life cycle was faster. A survey in Sichuan county[25] shows that in the older generation women began to help bring up their brothers and sisters from about an age of 6. By the time they were 10–12 years old they started some sort of social life and entered non-rewarding economic activities. By the age of 14, they were engaged and got married two years later. They had the first child at about 19, and thereafter childbirth occurred every 2.5–3.0 years. At age 38–40, they became grandmothers. Menopause was at about age 44.

Under the present conditions, girls start education at 6 and by the time they are 12 they leave school. Their menstruation starts a year earlier (it started at 15.5 for women born in 1961 observed in the Shanghai commune[26]) and ends a year later than it did for women in olden days. By 15, they commence socially productive labour and earn an income. By the time they are 20, they start mating, and get married at 23. Childbearing begins at age 25 and while they are breastfeeding their babies country women usually withdraw from labour participation, but return to work thereafter. They become grandmothers at ages 46–50 and retire from economically active life.

This simplified summary shows how life has quantitatively changed in rural China during the past thirty years. Among the qualitative changes are the reduction in male supremacy. Female infanticide, which was quite frequent before 1949 especially in some parts of China along the Yangzi River is now rarely heard of. But son preference persists, which may be revived by the tight policy of planned births. Negligence of girls resulting from son preference is the major killer of female children. In Huaiyuan region, Anhui, which is still notorious for female infanticide, the sex ratio is extremely unbalanced and men, when they come of age, find it very difficult to get married. They send people even as far as Sichuan to persuade young girls (sometimes through kidnappers) to marry them. The girls are offered attractive terms, which includes giving them authority to preside over the household.

International experiences demonstrate that females enjoy lower mortality than men. But the traditional forces in China had been so strong against women that their mortality was higher than that of men until they were 35 years old. In other words, only at about the age when women were reaching grandmotherhood, could their life expectancy be allowed to become higher than men's. Even to this day, there are places where female infant mortality rate is higher than that of male babies. For example, in Sifan county, Sichuan, the female infant mortality rate in 1974 was 3.62 per cent against 2.40 per cent for males. For a commune in Jiangxi, the zero age death for girls was 4.99 per cent in 1980 against 4.55 per cent for the boys. The 1982 census gives the infant mortality rate for 1981 at 3.37 per cent for females against 3.56 per cent for males. Life expectancy at birth for females was 69.3 against 66.4 for males, with a difference of only 2.9 years. In other countries or areas at a similar level of mortality, the difference is usually about five years. This may be a reflection of the remnants of the traditional masculinism.[27]

Before 1949, marriage was the most important thing for women. Arranged marriage was the norm. A survey in a village in Ding Xian, Hebei, shows that before the 1950s, 80 per cent of the marriages were arranged by parents, and brides met their men on the wedding day for the first time. But things have changed considerably. Among the couples married since the 1970s, 34.1 per cent had known each other for six months, and 61.5 per cent even longer, leaving only 5 per cent who had never met before marriage.[28]

The function of the matchmaker, who used to play a vital part, is also greatly curtailed. Now there is Jieshao (introduction), which is usually through the channels of relatives, neighbours or friends. Self-contact through social activities primarily occur to people with mobility. But in rural areas, introduction is very popular. A survey in a mountainous commune (Xiang) in Pengxian, Sichuan, indicates that 81.9 per cent of rural marriages (in a total of 254 first marriages) in the three years 1980–1982 were through introduction and the rest through self-contact. Marriage is contracted in three stages: Renshi (know)—engage—marry. The same survey shows that in 54.7 per cent of the marriages Renshi and engagement occurred simultaneously. In 31.5 per cent of them the couples were engaged after they became acquainted, and in 13.8 per cent the couples were engaged through self-contact. The mean waiting time from Renshi to marriage is 27 months with a range of between 4–96 months. The mode is twelve months. Marriage usually involves migratory movement because the Chinese villagers usually share the same family name. For the Pengxian sample, 47.8 per cent of the brides were from other areas. To be specific, 30.8 per cent were from other communes, the grassroot unit of administration, 36 per cent from other counties and 13.4 per cent from other prefectures. Only for 1.2 per cent of the bridegrooms change of residence was involved. These were marriages into the bride's family. This mountainous commune has a marriage market with a radius of about 50 kilometres.[29]

A mountainous area is usually considered backward, and the above data seems too rosy, but there are no other data as specific as for this commune. According to Professor Lei Jieqiong, President of the Beijing Society of Sociology, marriage by free choice is about 10 per cent in Beijing, arranged marriage is also about the same proportion. Most are through some sort of introduction and after a period of acquaintance.[30] This is consistent with the Sichuan data.

Mercenary marriage, rampant before 1949, was generally suppressed between 1949 and 1980, except in the bad years of the early 1960s when girls in some areas were weighed as the basis for extortion of money before a marriage was contracted. But after the responsibility system came in vague in 1980, mercenary marriage has been revived especially in some backward rural areas. A report in the *People's Daily* (January 17, 1985) says that 5,600 out of the 6,000 marriages contracted between 1980 and November 1984 in Xingguo county, Jiangxi (one of the old revolutionary bases) were through matchmakers. Marriage by choice was considered irregular there. Betrothal gifts at the lowest scale amounted to 3,000 RMB, which was higher than a farmer's yearly income in 1982, and they could be as high as 6,800 RMB.

The past thirty years have seen a rapid rise in marriage age. According to the One-in-a-Thousand Sample Fertility Survey in 1982, the mean age of women at first marriage rose from 18 in 1945 to 18.6 in 1949, and 23.1 in 1979. It has declined somewhat since then, after the Marriage Law of 1980 relaxed control on marriage age. Marriage age of urban women can be as high as 27, as found in Shanghai in 1975–1979. A husband about 2–3 years older is preferred, and this has even impaired the chances of some women getting married. Along the Yangzi River, women were often older than their husbands. In Ding Xian, Hebei in North China, in 1929, of the 766 peasant families studied, in 70 per cent of the cases wives were older than their husbands by an average of 4.3 years, 25 per cent of the husbands were older than their wives by an average of 8.5 years and the rest were of the same age. Professor Li Jinghan stated that older husbands occurred in poor peasant families whereas in better off families, which could afford to marry their sons young, wives were generally older than their husbands.[11]

Marriage is universal, though the age of marriage has gone up. In a commune in Jiangxi, before 1949, 14 per cent of the women were married before 15, 92 per cent before 20, and 98 per cent by 22. Almost all had eventually married. According to the 1982 census, 96 per cent women at age 15–19 were single. By age 25, 54 per cent had been married, and by age 30, 95 per cent. The census shows that less than 0.3 per cent of old women are unmarried.

The total fertility rate (TFR) before 1949 was somewhere around five births per woman. It rose with occasional, sometimes drastic, interruptions to about 6.5 in 1968 due to improvement in health which prolonged longevity and reduced birth interval. Births began to decline first in the urban areas in the early 1960s, and then in the countryside in the 1970s. By 1983, TFR was about 2.2. However, there is a great deal of variation. In 1981, the highest rate was 4.4 in Guizhou (Xizan being excluded) and the lowest, 1.3, in Shanghai, with a proportion of the first birth in the year's total births at 23.9 per cent and 87.0 per cent, respectively. In 1981 the fertility of illiterate women was over twice as much as for women with a college education. The total fertility rate in urban areas in 1981 was 1.4 against 2.9 in the countryside.

The rapid and drastic decline in fertility was due to a unique programme of planned birth by the government, which has taken the Chinese women on the path of contraception, an important change for them.

In 1982, 71 per cent of currently married women in the reproductive period were contraceptive users. Contraception sets the Chinese women free from the yoke of reproduction and helps break the taboo of sex. Sex education has entered the classroom all over the country. Widespread use of contraceptives plus the fact that over 85 per cent of the methods used are designed for females, helps to break the reserve on discussing contraception. A survey in a mountainous county in Hebei in 1983 reports that only 17 per cent of women in the reproductive period seldom talk about planned births, 48 per cent talk about it frequently, and the rest infrequently. The attitude to sex also has been liberalized as a consequence. A survey conducted in 1982 shows that 80 per cent of those interviewed considered pre-marriage sex immoral, but in 1985, this proportion was reduced to 60–65 per cent. Old people are more conservative. A survey in Beijing reveals that in 1985, only half the couples under 30 were against pre-marriage sex, whereas 75 per cent of those above 50 opposed it.[32]

The attitude to fertility has also changed greatly. During the era of natural fertility, reproduction, especially male offspring, had long been a blessing. But the consciousness of the rapid and persistent growth of population has led the Chinese to examine their old pro-natal attitude. In 1985, a provincial sample survey in Jilin polled its married women on the ideal number of births. The urban women put it at 1.65 against 2.01 for the rural women. Asked about the advantage of having children, 70 per cent of the urban married women as against 25 per cent of the rural women said that it was fun to have a family and 24 per cent of the urban women thought children would protect them in their old age, while 60 per cent of women thought so in the countryside. Apparently, this difference in old age security is due to the fact that urban people are mostly covered by an old age pension system while in the countryside people have to fend for themselves. Over two-thirds of the rural women as against 53 per cent of the urban women expect to live with their children in old age. Both groups agree that children must support their parents in old age: 73 per cent of the urban women and 76 per cent in the countryside.[33] Such data on attitude and opinion, however, needs to be accepted with a little reservation due to the volatile nature of the information, being very sensitive to the requirements of government policies.

A survey conducted in 1981 shows that unmarried women in Beijing prefer to marry at an average age of 25. About half (54 per cent) of the women interviewed considered it best to have a baby in the second year of marriage, and 97 per cent would like to have a birth before the fourth year of marriage. Less than 5 per cent of the women said that they had a baby because the parents of either party wanted it.[34]

In 1983, in a survey conducted by the provincial Association of Women in Anhui on 834 married women, 91 per cent of the respondents said they could make independent decisions in family affairs with occasional consultation with their husbands in serious matters. Only forty-five said that their husbands dominated the household affairs. This certainly indicates that women's status in the family has been substantially raised. But women have had to pay a price for this in that women today are much busier and shoulder responsibilities both inside and outside the family. The 1982 census reports a family size of 4.4 persons. Families having two and more generations account for 82 per cent of the total. Although in urban areas, many men share in household chores, women still do the major portion of it. In rural areas, men hardly share household chores. Many surveys show that women have to spend about 3–4 hours a day looking after the family in addition to their outside work. This weighs heavily on them. But a recent survey in six cities in Guangdon tells a different story. The survey is the result of monitoring round the clock the daily activities of 450 workers over two weeks. It transpires that women spend an average of 10.5 working hours per day at home and in the factory or office against 9.5 hours for men. About eight hours are spent on paid jobs. From this, it is estimated that about two-thirds of the household chores are done by women while men take care of the remaining one-third. But this is the average condition. The survey says that workers in the age group 26–56 spend most of their leisure in household chores among which shopping, cooking and washing take 82 per cent of the time. Cooking takes over three hours a day. This is primarily because 74 per cent of the families use coke and 18 per cent use firewood and grass. Only 8 per cent use gas, which is something people desire to have most as it would drastically ease housework.[35]

CONCLUSION

While the status of the Chinese women has substantially improved, the improvement is across the board and leaves considerable scope for further advance. Before 1949, not much outside the family was open to women. Today, they are found in every category of trade and all kinds of occupations. Women's conditions today are totally different from what they were less than forty years ago. Only a revolution can bring about such extensive and rapid changes. Without the revolution, political rights for women would very likely have received only lip-service. Women's economic value would have been at most partly recognized, mainly in urban areas, and universal employment would have been impossible. Women would still have been subordinate to men. All told, women probably have benefited the most from the present government.

Revolution can do in a short span what evolution does not. On the other hand, what evolution can achieve, revolution does not. Revolution can overthrow an old regime and start a new situation, but it leaves the implementation of details to the evolutionary process. For enduring change and a continuing improvement in the quality of life, the persistent process of evolution has to step in. An idealized balance of sex ratio in leadership jobs is not possible in the short run because bringing up women politicians takes time. So also in other lines of pursuits. Revolution can put all women in the working force, recognize their economic value and reward them accordingly. But it cannot sever the present from the past, and the marks left by history, old habits and old mentality will continue to work in the society as well as on the people.

The major advantages that women have derived from the revolution are economic. Without economic independence, there would be no freedom and equality for women. Universal employment had been maintained for many years by equalitarianism under which 'the iron bowl of rice' and the Dai Guofen (big rice cauldron) operated to protect women's economic status. But recent economic reforms, aimed at raising efficiency, have bypassed equalitarianism, and exposed women to competition for which they are not prepared. The opportunity was not exploited fully which could otherwise have been used to give women solid training so that they could compete on an equal footing with men. A more serious mistake was the negligence of exploring and establishing new systems and reforming the existing institutions so that they could best accommodate economically both men and women. The present system is built in favour of men, either consciously or unconsciously.

Prejudice against women in the enrolment of students, recruitment of workers, as well as promotion and retirement, is mainly rooted in the biological differences between the sexes. There is no economic institution that takes a positive attitude towards them and provides appropriate measures so that menstruation, pregnancy, childbirth and child rearing can be constructively assured in the evaluation of women's labour value. Ways must be found to give due consideration to such fundamental functions which only women possess, so that society would not discriminate against women on the mere fact of sex, and in the meantime attains efficiency. Economy should not be made to achieve social goals on a sacrifice from half of mankind.

Economic reforms have involved women in a new process of transition through which they must strive to work things out to the justice and dignity of women. Universal employment of women has received strong impetus from the extensive movement of contraception. Without such a vital revolution, women would have to remain under the natural rule of physiology and bear children constantly. Frequent pregnancy and child rearing would necessarily prevent women from being continuously socialized and confine them to their homes. This would definitely affect women's status, their way of life and its quality. In the olden days, women had children at about 20, and roughly every three years thereafter until they were in their forties. Contraception has transformed women's reproductive life by delaying their first birth to about 25 and end their reproductive life at about 30. Contraception has become the single most important pillar that sustains women's efforts towards their external emancipation from bounds the society has irrationally imposed on them.

The Chinese women's movement towards their goal of freedom and equality is also characterized by the disparity of development. This is the result of the swiftness of change brought about by administrative measures. While the majority of the masses press forward quickly, there are some who cannot catch up and are left behind. While more and more people have become liberal in their attitude to the sex of their children, there are also cases of female infanticide, in which most often old women have a hand. Among the same group of people, opposing ideas may exist simultaneously. Some old parents with customary attitudes interfere with their children's affairs, mostly marriage. There are also cases where young children oppose the remarriage of their widowed parents. Lack of spontaneity in arranged marriages causes great troubles. A lot of marriages through other forms also meet with problems. Unhappy marriages account for many crimes. In 1980, problematic marriages accounted for 32 per cent of homicide. Of those incurring the death penalty, 47 per cent were on the ground of troubles from marriages and love affairs. In 1982, fifty per cent of suicides were caused by marriage tragedy.[30]

Revolution has made a great impact on the Chinese women. But the changes are only a beginning, which may be a process of never ending changes. It may be easier to state the goal of women's movement than to specify how and when it can be finally achieved. We are not in a position to say what the final status will be. In olden days when arranged marriage was the absolute norm, the family was rather stabilized at the cost of the women's submissiveness. Marriage by free choice, while benefiting women, channels the family into a volatile situation where uncertainties supersede the fixed destiny defined by feudalism and rock the boat of stability. It would not be rash to predict that the Chinese family is heading for a bumpy road and may become unstable although the present level of marriage dissolution is low. The post-equalitarianism period, featured by the sweeping economic reforms, has diverted the movement of women's emancipation from a static and relatively cosy path traversed in the past thirty years into a situation full of threats and challenges. Women face a tough future and society must make fresh efforts to help them adjust to the vigorous battle for economic opportunities and transform them so as to be capable and really worthy of living a dynamic life of modern times.

Notes

1. Mao Zedong, 'Report on an Investigation of the Peasant Movement in Hunan,' *Selected Works of Mao Zedong* (Peking: Foreign Languages Press, 1967), vol. 1, p. 44.

2. Engels, F., 'Family, Private Ownership and the Origin of Nation,' in a book in Chinese on Women by Marx, Engels, Lenin and Stalin, pp. 131 and 135, for example (Beijing: People's Press, 1978).

3. Lu Xinhua, 'Shanghen' (The Scar), a chapter in *Shanghen*, edited by Liu Xinwu (Hong Kong: San Lian Book Store, 1978).

4. Mao Zedong, Speech at the opening ceremony of the Chinese Women's University, July 20, 1939, reported in *People's Daily*, August 25, 1966.

5. *Selected Works of Mao Tse-Tung* (Peking: Foreign Languages Press, 1975) vol. II, p. 419.

6. See *Zhongguo Tongji Lianqian, 1983* (Statistical Yearbook of China, 1983) (Beijing: China's Statistics Press, 1983).

7. Based on data given in the 1982 Yearbook of the Encyclopedia of China (Beijing: Encyclopedia of China Press, 1982).

8. 1982 Population Census of China (Beijing: China Statistical Press, 1985).

9. Li Jinghan, 'Statistical Analysis on the Rural Family Population,' *Social Science*, Vol. 2, No. 1 (Beijing: National Qinghua University, 1936).

10. Tuan, Chi-hsien, Yu, Jingyuan and Xiao, Zhenyu, *The Size of Family and Household in China*, 1985 (unpublished).

11. Lavely, W.R. and Li Bohua, 'Household Structure in Liaoning, Hebei and Fujian: A Preliminary Survey,' paper presented at the International Symposium on the One Per Thousand Fertility Survey, held in Beijing, October 14–18, 1985.

12. Tuan, Chi-hsien, *Wuyi City and Wuxi County—An Analysis of a Pilot Census* (Beijing: New World Press, 1987).

13. *Xiamen Ribao* (Xiamen, Fujian), May 30, 1985.

14. *Zhongguo Tongji Lianjian*, 1984 (China Statistics Yearbook, 1984) (Beijing: China Statistics Press, 1984).

15. Statistical Abstracts of U.S. 1985 (Washington, D.C.: Government Printing House).

16. More discussions on sex differences for various variables can be found in Tuan, Chi-hsien, *China—Employment Status, Industrial Structure and Occupational Composition* (Beijing: New World Press, 1986).

17. *Zhongguo Tongji Lianjian, 1984*, op. cit.

18. For more detailed discussion, the readers are referred to Tuan, Chi-hsien, *China— Employment Status, Industrial Structure and Occupational Composition*, op. cit.

19. Mao Zedong, *Sixiang Wan Sui*, 1969. This was a reprint of Mao's unpublished works which was smuggled out by the Japanese and leaked out during the Cultural Revolution years.

20. See, for example, *Zhongguo Funu Bao (Journal of Chinese Women)* (Beijing), January 30 and October 11, 1985. The January issue reports that scores required for females are often much higher than those for males. Although job recruitment should be based on the principle of choosing the better ones, local units bypassed it by adding a sex quota. Some required that males should not be less than half of the recruitment, others can go as high as 90 per cent.

21. *Shehui* (Society), 1984, no. 1, no. 2, no. 3, no. 4. See also Tuan, Chi-hsien, *China—Employment Status, Industrial Structure and Occupational Composition*, op. cit.

22. See *Zhongguo Funu Bao (Journal of Chinese Women)*, August 21 and October 11, 1985.

23. For a more detailed discussion, see Tuan, Chi-hsien, Yu Jingyuan, Xiao Zhengu, 'Education in China,' paper presented at the Workshop on China's 1982 Census, EWPI, Honolulu, Hawaii 1984.

24. See *Zhuozhuang Chengzhang De Zhongguo Ertong* (Healthy Growing up of China's Children)—Tabulations of the Sample Survey on China's Children, 1983 (Beijing: China Statistical Press, 1984).

25. See Li Xinggui, 'Marriage and Family—Report on 1000 Household Survey in Pengxian,' *Renkou Yanjui* (Beijing) 1984, No. 1.

26. Gao Ersheng, Gu Xingyuan, Zheng Xundai, Ding Xiangyun, Xu Genti, 'A Survey on Reproductive women in Qiyi Commune,' *Acta Academiae Medicine Primae Shanghai*, Supplement 1, 1982.

27. See Barclay, G.W., *et al.*, 'A Reassessment of the Demography of Traditional Rural China,' *Population Index*, October 1976, Vol. 42, No. 4.

28. See Zhou Hua, 'Dangdai Nuxin Shenghuo De Duoyuanhua' (Diversification of Life of Contemporary Women), *Zhongguo Funu* (Beijing), February 16–18, 1985.

29. See Li Yunsheng, Wang Xiaogao, Lo Hungchun, Zhang Feng, 'A Study on the Marriage Activities in a Mountainous Area in Pengxian, Sichuan,' *Renkou Yanjui* (Beijing), 1984, No. 1.

30. Lei Jiegiong, 'Problems of China's Marriage and Family,' *Shehui Yanjiu*, Sociology Department, Beijing University, 1985.

31. Li Jinghan, 'Demographic Analysis on Rural Families,' *Shehuikexue* (Beijing), Vol. II, No. 1, 1936.

32. *Mingpao* (overseas edition) (Hong Kong) February 7, 1986.

33. Chen Shenli, Li Zhen, Gao Yaging, Wang Shenjin, *A Study on the Relation Between Fertility and Living Standard of Jilin Province* (Jilin: 1985).

34. Duan Wei, Yang Yang, 'A Survey in Age at Marriage and at Birth,' *Renkou Yu Jingji* (Beijing) 1984, No. 4.

35. *Ta Kung-pao* (overseas edition) (Hong Kong), February 18, 1986.

The Status of Women in Thailand

SUCHART PRASITH-RATHSINT

Studies on the role, status and problems of Thai women in various areas have been carried out by a large number of scholars with varying scopes and objectives. The present paper is one of the earliest attempts to compile and review them, so as to put in perspective the various research papers, and the conclusions drawn by the researchers themselves. The topics in this paper include the areas covered in the planning of the development of Thai women, in order of presentation:

— a demographic profile;
— women in various sectors such as the economy, education, health, culture and society, politics and government
— special target groups of women;
— laws; and
— women's development plans.

A major limitation of the review is that the studies were based on different sets of data and samples collected at different times. In addition, the studies were carried out by different groups of people, whose interpretations are bound to conflict with one another. However, attempts will be made to highlight the significance of each study.

DEMOGRAPHIC PROFILE OF THAI WOMEN

Since the fourth five-year plan (1977–1981), the significance of the role of women in national social and economic development has been recognized. The fifth Plan (1981–1985) further stressed the need for a women's development plan as the role, status and problems of Thai women had drastically changed. Women were singled out as a major target group requiring special attention in development programmes. The sixth Plan (1986–1990) does not treat women's development as a special issue and women are no longer singled out as a special target group from overall development activities (NESDB 1986).

Size and Sex Ratio of Thai Population

Thai demographic data come from four major sources: population census, registration surveys and others. The 1960 census counted 26.2 million with a sex ratio (M/F) of 100.38 males to 100 females, and the 1970 census counted 34.4 million with a sex ratio of 99.13 males per 100 females (NSO 1978). The 1960 census shows that the great majority of the Thai population were young. Children under 15 years of age constituted about 45 per cent. The north-eastern region had the largest population, followed by the central, the north and the south regions. The percentage of females in the central region is larger than in the others (NESDB 1978). The 1980 Population and Housing Census shows that the country's population had increased to 44,824,540 in 1980. Women constituted slightly more than half of the population, 50.19 per cent. Children under 15 years of age constituted about 38.30 per cent. The north-eastern region had the largest population, followed by the central, the north and the south. Women in the central (including Bangkok Metropolis) and the south comprised more than half of the regional populations. According to the most recent population projections adopted for the sixth Plan, it is estimated that in 1990 Thailand would have a population of 56.34 million, children under 15 years of age constitute 33.39 per cent and those 60 years of age and over 5.96 per cent of the country's population, respectively. In the year 2000, the Thai population will reach 64.39 million with a sex ratio of 100.07. The aged population was estimated to be 7.5 per cent.

Nuptiality

According to the National Longitudinal Survey of Economic, Social and Demographic Change conducted by the Institute of Population Studies, Chulalongkorn University (Pitakthepsombut and Vibulsetr 1986), rural women marry at about 20 and men at 23.5 years, as compared to Bangkok women and men who marry at 21 and 26 years of age respectively. The difference in age at marriage to some extent reflects the differences in social and cultural backgrounds between urban and rural people.

A study based on the Longitudinal Survey data on the choice of spouse and housing after marriage shows that a majority of rural women choose their own spouses, who usually come from the same or a nearby village. Urban couples generally own their own houses. Those who cannot separate themselves from their families stay with the parents of the male spouse. In rural areas, patrilocal families are most frequently found.

A study of Thai women's nuptiality based on the 1970 census shows that social and economic factors affect nuptiality. Age at first marriage differs significantly between rural and urban people. It is the highest in Bangkok Metropolis and significantly differs according to their education and occupation (Chamratrithirong 1978). Another study of women's age at marriage points out that age at marriage of present-day Thai women is higher than in past decades. The proportion of women remaining single at 25 years of age has increased. Though some marry at a late age, the ratio of those who remain single has risen (Burapachana 1977).

Family Planning

Numerous KAP surveys on family planning have been conducted. A review of these studies leads to the conclusion that knowledge of birth control is fairly widespread among the Thai population. The practice of family planning has also accelerated. Between 1969 and 1975, the practice of contraception increased at about 4 per cent per annum and after 1975 it increased at a rate of 4.5 per cent per annum (Kamnuansilp and Kiratibutr 1980). The great majority of acceptors were female. However, there has been an increasing trend toward male contraceptive practice. For instance, in 1972 female sterilization was twenty-five times that of male sterilization. In 1976 the ratio was reduced to only nine times (Family Health Division 1976). A survey conducted for formulating policies on women's development also shows that 68.3 per cent of the women think that men should be the ones to be sterilized (Kannasuta 1981).

Fertility

Thailand's fertility used to be one of the world's highest, but at present, it is on a steady decline. Thai fertility is one of the areas that have been intensively studied. Some studies relating fertility to the role and status of Thai women show that women who have a higher educational status tend to have a smaller number of children (Knodel and Prachuabmoh 1973; Goldstein et al. 1972; Prasith-rathsint 1979), and that rural working women have a larger number of children than those who do not work (probably because the pressure of a large family has forced the former to go out to work and they are given more freedom to work outside the home). In Bangkok Metropolis, however, working women have a lower fertility than housewives. The explanation is that in urban areas, most families are nuclear, both spouses are working, and there are no elderly relatives to look after the children. Thus there is a conflict between motherhood and career. In the rural areas, the conflict is minimized by the nature of agricultural work and the presence of relatives in the household (Prasith-rathsint 1971).

A study of occupational fertility differentials based on a percentage sample of the 1960 census data shows that women in agriculture and trade had the highest fertility and professionals or administrative and clerical workers the lowest. Service workers and craftswomen were in the middle. The occupational fertility differentials are more obvious in the urban areas (Goldstein et al. 1972). Another study based on a 2 per cent sample of the 1970 census confirms the earlier findings. However, data from the Longitudinal Survey (two rounds) show that when the analysis is controlled by other variables, the relationship between occupation and fertility is minimal. Women engaged in clerical and managerial work average the lowest fertility. Women who earn wages or salaries before and after marriage have a low fertility. The relationship between fertility and husband's occupation is similar to that between fertility and wife's occupation (Chamratrithirong and Boonpratuang 1978).

A study of women's status and fertility in the south and Bangkok Metropolis carried out by the Institute of Population and Social Research, Mahidol University, shows a similar relationship between education, labour force participation and fertility to other previous studies (IPSR 1979). Another IPSR study on social and economic conditions of women in the non-slum areas of Bangkok Metropolis in 1979 finds a relationship between work status, occupation and fertility. Women who earn wages have the lowest fertility of any group (Setrpongkul 1980).

Mortality

Mortality is not a well-researched area. However, the available data show that death rates have been declining due to social and economic development and better public health. A survey of population change in 1974–1975 shows that the national death rate was 8.9 per thousand.

The male death rate was higher than that of the female, 9.8 as compared to 8.1 per thousand. The figure in non-municipal areas was 10.2 and 8.5 per thousand, respectively. Child and maternal death rates have also rapidly declined (Rachapachtayakom 1976). Thai women generally enjoy longer life expectancy at birth than Thai men. In 1964, life expectancy of women and men was 61.26 and 56.48 years, respectively. By 1984 this increased to 72.34 and 69.58 years, respectively (Prasith-rathsint 1986). The details of women's mortality will be given in the section on health.

Migration

Numerous studies have been conducted on migration and the findings are summarized here: The rates of migration of both male and female population have increased over the past decades. Most migration is for short distances. Intra-regional migration is higher and mostly between nearby provinces. Migrants are mostly at economically active ages, between 10 and 30 years of age. Women are increasingly tending to migrate into other areas and, in particular, to Bangkok Metropolis (Piampiti 1976). A review of literature on labour migrants will be presented in the next section.

In brief, a review of the literature on the demographic aspect of Thai women shows that during the past two decades women constituted half of the Thai population and that in the next decade, by 1990, women will number about 27.5 million, or 49.7 per cent of the total population. Thai women generally marry young and have a moderate sized family depending on their social and economic status. The population growth rate has been declining since the third Plan, and in 1986, at the end of the fifth Plan, Thai women will have an average of two children. In recent years, the country has witnessed an increasing rate of female migration, which is likely to have a significant social and economic bearing on families, the economy and society. This calls for a plan to face and remove the undesirable consequences. There is a serious need for policy-oriented research in this area.

WOMEN AND ECONOMY

The role of women in the economy is more generally accepted now than in the past. Women are given more opportunities to play a role in occupational activities and education. Changing social and economic conditions have also forced women to work outside the home. Thus women are found in various economic sectors including industry, handicrafts, agriculture, commerce and the service industry. Simultaneously, there has been an increase in the problems connected with women's increasing economic role, including rights and equal opportunities in promotion, wages and welfare, as well as problems associated with women's families.

The available data show that women's participation in the labour force is growing in importance. In 1979 there were 9.9 million women at an economically active age (about 66.3 per cent) in the labour force. Of those who were in the labour force, 9.8 million or 46 per cent of the total were gainfully employed. Those not in the labour force were housewives, school children, women waiting for the planting season and others. Female labour force participation has been on the increase, from 45.7 per cent in 1975 to 46.3 per cent in 1979. Unemployment also increased to 0.3 per cent in 1979 (NSO 1979).

Among the gainfully employed, women constitute 46.6 per cent. The majority of employed women, about 70 per cent, are engaged in agriculture or agriculture-related occupations. Fewer rural women are employed than men, who constitute only one-third of the unemployed. In addition, a greater percentage of rural women of age 11 to 19, that is, the school-going age, are working than those in the urban areas (NESDB 1978). More rural women have also become factory workers, most of them as unskilled wage labour, and problems of their welfare have arisen.

In the rural areas, female labour is as important as male labour (NCW, 1976). Traditional agriculture favours mutual help among relatives and neighbours in which children and women also participate. Rural women not only work alongside the men but also do household chores and attend to their husband's needs. In the past, when the labour corvee was operative, rural women had to take on all agricultural work to support their families and also do the unpaid housework.

Another study of the role and status of Thai women, conducted in the Chachoengsao and Lampang provinces in 1976–77, reports that rural women's labour is of great economic significance, 73 per cent of them earning an income jointly with their husbands in farming. The unemployed and dependent constitute only a small proportion (Chaiyasut 1978).

A National Labour Force Survey, conducted by the National Statistical Office during the same year to study labour utilization of men and women in both rural and urban areas, reports that the great majority of rural and urban women spend almost the same amount of time in occupational work, about 40–49 hours a week (NSO 1979). Urban workers are better educated and are frequently found in the service sector, whereas rural workers are mostly found in agriculture. Employment of rural women takes the form of family labour, and their status is neither of employer nor employee, whereas urban women are employees earning wages in a public or private business unit.

According to the 1979 National Economic and Social Development Board survey of factory workers in the Bangkok Metropolis, women constitute 56.4 per cent of all the factory workers. Only 2.5 per cent hold administrative posts. Most women are 21 to 25 years of age (NESDB 1978).

More opportunities are open for women's gainful employment. A study of female farmers in Nong Chok and Bang Pa In finds 60 per cent earning about half or more of the household income, 10 per cent less than half, and the rest takes in earnings equal to the household income (Kannasuta 1977).

Problems of Female Workers

While women increasingly share the burden of supporting their families through employment outside the home, their role and status in employment are not equal to those of men (Kannasuta et al. 1976). Women are discriminated against in promotional opportunities and income earning. In 1979, state enterprises employed over 200,000 people. The sex ratio of the employees was 3.6 men to 1 woman (Chansawang and Boripanbunpotedet 1981). In the civil service, there were about 0.27 million people in 1974, with a sex ratio (M/F) of 1.7 to 1 (Yotpetch and Utassatrsri 1981). A large number of female factory employees, 40 per cent, earn a relatively low income, about 500–1,000 baht a month (NESDB 1978). Less than 1.0 per cent of the women earn a monthly income of 5,000 baht. Thus there is considerable room for increasing women's participation in the labour force and promoting equality of economic opportunities.

According to some researchers, the stress in the culture and traditions of Thai society of lady-like virtues (NCW 1976, 1978; Pairoa 1976; Kamalnawin 1971) is among the factors adversely affecting Thai women's occupational opportunities in promotion and wages. Women are considered gentle, submissive and subordinate. Their duties are household chores, kitchen work, attending to their parents and husbands, and rearing children. Gainful employment outside the home is a secondary optional duty (NESDB 1978). Thai literature vividly reflects women's role and status in the family and society. Women are considered 'the hind legs of an elephant.' Their place is at home. They are of the tender sex and are like beautiful flowers. Women are sensitive, emotional, indecisive, and unoriginal. These beliefs and values have influenced the role and status of both men and women in employment.

Two other research works conclude that mores and traditions influence the belief that women are less competent than men. Women suffer from job discrimination, and have few promotion opportunities and low income because they lack training, work experience and self-confidence (Sirichunt 1976; Hungsasut 1976). Another study finds that only 3 per cent of women in the sample have secondary or higher education and 43.2 per cent have had little or no education or training (Chaiseree 1978).

A study of the status of female construction employees in Bangkok Metropolis (Sipipatanawitya 1977) shows that it is easier for employers to exploit female employees, who are mostly unskilled, in wages, working hours, holidays and welfare. Employed as casual labour, they are put to hard work, given low wages and work for longer hours for inadequate compensation.

Female labourers in textile factories in Bangkok Metropolis face job discrimination, wage discrimination and poor working conditions as employers disregard labour laws and officials from the Labour Department provide little regular supervision (Kosalwatana 1972). The labour laws themselves, while they protect the rights of women workers, also discriminate against women in one way or another.

Employed women also have unequal opportunities for skill development. The majority of female labourers are less educated. Employers, fearful of having to raise their wages, rarely encourage them to pursue further training to develop their skills (Thongchao and Suwanrojana 1981).

There have been numerous studies on the number of women's working hours. The findings are that women who work outside the home spend on an average about 7–9 hours a day at work; rural women spend an additional 3–4 hours a day doing house-work; married women in Bangkok Metropolis spend 2–4 hours a day doing household chores and looking after children; and single women spend about

1.6 hours a day doing household chores. In brief, women spend about the same amount of time in outside labour and more time than men doing household chores.

The NESDB working group on the long-term development of women (1982–2001) has conducted a number of small pilot studies on the status and problems of various groups of women, namely farmers, non-farmers, civil servants and state enterprise employees. Their reviews are presented in the section on special target groups.

It can be concluded that Thai women generally do not resent the fact that they rarely participate in activities at the district, provincial or national levels (Research and Evaluation Division 1978). Rather, they are content with the fact that they are given opportunities to make decisions on property and on the welfare of their families. Their attitudes may change when they become better educated. Only the better educated Thai women make demands for equal roles and participation in politics and households.

The major problems of Thai women are: job discrimination, unequal wages and lack of legal labour protection, particularly for women who migrate from the agricultural sector to urban areas and who are employed in the non-economically productive sector or in places where there is no legal labour protection. As long as the government is unable to solve the problems caused by migration to seek gainful employment or to generate employment in all regions, the great majority of women are certain to face problems of discrimination in employment, wages, and security.

Recommended Solutions

Attempts to solve these problems, first made in the third Plan (1972–1976), received more serious attention during the fourth Plan (1977–1981) with its stress on reducing inequalities and unbalanced growth.

Numerous studies have also been conducted. One study on the problems of female employees in the textile factories in Bangkok Metropolis (Kosalwatana 1972) suggests that to improve labour utilization, officials from the Labour Department should inform employers about their employees' problems and the employers should record the working hours and wages of their employees and supervise the factory floor. To improve labour protection, a minimum wage in each factory as well as methods of payment should be established by a wage committee consisting of employees'representatives, employers and government officials. To improve skill development, the government should provide vocational training at various levels.

Solutions to the problems of women in the service industry can be classified as preventive and corrective (Polsri 1974). Preventive solutions include curriculum readjustment and changes in methods of teaching at the compulsory level to encourage inquisitiveness, initiative, inventiveness and practicality in the student. Non-formal education, provincial industrialization, skill development training and labour protection should also be provided. The government should have a plan on the utilization of women's labour consistent with the national economic and social development plan. Corrective solutions cover vocational training which includes dress-making, hairdressing, an information service centre for migrant workers and more effective control over private job placement businesses.

Similar solutions are also proposed by another group of researchers (Kannasuta et al. 1976). For instance, the government should improve regulations of employment and encourage the private sector to do likewise. Vocational training centres should be improved, labour training encouraged, nursery services expanded for children of pre-school age to relieve the burden of working mothers, and women's organizations brought into the participation of solutions for women. Women should be encouraged to improve themselves and assist their less fortunate sisters. Problems of working mothers can be ameliorated by establishing communal nurseries or nurseries within factories for which the government should provide support, by evolving new family norms of division of labour and by letting women utilize new technological inventions to relieve the burden of household work.

Two studies made by the National Council of Women and the Faculty of Social Welfare of Thammasat University (Chaiyasu 1978) and by the Department of Community Development (Research and Evaluation Division 1978) in different areas similarly conclude that the major problems of rural women are income generation and family welfare. An increasing number of Thai women want to be income earners for their families and increase their knowledge and skills. For this, it is necessary to remove or minimize various social and economic barriers, including low education, job discrimination, and social prejudice against women's roles (NESDB and CUSSRI 1981).

WOMEN AND EDUCATION

In the past, the Thai educational system did not provide opportunities for women. During the Sukhothai period, education was offered only to men and women of the upper classes (Pairao 1976). Only with the change in the educational system during the Rattanakosin period did women begin to take an active interest in education. In 1868, a school was established to train people, mostly men, to enter the Thai civil service. Since 1874, when the first school for girls, Kulasatri Wang Lang (at present Vatana Academy), was established by American missionaries (Ministry of Education 1964), women have been encouraged to pursue education. After the revolution of 1932, the national educational plan stressed on equality in education. Boys and girls since then have had equal rights to education.

At present, women have the opportunity to educate themselves at all levels and in all subjects. In 1977, the number of boys attending school was slightly higher than that of girls. At the college level, during 1971–1973, the number of boys was higher by 16 per cent. In certain fields of studies, such as the social sciences and humanities, female students outnumber males (Chutikul and Thongchao 1981).

According to the 1960 Population and Housing Census, female illiteracy was higher than that of the male population, 25.2 per cent as compared to 1.1 per cent (NSO 1962). The illiteracy rate of older women was higher than that of younger women and higher in the north and the south than in the central and the north-east regions. Most women in the labour force had completed compulsory education. Over the past two decades, the percentage difference between male and female populations has been reduced from 28.3 in 1947 to 19.6 in 1960 and 14.1 in 1970 (NEC 1977). In 1980, the census results show that out of the population aged 10 years and over, 88.81 per cent were literate. The literacy rate for males was 92.45 per cent and for females was 85.26 per cent (NSO 1983).

A study of the effects of formal education development conducted in 1979 discovers that at the lower secondary levels, boys constituted 54.5 per cent of the school population at all levels (Kannasuta 1978). There were fewer boys than girls at the upper secondary and vocational levels in which the girls constituted 51.6 and 51.1 per cent respectively. The girls' rate of illiteracy has been on a decline and in the near future the rate will be about the same. It can be said that at present it is not sex but limitations of personal abilities, competence, inclination and intelligence which prevent women from gaining an education at any level.

In non-formal education, which has rapidly expanded to increase people's knowledge in various fields, more women are found to have enrolled than men, the percentage difference declining as the level of education increased. In vocational training, women have chosen what suits their traditional role, home economics being the most popular field. Business administration, mainly at the introductory level, is another subject that is gaining in popularity.

An analysis of the content of training courses during 1978–1980 shows that about 43 per cent of the course content is designed for women, 54 per cent for both sexes and 4 per cent for men (Thongchao and Suwanrojana 1981). At the primary level, traditional values and concepts of sexual division of labour are still found in daily socialization and in primary textbooks. Girls are still taught to be the weaker sex by being encouraged to play with 'girl toys', and to help their mothers cook and clean the house, whereas boys are taught to be tough by being encouraged to play with mechanical toys and to help in their fathers' farms.

At the secondary level, girls are taught how to be good wives, house-keeping, childbearing, supporting their husbands, and being faithful to them. At the same time, boys are taught to be stronger and more competent and to be responsible for supporting their families. They are not expected to be as well-behaved as girls.

Vocational training courses for women offered by the government and the private sector mostly aim at training them in the various functions of a housewife, such as cooking, dress-making and making imitation flowers, and overlook the importance of increasing women's skills in economic production, particularly among rural women who play as significant a role as men do.

The mass media and communications, which are influential, further impress on women their traditional roles by presenting them as sex objects and female beauties ignoring the creativity and intelligence of women that can be used to develop themselves, the community and society as a whole. There are few journals and magazines to serve women's needs. Furthermore, most programmes intended for women deal with household decoration, health care and beauty, cooking, manners and family planning but none on laws related to women.

Thus, even though the law protects women's rights and the educational system offers them the same rights that men have, the persistence of old values and customs decreases their opportunities for development. According to the NESDB working group, data show that the great majority of people, 70 per cent, want their boys to be better educated than their girls (Kannasuta 1981). The status of women's education will not change or probably will change slowly as long as there is no change in social values and attitudes, particularly with regard to boys' education relative to girls' and the conflict between preparing a woman to take on an occupation or to be a good wife. These values and conflicts indicate the obstacles that must be overcome before women can fully participate in social, economic and political development.

WOMEN AND HEALTH

Research on the role, status and problems of women and health is scarce. According to one study, the health problems of women vary by age group. The main health problems of adolescents aged 11–14 years are malnutrition and adaptation of sex behaviour. Women of the age group 15–44 years face high mortality risk due to childbirth and spontaneous abortions as well as mental health problems. Those aged 45–49 years face problems of personal adjustment to physical and mental decline, and those who are 50 years and above face increased bodily malfunction (Boonthai and Chanwimol 1981).

Maternal and child health statistics indicate women's health problems. In 1980 in non-municipal areas, 18.4 per cent of the women underwent delivery at a public hospital, 7.9 per cent at a health or midwifery station, 5.7 per cent at a private clinic, and the rest were delivered by traditional midwives, neighbours, husbands or relatives. The result was high infant and maternal death rate. There are other problems such as malnutrition and poor spacing of children. About 47.5 per cent of urban women underwent delivery at a hospital or a health station and 38.9 per cent at home (NESDB and CUSSRI 1981). Women in rural and slum areas know little about nutrition, prenatal care, infant feeding and care, and child development. Poverty and poor education affect maternal and child health. Child malnutrition is fairly high, and mothers are not in a position to help themselves, families or communities.

Women are regarded as child producers and rarely considered as persons whose energy can be used to develop society (Kannasuta 1981). Indicators on women's health are consequently related to births. Although the fourth Plan has improved public health services, there are still significant urban-rural differences. The ratio of doctor to population is 1:1, 289 in urban areas and 1:17,280 in rural areas. The ratio of nurses to population is 1:2,372 in urban areas and 1:120,431 in rural areas. Health stations also vary by region. The ratio is 1:441 people in the central region, 1:626 in the south, 1:964 in the north and 1:1,472 in the north-east.

To improve women's health several measures have been proposed, including increasing family health services, promoting nutritional programmes, increasing people's knowledge of birth and child care, family planning, health insurance, and social welfare. These measures are expected to enable women to improve themselves and contribute to national development.

WOMEN AND SOCIETY

Thai society was influenced by both Indian and Chinese cultures through Brahminism and Buddhism. In both cultures, a woman's status is much lower than a man's, significant value is placed on large families and boys over girls. Nonetheless, a Thai woman's status comparatively is much better than that of an Indian or Chinese woman. In Thai society, men have been taught to be the leaders of families, communities and society while women are taught to take care of household chores and children (Sub-committee 1980).

In a survey of attitudes of household heads conducted by the National Council of Women and the Faculty of Social Welfare, Thammasat University, the great majority of men, 95 per cent, concur that mothers are important to personality formation and for the future of children and that husbands and wives should equally share family responsibilities. About 87 per cent state that wives have the right to make decisions in the family's affairs, and 96 per cent want to see their wives participate in the development of their villages. In other words, men generally expect women to play various kinds of roles in the family and community.

A survey of the role and status of working women in Bangkok Metropolis conducted by the Association of Business and Professional Women of Thailand in 1975 finds that the majority of women incline towards liberalism and individualism; about 78 per cent say that women should help themselves first before they help society; 70 per cent stress the role of women in societal work; 59 per cent say that social inequalities are the product of society, and 91 per cent say that people should also have a role to play in social change and not leave it to the wish of the ruling elite (Kannasuta et al. 1976).

Men and women share similar social values. However, while men stress achievements in life (better education, freedom and equality), women stress love, familism and dependency and are more superstitious than men (Komin and Samakkarn 1979).

Regarding the role and status of women in family, the first primary social unit, studies show that in 1980 over one-fourth of the women chose their own spouses and for 56 per cent of the women, parents and siblings participated in the decision (NCW 1980). However, as family ties weaken, it is expected that more women will make the decision on their own. Within families, husbands still make the final decision in a number of areas but generally share decision-making with their wives (Kannasuta 1981).

The percentage of divorced men and women has remained relatively constant over a long period of time. In 1974, about 1.1 per cent of men and 2.8 per cent of women, 15 years of age and over, were divorced. In 1970, 1 per cent of men and 2.9 per cent of women were divorced (Prasith-rathsint 1981b). The slightly higher percentage of divorced women is due to the ease with which men can remarry (NCW 1976). Women generally agree to divorce in cases of adultery, irresponsibility or incompatibility (Kannasuta 1981).

The role and status of Thai women have considerably changed particularly during the past decade. Before the Rattanakosint period, Thai women's roles were limited by custom and tradition to the family. In the early Rattanakosint period and after the change of government in 1932, the role and status of women began to change. King Rama IV prohibited forcing women into concubinage and allowed parents to arrange marriages only with the children's consent (Nakhonchat 1965). The most significant factor in changing women's role was the educational reform of 1898 (Sub-committee 1980).

Between the 1932 change in government and World War II, the growing influence of the mass media influenced political movements which demanded political rights, freedom and equality. The first Constitution and Election Law in 1933 declared equal political rights for men and women. During 1932–1949 there were eleven elections of people's representatives. The first woman was elected to parliament in 1949. Various organizations related to women's activities were established. An office of women's culture was established in 1953 in the National Cultural Council; the National Council of Women was established in 1959, and the Social Welfare Council in 1963 (Kannasuta et al. 1976).

Rural development began in 1962. During the first five years, as many as 6,000 women were trained in groups on home economics, and women's clubs were established in 675 villages but later abandoned because women themselves were not ready for them (Dejarint 1981). As far as the training courses organized by various agencies, public and private, were concerned, 35 per cent of women were trained in family planning and 12 per cent in vocational activities and sewing. Data also show that 75 per cent of women were idle during March and April. Only 13 per cent of women participated in activities of some activity groups even though 53 per cent were members of the groups. The great majority of rural women, 85 per cent, wanted to work outside the home to earn an additional income (Research and Evaluation Division 1978).

A small survey interviewing 448 women in four provinces found that one-third of them had participated in discussions on village problems, such as keeping the village and household clean, slightly over one-third had participated in village development activities, and only 11 per cent considered it unnecessary to participate in the village development programme (Keetasungka 1979). However, another study of agricultural housewives and development, which interviewed 193 female respondents and 139 male respondents in Nakhon Prathom province, finds that of the women who have taken part in community development, 67 per cent of the housewives know of various community problems, 70 per cent participate in community development projects, but only 40 per cent have ever discussed the problems with the village headmen (Chansawang 1980).

In brief, Thai women are increasing their participation in community affairs, and attitudes toward women's role and status are also changing. In the near future women's role and status are expected to be equal to men's.

WOMEN, RELIGION AND CULTURE

Women's religious status is inferior to men's. In Buddhism, men have superior religious value. Thus parents prefer to have boys. Women's religious role is in strict observance of religious principles and involvement in religious ceremonies (Sub-committee 1980). A study of 20,000 nuns finds that nuns play a functional role in religion, but their status is not officially recognized. They are confined to the temples where they help the monks keep the compound clean and prepare food for the monks. There is no organization to provide support for the nuns to assist them in improving themselves and serving society (Panchapun and Pruetatorn 1981).

No direct research has been conducted on women in arts and culture. However, it has been observed that women are the guardians of tradition, art and culture. Traditional games, folk plays, dancing, flower arrangement and making household items have been continued by women. Thus they play a very crucial role in conserving Thai culture, tradition, customs and practices.

WOMEN, POLITICS AND ADMINISTRATION

After the 1932 change of government and the 1933 election law, Thai women began to play a greater role in politics. In 1957, women constituted 40 per cent of the voters, or about 34 per cent of eligible women. In 1969, the percentage rose to 43 of all those elected to parliament, and a number of women were appointed senators. At the sub-national level, women were elected as members of the municipal council, chairmen of the council and councillors.

A study conducted in Chachoengsao and Lam Pang provinces finds that in 1977 as many as 78 per cent of the women in both provinces went to the polls. The great majority, 86 per cent, took their own decision on whom to vote for. The rest were advised by their husbands, village headmen, Kamnan (heads of sub-districts), or vote leaders (NCW and Faculty of Social Welfare 1977). A 1978 study by the Department of Community Development on the question of women's willingness to participate in various committees of village and sub-district councils found that about 43 per cent of women wished to participate in the councils if they were given the opportunity.

One study found that 57 per cent of women voted on their own in an election for Kamnan. The rest were influenced by the village headmen, Kamnan, their husbands, neighbours and government officials. The same study shows that about 59 per cent of women voted on their own in a parliamentary election; 23.7 per cent on the advice of the Kamnan, and the rest on the advice of their husbands and government officials (Chansawang 1980).

Thus it can be concluded that even though women increasingly play a great role in politics and administration by voting in elections, their participation as candidates is still at a low level. There is a need for research into factors affecting their willingness to participate in politics and administration in a more dynamic manner.

Educational attainment is a prerequisite for leadership (Prapuetdee et al. 1977). Most women leaders, 86 per cent, in this small study, have at least a bachelor's degree. They assumed leadership when they were 40-45 years of age. Most of them had high esteem of their abilities to decide on various problems in their organization and families. The great majority of them delegated authority to their subordinates according to their abilities. However only 54 per cent of them expressed total dedication to their profession. About 55 per cent believed in the equality of the sexes.

A research work on the long-term development of women in politics and public administration finds that 58 per cent of women believe that in the next ten years Thai women will be capable of being governors and 23 per cent believe that women are even now capable of being governors (Kannasuta 1981). At the local level, about 64 per cent of women are ready to be candidates for the post of village headman, 26 per cent for provincial councillor or municipality councillor and 55 per cent for member of parliament. It is evident that an increasing number of women wish to participate actively in politics and public affairs.

WOMEN AND LAW

Thai laws have provisions endorsing women's rights of various kinds. However, in practice, there are still regulations and orders discriminating against women. There is an obvious need to study these regulations and orders in detail.

The NESDB working group has conducted a study of laws for women's development by comparing Thai law with the 1967 United Nations declaration on women's rights in five major areas, namely (*a*) physical rights, (*b*) family rights and naturalization, (*c*) education and vocational training, (*d*) social and economic rights and (*e*) political rights (Singhaviriya 1980).

A study was conducted on proper legal measures and incentives to encourage people to have a small family, ideally with two children. These incentives include measures designed to encourage people to practise family planning, such as tax incentives, social benefits provided for a small family, educational assistance, incentives or rewards to those who induce people to practise birth control, tax exemptions for donations to population activities, and disincentives to those who have a larger family size. Each woman also needs to work at improving her own education, select her mate, decide when to get married and learn how to carry out the decision-making process in the household. There was also a study of family law and national security which outlines the role of women in great detail.

TARGET GROUPS

In the women's development plan in the fifth Plan, pilot studies were made on special target groups of women which included (*a*) agricultural women, (*b*) non-agricultural women, (*c*) government officials and public enterprise employees, (*d*) minority groups, (*e*) prostitutes and women in the service sector, and (*f*) female prisoners.

A study finds that 7 million women work on farms, or about 77 per cent of the entire female labour force (Pongpaichitr 1981). Women participate in production activities as well as take care of household chores. Women recognize the importance of being farmers and are eager to learn more about new agricultural technology, to increase their earnings.

Men have more opportunities to use labour-saving machines than women do. Women labourers earn a lower income and work for longer hours than men. Women spend 1,644 hours a year on the farm, while men spend 2,294 hours, but in household work women spend 3,894 hours and men spend much less time. In addition, women suffer from irregular employment, lower wages, fewer opportunities to work outside the home, poor health and low education. In the past, government efforts to develop rural women focused on the role and functional activities of a housewife but they lacked inter-agency coordination. In 1980, the government launched a nationwide rural job creation programme, but only 13.2 per cent of women were employed by the programme. The study recommends extending the years of compulsory education to give women more education, designing and developing vocational training according to women's own needs, encouraging various groups of women, improving the marketing system for agricultural products and enacting laws on working hours, minimum wages, and welfare of agricultural labourers and on equality in housework and gainful employment (Pongpaichitr 1981).

A study was conducted on reasons for non-agricultural women working outside the home, employment opportunities, work status, wages, promotion and working women's needs (Raviwongse 1981b). Based on the census and labour force survey data, the study finds that in 1978, there were 2.5 million non-agricultural women; 42.4 per cent lived in municipal areas and 57.6 per cent in non-municipal areas. Over one-third of them were private employees; 28.8 per cent worked on their own; 25.7 per cent were employed in family business without pay; and one-tenth were state employees. Less than 1 per cent were employers.

The majority of the non-agricultural women are poorly educated. The problems facing them consequently are fewer job opportunities than men, lower wages, fewer opportunities for promotion, lack of appropriate skills and security, and lack of coordination among organizations dealing with women. The same study recommends the extension of compulsory education, enforcement of labour laws, changes in labour laws to protect women's labour, provision of social security, increasing job security, provision of ways and means to assist working women, e.g., child care centres and flexible working hours.

Two studies have also been conducted, one on government employees and the other on state enterprise employees (Yotpetch and Utasatsri 1980; Raviwongse 1981). The studies focus on the problems and needs of female employees, job opportunities, recruitment processes, promotion, salary increase, and ways to improve their status. The details of the studies are presented in the long-term development plan for women (1982–2000).

There are few studies of the role, status and problems of minority women, namely, Thai Muslims, refugees and tribals. The Thai Muslims live mostly in the south, in the provinces of Yala, Patani, Satun and parts of Songkla. Out of the national population of 1,867, 107, about 956,462 live in these provinces. The hill tribes comprise about 114,000 people (Veerawongse and Sirisumpunt 1981).

Owing to social and cultural differences and specific kinds of culture, the problems of each of the minority groups differ, regarding population growth rate, health, educational opportunities and employment. No general solutions can thus be prescribed for all minority groups.

Prostitutes and women in massage parlours and tea houses are also one of the target groups. Their problems have been studied by a number of researchers but on a small scale and a variety of topics (Panchapun, Harntrakul and Pruetatorn 1981; Muengman et al. 1979; Pongpaichitr 1980; Eimbutrop 1977). As yet, there is no conclusion on how to deal with their problems. The number of these working women has rapidly risen, and the NESDB working group estimates that in 1980 there were about 500,000 to 700,000 such women. The increase is in the number of women working as masseuses and sexual partners in massage parlours, tea houses and nightclubs, whereas the number of those working in hotels and brothels has declined.

Another target group is women in prisons. At present, out of about 64,000 people in prison, 15,000 are women (Ratanaserewongse and Areeya 1981) and their number is on the increase. It is argued that economic and social pressures are the primary cause for this increase.

Also included in the target group are the nuns. The problem of nuns is mainly that they are not recognized by the public. Their status and role are ambivalent. They also need some kind of public welfare and training to be more productive in society (Panchapun and Pruetatorn 1981).

With respect to female migrant labour, it is found that women who tend to migrate more to urban areas enter the tertiary sector. Women who migrate from the north-east constitute an increasing proportion of migrant labour (Prasith-rathsint 1981a).

Other target groups include women who have compulsory primary education and are out of school and the aged (Prasith-rathsint 1981b). A greater percentage of girls than boys leave school after obtaining a primary education. The girls at this age constitute quite a significant percentage of the female migrants. As the rural young migrate into urban areas, the aged are left behind unattended. In the past they were taken care of by their children. Some kind of social security for them is recommended.

There are also other studies in connection with the long-term planning for the development of women. They are social indicators for women (Prasith-rathsint, 1980), evaluation of projects related to development of women (Vuthimedhi 1981), desirable models of Thai women and evaluation of the work of the National Council of Women (NESDB and CUSSRI 1981).

In brief, studies on the role, status and problems of Thai women in various social and economic sectors have been spotty, most of them being based on scanty data or relatively small surveys. Although pilot studies, some have made generalizations beyond their sample. Nevertheless, all serve as a basis for further inquiries into the subject. The work of the NESDB working group on long-term planning for development of women is also of similar value. Indeed, for policy formulation, a great deal of serious research on some of the topics is needed. Research should be conducted by well-qualified social scientists competent in conducting field surveys and data analyses. Among topics that need further research are the role, status and problems of the aged, the out-of-school teenagers, female migrant labour, office regulations directly and indirectly discriminating against women and evaluation of women development projects.

REFERENCES

Sources available in Thai unless stated otherwise

Boonthai, Chalermsuk and Pissamai Chanwimol, 1981. 'Health of Thai Women,' NESDB Working Group.

Burapachana, Napaporn, 1977. 'Fertility Research in Thailand,' *Newsletter*, Institute of Population Studies, Chulalongkorn University, March 1977.

Chaiseree, Nongyao, 1978. 'Women and Economic Growth,' a paper in the seminar on *Women's Participation in Social Development* organized by Kasetsart University and Agricultural Development Council.

Chaiyasut, Nanthanee. 1978. 'Status of Rural Women,' a paper in the seminar on *Women's Participation in Social Development*, op. cit.

Chamratrithirong, Apichat, 1978. *Thai Marriage Pattern: An Analysis of the 1970 Census Data*, Research Monograph (Bangkok: Institute for Population and Social Research, Mahidol University) (in English).

Chamratrithirong, Apichat and Supranee Boonprathueng, 1978. *The 1971 Population and Housing Census; Fertility: An Analytical Report* No. 3 (Bangkok: National Statistical Office).

Chansawang, Apornpunt, 1980. 'Farm Housewives and National Development' (Bangkok: Office of Information, Supreme Command Headquarter) (mimeo).

Chansawang, Apornpunt and Saksri Boripanbunpotedet, 1981. 'Problems and Needs of the State Enterprise Employees,' research paper of the Working Group on Long-term Development of Women.

Chutikul, Saisuree and Viboonluck Thongchao, 1981. 'Education and Occupation Preparation,' a paper presented to the NESD Working Group.

Debavalya, Nibhon, 1977. 'Female Employment and Fertility: Cross-sectional and Longitudinal Relationships from a National Sample of Married Thai Women,' Working paper No. 24 (Institute of Population Studies, Chulalongkorn University) (in English).

Dejarint, Pairat, 1981. 'Social, Political and Administrative Participation of Thai Women,' Research paper for the NESDB Working Group.

Eimbutrop, Korkiat, 1977. 'Attitudes of Crime Suppression Policemen toward Registration of Prostitutes,' Research paper of Faculty of Social Sciences and Humanities, Mahidol University.

Goldstein, Alice and Penporn Tirasawat, 1972. *The Influence of Labor Force Participation and Education on Fertility in Thailand*, Research Report No. 9, Institute of Population Studies, Chulalongkorn University.

Hungsasut, Chitchan, 1976. 'Short Course Schooling in Factories,' *Journal of Woman Labor* (Vol. 1, May 1976), pp. 37–42.

Kamnuansilp, Peerasit and Supa Kiratibutr, 1980. 'Contraceptive Prevalence in Thailand,' paper presented at a seminar on *Regional Development and Fertility Difference*, organised by the Thai Population Committee, pp. 13–31.

Kamolnawin, Sinee, 1971. 'Changing Status of Thai Women,' *Journal of Development Administration* (Vol. 11, No. 3), pp. 401–442.

Kannasuta, Kattiya, et al., 1976. *Reflections of Thai Women* (Bangkok: Thai Kasem Printer), p. 35.

Kannasuta, Kattiya, 1977. 'Thai Women Farmers: A Case study of Woman Farmers in Nong Chok and Bang Pa In Districts' (Bangkok: Research Center of the National Institute of Development Administration).

Kannasuta, Kattiya, 1978. 'Education and Development for Thai Women' in *Aspect of Thai Women Today*, Background Document to World Conference of the United Nations Decade for Women, Copenhegen, July 14–20, 1978 (in English).

Kannasuta, Kattiya, et al., 1980. 'Evaluation of the work of the National Council of Women During 1977–1979,' Research Center, Institute of Development Administration (mimeo).

Kannasuta, Kattiya, 1981. 'National Survey on the Attitudes Towards Thai Women 1980,' Research paper for the NESDB Working Group.

Keetasungka, Maka, 1979. 'Development of Rural Thai Women,' Thaikadee, Thammasat.

Knodel, John and Visid Prachuabmoh, 1973. *The Fertility of Thai Women*, Research Report No. 10, Institute of Population Studies, Chulalongkorn University.

Komin, Suntharee and Sanid Samakkarn, 1979. 'Thai Social Values System: Methodology of Measurement,' Research Center, National Institute of Development Administration.

Kosalwatana; Napaporn, 1972. *Working Conditions of Women and Children in Textile Industries in Bangkok-Thonburi*, M.A. thesis, School of Public Administration, National Institute of Development Administration (unpublished).

Limanonda, Bhassorn, 1976. *Mate Selection and Post Nuptial Residence in Thailand*, M.A. thesis, Cornell University (in English) (unpublished).

Muengman, Dheppanom, Somsakdi Nunta, et al., 1979. 'Knowledge and Attitudes of Massage Girls.'

Nakhonchat, Arb, 1965. 'The Role of Housewives in National Economic and Social Development,' Department of Agricultural Economics, Kasetsart University.

Pairoa, Boonthun, 1976. *Status and Role of Thai Women Today*, M.A. Thesis, Chulalongkorn University (unpublished).

Panchapun, Naengnoi, 1981. 'Nuns', Research paper for the NESDB Working Group.

Panchapun, Naengnoi and Nilamol Pruetatorn, 1981. 'Nuns, Attitudes towards Their own role and Status,' Research paper for the NESDB Working Group.

Panchapun, Naengnoi, Sukanya Harntrakul and Nilamol Pruetatorn, 1981. 'Some Service Women, Prostitutes and Masseurs,' Research Report to the NESDB Working Group.

Piampiti, Suwanlee, 1976. 'Changes in the Pattern of Migration in Thailand: 1960–1970,' *Journal of Development Administration* (Vol. 16, No. 3).

Pitakthepsombut, Pichit and Suwattana Vibulsertr, 1986. *Summary of Findings of the Longitudinal Survey of Social, Economic and Demographic Change*, Research Monograph, Institute of Population Studies, Chulalongkorn University.

Pongpaichitr, Pasuk, 1980. *Causes of Migration of Rural Women to Become Massage Girls and the Effects on Their Families* (mimeo).

Pongpaichitr, Pasuk, 1981. 'Agricultural Women,' Research paper for the NESDB Working Group.

Polsri, Somkit, 1974. *Utilization of Women Labor in Service Establishments and Manpower Development, A Case study of Masseurs in Massage Parlours*, M.A. thesis, Faculty of Economics, Thammasat University (unpublished).

Prapuetdee, Bovorn, Thiparporn Pimpisuthi and Chalermpol Srihongse, 1977. *Thai Women: Role of Administrative Leaders*, Faculty of Political Science, Ramkhamhaeng University (mimeo).

Prasith-rathsint, Suchart, 1973. 'The Relationship between Female Labor Force Participation and Fertility of the Rural Thai Women,' *Journal of Social Science*.

Prasith-rathsint, Suchart, 1979. *Fertility Threshold Values of Income and Education in Thailand*, Department of Demography, School of Applied Statistics, National Institute of Development Administration.

Prasith-rathsint, Suchart, 1981a. 'Female Migrant Labor,' Research paper for the NESDB Working Group.

Prasith-rathsint, Suchart, 1981b. 'Social and Economic Status of Thai Women and Target Groups,' Research paper for the NESDB Working Group.

Prasith-rathsint, Suchart, 1986. *Adjust of Mortality Statistics and Life Table Construction in Thailand* (Bangkok: National Institute of Development Administration).

Pruekpongsawalee, Malee, 1981. 'Laws for Development of Women,' Research paper for the NESDB Working Group.

Rachapachtayakom, Jawalaksana, 1976. 'Trends and Differentials in Mortality,' in Economic and Social Commission for Asia and the Pacific, Country Monograph Series, No. 3, Population of Thailand (Bangkok: United Nations) (in English).

Ratanasereewongse, Saengchai and Kothom Areeya, 1981. 'Women Prisoners,' Research paper for the NESDB Working Group.

Raviwongse, Vichitr, 1981. 'Agricultural Women,' Research paper for the NESDB Working Group.

Research and Evaluation Division, Department of Community Development, Ministry of Interior (Thailand), 1978. 'Problems and Needs of Rural Women' (mimeo).

Ruengsuwan, Chavaeng and Sinee Kamolnawin, 1970. *Economic Roles of Thai Women* (Bangkok: National Institute of Development Administration).

Setrpongkul, Suppamas, 1980. 'A Study of the Relationship between Female Labor Participation and Fertility in Bangkok Metropolis,' M.A. thesis, Mahidol University (unpublished).

Singhaviriya, Sahas, 1980. 'Family Law and National Security,' Thesis of the National Defence College.

Sipipatanawitaya, Vichjuta, 1977. 'Working Conditions of Female Employees in Construction Work,' M.A. thesis, Faculty of Economics, Thammasat University (unpublished).

Sirichunt, Charoen, 1976. 'Labor Protection Law,' *Journal of Women Labor* (Vol. 1, No. 1, May), pp. 7–12.

Sub-Committee on Development of Activities and Roles of Women, NESDB, 1980, 'Present Status of Thai Women.'

Thailand, Election Division, Ministry of Interior. 'Report on the Election of the Members of Parliament' (mimeo), 1983.

Thailand, Family Health Division, 1976. 'Sterilization Expansion Program,' *Journal of Family Health* (Vol. 6, No. 1).

Thailand, Institute of Population and Social Research, Mahidol University, 1979. 'Women's Status and Fertility: A Case Study of a Southern Community Compared to Women in Bangkok Metropolis,' a research paper for the Third Training Course on Population and Family Planning Research.

Thailand, Ministry of Education, 1964. *History of the Ministry of Education* (Bangkok: Kurusapa Printing House).

Thailand, National Council of Women, 1971. 'Impact of Thai Women's Social Values on National Development,' a seminar paper organized by the Council of Bangkok, August.

Thailand, National Council of Women, 1976. *Thai Women* (Bangkok: Vitayakhon).

Thailand, National Council of Women and Faculty of Social Welfare, Thammasat University, 1977. *Survey of the Status of Thai Rural Women in Two Provinces*, September (mimeo).

Thailand, National Economic and Social Development Board, 1978. *Seminar Papers on Thai Women's Status*, Pattaya, 6–9 September, p. 1.

Thailand, National Economic and Social Development Board and Chulalongkorn University Social Science Research Institute, 1981. 'Implementation Plan for Development of Women' (mimeo).

Thailand, National Education Council, 1977. *Statistics on the Illiterate of Thailand (1947–1970)* (Bangkok: Thoupraditkarnoim).

Thailand, National Statistical Office, 1962. *The 1960 Population and Household Census* (Bangkok: National Statistical Office).

Thailand, National Statistical Office, 1978. *Survey of Population Change (Second Round)*, July-September, 1978 (Bangkok: National Statistical Office), (in English and Thai).

Thailand, National Statistical Office, 1983. *The 1980 Population and Housing Census* (Bangkok: NSO).

Thailand, Population Projection Working Group, 1981. *Population Development Plan: 1982–1986* (Bangkok: Ruenkaewkarnpim).

Thailand, Social Development Projects Division, 1981. *National Economic and Social Development Board, Draft of Plan for Five-Year Women Development (1982–1986)* (mimeo).

Thailand, NESDB Working Group, 1981. *Draft: Long-term Plan for Development of Women 1982–2000*, pp. 55–61 (mimeo).

Thongchao, Viboonluck and Pornthip Suwanrojana, 1981. 'Basic Educational Status and Vocational Preparation of Women,' Research paper for the NESDB Working Group.

Veerawongse, Suriya and Napas Sirisumpunt, 1981. 'Cultural Groups,' Research paper for the NESDB Working Group.

Vuthimedhi, Yuwat. 1981. 'Evaluation of Women's Development Project,' Research paper for the NESDB Working Group.

Yotpetch, Sasipatana and Surongratana Utasstrsri. 1981. 'Roles, Problems and Needs of the Female Civil Servants.' Research paper of the Working Groups on Long-term Development of Women.

Status of Women in Taiwan

Lan-hung Nora Chiang

Historically, the position of women in China is inextricably linked to the structure of the family. As a result of patriarchal familial values, inequality between men and women existed, as reflected by the absence of women's right to own property, to hold religious positions, and even to have their full names written in the ancestral records. Women's subordination in the family lasted for centuries and their positions were determined by a life cycle throughout which they devoted themselves to the needs of their families. Both single and married women were subject to innumerable social constraints, which included women holding multiple roles at home, producing male offspring, carrying out household chores and obeying their in-laws. Their lives were constrained by obedience, forbearance and tolerance, even of the polygamous marriages by their husbands. Disobedience to their husbands and their in-laws could result in being expelled from their families upon which they were economically dependent. As victims of social mores, the exclusive route to escalate their status as women was to produce male offspring.

Before the war, the status of women of Taiwan paralleled that of women in agrarian societies (Duley and Edwards, 1986:241). Although the Constitution adopted in 1931 gave women equal opportunities to participate in politics as well as in education and employment, the ideology towards women's status has changed only gradually. Women's roles have broadened to include social, economic and political aspects. However, the family is still their exclusive domain and responsibility.

STATUS OF WOMEN IN TAIWAN: RESEARCH FINDINGS

Margery Wolf (1972) who has worked on this subject since 1958 wrote that there were crucial differences in the status of Chinese women according to their position in the life cycle. From the moment of birth, a girl was at risk: the valuation of females was such that female infanticide was widespread. Childhood role socialization prepared boys and girls early and well for their adult destinies. Even the marriage. ceremony symbolized a woman's place in the patriarchal society. If a women had sons who remained at home with their brides, she occupied a key role in the extended family, influencing many household decisions.

Sung, an anthropologist who carried out fieldwork in northern Taiwan between 1972 and 1981 found that Taiwanese women in the rural areas were not powerless by any means (Sung 1983). He reported that they took active part in family affairs and management and in certain matters were always considered to be the decision makers. Sung's argument was that as a woman went through different stages in her family, her status changed.

Even as women entered the paid labour force, particularly in industries, their status in the family did not seem to change. Gallin (1982) demonstrated that daughters who turned in a good portion of their wages did not win equal opportunity. This was so because most lack skills and knowledge that would enable them to have alternatives to marriage and family. Gallin concluded that development in Taiwan has neither altered cultural definitions of male and female roles nor transformed the structure of status and authority within the family.

Lu's (1981) in-depth interview of 58 women in the three rural communities found that women's participation in the industrial labour force had not been accompanied by a significant change of their family status and role playing during the process or the family's adjustment to women's employment.

Hu's (1985) counter argument to the above statements is based on the fact that as a result of rural industrialization, the male family head has less control over the younger generation who are engaged in industrial work. In all types of families, daughters and daughters-in-law now enjoy more autonomy, whereas the status of mothers-in-law has become lower. In two other regards, young women's status has improved. First, a working girl's parents usually transfer all bride price into dowry and give them extra money to raise their marriage status; and second, married daughters maintain closer ritual relations with natal families.

Kung(1983) analysed the effects of women's work on their position and self-image and concluded that while working does allow women physical mobility and provide money for better clothing and recreational activities, new economic roles do not evolve into higher familial status. A recent study of urban women by Tsui (1985) focuses on parental investment in children's education as well as the subsequent role changes of highly educated working women in relation to their families. She has shown that by continuing economic relationship with their natal families after marriage, these women have improved their positions in the family.

The above studies show that the impact of women entering the wage labour force on women's upward mobility and social status has not been uniform. This paper will examine three aspects of women's status in Taiwan: women's reproductive role and its relationship to status is first introduced. Second, women's attainment in education which would make the best promise for advancing women's status in the future is discussed. Third, women's role in economic development would be reflected by their contributions in the labour force.

FERTILITY AND THE STATUS OF WOMEN

Taiwan's demographic transition began with high growth rates in the post-war years and declined to 15 per thousand at present. A high population density of 528 persons per square kilometre which is only second to that of Bangladesh in the world deems it necessary to restrict population growth. Family planning programmes which were implemented since 1969, together with socio-economic changes, have contributed to fertility decline. Although the birth rate is declining, the rate is still low. Many obstacles exist in the implementation of family planning on the island. The major ones are: (*a*) a large number of women still have not accepted family planning before they have had the number of children they want, (*b*) son preference is common among men and women, resulting in large numbers of children,[1] (*c*) small family size norms have not been widely accepted by women of child-bearing age, nor husbands, or parents-in-law, (*d*) contraceptive methods which are available to men have not been promoted to an equal extent as to women,[2] and to some extent (*e*) adolescent pregnancy

[1] A value of children study carried in 1974 showed that 62 per cent of the women interviewed wanted to have two boys and one girl. Since then the percentage of wanted combination has declined, particularly among urban working women. However, the combination of two boys and one girl accounts for 23 per cent, the largest proportion in the various combinations of number and sex of children in a survey of 1,430 married women in Taipei in 1982 (Chiang 1985).

[2] A survey conducted in Taipei city shows that the percentage of men who accepted sterilization and condom are respectively, 0.07 per cent and 30.2 per cent among 1,420 women of child-bearing age (Chiang 1985).

before marriage leads to early childbirth in marriage and illegitimate childbirths.

Recent studies have demonstrated a close negative relationship between modernization and fertility levels. Chiang (1985) demonstrated that women with non-traditional experiences before marriage such as receiving higher education, working outside home, keeping most of their earnings, and deciding their own marriages, tend to have lower fertility. It is likely that improving the status of women would be a pertinent solution to the further lowering of fertility levels. As society depends less on male children for supporting older parents, an increasing dependence on daughters for maintaining the parents' economic well-being in old age would occur, hence reducing the need for many sons. Enabling women to take more active roles in childbearing decisions and encouraging the use of contraceptives and sterilization for males would have strong implications for a breakthrough in fertility decline. Educating women to pursue a life goal beyond their marriage and reproductive roles would have indirect repercussions on their fertility behaviour. In the long run, society should be more receptive to the fact that having daughters is just as important as having sons.

WOMEN'S ACCOMPLISHMENT IN EDUCATION

Since the beginning of the post-war period, education levels of Taiwan's population have risen considerably. Over the last decades, the literacy rate has increased from 57.9 per cent in 1952 to 91.2 per cent in 1985. While only 2.1 per cent and 0.4 per cent respectively of male and female population aged fifteen and over received college and above education in 1951, the proportion had increased to 13.1 per cent and 7.8 per cent respectively for men and women in 1983. Not only have both men and women benefited from their improvement of education, but the discrepancy in the number of years of schooling has been closing in the last thirty years. In 1951, the number of years of schooling was 1.407 for women compared to 3.921 for men. This has changed to 7.359 for women, and 8.875 for men in 1983 (Tsai 1985). These statistics indicate that besides an overall improvement in the educational attainment for both men and women, the increase is faster for women than for men, at all school levels. Among the population aged 15–19 and 20–24, the number of years of schooling between men and women is the closest of all the age groups. The advancement in education for women not only reflects better opportunities arising from the prolonged years of free education, but also parents' changing attitudes toward education for girls, who, in the past, were not as likely to receive an equal opportunity for education as men. Today, it is still the case that parents think it is more worthwhile to invest in a son's education rather than a daughter's. However, young females are provided with the same educational opportunities as males, unless the family is in hardship (Tsui 1985).

In terms of the structure of educational achievement, discrepancies can still be found. In the levels of educational attainment, the proportion of women who reached senior levels[3] is still lower than that of men and the increase over the years has been slower than other levels of education. Moreover, women college students are overwhelmingly concentrated in liberal arts and humanities and many are enrolled in vocational, normal, or supplementary schools. This led one to believe that while better economics provides improved opportunities for women to receive education as often as men do, the socialization process continues to substantiate differences in the type of education received by women.

Historically, women were deprived of an equal opportunity to receive education as men did. What remains today are qualitative differences. Government policies of compulsory education have benefited women in Taiwan to a large extent, but what is needed are policies to correct biases in the socialization process, as reflected in differences in the levels of educational attainment between men and women.

ECONOMIC ROLE OF WOMEN

The pattern of structural changes in the female labour force, from predominantly agricultural to industrial occurred as a reflection of the transformation of the economy of Taiwan in the last three decades.

As a newly industrialized country in Asia, Taiwan has emerged from a period of labour-intensive (1965–1973) to capital-intensive and technologically oriented economy (1973 to present). In the first period of industrial growth, the availability of female workers was an important factor in the development of light industries, led by textiles, electronics and plastics. Involvement of the island economy in the international market creates a demand for unskilled and relatively

---

[3] The last two years of five-year junior college, three-year junior college, and above.

cheap labour. Not only are wages kept low in order to compete in the world market, but also, the supply of female labour force has been kept flexible to meet peak demand and economic depression.

From 1965 to 1973, the labour participation rate of females increased from 33.1 per cent to 41.5 per cent, representing an increase from 1,028,000 to 1,837,000. The annual growth rate of 7.5 per cent is much higher than that of the male labour force which is 3.1 per cent. In the second period (1973 to 1984), Taiwan faced competition from other developing countries in their supply of low cost and plentiful labour. The government decided then to pursue the path of capital-intensive and technologically oriented industrial economy. The growth of the female labour force (an annual rate of 3.4 per cent) is slower than the first period and faster than the annual rate of growth (2.7) of the male labour force.

The demand for cheap female labour in the economic development process is one major reason for the growth of the labour force at an early stage, during which many elementary and junior high school graduates suddenly poured into the labour market. Recently, women are increasingly employed in white-collar jobs. In 1982, the proportion of employed women in the white-collar class has exceeded that of the blue-collar working class and the types of work that women are involved in have increased particularly in the tertiary sector such as retail business, social work, insurance, and commerce. Increasingly, jobs which are traditionally performed by men such as chemists, architects, engineers and computer scientists are performed by women, resulting in a greater diversity of jobs held.

Increase of the female labour force has been associated with a great demand of industrialization for labour, a rise in the educational level of females, changing attitudes towards women, technological advances that simplified household work; and family planning, which has enabled more women to join the labour force.

As their college training is limited to social rather than physical sciences, women are much more highly represented than males in teaching and clerical jobs. At the same time, women are considerably under-represented in fields like engineering, architecture, medicine and other sciences. Female representation is still small at the professional, managerial and executive levels and large in lower-level occupations. As a result of shorter or interrupted years of work, and their responsibilities for caring for the family, women are less likely to be promoted as men, and remain in the lower rungs of the occupational ladder. Among government female employees in 1985, only 0.4 per cent have been promoted to the high rank while 3.7 per cent of male employees were promoted.

Woman's participation in the labour force is closely intertwined with her life cycle. Women enter the labour force earlier than men due to a relatively shorter period of education. While employment rate for women is the highest in the 20–24 age group, it declines and rises again at the age between 35 and 44. Many women still leave work after marriage or the birth of the first child and seldom do they re-enter the labour force at a later stage of their lives.

Discrepancies in salaries received by men and women performing the same work are found particularly with women at a lower educational level. It is estimated that women earn only up to two-thirds of salaries paid to men of the same educational levels.

CONCLUSIONS AND POLICY IMPLICATIONS

The emergence of women in social and economic aspects of society forms a major dimension of social change in Taiwan. Although the status of women has improved in the last thirty years, there are still many impediments to change. The socialization process between men and women is different, as in most Asian countries. Sex role stereotyping begins at home, in the kindergarten classroom and throughout our experiences in education and places of work. Beginning with early childhood, boys are rewarded for aggressive and competitive behaviour while girls are rewarded for dependence and docility. A typical example is that girls are discouraged from showing interest in science subjects and boys, on the other hand, are encouraged to study engineering and technical subjects. One psychologist (Chia 1985:33) who studied Chinese women pointed out that achievement motives differ between men and women in that while females have greater concern over the family, it may hamper their motivation to maximize their achievement. Chinese traditional value systems and social pressures still have an immense impact upon women's attitudes towards their own status and roles in life.

Based on his long-term interest in Taiwan's population, Freedman (1986:96) pointed out that:

Questions about the status of women in Taiwan's changing social and economic system are likely to become increasingly a subject of policy discussion. Young Taiwanese women have experienced rapidly rising levels of education, and more and more of them are marrying later and entering the non-familial labour force. They will be pressing for better positions in the economy.

It is the responsibility of colleges and universities to help women see their lives in a wider context beyond marriage and family and give them the skills they need to begin appropriate social participation. It is also the moral obligation of our educational system to help women expand their roles beyond those in families and to put their education to good use. Policies should be addressed to problems and needs of women in the labour force. Government should take the lead in implementing employment and social policies such as providing vocational, and leadership training, and various other supporting services.

Women of Taiwan should seek to aspire and attain a fuller human life for themselves; for it is through developing their talents that they would not only contribute to the well-being of their own families, but also to society. In the long run, women should be a part of the human resource that should not be wasted. They should be considered seriously as part of the national development process.

REFERENCES

Chia, Rosina C., 1985. 'Suggestions for Developing an Achievement Motivation Theory Applicable to Chinese Women,' Proceedings of ACUCA 1985 Symposium on the *Future Role of Women in Asia*, September 9–10, 1985, Taipei, Soochow University.

Chiang, Chien-dai, 1985. 'Follow-up Survey on the Tubal Ligation Acceptors in Taipei City,' paper presented at the Conference on the *Role of Women in the National Development Process in Taiwan*, March 14–16, 1985, Population Studies Center, National Taiwan University.

Chiang, Nora Lan-hung and Yenlin Ku, 1985. *Past and Current Status of Women in Taiwan*, Monograph 1, Women's Research Program, Population Studies Center. National Taiwan University.

Diamond, Norma, 1973. 'The Status of Women in Taiwan: One Step Forward, Two Steps Back,' in *Women in China*, edited by Marilyn B. Young. (Ann Arbor: University of Michigan, Center for Chinese Studies).

Duley, Margot I. and Mary I. Edwards (eds.), 1986. *The Cross-Cultural Study of Women* (New York: The Feminist Press).

Freedman, Ronald, 1986. 'Policy Options in Taiwan after the Demographic Transition,' *Population and Development Review* (Vol. 12, No. 1), pp. 77–100.

Gallin, Rita S., 1982. 'The Impact of Development on Women's Work and Status: A Case Study from Taiwan,' Michigan State University, WID Working Papers 9.

Hu, Tai–li, 1985. 'The Impact of Rural Industrialization on Women's Status in Taiwan,' paper presented at the Conference on the *Role of Women in the National Development Process in Taiwan*, cited above.

Kung, Lydia, 1983. *Factory Women in Taiwan* (Ann Arbor, Michigan: UMI Research Press).

Li, K.T., 1985. 'Contributions of Women in the Labor Force to Economic Development in Taiwan, the Republic of China,' *Industry of Free China* (Vol. 64, No. 1), pp. 1–8.

Lu, Yu-hsia, 1981. 'Career Attitudes of Women in a Changing Society,' *Bulletin of the Institute of Ethnology*, Academia Sinica 50: 25–66.

Sung, Lung-Sheng, 1983. 'Chinese Women, Family and Property in Northern Taiwan,' *Journal of Women Studies* (Vol. 6, No. 1) pp. 54–64.

Tsay, Ching-lung, 1985. 'Sex Differentials in Educational Attainment and Labor Force Development in Taiwan,' paper presented at the Conference on the *Role of Women in the National Development Process in Taiwan*, cited above.

Tsai, Hong-Ching and Lan-hung Nora Chiang, 1985. 'Women's Role in Demographic and Social Changes in Taiwan,' paper presented at ACUCA 1985 Symposium on the *Future Role of Women in Asia*, cited above.

Tsui, Elaine Yilan, 1985. *Education and the Changing Role of Working Women in Urban Taiwan*, Ph.D. dissertation in Anthropology, University of Hawaii.

Wolf, Margery, 1972. *Women and the Family in Rural Taiwan* (Stanford: Stanford University Press).

Yao, Eather S. Lee, 1983. *Chinese Women, Past and Present* (Mesquite, Tex.: Ide House).

The Status of Women in Malaysia

Hamid Arshat and Masitah Mohd. Yatin

Background

Malaysia is a nation of approximately 15 million people in 1985 and almost half are women. Since its independence in 1957, the population of Malaysia has experienced rapid socio-economic development. The status of Malaysian women too has changed tremendously since then. Women now have access to almost all opportunities and more are encouraged to play their role in the development of the country.

Malaysian women's movements like the National Council for Women Organisation have been long active in calling for equal opportunities for women. It was not, however, until after the 1975 Mexico Declaration on Integration of Women in Development that the Malaysian Government responded more positively to that call. A National Council for Integration of Women in Development or NACIWID was established in 1976 to advise the Cabinet regarding matters related to women and it operates through the Department for Women's Affairs (HAWA) which coordinates women's activities.

The integration of women in development through greater education and occupational opportunities had emancipated women from their traditional role of wife, mother and very often unpaid family worker to that of wife, mother and paid worker. Increasing demand for labour by the manufacturing industries, particularly the electronics, as a result of rapid industrial growth stimulated by national industrialization policies, has provided more opportunities for women to participate in the labour force. This does not mean that in the past women were excluded from participating in the labour force, because the agricultural sector such as the rubber and oil palm plantations has always had a significant number of women employed although at low wages. Employment opportunities have helped women to either free themselves from economic dependence on the family or be able to help supplement their family income.

Women's labour force participation has often been used as the main indicator for evaluating the status of women. There are, of course, other factors which determine the status of women, namely, education, health, social and legal position. A woman plays a significant role not only at work but also in the family. Her decision can affect herself as well as her family. In order to be able to make a rational and responsible decision, a woman must be knowledgeable, free from diseases and the burden of repeated pregnancy and childcare and have equal rights socially as well as legally.

Today, Malaysian women can be proud of themselves because they have made great strides in education, health, and both socially and legally. In the past, literacy rate and educational attainment among women was low because of low parental aspirations towards the education of daughters. Educating daughters was regarded as wasteful because they were expected to eventually get married and remain housewives and mothers whose role was assumed as not requiring formal education. Free primary education policy has helped towards eradicating this attitude and made parents aware of the need to educate their children regardless of their sex. Women are now represented in almost all types of occupations although the numbers are still comparatively small.

Malaysian women now have a life expectancy at birth of 72 years old.[24]. Infant and maternal mortality are low compared to other developing countries within Asia and the Pacific region. But, within the country itself maternal mortality for rural mothers is still high because of their traditional belief in home delivery. Generally, however, the number of maternal deaths has decreased from 1.5 per thousand live births in 1970 to 0.6 in 1980 and 0.4 in 1984/(25). The level of family planning prevalence rate among married women, in the reproductive age may well be over 50 per cent in Peninsular Malaysia.[25] Family planning in Malaysia is for the health and welfare of the family, and this indirectly has helped women, particularly those from the low-income group, to space their births and thus contribute towards building up their health status.

Cultural and social norms of a society together with their legal rights are some of the factors determining the social status of women. Malaysian women have the right to vote so long as they meet the legal requirements. Marriage and divorce are according to the religious, civil, and common law. The lowest age limit for marriage is 18 for men and 16 for women. Women can own and inherit property according to religious and civil law.

Generally, the position of women in Malaysia is favourable but there is still plenty of room for further improvement.

DEMOGRAPHIC PROFILE

Women, Marriage Pattern and Legal Rights

Marriage Pattern

The population of Malaysia was approximately 13 million in 1980 and approximately 15 million in 1985. Out of this 50 per cent are women. The sex ratio was 100.6 males per 100 females in 1980. Like most populations, the proportion of females has been fairly constant except at old age. In 1970 females formed 48 per cent of the population aged 55 and over and 51 per cent in 1980.[20] Longer female life expectancy means there are more women among the aged. Malaysian social norms and culture do not permit births outside marriage and although such incidences could have occurred, no record is available. Although the minimum age requirement for marriage is 16 for women and 18 for men the mean age at first marriage for both men and women 10 years and over has risen. For men it was 23.8 years in 1957, 25.8 years in 1970 and 26.9 years in 1980. In the case of women it was 19.4 years in 1957; 22.3 years in 1970 and 23.8 years in 1980 (Table 1). Higher mean age at first marriage is one of the contributory factors to fertility decline in Malaysia. Rising age at marriage is particularly marked among the Chinese community as compared to Indians and Malays.[27] 'Marriage squeeze' is said to be one of the reasons for the increase in the proportion of single women.[26] Tables 2 and 3 show the latest mean age at first marriage by ethnic group and sex derived from a study on marriage and marital dissolution in Peninsular Malaysia among the married couples.[28] Education level is partly influential in the mean age at first marriage.[28]

TABLE 1
*Mean Age at First Marriage of Women 10 Years and Over
for the Years 1957, 1970 and 1980 for
Peninsular Malaysia*

	1957	1970	1980
Male	23.8	25.8	26.9
Female	19.4	22.3	23.8

Source: Calculated from Population Census, 1957, 1970, 1980.

TABLE 2

**Mean Age at First Marriage by Ethnic Group and Place of Residence
for Women Aged 25 Years and over
Who Married before Age 25 Years**

Ethnic Group	Place of Residence		Total
	Rural	Urban	
Malays	17.2	18.9	17.8
Chinese	20.3	21.0	20.5
Indians	17.7	19.3	18.6
Total No. of Cases	18.0 (1,072)	19.5 (627)	18.5 (1,699)

Source: Tan Poo Chang, Paul Chan Tuck Hoong, Lee Kok Huat, Shyamala Nagaraj, 'The Study of Marriage and Marital Dissolution in Peninsular Malaysia', *The Married Couples*. September 1986.

TABLE 3

Mean Age at First Marriage of Men Aged 30 Years and Over

Ethnic Group	Place of Residence		Total
	Rural	Urban	
Malays	17.2	18.9	17.8
Chinese	20.3	21.0	20.5
Indians	17.7	19.3	18.6
Total No. of Cases	18.0 (1,002)	19.5 (608)	18.5 (1,610)

Source: Same as Table 2.

TABLE 4

**Per cent Divorced/Separated for Women Aged 10 and over by
Ethnic Group—1970 and 1980**

Year	Community Group				Total
	Malay	Chinese	Indian	Others	
1970	1.7	0.5	0.7	1.2	1.2
1980	2.5	0.7	1.0	2.3	1.7

Source: Calculated from 1970 and 1980 Populated Census.

A similar trend is seen for divorce rates which show an increase from 1.2 per cent in 1970 to 1.7 per cent in 1980. This increase is highest among the Malay community because divorce practice is much simpler in Muslim than in civil law (Table 5). The Sya'riah court is now more strict with regard to marriage and divorce in order to protect Muslim women and their children from discrimination and abuse. Divorce is least common among the Indian community and lesser among the Chinese partly due to their socio-cultural beliefs and practices. Remarriage is also most common among Muslim women but such incidences are not well recorded.

TABLE 5

Percentage Distribution by Number of Times Married of Men and Women Aged 45–49 Years by Ethnic Group

Ethnic Group	Place of Residence	Number of times married		Total	No. of Cases
		1	2+		
Wife					
Malays	Rural	83.8	16.2	100.0	80
	Urban	85.0	15.0	100.0	40
Chinese		98.2	1.8	100.0	57
Indians		100.0	0.0	100.0	35
No. of Cases		192	20		212
Husband					
Malays	Rural	82.8	17.2	100.0	116
	Urban	89.8	10.2	100.0	59
Chinese		97.7	2.3	100.0	88
Indians		98.1	1.9	100.0	54
No. of Cases		288	29		317

Source: Same as Table 2.

On the whole, the marriage trend among women in Peninsular Malaysia during this period appears to be heading towards a decline in the proportion married, rising age at marriage and increasing divorce rates, particularly among Muslim women. Currently, efforts are being made to disseminate knowledge on family life education for both men and women through the national family development programmes.

Social Practices and Legal Rights of Marriage and Divorce

Legal rights are meant to protect the individual from discriminatory treatment but social practices sometimes are contradictory to what is provided for by the law. There are four main types of marriage recognized legally in Malaysia, namely Muslim Sya'riah Law, civil law, Christian and common law or customary marriages.

Muslim Sya'riah law marriage and social practices: All Muslims are required to marry and divorce according to Muslim Law. A Muslim man shall not marry a non-Muslim woman unless the latter converts to Muslim religion. Similarly a Muslim woman is not allowed to marry a non-Muslim man until the latter too becomes a Muslim. A couple has to apply to the registrar for permission to marry. Permission will be granted only when the Registrar is satisfied regarding the legality of the marriage and that the matters stated in the application are true. All marriages conducted in the area will be registered in accordance with the Act in force for that area. A Muslim couple wishing to take a second wife have to apply for permission in writing from the Sya'riah (Muslim) Judge who will only agree if the reasons given are logically valid. There is a slight variation in implementation in the different states of Malaysia. These are some of the statutory declarations that the man is required to make before taking a second wife:

1. The grounds on which the proposed marriage is considered to be just and necessary;
2. His present income and details of his commitments and financial obligations and liabilities;
3. The number of his dependents including persons who would be his dependents as a result of the proposed marriage;
4. Whether the consent or views of the existing wife or wives to the proposed marriage have been obtained.[32]

The permission will be heard in court in camera (not open to the public) in the presence of the applicant and his existing wife or wives. Permission will then be granted by the court only if it is satisfied that:

1. The proposed marriage is just and necessary unless the circumstances include among others, sterility, physical infirmity, physical unfitness for conjugal relations, wilful avoidance of an order to restitution of conjugal rights or insanity on the part of the existing wife or wives,
2. That the applicant has the means to support all his wives and dependents including the woman he proposes to marry and her dependents;

3. That the applicant will be able to treat all his wives equally;
4. That the proposed marriage would not cause harm according to what is normally recognized by Islamic Law, affecting a wife in respect of religion, life, body, mind or property;
5. That the proposed marriage would not directly or indirectly lower the standard of living that the existing wife or wives and dependants had been enjoying and would enjoy were the marriage not to take place.[31]

Appeal is allowed if any party, that is, either the applicant or his existing wife or wives is not satisfied with the decision of the Sya'riah judge.

A person who is found to have given false information is required to pay immediately the entire amount of the dowry due to the existing wife or wives plus M$1,000 and may, in addition, even be imprisoned not exceeding six months.

These provisions are meant to deter men from committing polygamy but in practice these rights are abused. Wives are obliged to agree to the second marriage in order to avoid family break-up and ensure the children's maintenance.

Customary Law Marriages: These are practised by Hindus and Chinese based on traditions, customs and common practices in their own communities. Customary marriages are conducted under religious rites and the customs of the various communities of Malaysia.

Culturally, an ideal Chinese family is a large extended family consisting of several generations. It is patriarchal, patrilineal, and patrilocal. But this is gradually disintegrating due to modernization and western influence in family life. Although customary marriage is still prevalent, most marry according to civil law. Civil marriage permits only one wife. The Marriage and Divorce Law Reform Act 1976 no longer allows polygamy among non-Muslims, but polygamous marriages which were allowed under customary or common law marriage and contracted before this Act came into force in March 1982, are still recognized and deemed to have been registered on the date the Act came into force.

In the past, Chinese customs recognized mistresses and polygamous marriages. Love marriage was not encouraged. Customary marriages are normally conducted under religious rites and customs and performed in temples.

Indian customary marriage was imported into Peninsular Malaysia by the Indian population which comprises Tamils and Telugus (83.4 per cent), Malayalis, Punjabis and others (approximately 12.5 per cent) and Sri Lankans (about 3 per cent). More than 80 per cent are Hindus, 8 per cent Christians and 7 per cent Muslims.[28] Hindus believe that marriage is a sacrament which enables a person to fulfil Dharma or religious as well as social obligations towards the family, community and society, Praja (progeny) and Rati (pleasure).[30] Once the rites of marriage are performed, it is irrevocable. Ideally, marriage in the Hindu scriptures is monogamous and the wife should be devoted to the husband alone. Child marriages are not allowed in Peninsular Malaysia and there is little evidence of such practices. Although Indian girls are encouraged to marry early, employment opportunity tends to provide them with an alternative to early marriage. Polyandry is not practised among the Hindus in Peninsular Malaysia. Socially, polygamy has been tolerated in certain Hindu communities but this is now not allowed by the Reform Act of 1976

Christian marriages are normally performed in the church by an assistant registrar as may be permitted by the religion or custom professed by either party to the marriage. It is the responsibility of the church group to give notice of the intended marriage to the Registration Department. Polygamy is not permitted under the Reform Act of 1976. Socially illegal polygamy did occur in the past and was tolerated.

Divorce: Divorce is not encouraged by any community in Malaysia although there is provision for divorce under the Sya'riah Law as well as the Reform Act 1976. As shown by the findings of a study in Table 6, all ethnic groups disapprove of divorce.

A Muslim husband can divorce his wife by stating his intention to his spouse witnessed by the Sya'riah judge. He is permitted to declare his intention to divorce or 'talak' once, twice or three times. The first and second declaration permits reconciliation and thus annulment of the divorce declaration but the third declaration is final. A Muslim woman cannot declare her intention to divorce but can seek separation or divorce by three means, namely:

1. 'Cerai taklik' meaning an agreement with the husband at marriage that she can seek divorce if the husband fails to fulfil the conditions agreed upon at the signing of the marriage vows.

2. 'Khuluk' or 'Cerai tebus talak', where a wife can seek divorce when the husband agrees to receive alimony from the wife.
3. 'Fasakh' means a woman can divorce the husband if his whereabouts are not known for one year or more; that the husband has not given financial support for a period of three months; that the husband is in prison for three years or more; that the husband cannot or has not performed, without reasonable cause, his marital obligations (sexual obligations) for a period of one year; that the husband was impotent at the time of marriage and remains so.[31]

TABLE 6
Percentage Distribution by Opinion on Divorce by Ethnic Group

Opinion	Ethnic Group			
	Total	Malays	Chinese	Indians
Wife				
Common	5.4	2.6	12.8	2.7
Not good, but at times have to take such a step	70.9	80.0	63.3	41.9
Disgraceful	20.8	14.6	21.1	52.7
Do not know	2.9	3.0	2.9	2.7
Total (%)	100.0	100.0	100.0	100.0
Husband				
Common	7.7	4.6	16.2	3.8
Not good, but at times have to take such a step	69.3	78.1	61.3	42.2
Disgraceful	20.1	13.9	20.4	52.1
Do not know	2.9	3.4	2.1	1.9
Total (%)	100.0	100.0	100.0	100.0

A divorced wife is entitled to maintenance for a period of three months whilst the children are entitled up to 18 years of age or higher if they proceed to higher education. If a woman is divorced without just cause she may apply to the court for consolatory gift.

As regards division of property under the Muslim law, the woman is entitled to a share of the matrimonial asset. If she has contributed some money, then she is entitled to half of the asset. In case the husband tries to dispose of the assets to evade claims from his wife, the court can invalidate such transactions if they take place within the preceding three years. As for the custody of a child, paramount consideration is given to the welfare of the child.

Before the Reform Act of 1976 was enforced, divorce under the common law or customary marriage depended on the agreement of both parties and not on the civil court. A husband could divorce his wife if she talked too much; if she did not behave like a daughter to the mother-in-law, committed adultery, was sterile, stole the husband's property to help her own family, or was jealous or sick. A common law wife could not divorce the husband but agreement in writing from both parties would free the woman. This is true also of the Chinese community. Hindu custom does not allow divorce. A wife would be returned to her parents' home if the husband had ceased loving her.

The Reform Act of 1976 abolished polygamy among Muslims; required all marriages to be registered; raised the minimum age at marriage to 18 for men and 16 for women and allowed divorce only on agreement by both parties. These provisions were meant to protect women but their implementation, particularly with regard to Muslim laws, has not been entirely satisfactory. The government has taken steps to provide training for Sya'riah court (Muslim court) officials in the new law so as to ensure proper implementation. Civil law is implemented by the civil courts which have trained officials and qualified lawyers. Now a Muslim couple seeking divorce has to satisfy the Sya'riah court that both spouses are agreeable to it. The father has a superior right for the custody of the children but the Act provides an additional clause which gives priority to the welfare of the child.

A divorced Muslim woman is entitled to maintenance only during the Edah (period) of three months after the divorce. The Muslims are governed by the Muslim Family Law Act 1984. The Muslim court has the same power as the civil court to order division of assets acquired by the parties during the marriage based on the following principles:

1. The extent of the contributions made by each party in money, property, or labour towards acquiring the assets;[31]
2. Any debts owing by either party that were contracted for their joint benefit;[31]
3. The needs of the minor children of the marriage, if any.

Thus the family enactments indirectly have helped in recognizing and putting value to the work of the wife and mother in the home.

Fertility, Family Planning and Breastfeeding

Fertility

Studies have shown that age at menarche is a significant determinant of ages at first marriage and first birth. According to an analysis on age at menarche by Tan Boon Ann et al., using data from the 1976, 1977 Malaysian Family Life Survey, the average age at menarche in Peninsular Malaysia is 13.7 years (see Figure 1) although it varies with ethnicity. A decline in age at menarche is observed among Chinese and Indian girls but little change is seen among Malay girls.[8]

Figure 1: Cumulative Frequency Distribution of Age at Menarche in Malaysia, Italy, and Venezuela

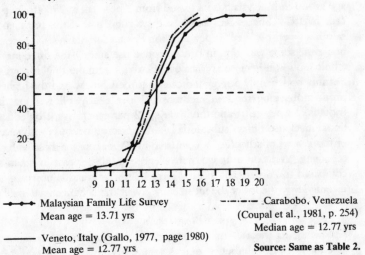

●—●—● Malaysian Family Life Survey
Mean age = 13.71 yrs

————— Veneto, Italy (Gallo, 1977, page 1980)
Mean age = 12.77 yrs

—·—·—·— Carabobo, Venezuela
(Coupal et al., 1981, p. 254)
Median age = 12.77 yrs

Source: Same as Table 2.

Research on biological correlation of the timing of menarche reveals that ethnicity and nutrition are the principal biological determinants of menarche. Well-nourished girls have earlier menarche than under-nourished girls. The socio-economic status of the ethnic group differs particularly among earlier cohorts, i.e. among those born before 1960.[8] In a study on old age some questions were asked on menopause and the findings suggest that the average age at menopause is 48.7 years, a level that falls within the range of 45 to 53 documented in the industrial societies.[32]

There has been a decline in fertility in Peninsular Malaysia since the 1960s. Crude birth rate declined from 40.3 per thousand population in 1961 to 32.4 in 1980. It is projected that it will decline further to 16.2 in 2030 if everything else remains the same. Total fertility rate declined from 6.8 in 1957 to 3.7 in 1980.[20] Rapid socio-economic development and rising age at marriage are contributory to the decline in fertility in Malaysia. Fertility decline is most rapid among the Chinese community followed by the Indians and then the Malays. These differences in the decline of CBR among the three ethnic groups could be due to both their differences in socio-economic status and cultural values.

Family Planning

Family Planning practice among married women in the reproductive age group in Malaysia has increased from 8 per cent in 1966 to 36 per cent in 1974. Successive sample surveys suggest that the prevalence rate may well be over 50 per cent for Peninsular Malaysia. There is, however, some variation in contraceptive use among the three major ethnic groups in Peninsular Malaysia.[8] Findings from the 1974 Malaysian Fertility and Family Survey indicate that the Chinese had the highest proportion using modern methods (41 per cent), followed by the Indians (38 per cent) and the Malays (22 per cent). Usage by educational level also differs substantially—40 per cent for those with seven or more years of schooling as compared to 22 per cent for those with no schooling. Variation in usage by residence was 40 per cent in urban as compared to 26 per cent in rural areas. A similar trend is observed by income level: the lower the income, the lower the contraceptive use.[22]

Breastfeeding

According to theories on breastfeeding, the duration of lactational amenorrhoea is lengthened due to temporary cessation of ovulation and thus cessation of menstruation after the birth of a child. Potter and Bongaarts, in their study on breastfeeding, found that full breastfeeding can lengthen the post-partum infecundity interval to one year or more. Breastfeeding practice is not only good nutrition for infants but can act as a contraceptive for women by delaying their post-birth menstruation cycle, thus helping in birth spacing.

In Malaysia, the percentage of initial breastfeeding and duration of breastfeeding has declined between the period 1960–1974. The percentage of infants breastfed initially dropped from 89 to 74 and the percentage breastfed for more than three months declined from 75 to

53 during the same period. Aziz Othman in his analysis found that higher educated women are less likely to start breastfeeding and, if they do start, the average duration of breastfeeding is short. Women with lower and no education are more inclined to breastfeed and for longer duration (see Table 7). Othman does not rule out the possibility of employment of higher educated women as the determinant for the shorter duration of breastfeeding among higher educated mothers.[10] A breastfeeding campaign was initiated by the Government in 1976 and it has continued since then. More child care centres will be needed at the place of work if breastfeeding is to be encouraged among working mothers.

TABLE 7

Mean Length of Breastfeeding (in month) by Number of Children ever Born and Level of Education

Education	Total	Less than 4 Children	4 or more Children
None	8.84	10.47	8.432
	(837)	(189)	(648)
Primary	6.48	5.67	6.83
	(816)	(262)	(554)
Secondary and Above	3.14	2.39	6.83
	(100)	(107)	(53)

Note: Figure in bracket refers to sample size.
Source: Aziz Othman, *Malaysia Journal of Reproductive Health* (Vol. 3, No. 1), June 1985.

Abortion

Abortion is illegal in Malaysia. Hence a clear record on abortion is not available. The 1966 West Malaysia Family Survey revealed that at least one per cent of the women interviewed admitted to having had one induced abortion during their reproductive life. Of the eligible respondents interviewed in the Malaysian Fertility and Family Survey (1974) 2.5 per cent reported having had an induced abortion.[22] In another study called Maternal Health and Early Pregnancy Wastage in Peninsular Malaysia conducted in 1977, it was found that the prevalence of induced abortion was 4.3 per 100 live births and 3.9 per 100 pregnancies.[17] The number of spontaneous abortions was 5.3 per 100 pregnancies and 6.0 per 100 live births (see Table 8).[17] In terms of ethnic distribution for induced abortion the study reveals that the prevalence is highest among the Chinese and lowest among the Malays (see Table 9). Spontaneous abortion is highest among the Indians.

TABLE 8
Induced and Spontaneous Abortion Ratios by Age and Residence

Ratios	Age Group	Urban		Rural		All Areas	
		I.A.	S.A.	I.A.	S.A.	I.A.	S.A.
	15 to 19	8.5	8.5	3.6	8.3	5.7	8.4
	20 to 24	8.3	6.4	2.1	5.0	4.7	5.6
Per 100	25 to 29	7.1	5.6	1.9	4.4	4.4	5.0
Pregnancies	30 to 34	6.2	5.9	1.9	4.5	3.9	5.1
	35 to 39	6.7	6.4	1.4	4.4	3.8	5.3
	40 to 44	5.7	6.4	1.4	5.0	3.3	5.6
	All Ages	6.5	6.2	1.7	4.6	3.9	5.3
	15 to 19	10.2	10.2	4.2	9.7	6.7	9.9
	20 to 24	9.9	7.6	2.3	5.5	5.3	6.3
Per 100	25 to 29	8.2	6.5	2.0	4.8	4.9	5.5
Pregnancies	30 to 34	7.2	6.8	2.1	4.9	4.4	5.8
	35 to 39	7.8	7.5	1.5	4.8	4.3	6.0
	40 to 44	6.6	7.4	1.6	5.5	3.7	6.3
	All Ages	7.6	7.2	1.8	5.1	4.3	6.0

Source: Maternal Health and Early Pregnancy Wastage in Peninsular Malaysia, 1977.

MORTALITY/MORBIDITY AMONG MOTHERS AND CHILDREN

Maternal and infant mortality rates have declined substantially in Peninsular Malaysia during the period 1967–1977.[23] In 1967 maternal mortality rate was 1.68 per thousand live births and this declined to 0.6 in 1980 and 0.4 in 1983. During the same period neo-natal mortality decreased from 24 per thousand live births in 1967 to 19 in 1977. Infant mortality rate declined from 45 per hundred live births in 1967 to 32 in 1977 and 20 in 1983. Child mortality (1–4 years old) also declined from 5 per thousand children of this age in 1967 to 2.9 in 1977 and 1.8 in 1983. Babies born to mothers below 19 years of age and 40 years and above are more likely to die due to prematurity and close birth interval. Such births are more common among low income families. Poor sanitation is one of the factors contributing to infant death. Breastfeeding would help reduce deaths due to contamination of children's food. Improvement in the socio-economic status of rural mothers has helped in reducing infant mortality in Malaysia.

TABLE 9
Induced and Spontaneous Abortion Ratios by Community Group and Residence

Community Group	Urban		Rural		All Areas	
	I.A.	S.A.	I.A.	S.A.	I.A.	S.A.
	ER 100 Pregnancies					
Malay	2.8	5.9	0.6	4.3	1.2	4.8
Chinese	9.2	5.7	3.7	5.0	6.9	5.4
Indians	2.8	7.7	0.4	4.9	1.5	6.2
Others	3.6	8.3	10.9	8.7	5.0	8.4
All Communities	6.5	6.2	1.6	4.7	3.8	5.4
	ER 100 Live Births					
Malay	3.1	6.6	0.6	4.6	1.3	5.2
Chinese	11.0	6.8	4.1	5.6	8.0	6.3
Indians	3.2	8.9	0.4	5.4	1.7	7.0
Others	4.2	9.6	14.3	11.4	6.0	10.0
All Communities	7.5	7.2	1.8	5.1	4.3	6.0

Source: National Health and Early Pregnancy Wastage in Peninsular Malaysia, 1977.

Maternal mortality is highest among rural mothers, particularly the Malays (0.53 in 1983) because of their preference for home delivery which put them at a higher risk (see Figure 2). The Chinese community experience the lowest maternal mortality (0.13) followed by the Indians (0.17) for the same period.[23]

WOMEN AND EDUCATION

Education is a key factor in the socio-economic development of women and the most powerful liberating force. Yet women have been deprived of equal education opportunities in the past by parents who regarded it as more important to educate sons than daughters. In recent years, women's educational opportunities have improved a great deal not only due to increasing awareness on the importance of education among parents but also due to the changing educational opportunities provided by the government. However, literacy rates are still lower among the female population, 64.1 per cent, compared to the males (80.4 per cent in 1980) although the rate has improved since 1970 when it was only 46.8 per cent (see Table 10).[21] Women's status in society is governed by their ability to read and write as well as their

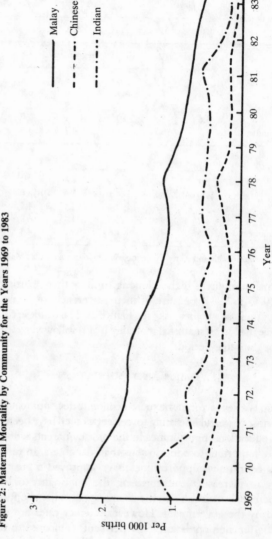

Figure 2: Maternal Mortality by Community for the Years 1969 to 1983

TABLE 10
Literacy Rate of Female Population Aged 10 Years and Over—Malaysia: 1970 and 1980

Age Group	1970 Literate	1970 Semi-literate	1970 Illiterate	1970 Total	1980 Literate	1980 Semi-literate	1980 Illiterate	1980 Total
10-14	66.1	6.4	27.4	100	85.0	4.1	10.9	100
15-19	74.7	3.7	21.6	100	88.1	1.6	10.3	100
20-24	66.8	4.1	29.1	100	83.0	2.3	14.7	100
25-29	52.1	4.6	43.3	100	77.4	3.0	19.5	100
30-34	39.0	4.7	56.3	100	67.7	4.0	28.3	100
35-39	27.2	4.5	68.3	100	53.4	4.7	41.9	100
40-44	22.4	4.1	73.5	100	40.5	5.0	54.5	100
45-49	16.8	3.5	79.7	100	28.6	4.9	66.5	100
50-54	11.5	2.8	85.7	100	23.5	4.4	72.1	100
55-59	8.5	2.4	89.1	100	17.7	3.8	78.5	100
60-64	5.4	1.8	92.8	100	12.5	3.1	84.4	100
65+	3.7	1.3	95.0	100	7.5	2.8	90.2	100
Total	46.8	4.3	48.9	100	64.1	3.4	32.5	100

Source: 1970: General Report Population Census of Malaysia, Vol. II.
1980: Calculated from 1980 Census of Malaysia.

educational attainment. Illiteracy and low educational achievement have placed women in low paid employment and unskilled occupation. Educational attainment among the females is also much lower than among the males at all levels (see Table 11). In 1970, only 61.4 per cent of the females had at least some education as compared to 84.6 among the males. The respective figures for 1980 were 71.9 per cent and 85.4 per cent. Nevertheless, the women's educational achievement is improving steadily, which will help uplift the status of women as housewife, mother, wife and worker.

WOMEN IN EMPLOYMENT

In the course of development, the responsibilities of women have changed from their basic functions as wife and mother to also as breadwinner. The accepted definition of labour force does not include housewifely activities. But the view that housewifely duties do not have high economic and social value is gradually changing as society begins to recognize the value of parenting in determining the well-being of the individuals and family and therefore society. However, an economic value is yet to be recommended for housewives' activities.

Women have always been part of the labour force but mostly as unpaid family worker (see Table 12).[21] Underutilization of labour is higher among women and in particular among rural women. In 1970, only 31.7 per cent of the females were employed compared to 65.3 per cent males (see Table 13). Women's employment rate increased to 34.6 per cent in 1980. A large proportion of the females in 1970 were out of the labour force (66.6 per cent) and this rate decreased slightly in 1980 (63.3 per cent). Among the women who were outside the labour force in 1970, 45.3 per cent were housewives and 16.3 per cent were students. In 1980, the housewives' rate decreased to 38.9 per cent. Underutilization of the female labour force is a loss to the country and more needs to be done to encourage women to participate in the labour force.[10]

The employment pattern of women has changed from rural to urban concentration (see Table 14). Rural/urban migration of females has increased from 88.2 per cent in 1970 to 92.1 in 1980 due to greater availability of employment opportunities in the capital city and large urban towns. These women are employed mainly in the manufacturing, particularly the electronics, industries. Figure 3 illustrates the distribution of female employment by age group for the years 1970 and 1980.

TABLE 11

Percentage Distribution of Population by Educational Attainment and Sex—Malaysia, 1970 and 1980

Educational Attainment	1970						1980					
	Male		Female		Total		Male		Female		Total	
	No.	%	No.	%	No.	%	No.	%	No.	%	No.	%
At least some education (7 Years +)	3,260,660	84.6	2,452,401	61.4	5,720,061	71.3	4,490,518	85.4	3,820,366	71.9	8,310,984	78.6
At least Form I (13 Years +)	861,676	27.8	527,363	16.9	1,389,039	22.4	1,889,803	44.8	1,477,068	34.2	3,366,871	39.5
At least Form II (15 Years +)	573,015	20.2	336,332	11.8	931,807	16.4	1,409,244	36.3	1,090,116	27.3	2,499,360	30.0
At least School Certificate (17 Years +)	184,959	7.1	96,217	3.7	182,176	5.4	697,930	20.0	402,396	10.9	1,100,326	13.1
At least HSC with Certificate (18 Years +)	29,814	1.2	10,864	0.4	40,678	0.8	152,756	4.5	77,800	2.2	230,556	3.3

Sources: 1970: Table 4.6, 1970 General Report Population Census of Malaysia, Vol. 1.
1980: Calculated from 1980 Census of Malaysia.

TABLE 12
Employment Status of the Labour Force Aged 10 Years and Over for Malaysia, 1970 and 1980

Employment Status	1970						1980					
	Male		Female		Total		Male		Female		Total	
	No.	%	No.	%	No.	%	No.	%	No.	%	No.	%
Employer	96,731	4.2	25,315	2.3	122,046	3.6	131,906	4.2	40,529	2.6	172,435	3.7
Employee	1,139,755	49.3	412,257	36.9	1,552,012	45.2	1,855,697	59.2	820,083	53.6	2,675,780	57.3
Own Account Worker	736,873	31.9	201,187	18.0	938,060	27.3	874,728	27.9	366,191	23.9	1,240,919	26.6
Unpaid Family Worker	253,230	10.9	121,250	37.7	674,480	19.7	230,402	7.3	273,577	17.9	503,979	10.8
Seeking First Job	85,644	3.7	57,430	5.1	143,074	4.2	42,530	1.4	30,327	2.0	72,857	1.6
Total in Labour Force	2,312,233	100.0	1,117,439	100.0	3,429,672	100.0	3,315,263	100.0	1,530,707	100.0	4,665,970	100.0

Sources: 1970: Table 4.6 1970 General Report Population Census of Malaysia Vol. 1.
1980: Calculated from 1980 Census of Malaysia.

TABLE 13

Percentage of Labour Force Status of Population Aged 10 Years and Over, Malaysia 1970 and 1980

Labour Force Status	1970		1980	
	Male	Female	Male	Female
In the Labour Force	65.34	31.67	69.26	34.57
Employment	62.52	29.53	65.46	31.14
Unemployment	2.82	2.14	3.80	3.43
Out of the Labour Force	33.19	66.62	29.59	63.36
Looking After House	3.06	45.37	2.16	38.91
Student	20.33	16.34	22.75	21.49
Others	9.80	4.91	4.68	2.96
Not Reported	1.47	1.71	1.15	2.07
Total	100.0	100.0	100.0	100.0

Sources: 1970: General Report Population Census of Malaysia Vol. II (Table 2.22).
1980: Calculated from Census of Malaysia 1980 Vol. 2 Table 6.2.

TABLE 14

Females Sector Employment Rates for 1970 and 1980—Malaysia

Stratum	1970	1980
Urban	88.2	92.1
Rural	95.2	90.8
Total	93.6	91.3

Source: Population Census of Malaysia, 1970, 1980.

Figure 3 indicates that women's employment decreases with higher age perhaps due to more women leaving their employment after marriage.

The Employment Act 1955 (revised 1981) provides protection of employment for all workers, but there is no provision laying down the minimum wage that workers should be paid or to prohibit discriminatory wage practices. Equal pay for equal work has not yet been legally adopted in Malaysia. Although this concept has been implemented in the public sector, in the private sector women workers are still subject to discrimination in pay.[19]

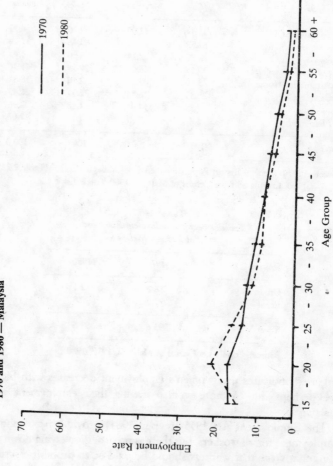

FIGURE 3: Percentage Distribution of Females Employed by Age Group 1970 and 1980 — Malaysia

Maternity leave is given for sixty consecutive days upto the fifth child and maternity allowance during the eligible period for the first three surviving children. Women employees in the public sector are entitled only to forty-two days of maternity allowance. In practice, however, these 'protective' provisions may adversely affect women. In the plantation sector, women having less than three children are not employed, in order to avoid giving maternity leave and allowance.

WOMEN IN POLITICS

In politics, women have equal rights to vote as well as stand for election. Women's involvement in politics has increased after independence in 1957, but the number of women actively involved in politics is still small. There are now three women ministers and one deputy woman minister in the Government of Malaysia.

WOMEN AND VOLUNTARY ORGANIZATIONS

There are two types of voluntary organizations in Malaysia, namely (a) organizations consisting of only women members and (b) organizations consisting of both sexes. The latter are normally religious, political, trade unions and youth organizations whilst the former cater exclusively to women. Examples of the first type are the Women's Institute, the Women's International Club, the Girl Guide Association, the Malaysian Women Journalist Association (PERTAMA), University Women's Association, the Malaysian Association of Graduate Women and others.[7]

The voluntary associations are basically oriented towards welfare and social activities. They serve their own members as well as the community. Malaysia has an active voluntary women's movement although there is some inefficiency because of the same person getting involved in more than one organization and sometimes simultaneously holding the same responsibility in both organizations. Another common problem is the lack of interest among educated women to participate actively in these organizations.

CONCLUSION

The status of Malaysian women has indeed improved tremendously as a result of the awareness on the need to develop women. Today

Malaysian women can be seen participating in various sectors of the economy. They are now recognized as a significant part of society and the family. Malaysian women are now aware of their rights although discrimination has not been completely wiped out.

It is important, however, for Malaysian women to continue pressing for equal opportunities as well as taking the opportunities given to them. They need to create awareness among the majority of women to develop themselves socially, economically, healthwise and psychologically. More women need to be given family life education to ensure their ability to cope with their role as mother, wife and in some instances as breadwinner and worker.

NOTES

1. Hing Ai Yun et al., *Women in Malaysia*, Pelanduk Publications, 1984.
2. Datin (Dr) Noor Laily Aziz, 'Women in Development,' Puvan Memorial Lecture, April 1980.
3. Family Planning Association. Women Today in Peninsular Malaysia, 1978.
4. James Lochhead, Vasanthi Ramachandran, 'Women and Employment: Some Malaysian Observations,' KANITA/NACIWID, 1983.
5. NCWO, 'Women in Malaysia: Achievement and Future Challenges,' September 1982.
6. Virginia A. Miralao, *Some Guidelines for the Integration of Women in National Development Plans*, Occasional Paper No. 2, Integration of Women in Development Programme, Asian and Pacific Development Centre, Kuala Lumpur, Malaysia, 1984.
7. Nik Safiah Karim, 'National Policy on Women and Development,' NACIWID, June 1976.
8. Hamid Arshat et al., *Malaysian Journal of Reproductive Health*, Vol. 1, December 1983.
9. Hamid Arshat et al., *Malaysian Journal of Reproductive Health*, Vol. 3, June 1985.
10. Proceedings of the Seminar on *Economic Activities of Women in Malaysia*, National Family Planning Board, Malaysia, 1983.
11. NFPB Research Series No. 2, *Child Care Needs of Low Income Women in Urban Malaysia*, National Family Planning Board of Malaysia, Kuala Lumpur.
12. *Women's Studies in Asia and the Pacific: An Overview of Current and Needed Priorities*, Integration of Women in Development Programme, Asian and Pacific Development Centre (APDC), Kuala Lumpur, Malaysia, November 1983.
13. Majlis Kebangsaan Pertubuhan—Pertubuhan Wanita Malaysia, Lapuran Kegiatan-kegiatan dan Kejayaan MKPW, 1974–1976.
14. Abdullah Malim Baginda, Women in Development Project (WID), ASEAN Population Programme, Phase II (1980–1983).
15. Report on Seminar *Wanita Negeri Johor*, November 21–23, 1983.

16. Report on Symposium on *Women in the New Economic Era*, Intan, Petaling Jaya, May 16, 1985.

17. *Report on Maternal Health and Early Pregnancy Wastage in Peninsular Malaysia*, Federation of Family Planning Associations, Malaysia and International Development Research Centre, Canada, 1977.

18. Dr Noor Laily Aziz, *Malaysian Women in the 1980's*, National Family Planning Board, Malaysia, 1980.

19. Noor Faridah Ariffin, Legal Protection for Women Workers within and Outside the Home, UWA/APDC Seminar on Women and Employment, Kuala Lumpur, April 16–17, 1984.

20. Proceedings of the Seminar on *Socio-Economic Consequences of the Ageing of Population in Malaysia*, Melaka, Malaysia, May 9–12, 1985.

21. General Report Census 1957, 1970 and 1980, Department of Statistics, Malaysia, Kuala Lumpur.

22. R. Chander, V.T. Palan, Noor Laily Aziz, Tam Boon Ann, Malaysian Fertility and Family Survey, 1974.

23. Datin (Dr) Noor Laily binte Dato Abu Bakar et al., *Facts and Figures, Malaysian National Population and Family Development Programme*, 1982.

24. Datin (Dr) Noor Laily binte Dato Abu Bakar et al., *The Changing Ethnic Patterns of Mortality in Malaysia: 1957–1979*, National Family Planning Board, Research Paper, No. 6, February 1983.

25. Department of Statistics, *Quarterly Review of Malaysian Population Statistics*, January, April and July, 1986.

26. Gavin W. Jones, 'Social Science Research on Population and Development in East and Southern Asia,' January 1978.

27. Gavin W. Jones, Population Growth and Fertility Change in Peninsular Malaysia since 1957, Seminar proceedings on *Malaysian Fertility and Family Survey, Population and Development*, June 1979.

28. Tan Poo Chang, Paul Chan Tuck Hoong, Lee Kok Huat, Shymala Nagaraj, *The Study on Marriage and Marital Dissolution in Peninsular Malaysia: The Married Couples*, September 1986.

29. Islamic Family Law (Federal Territory Act 1984), published by MDC Sdn. Bhd., Government Printers Malaysia, Ministry of Trade and Industry, 1985.

30. Man Singh Das and Panos D. Bardis, *The Family in Asia*, George Allen and Unwin, 1979.

31. Country Paper—Malaysia, Regional Inter-government Preparatory Meeting for the World Conference of the United Nations Decade for Women, 1985, Tokyo, March 26–30, 1984.

32. Tey Nai Peng and Nizileh Ramli, Age at Menopause and Menopausal Symptoms among Malaysian Women, paper presented at the National Seminar on *Socio-Economic Consequences of Ageing in Malaysia*, March 25–27, 1988.

Bangladesh Women in Transition: Dynamics and Issues

Asfia Duza

Serious study about women's status and gender role is a recent phenomenon on the world scene. In Bangladesh also a series of articles, books and monographs exploring the multifarious dimensions of women's status and role have been published during the Decade of Women. All these reveal the universal fact that women in Bangladesh occupy a secondary and an inferior position to that of men. In all aspects of life—education, work and employment, health and nutrition, politics and law, in short in most spheres of economic and social activities including the family—women have limited opportunities. This paper aims at shedding some light on the situation of women, the dynamics of their status and role in relation to development efforts.

The factors most commonly referred to as reflecting the position of women in a society are the following:

— opportunity to survive
— food consumption and nutritional level
— reproductive and family role
— right to work
— educational facilities available
— health and medical care
— political participation
— rights given by law

However, the socio-cultural context cuts across all these factors, and these need to be generally understood before we can appreciate the true nature of the status of women in Bangladesh. The first important thing is to have a brief review of the country's religio-cultural and economic realities and their ramifications.

Islam, the main religion of Bangladesh, originated in a completely different environment. In its sojourn to this area through time and space, it was influenced by various beliefs and practices, especially by Hinduism and other local religions. Many of the religious rites, rituals and beliefs commonly considered Islamic are a compound mixture with existing customs, traditions and other religions. Needless to say, the social consequences of such phenomena are both intricate and profound.

One of the least developed countries on the world map with a limited land area of 143,778 sq km, a large population of over 105 million and a current growth rate of 2.26 per cent per annum, Bangladesh poses a formidable challenge to the economist, the demographer and the policy maker (Bangladesh 1985; World Bank 1984). After the war of independence in 1971, the country suffered serious economic and demographic dislocations. Population density is one of the highest in the world (700 per square kilometre) with a land-man ratio of 0.29 acre in 1981 (Bangladesh 1985a). The dependency ratio (persons less than 15 and over 65 years of age as ratio of those 15–64) is also high (93), with 45 per cent of the population below 15 years of age. The rate of annual GDP growth, showing a declining trend, is 3.8 per cent in the 1980–85 period, with per capita income of US$ 140 (World Bank 1984). Land being the main economic resource, the high frequency of floods, droughts and cyclones means considerable disruption of the economy and people's lives.

Gender as a determinant of roles and as a principle of social organization is a universal phenomenon. But each society has its own social and religio-cultural traditions, beliefs and practices which are translated into normative pattern. In Bangladesh, its patriarchal culture, predominantly 'Islamic ideology' and socio-religious commentaries assigned women with their roles in society and detailed their rights and obligations. Accordingly, women in Bangladesh have always been dependent on men and they have rarely had any opportunity to participate in social, political and economic decisions, though they contributed heavily to the country's economy by their participation in agriculture, along with the household chores. The sources of power— formal as well as informal—were vested in the male; society was dominated by men, and women formed an especially neglected and deprived group. The uncritical acceptance of male superiority and women's deprived position with grace was glorified by cultural norms. Women belonged to a world different from that of men. Their segregation at physical, social, political, economic and psychological levels is symbolized by a system of Purdah which confines them within the home and to control by men (Abdullah 1974; Noman 1983; Jahan 1973; Arens and Beurden 1977; Zeidensteins 1973; Schaffer 1986; Yunus 1982).

However, the considerable socio-economic changes that have swept over Bangladesh society in the past few decades have shaken the secluded world of women. The sojourn of women from Mexico to Nairobi (1975–1985), during which the women's world, supported by their collective effort has changed profoundly, has germinated seeds of change in Bangladeshi women too. One of the distinct features of the last decade in Bangladesh has been the emergence of women in the 'men's world'. Modernization, industrialization and rapidly growing communication with the modern western world are bringing about rapid social change in the country and the traditional social set-up is giving way to a new order. There is noticeable change in women's thinking, living, and aspirations also. Like the women of the developed world, Bangladesh women are also asking to be viewed as individuals, allowed to discover their needs and respond to them. They are no longer willing to restrict their self-expression only as docile daughters, compliant wives and dependent mothers.

The planners, reformers, social thinkers and donors are taking note of the needs and demands of society. Women's development, thus, has become a major focus of intensive development efforts by many agencies—governmental, non-governmental, foreign and indigenous. The key issues in the process relate to the dynamics and mechanisms of integrating women with various operational programmes at different levels to bring about desired change in women's role and status.

Socio-Economic Changes in Female Status

Social Status

Islam, though mingled with many local customs, rites, beliefs, etc., has been the most important factor in assigning the traditional position to women in Bangladesh. To begin with, inequality of the sexes is manifested in the different moral standards applied by the religio-cultural system to men and women. Sexual laxity in men is often tolerated but a rigid code of sex mores is imposed on women. The Purdah—the degree of seclusion to which a woman must conform—depends upon her locality and social class. Purdah is often an index of social status in poverty-stricken Bangladesh where only well-off families can afford the cost of the observance of Purdah. The poor majority only aspire to it. As such, though one can argue that Purdah as a social system does not hamper women's development—because the majority of the women do not or cannot observe it—Purdah is still emblematic of the general socio-cultural attitudes about women; the concept which underlies it hampers their education and employment. However, seclusion is becoming less stringent and a growing number of women from different classes and regions are coming out of their homeshells. At present, the rules of Purdah are not as rigid as before (Abdullah 1984, Yunus 1982).

As in many other developing countries, in Bangladesh also boys are much preferred, the birth of a girl being a disappointment. Engendered partly by the patriarchal nature of the society and partly by the socio-economic context of the country, the economic value of sons is expressed by preferential attention, health care, and family resource use (Amin 1987; Schaffer 1986; BFS 1975; Chen et al. 1981).

The position of woman being defined in terms of her marital status, marriage is virtually universal. Unmarried women are generally considered redundant. Early marriage is traditional (see Table 10). It caters to the social imperative of protecting the chastity of a girl and of making the wife compliant and submissive to the absolute power of the husband and the in-laws.

Payment of dowry (in cash or kind) is an important indicator of women's status. As a form of gift, some sort of dowry system has long been prevalent, but dowry as a means of systematic exaction of as much money and goods as possible by the groom and his family from the bride's parents is a recent phenomenon. Dowry also has an economic angle. Because of the rigid code of sex mores for girls, the bride's parents are eager to marry off their daughter as early as possible. But the groom's family is not financially capable of accepting the burden and cost of marriage and to commence a new family without dowry or the promise of dowry. Unfortunately, most indigent parents can satisfy little or none of the dowry promises and in consequence the brides often suffer maltreatment, desertion and divorce and are driven to utter destitution with their children. Such women often join the growing floating population; some resort to begging and prostitution. According to a survey done in 1985 by CARITAS, a voluntary organization, 36.7 per cent of the prostitutes in Bangladesh were either deserted or divorced women (CARITAS 1986).

There is not much data on violence against women. However,

booklets, pamphlets, reports and issue papers make it clear that male violence against women is in line with the latter's marginal status in society. Teasing, harassment, acid throwing, kidnapping and even rape and murder are increasing alarmingly. This has led to efforts to create some pressure on the existing legal system to bring about some positive changes. The Mahila Parishad—a leading non-government women's group—Mahila Ain-Jibi Samity, Nari Pakkha, Women for Women and many other women's organizations have successfully worked to bring about some legal measures to safeguard the cause of women, and protect them from violence and oppression. The Dowry Prohibition Act was promulgated in 1980, and again amended in 1982. The Muslim Family Ordinance (1961) also was amended in 1982 in favour of women. The Cruelty to Women (Deterrent Punishment) Ordinance (1983) and establishment of family courts are some of the major steps towards alleviating the suffering of women, and integrating women in development.

But this is only the beginning. How far the judicial and executive system and ethos can favour women's rightful position depends on many other variables. Conformity to social mores and customs overrides conformity to law. It is therefore more important to change the attitudes and practices that downgrade women.

Women and Education

The high rate of illiteracy in Bangladesh contributes to perpetuating the traditional cycle of ignorance and a subsistence economy. The education system begins with the primary stage. Kindergarten and pre-primary schools are rare and serve only the urban affluent. Although primary education is free for both sexes, the economically hard pressed system cannot accommodate all eligible children. There is also a lack of coordination between the systems of education and labour force participation irrespective of gender role. There are some noteworthy sub-features: public system or mass education, private tutoring to supplement formal schooling, and private schools, the last being beyond the reach of ordinary people.

Education is recognized as a basic human right, but in reality a woman's right to education has never been considered seriously by society until very recently. Table 1 reflects how female literacy lags far behind the male and how the gap widens with increasing age. It further reveals that male-female disparity is less in urban than in rural areas. Social attitudes and institutions positively support males over females in every aspect of life including education. Because most families cannot afford schooling for all children, the choice naturally falls on the boys—for as the proverb goes, 'investment in girls is like watering someone else's garden.'

TABLE 1
Per cent of Literate Population (Aged 5 and over)

Year	Male	Female
1961	31.4	10.7
1974	32.9	14.8
1981	31.0	16.0

Source: National Censuses.

Of late efforts are being made to make the education system more effective in development terms. There is also an effort to reduce the gap in education opportunities for the sexes. Previously the planners supported female education on the grounds of better child-rearing and domestic management. The Education Commission Report (1974) recommended a change in the curricula to equip girls for better household management as well as for earning a living and acknowledged the need for female education in development terms (Islam 1982). This is indeed a significant shift in orientation.

The second five-year plan (1980–1985), admitting the 'imbalance in enrolment and drop-out rate between the two sexes' and the 'gap in education facilities for boys and girls' took some major steps to promote female education like reservation of seats for girls in various faculties of the universities, special scholarship for girls at all levels of education, and establishment of more girls' schools and colleges specially in rural areas (Bangladesh 1980).

Even after all these efforts, the picture is rather gloomy. Enrolment of both females and males has risen. Though female enrolment at secondary level has increased to one-fifth of the total eligible age group in 1985 from one-tenth in 1975, the overall female enrolment still markedly lags behind that of male (Table 2).

In university education, women constitute only 27.4 per cent of the total enrolment. According to the latest available figures women constitute only 4.5 per cent of the total students of Bangladesh University of Engineering and Technology. The ratio of female students in medicine to total enrolment is 23.2 per cent. Other technical and commercial education also is predominantly male-oriented. All this

TABLE 2
Per cent of Eligible Age Group Enrolled at Primary and Secondary Levels

Year	Male		Female	
	Primary	Secondary	Primary	Secondary
1951	48.0	12.0	13.0	0.5
1961	53.0	17.0	21.0	2.0
1975	66.0	30.0	40.0	10.0
1985	73.0	42.0	38.0	19.0

Source: Shamina Islam, 1982. *Women's Education in Bangladesh: Needs and Issues* (Dhaka: FREPD).

shows that women receive a meagre share of government allocation for education (Bangladesh 1985).

The principal factors contributing to the unequal access of women to educational opportunities are poverty and socio-cultural attitudes and practices. The mass media, textbooks etc., still portray women as performing a domestic role and as being economically non-productive. The whole system is thus a self-perpetuating vicious circle by limiting skill development and access to better paid jobs for women.

Women and Work

With minimal access to education and skill, women have peripheral economic status. By most definitions of economic status such as the degree of access to economic resources as and when needed and the degree of control over economic activities, most women are at a disadvantage.

Women in Bangladesh are engaged in various economic activities at family level. But their work has not been quantified in monetary terms, and as such, cannot include the full connotation of economic partici- pation. Most women, though they contribute to the production pro- cess, are classified as economically inactive. The men monopolize the credit for whatever little is produced while the average woman lives in a pitiable state of dependency and low status.

This neglect of women's role in the economy, particularly their contribution to agriculture, restricts the planners' vision for develop- ment. For when the economy is basically subsistence-oriented and the labour mainly self-employed, women's contribution, even if not directly income-generating, is a significantly relevant issue which must be addressed properly. Without wage-oriented production targets and employment, income-generating aims of women are thwarted and they are caught in a perpetual trap of economic vulnerability. Besides, the basic structural weakness of the economy forces women to depend on employment generated in agricultural and para-agricultural tasks around the homestead like threshing, husking, parboiling of paddy, preparation of food, cleaning, washing, raising cattle and caring for the children, the old and the sick. These works are labelled as domestic work and conveniently excluded from employment measurement or in the estimation of Gross National Product (GNP).

Published figures thus provide a gross underestimation of women's work. Table 3 shows that overall participation rates for the age group

TABLE 3
Distribution of Population by Economic Activity, Sex and Residence (per cent)

Economic Activity, Sex and Residence	1961		1974		1981	
	Male	*Female*	*Male*	*Female*	*Male*	*Female*
National						
Population aged 10-plus	64.26	61.63	66.04	63.37	67.48	66.11
Civilian Labour Force	87.57	17.22	80.41	4.13	73.93	4.30
Employed	87.57	17.22	78.37	3.67	73.93	4.30
Unemployed	5.92	—	2.04	—	—	—
Others	12.43	82.78	19.59	96.33	26.07	95.34
Household work	—	73.51	—	76.61	3.96	74.55
Inactive	12.43	9.27	19.59	19.73	22.11	20.79
Rural						
Population aged 10-plus	63.70	61.96	65.37	63.41	66.13	65.66
Economic Participation						
Civilian Labour Force	87.97	17.93	80.82	3.19	73.00	4.18
Employed	87.34	17.93	79.45	3.48	75.00	4.18
Unemployed	0.63	*	1.83	*	—	—
Others	12.03	82.07	18.72	96.02		
Household work	—	73.10	—	77.11	4.00	76.57
Inactive	12.03	8.97	18.72	18.91	21.00	18.83
Urban						
Population aged 10-plus	68.75	63.64	74.29	66.67	74.32	68.97
Economic Participation						
Civilian Labour Force	81.82	14.29	73.08	5.56	69.00	5.00
Employed	81.82	14.28	69.23	5.56	69.09	5.00
Unemployed	*	—	3.85	*	—	—
Others	18.18	85.71	26.92	94.44	30.91	95.00
Household work	—	71.43	—	66.66	3.94	62.50
Inactive	18.18	14.28	26.92	27.78	27.27	32.50

* Less than 50,000

Source: *Statistical Pocket Book of Bangladesh, 1983.*

10 and above were 73.9 per cent and 4.3 per cent for males and females respectively in 1981 against the corresponding figures of 87.6 per cent and 17.22 per cent in 1961. The higher participation rate for females in the 1961 census was due to counting of some house-wives as working women. Agriculture being the main economy, this accounts for about half of the GDP. In 1982, 74 per cent of the labour force was employed in this sector (unpaid family labour included) (UN University 1986).

Whether recognized or not, crop-related activities of Bangladesh suggest that women's labour accounts for at least 25 per cent of the value added from sowing onward in the production process of rice. Time series studies carried out in different parts of the country during 1974 to 1985 also reveal that women work longer than men (Chowdhury 1984). A typical time-table of rural women (Table 4) will show the 'occupational multiplicity' they are involved in.

TABLE 4
A Rural Woman's Timetable

5	a.m.	Rising, washing and cleaning the house and compound, releasing the poultry, collecting eggs.
6-7	a.m.	Preparing the early morning meal for the working members of the family before they go out to the fields.
7-8	a.m.	Milking, collecting fuel, making dung cakes, tending to the kitchen garden, cleaning the cowshed and compound, drying straw to burn it.
8-9	a.m.	Preparing the midday meal, grinding spices, peeling vegetables.
9-11	a.m.	Husking paddy, winnowing and sifting, preparing rice products.
11-12	a.m.	Cooking.
12-1	p.m.	Washing clothes, bathing, fetching water, feeding the animals and the poultry.
1-2	p.m.	Washing jute and paddy, putting other stores out in the sun to dry.
2-3	p.m.	Feeding her husband and family, and eating the leftover herself.
3-4	p.m.	Making articles such as baskets and quilts for home use or for sale.
4-5	p.m.	Preparing and cooking the evening meal.
5-6	p.m.	Praying, bringing the children home, shutting up the poultry and animals.
6-7	p.m.	Eating the evening meal and cleaning up.
7-8	p.m.	Rest period, sitting on the verandah talking and smoking before going to bed.

Source: Report on Feasibility Survey of Productive/Income-Generating Activities for Women, UNICEF.

Since most of these activities are performed within the family setting, and are of subsistence nature, these do not enter into the market economy. Besides, the earnings of women e.g., from the sale of surplus vegetables, eggs, chickens or cottage crafts are diluted as there is no opportunity to market their products.

A look into the Manpower Survey helps in the better understanding of women's economics. The 1980 Manpower Survey, giving rural-urban occupational patterns separately shows that of the so-called employed women, 74 per cent of the urban employed women were engaged in services followed by clerical work, sales work etc., and about 55 per cent of the rural employed women were engaged in agricultural work, followed by manufacturing, transport and related activities (Table 5). Table 6 reveals the tangential role of women in Bangladesh Secretariat.

TABLE 5

Distribution of Employed Women by Major Occupation, 1980 (per cent)

	Total	Rural	Urban
Professional and Technical	2.4	2.1	4.5
Administrative and Managerial	—	—	—
Clerical	1.5	0.5	7.7
Sales	4.2	2.9	5.7
Service	19.6	11.6	74.4
Agriculture	47.6	54.7	4.5
Manufacturing, Transport and Others	24.7	28.2	3.2
Total	100.0	100.0	100.0

Source: '1980 Manpower Survey,' *Statistical Pocket Book 1983.*

TABLE 6

Female Employment in the Secretariat

Class		
	I	5%
	II	4%
	III	4.5%
	IV	5%
Total		4.7%

Source: Government of Bangladesh, Ministry of Establishment (unofficial estimate).

Women account for about 9 per cent of the officially estimated non-agricultural employment in the country. Though there are no definite data about actual participation of women in employment some knowledge could be gained from different studies and official reports. Among the working women in urban areas one can identify three broad groups: (*a*) destitutes, (*b*) middle class women and (*c*) women elite. The destitute women are mainly migrants who take recourse to any available job—house maid, construction work, etc., to earn a living. The middle class, which constitutes the majority, goes for a variety of jobs from factory work, telephone operating, nursing, etc., to teaching, medical profession, etc. The third group is minuscule. The vast majority is engaged in garments, pharmaceuticals, electric works, confectionery, cosmetics and jute packaging. They are predominantly rural in origin (83 per cent), aged between 16 and 24 (91 per cent), unskilled (70 per cent), and therefore falling in the low income and status group. Among the rural industrial workers 37 per cent are women and the majority of them (77 per cent) are engaged in the production of goods like Kantha, coir products, jute products, paper bags, bidi making, silk weaving, handloom products, pottery, fishing nets, etc. Female workers are paid less than male workers. Technological improvements in all these activities have worsened the employment situation for women with their restricted access to training and other resources (Bangladesh 1983; Bangladesh 1980; RISP 1981; Ahmed et al. 1985).

In the absence of definitive statistics, it is believed that 85 per cent of women in Bangladesh live in rural areas, the vast majority of them being involved directly or indirectly in agricultural activities. Pre-harvest work and post-harvest processing of crops such as processing and storing seeds, threshing, parboiling, soaking, drying, husking and storing of different crops are mainly women's jobs. But here too, mechanization and technological innovation has adversely affected women. With the introduction of high-yielding varieties and seed-irrigation-fertilizer technologies, there has been a 'massive increase' in the production of paddy which is milled in small rural or large commercial mills displacing a substantial number of female labourers. With the establishment of some 10,000 steel hullers in rural areas, between 1.4 million and 2.0 million women have lost a traditional source of productive part-time employment. Every year 700 new mills are being set up, displacing another 100,000–140,000 women (World Bank 1984).

Undoubtedly, technology is needed to release women from drudgery, to save their time and energy and to enable them to earn more to lead a better life. But there is an urgent need to plan a strategy for involving women in agricultural development activities and for technological change that allows the best possible end result in terms of women's employment.

Women, Politics and Law

The Constitution of Bangladesh (1979) clearly grants equal rights to women with men in all spheres of state and public life. It further affirms that the State shall not be prevented from making any special provisions in favour of women. Nevertheless, politics remains a male domain. The recent emergence of two female leaders—Sheikh Hasina and Begum Khaleda Zia—in the forefront of national politics is an incidental phenomenon. It would be fallacious to relate this to women's participation in politics or to see this as the epitome of women's power. Both the leaders emerged as mere 'symbols' of departed male leaders; their political philosophy and commitments, their party programmes and activities have no particular emphasis on women's development issues. However, the fact that they are women in extraordinary roles, combined with the objectives of the time (Women's Decade), is having its own impact on women's development in general.

In the National Parliament, thirty seats are reserved for women over and above their right to contest general seats. But this reservation is working to their detriment. Very few women are nominated to contest directly as each party feels that its potential women candidates can be accommodated in the reserved seats if and when it gains majority, and a majority of the 300 members elected directly does this nomination. Thus, women have no opportunity to develop initiative and competitiveness through electoral politics. The situation is similar in the Local Bodies—Union Parishad, Upazila Parishad, Zila Parishad and Pourashivas with their reserved seats for women. Without a political forum, the women in reserved seats are vulnerable to all sorts of manipulations and the whims of male politicians and power brokers (Alam 1985). The socio-cultural impediments faced by women are felt most acutely in politics.

In the last election held in May 1986, out of a total of 1,527 contestants, seventeen women stood for election, none of them from the party which obtained a majority. Three of them won (Election Commission Report 1986).

Constituting almost half of the country's electorate, women as voters should be important. But being politically inarticulate, they regard politics as man's business and often are manipulated by different kinds of familial loyalties and relationship. In legislation also women do not make much impact, with poor involvement in party organizations and activities.

Under the Constitution, Bangladesh women have equal rights with men but the reality is different. Their low status in social, economic, educational and political spheres amidst the widespread prevalence of poverty and illiteracy, has negatively affected their real legal status.

status. To protect and promote the legal status of women, some new legislation has been promulgated. A Legal Aid Cell has been set up in the Women Affairs Department to counsel and assist women. A number of private voluntary organizations also render legal services to women. But for the vast majority of women, still ignorant of their legal rights or disabled from going through the complex legal procedures, legislation protecting their rights hardly makes a difference. Most often legal issues relating to women are settled by patriarchal community leaders, for whom the law that upholds equality of women with men means nothing.

DEMOGRAPHIC PROFILE OF WOMEN

The linkage of female status with the dynamics of reproduction, longevity, health, nutrition and quality of life is pivotal in the context of family as well as society. An understanding of the demographic profile of Bangladeshi women is thus an essential precondition for addressing the issues of women and development.

It is indeed revealing that issues like early marriage and high fertility of women—raised by Anne Besant in her preface to a book on population as early as in 1914—are still persistent in many parts of the developing world, including Bangladesh. By and large Bangladeshi women are still trapped in the vicious circle of underdevelopment, early marriage, burden of high fertility, ill health, and malnutrition—worse than the high and unacceptable levels that their male counterparts themselves are subject to.

The population of Bangladesh as of mid-1987 is estimated to be 105 million (Mabud 1987). Table 7 presents vital rates and rates of natural increase of the population since the early part of the twentieth century. It is shown that both birth and death rates remained stable at the traditional high level until the middle of the century. Since then mortality declined rather rapidly. The recent CDR of 15 per thousand is about a third of the figure noted at the beginning of the century. The modest decline in the birth rate, recorded since the late 1960s, has failed to cope with the rate of mortality decline with inevitable escalation in population growth. Assuming a nearly 50 per cent reduction in CBR and 33 per cent reduction in CDR between 1980 and 2000, the projected population by the end of the century could be of the order of 130 million (Duza 1985). The corresponding pressure on the socio-economic infrastructure and debilitating consequences for the already disadvantaged females of the society would thus continue to pose a formidable challenge to the policy maker.

TABLE 7
Estimated Birth Rate, Death Rate and Rate of Natural Increase

Years	Birth Rate (per thousand)	Death Rate (per thousand)	Rate of Natural increase (% per year)
1911	53.8	45.6	0.82
1921	52.9	47.3	0.56
1931	50.4	41.7	0.87
1941	52.7	37.8	1.49
1951	49.4	40.3	0.91
1961	51.9	29.7	2.17
1976	47.0	16.0	3.10
1986	38.0	15.0	2.30

Source: M.A. Mabud, 1987. 'Levels and trends of Infertility and Demographic Prospects in Bangladesh (Dhaka: Planning Commission).

The young age structure of the population, shown in Table 8, reflects the persistent high fertility and heavy dependency burden for the working population. The same table records high sex ratio (males per 100 females) in the total population, and virtually in all age groups. This could be attributed to possible under-enumeration of females owing to the system of Purdah and related factors, and more important, to higher female mortality (cf ESCAP 1981: 35), resulting from 'some socio-cultural deprivations of women' (Khan 1985: 68). Chen and others (1981), investigating sex bias in rural Bangladesh families, provide definitive evidence of lower calorie and protein intake by females compared to males, and better attention to the latter with respect to diarrhoea treatment.

TABLE 8
Per cent Population and Sex Ratio

Age	Sex Ratio		Percent population in age group	
	1974	1981	1974	1981
0-4	99.3	101.4	16.9	17.1
5-9	101.2	102.5	18.3	16.2
10-14	118.9	115.1	12.8	13.4
15-19	114.1	101.6	8.3	9.5
20-29	95.2	97.6	13.7	15.2
30-39	106.9	107.1	11.0	10.7
40-49	119.6	127.7	8.1	7.4
50-59	122.5	116.2	5.2	4.9
60+	129.9	122.5	5.7	5.6
Total	107.7	106.1	100.0	100.0

Source: Bangladesh Census 1974 and 1981.

Table 9 shows that while overall expectancy of life has more than doubled—from mid-twenties to around mid-fifties—since the beginning of the century, female longevity has continued to lag behind male longevity. This is attributable not only to relatively high mortality of women in the reproductive years, compared to mortality of men in corresponding ages (Ahmed 1987), but also to reportedly higher child mortality among females, relative to males, as evident in Table 10. Commenting on higher mortality of female children, compared to males, Mosley (1970) corroborates that this mortality differential is apparently due to the fact that parents are more cautious about the health of their sons. We have already noted son preference as a societal norm (Amin 1987). This factor indicates important areas for public education and policy interventions directed at enhancing the status of women and mitigating the socio-cultural deprivations they suffer from.

The high fertility norm of the past, backed by societal prescription of early and universal marriage, logically led to the traditional high mortality situation. As reflected in Table 11, low female age at marriage—closely following puberty—was prevalent until about two

TABLE 9
Expectancy of Life at Birth

Year	Male	Female
1901	23.6	23.9
1911	22.6	23.3
1921	19.4	20.9
1931	26.9	26.6
1941	32.1	31.4
1962–64	49.2	46.9
1973–74	51.6	49.7
1982	55.2	52.7

Source: Ashraf Uddin Ahmed, 'Mortality and its Prospects in Bangladesh' (Dhaka: Planning Commission).

TABLE 10
Child Death Rate (per thousand) for Ages 1-4 Years

Year	Male	Female
1966–69	22.5	29.6
1974	18.3	32.9
1976	22.5	33.9
1980	18.5	32.9
1981	20.3	29.6
1982	19.3	36.5

Source: ICDDR, B, Annual Reports.

TABLE 11
Singulate Mean Age at Marriage

Year	Male	Female
1921	21.9	12.3
1931	18.7	10.8
1941	21.7	13.4
1951	22.4	14.4
1961	22.9	13.9
1974	24.6	15.9
1981	23.9	16.8

Source: ESCAP, 1981, *Population of Bangladesh* (New York: United Nations) and Bangladesh Census 1981.

decades ago, and the singulate mean age at marriage for females ranged from about 11 to 14 years between 1921 and 1961. The last two censuses, however, have shown a definite upward trend in this respect, the 1981 figure being nearly 17 years.

This trend is further enhanced by the growing percentage of never-married population in the younger ages (Table 12). In 1961 two -thirds of the female population aged 10–14 were never married, which rose to 98 per cent by 1981. Similarly, in the next age group, 15–19, only one out of every twelve females was yet to marry in 1961, compared to about one in every three in 1981. Male age at marriage too has risen, but the increase has been much less pronounced.

Postponement of marriage used to be limited to the relatively better urban socio-economic classes in response to educational expansion

TABLE 12
Percentage of Never Married Population Aged 10-24

Age	Male			Female		
	1961	1974	1981	1961	1974	1981
10-14	97.8	99.3	99.9	67.4	90.5	98.0
15-19	87.7	92.3	93.3	8.3	24.5	31.3
20-24	49.7	60.1	59.7	1.3	3.2	5.1

Source: Bangladesh Census 1974 and 1981, and Pakistan Census, 1961.

and rising achievement orientations. The spread of education in rural areas has begun to exert some effect toward rising age at marriage. In addition, the pressure of dowry also seems to be playing a role in marital postponement in the lower socio-economic strata, and among uneducated girls in the countryside.

Delayed marriage is likely to have far-reaching implications for the fertility behaviour and contraceptive response of women, and for their role and status in the family and society. A relatively mature bride is likely to have qualitatively different equations in intrafamilial relationships with husbands, in-laws and children; and is likely to have more say in marital decision making. When reinforced with education and training, possibilities of income generation, and exposure to communications for social change, the brides of tomorrow are likely to be quite different from their mothers and grandmothers.

As to fertility level, child-woman ratios provide a confused picture in the trend. The ratios of children 0–4 to women 15–49 show progressively higher figures for the past decades—from 537 in 1921 to 867 in 1961. Even for the 1974 and 1981 censuses, which ostensibly have been affected by the recent fertility declines, the figures are only slightly lower—851 and 807 respectively, compared to the 1961 figure (Mabud 1987). This is because of the offsetting effect of substantial mortality decline, leading to increasingly greater number of surviving children in recent years.

On the basis of estimates of total fertility (TFR) however, the declining trend in recent fertility is clearly noticed. Compared to TFR estimates exceeding 7 on the basis of PGE (population growth estimation) figures for 1963–65, BFS (Bangladesh Fertility Survey) 1975 provides a figure of 6.35, and the 1986 estimate on the basis of the National Family Planning and Fertility Survey, gives a figure of 5.55. Corresponding figures on age-specific fertility rates show increasing shifts from too early and too late age of reproduction on the part of mothers to age groups 20–29 (Mabud 1987).

That such emerging patterns in reproductive behaviour are a result of growing contraceptive dissemination is also evidenced by recent figures. It is true that there is still a wide KAP gap in the country and the level of contraceptive use is limited. Even so, recent contraceptive diffusion is not a mean achievement when seen against the backdrop of traditionalism and pervasive socio-economic underdevelopment. As shown in Table 13, the ever use rate for any contraceptive method has

TABLE 13

Per cent of Currently Married Women under 50 Years of Age Reporting ever use *and*
Current Use *of Contraceptives*

Method	Source and Year				
	1975 BFS	1979 CPS	1981 CPS	1983 CPS	1985 CPS
Any Method					
Ever use	13.6	19.6	35.7	33.4	32.5
Current use	7.7	12.7	18.6	19.1	25.3
Modern Method					
Ever use	10.0	15.8	20.2	23.8	25.9
Current use	4.7	8.9	10.9	13.8	18.4

Sources: Bangladesh Fertility Survey 1975 (Dhaka: Ministry of Health and Population Control) and Contraceptive Prevalence Survey 1975–85 (Dhaka: Mitra and Associates).

increased from about 14 to 33 per cent, and current use from 8 to 25 per cent. The use rate of modern methods is somewhat lower than these figures, but still nontrivial.

The option of small family norm and related nuptiality and contraceptive behaviour are positively associated with such modernity variables as education, urbanization and wage employment (Chowdhury and Ahmed 1979; CPS 1979–1985; ESCAP 1981; Mabud 1987). Various government and NGO outreach programmes are also making significant headway in diffusing the small family and contraceptive message to the population, including poor and illiterate masses in the rural areas. All these do provide some element of optimism. They dissipate the myth of the traditional woman, stubbornly non-responsive to forces of planned change. Instead, they demonstrate that provided with effective options, women can make a rational choice toward redefining their demographic and socio-economic parameters.

It is in this context that ongoing efforts directed at reproductive modernization have profound significance for female roles and status in Bangladesh. Among others, the prospect of new nuptiality, fertility and contraceptive behaviour could open up immense potentials in the women's world. Initiating marital life as mature persons, freedom of reproductive decision making, health and longevity, corollaries of having fewer children, and consideration of non-familial options— including wage employment—are some such important possibilities. They would certainly demand attention by their own right. In addition, they would deserve careful consideration for the wider policy framework for enhancing the status of women.

WOMEN, MODERNIZATION AND EMANCIPATION

Throughout the ages in Bangladesh, woman's personal self-fulfilment was realized by performing her foreordained role as wife/mother and housewife. She was the centre of communication and all familial activities which were important for life. But with growing urbanization and socio-economic development, the setting is changing. The close social living of traditional rural society is giving way to modernized living. In the process the role of woman is also changing; the modern woman has moved quite a distance from her predecessors, in education and accomplishment, attitudes toward husband and in-laws, in her work roles and social activities, etc. Notwithstanding the accompanying criticism the concept of women's emancipation is gaining momentum. Women are trying to choose their own course of action, struggling for freedom to pursue a life of their liking and to achieve equal status with men, the responses from society being sometimes positive, but often negative.

The partition of India, with the attendant large shifts in population and resources, brought about a major structural change in society. Only after partition Bengali Muslim women started to redefine their life in light of new ideas and societal needs; their values, behaviour patterns and attitudes changed and a number of women's organizations appeared intending reform.

However, women's organizations during the 1950s and 1960s could not develop into a mass movement; they were limited to certain specific groups of urban women and to welfare activities. Only after the independence of Bangladesh in 1971, there was a major shift in their orientation. The leadership of some organizations like Mahila Parishad, Jatio Mahila Sangstha, Women for Women, and Mahila Samity became concerned with basic women's development issues and aimed at bringing about emancipation of women in all aspects of life.

For this shift of orientation three main factors can be identified, among others: (a) the Liberation War of 1971, (b) the research findings that there is an inseparable linkage between women's reproductive behaviour and their resources needs and means of meeting these needs, and (c) the journey of the world's women from Mexico (1975) to Nairobi (1985).

The Liberation War of 1971 is of special relevance in understanding the pattern of the changing role and status of women in Bangladesh. To rehabilitate distressed and war-torn women, the Women's Rehabilitation Board was established in 1972. The Director of the Board announced in December 1972 that about 1,400,000 women were oppressed in some form or the other; thousands had been dishonoured; a good number of families had been disrupted, women in the thousands had become destitute having lost their male breadwinners. In this difficult situation, women opted to live and came out of home in search of a means to earn a livelihood. Society became ambivalent about accepting Xenophone's age old declaration that 'The gods created women for indoor duties and man for all others . . . It is improper for women to loiter outdoors.' By an Act of Parliament (Act No. L1 of 1974) in July 1974 the Rehabilitation Board was converted into the Bangladesh Women's Rehabilitation and Welfare Foundation with specific responsibilities of formulating rehabilitation programmes for war-affected women.

Soon it was realized that such welfare-oriented programmes would not match the social necessities engendered in the world situation of the 1970s. From pure rehabilitation, the government gradually moved into income-generating programmes for women. The clear indication in research conducted abroad and in Bangladesh about the relationship between the status of woman and her fertility behaviour, and the identification of population growth as the number one problem in Bangladesh led development planner and donors to argue in favour of policy interventions to raise the status of women in society by involving them in development work (Bangladesh 1973). The World Population Conference (Bucharest 1974), the International Women's Conference (Mexico City 1975), and the subsequent United Nations Declarations of the Women's Decade 1975–85, with end of the decade conference in Nairobi (1985), had great influence all over the world including Bangladesh in terms of examining women's status and planning for their integration into the development process.

Conforming to the policy of raising the status of women and integrating them into development activities, the government took various steps and, in 1978, a separate Ministry of Women's Affairs was created. Bangladesh was one of the pioneering countries which established a national machinery for women's development. Besides these sectoral programmes, a number of multisectoral women's activities started functioning to provide women with income-earning opportunities through education, training and credit with focus on rural women. Side by side many non-governmental organizations (NGO), realizing that women's participation is essential to achieve developmental goals, have sprung up and made their presence felt by attacking the poverty, ignorance, and despair and dependency of women.

All efforts by the government of Bangladesh, NGOs, and women themselves can claim some achievements. But the basic drawback remains; the country has not been able to develop a clear philosophy of women's development which could gear an appropriate and comprehensive policy on women's development. The government's policy statements are sporadic, ad hoc and often it is difficult to find their relevance to current needs. Moreover, an unfortunate gap often exists between policy objectives and their implementation. In the confusion as to the philosophy and actual orientation of women's development lies the tragedy of the Bangladesh woman. As the Forward Looking Strategy document of the Nairobi Conference puts it: 'because the issue of women in development has been perceived as a welfare problem, it has received low priority, viewed simply as a cost to society rather than as a contribution.'

The fundamental obstacle to enhancing the status of women is bound up with cultural factors, traditional-ethical systems and the outlook of policy planners and administrators. For example, the low socio-economic status of women—their poverty, malnutrition, drudgery, illiteracy—has not been considered as a critical issue even though they constitute half of the population. The traditional stereo-typing of women has led to women's development being regarded as a 'specific interest issue' to be addressed ad hoc. Currently a controversy is brewing about whether or not women-specific projects should be more effective. An empirical investigation is called for to arrive at a conclusion. However, one could hazard some guesses.

In the kind of socio-cultural context found in Bangladesh, women-specific projects naturally tend to be small in scale and few in number. Consequently, they command only a fraction of the funds devoted to development efforts. One often forgets the most important fact that women's development is a means to the ultimate goal of total social development. In Bangladesh, women are being included in develop-ment projects but without a clear vision about the interrelationship of such inclusion and total development efforts; projects are not fully integrated into general schemes. Any attempts to enhance the status of women are based largely on specific activities such as literacy work and imparting training in some skill development such as domestic, agricultural or certain craft techniques. The attempts are, no doubt, important but are not sufficient to counter attack the socio-cultural barriers, to inform and motivate women and the community as a whole.

It is at this point that we need to add the most pertinent dimension of the problem of the submission/emancipation of women. The then Director General of UNESCO, Amadou-Mahtar M'Bow in 1980 clari-fied the basic fact of life by saying, 'Men and women form a complex whole of reflexes, thoughts, feelings, attitudes, certainties and pre-judices that are all the more difficult to uproot . . .' Following this statement one may delineate several issues which are relevant to reflecting on women's emancipation in Bangladesh. What type of socio-political support is available for emancipating women? How organized and serious are women themselves? What is the role model for change? Some of these issues have been addressed in the preceding discussions. Even so, some additional comments are called for.

First, as we have seen, the type of socio-political support is an ambiguous one. The Constitution of Bangladesh grants equal rights to women with men but the traditional outlook and limited opportunities are obstructing the exercise of such rights by women. Some of the laudable efforts by the government and voluntary groups to uphold the cause of women's development could not become internalized in the socio-political structure of the country so as to become a sustained force (Khan 1985). Most men are still reluctant to accept any other role for women than in the historically allotted place in the home, though traditional male behaviour is changing. Women themselves are often fearful of a change in their role, and feel vulnerable in a society that still discriminates in favour of men.

The nature of women's organizations and their seriousness is some-what disappointing. Broadly speaking, women of Bangladesh represent a separate interest group. But by no means they are a homogeneous group. They differ considerably in educational qualification, economic competence, household burden, availability of free time, motivation for work outside the home and perception about life and living. Accordingly, their needs and priorities also vary in terms of their residence, class position, socio-cultural orientation, etc. Most women's organizations are aware but do not take note of the implications of all these factors in achieving their goals. The participation of many members is rather a result of temporary zeal or fad; a normative pattern, a psycho-social infrastructure of women's participation has not developed. Whether the existing organizations can foster a strong women's movement superseding the differences among themselves and whether they can make concerted effort to propagate their con-sensus views on their rights and obligations is to be seen.

Finally comes the central question of role models that Bangladeshi society seeks to follow. In the transition of their status what specific role changes do women desire? The history of women's development in Bangladesh is too short to provide a definitive answer. But what appears from an observation of the society, gleaned mainly through the development projects and government-donor interaction, is that society as well as women are perplexed as to the direction they should take. But this much is clear: real emancipation can never be achieved at the cost of someone else, it is the women who will have to work hard. There seems to be no clear notion that the dynamics of women's roles and status are interwoven with men's roles and status in society, for men and women together constitute a single unit of the species. In any development planning for women one needs to take into account the men's point of view of women and themselves versus women's point of view of men and themselves; whether the current change in women's roles has significance to these views; whether these role changes of women are compatible or contradictory to that of men; how these views are negotiated in life, etc. To understand and guide the emancipation of women, one must reflect on the role and status of men, specially in a subsistence society like Bangladesh. Are the menfolk in Bangladesh liberated? Can they choose their own course of action, pursue a life of their liking?

What Birgitta Leander said very much fits the Bangladeshi context:

the liberation of woman may never be effective without the simultaneous achievement of the liberation of man; liberation from a life removed from the affection and the touching experiences of seeing his children growing up, liberation from being the only economic support and the undisputed head of the family, liberation from exaggerated careerism and the violence it involves, liberation from the need to find dialogue and companionship outside home (Leander 1985).

Transcending mere slogans for improvement in the status of women requires serious attempts to address these issues. Else, emancipation of women in Bangladesh will forever remain a mirage.

REFERENCES

Abdullah, Taherunness Ahmed, 1985. 'Women in Poor Families: Some Problems and Causes' in K.S. Huda et al., (eds.), *Focus on 50 Million: Poverty in Bangladesh* (Dhaka: ADAB).

——————, 1974. *'Village Women as I Saw Them'* (Dhaka: Ford Foundation).

Ahmed, Ashraf Uddin, 1987. 'Mortality and its Prospects in Bangladesh,' paper presented at the *National Seminar on Recent Trends in Fertility and Mortality in Bangladesh* (Dhaka: Planning Commission).

Ahmed, Q.K. et al. (eds.), 1985: *Situation of Women in Bangladesh* (Dhaka: Ministry of Social Welfare and Women's Affairs, Government of Bangladesh).

Alam, Bilquis Ara, 1985: 'Women's Participation in Local Government' in *Women Politics in Bangladesh* (Dhaka: Centre for Women and Development).

Amin, Ruhul and A.G. Mariam, 1987. 'Son Preference in Bangladesh: An Emerging Barrier to Fertility Regulation' in *Journal of Bio-Social Science*, 19: 221–228.

Arens, J. and Jos Van Beurden, 1977. *Jhagrapur: Poor Peasants and Women in a Village in Bangladesh* (Calcutta: Orient Longman).

BBS (Bangladesh Bureau of Statistics) 1985. *Statistics Yearbook* (Dhaka: BBS).

Bangladesh, Government of, 1985. *The Third Five Year Plan of Bangladesh (1985–90)* (Dhaka: Planning Commission).

——————, 1973. *The First Five Year Plan of Bangladesh (1973–78)* (Dhaka: Planning Commission).

——————, 1983. *The Second Five Year Plan of Bangladesh (1980–85)*. (Dhaka: Planning Commission).

Bangladesh Unnayan Parishad, 1980. *Survey of Female Industrial Workers in and around Dhaka* (Dhaka: Bangladesh Unnayan Parishad).

BFS (Bangladesh Fertility Survey), 1975 (Dhaka: Ministry of Health and Population Control).

BIDS (Bangladesh Institute of Development Studies), 1981. *Rural Industries Survey Project (RISP)* (Dhaka: BIDS).

Caritas Bulletin (July 1986) (Dhaka).

Chen, L.C., E. Huq and S. D'Souza, 1981. 'Sex Biases in the Family Allocation of Food and Health Care in Rural Bangladesh,' *Population and Development Review*, 7:·1.

Chowdhury, N., 1984. *Re-evaluation of Women's Work in Bangladesh* (Dhaka· BIDS) (mimeo).

Chowdhury, R.H. and Nilufar, R. Ahmed, 1979. *Female Status and Fertility in Bangladesh* (Dhaka: BIDS).

CPS (Contraceptive Prevalence Survey), 1975–85 (Dhaka: Mitra and Associates).

Duza, M. Badrud, 1985. 'Fertility Regulation in Bangladesh: Policy Evolution and Execution,' Working Paper No. 10 (Cairo: Cairo Demographic Centre).

ESCAP, 1981. *Population of Bangladesh*, Country Monograph No. 8 (New York: United Nations).

ICDDR, B. 1966–82. *Annual Reports*.

Islam, Shamima, 1982. *Women's Education in Bangladesh: Needs and Issues* (Dhaka: FREPD).

Jahan, Raunaq, 1973. *Women in Bangladesh* (Dhaka: Ford Foundation).

Khan, A.R., 1985. 'National Health Policy on Women' in End Decade National Conference on Women and Health (Dhaka: Women for Women).

Khan, Salma, 1985. 'Women's Development and Public Policy in Bangladesh' in *Integration of Women in Development* (Dhaka: United Nations Information Centre).

Leander, Birgitta, 1985. 'Women on the Move—Towards What' in *Women—From Witch-hunt to Politics* (Paris: UNESCO).

Mabud, M.A., 1987. 'Levels and Trends in Fertility and Demographic Prospects in Bangladesh,' paper presented at the National Seminar on *Recent Trends in Fertility and Mortality in Bangladesh* (Dhaka: Planning Commission).

M'Bow, 1985. 'Towards a New Order with Regard to the status of Women' in *Women from Witch-hunt to Politics* (Paris: UNESCO).

Mosley, Henry et al., 1970. *Demographic Characteristics of a Population Laboratory in Rural East Pakistan* (Dhaka: Cholera Research Laboratory/ICDDR, B).

Noman, A., 1983. *Status of Women and Fertility in Bangladesh* (Dhaka: The University Press).

Schaffer, T., 1986. *Profile of Women in Bangladesh* (Dhaka: US AID).

U.N. University, 1986. 'Comparative Study of Women's work and Family Strategies in South and South-east Asia,' Working Paper No. 1, Tokyo.

Yunus, M. (ed.), 1982. *Jorimon of Beltoli Village and Others: In Search of a Future* (Dhaka: Grameen Bank)

World Bank, 1984. *World Development Report.*

Zeidenstein, Sandra and Laura Ziedenstein, 1973. *Observations on the Status of Women in Bangladesh* (Dhaka: Ford Foundation).

Female Status in Pakistan:
Where are We Now?

NASRA M. SHAH

The focus on studying female status as a topic in its own right is relatively new in Pakistan, as in several other developing Asian countries. The year 1975, celebrated by the United Nations as the International Women's Year was a critical point in the historical evolution of studies on women. The proclamation of the women's decade was equally important in the maintenance of interest in the subject. An important implication of such interest is the heightened political and social awareness regarding the subject. Such awareness has resulted in specific plans and actions aimed at changing the status of Pakistani women.

Prior to 1975, the status of women was a non-issue. Development plans did not focus on women as a separate group in need of special development programmes. Research on women was incidental rather than planned. Demographic studies on the sex ratio and mortality indicated that unlike the pattern in most countries, females had a higher mortality rate and a lower life expectancy than males (Rukanuddin 1967). A few studies focussed on aspects such as the labour force participation or the educational levels of the female population (Farooq 1975; Jillani 1964). Other studies dealt with the traditional roles of women and customs such as Purdah (Papanek 1973; Pastner 1974).

With the increased interest in the subject, several institutional and other changes have taken place that may result in some status changes for Pakistani females. Before outlining the relevant institutional reforms, however, it is necessary to specify those indicators which are likely to be affected by government plans and actions. Since the status of women is a multifaceted concept, several different variables (and their interactions) need to be considered in such measurement (Oppong 1980; Oppong and Abu 1985). Among the indicators of female status, two broad categories, i.e., qualitative and quantitative, are basic.

Within qualitative indicators, one may include the 'position' a woman holds in society, or the power, prestige and authority she wields in various situations (Dixon 1978; Oppong 1980). These indicators show the image that a society has of a woman, and the value it places on her. While it is possible to measure these qualitative aspects of a woman's status, such measurement is likely to be less specific and concrete than the one permitted by other, more quantitative measures listed below.

Among the quantitative indicators that are relatively easier to measure are: education, occupation, health and mortality, fertility level and fertility control, and marital status and age at marriage. Each of these indicators represents a different aspect of female status and the role she is likely to perform as a result of this status. While conceptualizing the various roles of women Oppong (1980) identified seven distinct (though interrelated) roles, namely individual, community, domestic, kin, occupational, conjugal and parental. She further pointed out that certain roles may be in conflict with each other (inter-role conflict), or there may be conflicting strains within the same role (intra-role conflict).

The various quantitative indicators specified above represent different aspects of female roles. For example, a woman's educational level provides some information about her individual role; her marital status provides some indication about her conjugal role, etc. Thus, an examination of the current level of the quantitative indicators enables some conclusions about the current status of women. Also, an examination of the changes in these indicators over time gives an idea of the pace and volume of change in female status. An attempt was recently made by me (Shah 1986b) towards assessing the changes in female roles in Pakistan, and the adequacy of change in terms of volume and pace. The specific question addressed there was: Are the changes in female role in Pakistan adequate in terms of pace and volume?

In this paper, a related question is addressed as follows: In view of the evolution that has occurred in the roles and status of women in Pakistan, where do we stand now? An obvious, and related question is: what does the future look like? While concentrating on the former question, some discussion of the latter is also included in this paper.

The indicators on which I have focussed include both the quantitative and the qualitative ones specified above.

QUALITATIVE ASPECTS OF FEMALE STATUS IN PAKISTAN

In order to describe the position of women in Pakistani society, a few qualifications must be made at the outset. First, it is difficult to make generalizations about the whole society since the situation may differ drastically according to such factors as rural vs. urban residence, cultural, region of residence, and the level of socio-economic status. Second, any assessment of the position of women is likely to be influenced by the researcher's own cultural milieu. The religious orientation with which a researcher/writer approaches the subject is of particular importance in the Pakistani society.

Pakistan is a Muslim society that has been shaped by centuries of interaction with other faiths such as Hinduism and Christianity. The perception of women's appropriate roles is therefore likely to have been influenced by historical traditions and circumstances (see Shah 1986a for details). Even within the Muslim religion, there is no universal agreement among the various sects and schools of thought on what the appropriate roles of women are. The religious dictates are not always interpreted uniformly. The influence of religious prescriptions on actual behaviour also varies substantially across the society. Thus, there is a certain amount of discord and conflict between the prescriptions as provided by religion and the actual status of women as it exists today. The quest for a resolution of the existing conflicts is perhaps stronger today than it was before, as witnessed by some institutional changes in this direction.

Third, the position of women is not unidimensional, just as her roles are not. In some roles, she has a high position; in certain others, her position leaves a lot to be desired. An example of the earlier situation is provided by her as a mother. To become the mother of children, especially males, is a very effective means of elevating a woman's social position. Participation in the labour force, on the other hand, may not result in a similar elevation of position, especially if the woman is engaged in a low paying job carrying a low social value.

Given the above qualifications, and complexities, the following generalizations about the position of women in the Pakistani society can be made.

1. *Societal perceptions accord a lower value to females than males*: The birth of a male child is seen as a reason for much more rejoicing than that of a girl. One word that describes the sentiments evoked by the birth of a female child across almost all strata of society is 'burden'. Different colloquial expressions describe a female child as a responsibility, a duty, a guest in her parents' house, someone whose fate is to be feared, etc. The presence of female children makes the family's position vulnerable to potential shame and insult. Any non-traditional

behaviour by a girl (e.g. emotional involvement with a male or behaviour resulting from such involvement) can cause enough shame for a family for them to kill her, in some cases. The male partner engaged in such involvement is usually not so punished by his family.

One reason for the perception of 'burden' concerning female off-spring is the dowry system which is still highly prevalent in the Pakistani society. The expectations regarding the gifts that one girl's parents should give to their daughter and her in-laws are certainly increasing, despite a legislation which sets a very conservative limit on the amount of dowry permissible legally. It should be noted here that the Muslim inheritance law allows the female to inherit property and wealth from her relatives. Clear guidelines concerning the amount of inheritance are provided in the Muslim holy book, the Quran. However, relatively few families actually give the daughters their due share in property. Instead, the dowry is usually considered a substitute for her share.

2. *There is a very strict division between male and female roles*: The basic role of a woman is defined in terms of a wife and mother: that of a man in terms of a breadwinner and protector of the family. He is defined as the head of the household, except in cases where the family may be supported by a widowed mother. Only about 1 per cent of all household heads were reported to be female in 1973 in Pakistan.

3. *The wife-mother role is the primary role while the occupational and community roles are secondary*: Deviations from the strict division of roles mentioned above exist, particularly when females begin to take up occupations that could very well be performed by males. Such deviations are tolerated by society to varying degrees, depending on several factors, such as the perceived threat to segregation between the sexes, the social desirability and prestige of the occupations, and the socio-economic status of the employee in question. The secondary nature of the occupational role is evident from the low level of participation by females in this role. In some cases, the woman is in fact a productive member of the labour force but she is either not perceived to be so, or is not reported to be so in censuses and surveys.

4. *Government policy concerning the appropriate role of women in society is not well specified*: In order to accommodate the demands of the time, and project a positive developmental image, a fair amount of overt attention has been given by the government to the improvement of women's status in Pakistan. Government speeches and documents often talk about the 'integration of women in development.' These

terms are, however, not usually well specified. The two innocuous and non-controversial indicators on which there is general agreement consist of providing education and good health care to women. However, the basic issues concerning how women can contribute towards the development of the country, or how the societal values and attitudes towards women should change still remain at the level of questions. In fact, these questions were raised by the President of the country himself in his address to a woman's conference in 1980 (Shah 1986a: 25–26).

A policy guideline and agreement on the relevant issues concerning the status of women is of course necessary for any concrete changes in it. A few steps towards the evolution of such a policy are embodied in the creation of a Women's Division within the government and the consideration of women as a special group in the latest development Plan, as discussed in a later section of this paper.

5. *Changes in women's status are intrinsically related with the overall development of the country*: While the perceptions regarding the worth of a female, or her appropriate roles in society may be culturally determined and modified, changes in the country's economic situation may result in dramatic improvements in certain aspects of female status. Quantitative indicators such as education and health are the ones most likely to be affected. Some of the Gulf countries such as Kuwait present a good example of the rapid advancements that are possible in several different aspects of women's lives in the wake of rapid economic development of the country (Shah 1986c).

Pakistan is among the low-income countries of the world with an annual per capita GNP of US$ 380 in 1985. The economic growth rate is considered satisfactory but is seriously undermined by the high rate of population growth.

QUANTITATIVE ASPECTS OF FEMALE STATUS IN PAKISTAN

It has been stated in the introductory section that certain indicators, such as education and occupational participation, lend themselves to relatively more specific quantification than certain others discussed already. In this section, an evaluation is made in terms of the current level of various indicators to judge where the status of women stands now. The current status of various indicators is estimated by the use of the latest available census or survey data, and a comparison of these data with those pertaining to earlier time periods.

TABLE 1

Quantitative Indicators of Female Status in Pakistan according to the Latest Available Data

	Total	Urban	Rural
EDUCATION (1981 Census)[a]			
Per cent:			
Literate among persons aged 10+	26.2	47.1	17.3
Literate among males (10+)	35.1	55.3	26.2
Literate among females (10+)	16.0	37.3	7.3
Females with primary education	7.0	14.5	3.9
Females with B.A. or higher education	0.5	2.2	0.1
Girls aged 10–14 enrolled in schools	17.3	41.1	7.3
EMPLOYMENT (1981 Census)[a]			
Per cent:			
Age 10+ in labour force	3.2	3.5	3.0
Employed as unpaid family worker	27.9	5.9	38.2
Employed in professional occupations	16.5	33.9	8.4
Employed in service occupations	8.4	16.8	4.5
Employed in agricultural occupations	38.2	3.1	54.7
HEALTH AND MORTALITY			
Expectation of life at birth—females[b]	51.8	54.9	51.3
Expectation of life at birth—males[b]	52.9	56.4	52.1
% severely or moderately malnourished among children 5 years[c]	16.7	15.9	17.0
% mildly malnourished among children < 5 years[c]	43.4	42.3	43.7
Maternal deaths per 1000 live births[c]	6.8	—	—
FERTILITY AND FERTILITY CONTROL[d]			
Total fertility rate 1970–1975	6.3	6.2	6.4
% ever used any contraceptive method, 1975	10.5	21.9	6.3
% currently using any contraceptive method, 1975	5.2	12.4	2.7
% who never used and do not intend future use, 1975	42.6	46.9	41.3
MARITAL STATUS AND AGE AT MARRIAGE (1981 Census)[a]			
% single women in ages 20-24	26.5	53.7	23.2
% single women in ages 35-39	1.7	4.1	1.7
% divorced women among those aged 15+	0.4	0.3	0.4

Note: — Not available.

Sources: a. Statistics Division, 1984
　　　b. Based on 1968–71 Population Growth Survey data
　　　Nasra M. Shah, 1986. *Pakistani Women. A Socioeconomic and Demographic Profile* (Islamabad and Honolulu: Pakistan Institute of Development Economics and East-West Center), pp. 70, 71.
　　　c. ibid., pp. 188–189.
　　　d. Based on Pakistan Fertility Survey data (Alam and Shah in ibid., pp. 73, 80).

Literacy and Education

About 26.2 per cent of the population aged 10-plus was defined to be literate (i.e. had the ability to read or write a simple letter) in the latest census held in 1981 (Table 1). The per cent literate among males was 35.1 compared with 16.0 among females. The difference in literacy level in rural vs. urban areas was large among both sexes, but was particularly so among females. Only 7 per cent of the rural females aged 10-plus were literate in 1981 compared with 37 per cent in urban areas. The percentage of literate females increased slightly between the last intercensal period, 1972–1981. Within rural areas, for example, the per cent increased from 4.7 to 7.3. Despite the increase, the level remains pitifully small.

Female status was even lower when examined by the level of educational attainment. Table 1 shows that only about 15 per cent of the urban and 4 per cent of the rural females had a primary level education. The per cent with a college level education was only 2.2 in urban and 0.1 in rural areas. Within the urban areas, the percentage of women with college or B.A. level education increased from 1.0 in 1973 to 2.2 in 1981. However, the minute percentage of college-educated women emphasizes the fact that such women indeed represent a very small minority in the country as a whole. This group of women is nevertheless a highly visible and vocal one and contains the potential for bringing about a change in the status of Pakistani women.

Employment

On the surface, employment appears to be an easy concept to measure but research from several different countries has shown that the accurate estimation of female work participation is quite problematic, especially when this pertains to the informal sector. Several innovative methodologies for measuring labour force participation have been tried (e.g. Zurayk 1985), and specific biases in data collection have been noted and solutions suggested (United Nations 1980).

In Pakistan also, research on the problems of measuring female work has been conducted (Shah et al. 1977; Allauddin n.d.; Abbasi 1982). One finding that is important in this context is that relatively higher under-reporting occurs when the male respondent answers the labour force questions rather than the female worker herself. Also, it is generally agreed that participation in agricultural activities as well as in the informal sector is often under-reported. Finally, the evidence suggests that the censuses report the female activity rate to be lower than household surveys; information in the former is usually always provided by the male household head while the surveys in question have focussed on the female worker.

Over the last four censuses (1951–1981), female work participation rates have ranged between 3.1 in 1951 and 9.3 per cent in 1961. The highest national level rate for currently married women was reported by the National Impact Survey of 1968–69 (18.7 per cent). The latest (1981) census revealed the rate for the labour force participation to be 3.2 per cent among women aged 10-plus. Also, the rate in rural areas appeared to be lower than in urban areas (3.0 per cent and 3.5 per cent, respectively). The discrepancies between data sources and over time make one point clear: the measurement of female economic activity continues to be a very serious problem in the Pakistani censuses, and the level of under-reporting of such activity has not decreased.

In Pakistan, as well as other South Asian countries, a high rate of labour force participation should not be interpreted as a positive change in the status of women necessarily. My research shows that a majority of Pakistani women participate in economic activity as a result of sheer economic need rather than a desire for self-expression or self-fulfilment. In several cases, the work participation actually results in status reduction rather than status enhancement—in so far as social prestige is concerned. Furthermore, the woman withdraws from the labour force when she no longer needs the economic subsidy, thereby enhancing her social status. Rarely is the work role seen as an alternative to the wife-mother role; the former is usually combined with the latter across all strata of society.

Even though the work role is secondary, it does provide some potential economic independence to women, particularly in the urban, educated segments of society. There is also some evidence that work participation results in delaying marriage. However, the impact of such participation on fertility has been found to be insignificant. Whatever the implications of work participation, the data suggest that only a small proportion of the females are affected by such activity.

Health and Mortality

Pakistan continues to be one of the few Asian countries with a higher female than male mortality. The life expectancy at birth is about 51.8

years for females and 52.9 years for males. The differentials between rural and urban areas among both males and females are large, as shown by the data in Table 1. The differential in life expectancy between the two sexes has declined over time even though female mortality is still higher.

Estimates of the infant mortality rate by various demographers and data sources vary between 105 and 143. The Pakistan Fertility Survey (PFS) data showed the infant mortality rate for 1970–1975 to be 152 for females and 135 for males. Thus, despite data discrepancies it seems clear that well over 100 infants born annually do not survive upto their first birthday; and the mortality among female children is higher than among males. Two of the major reasons for the mortality differential between the sexes probably include the lower levels of nutrition and health care provided to female than male children, as found in other South Asian countries (Chen et al. 1981).

About 17 per cent of the children aged less than five are either severely or moderately malnourished i.e., their weight is less than 80 per cent of the standard weight for height for age, and their height is either less than 90 per cent of the standard (severely malnourished) or more than 90 per cent of the standard (moderately malnourished). Again, the rural children are at a somewhat greater disadvantage than urban children, as shown in Table 1. In addition to the severely malnourished children, about 43 per cent are mildly malnourished i.e., their weight is above 80 per cent the standard weight but their height is less than 90 per cent the standard height for age. Malnutrition is an important factor which determines the morbidity profile of the population, and predisposes the affected respondents to disease and death.

The high rate of infant deaths is also related to maternal mortality. The maternal mortality rate has been estimated to be 6.8 per thousand live births during the mid-1970s, which is very high compared to a rate of 0.15 in the United States. The large number of deaths at childbirth is not surprising in view of the highly unhygienic conditions in which deliveries usually take place. Even in the cities, about 90 per cent of the deliveries occur at home and under the supervision of the traditional midwife (dai) who has no formal training in midwifery. In rural areas, almost all deliveries take place at home. Efforts are being made by the government to increase the number of trained dais as rapidly as possible.

Fertility Level and Fertility Control

Given the centrality of the wife-mother role in the Pakistani society, the level of fertility remains a very important question. The total fertility rate (TFR) has remained consistently above six children as research from various sources indicates. It had been shown by previous analyses that the fertility level fell from about 7.1 children per woman during 1960–1970 to about 6.3, as reported in the World Fertility Survey. It has recently been pointed out, however, that the observed decline may in fact have been spurious and that the actual fertility level is around seven children (Retherford et al. 1987).

The number of children an average Pakistani woman bears has not shown any signs of decline. The absence of fertility decline is consistent with the low level of contraceptive use. In 1975, only 6.3 per cent of the married women in rural areas reported that they had ever used any method, while 2.7 per cent were using any contraceptive (Table 1). More recent data from a 1970–1980 survey suggest that the levels of contraceptive use may have in fact fallen further. Also, a large percentage (42.6) of those who have never used any contraceptive method state that they will not do so in the future (Table 1). One of the major reasons for this is stated to be religious taboos.

The foregoing analysis suggests that the normative values in Pakistan continue to be extremely pro-fertility. A government family planning programme has been in place since 1965 but does not appear to have made any major dent in population growth. This fact is of course of great concern for development planners. A high rate of population growth is bound to retard economic development; and a low rate of economic development is likely to have relatively more negative implications for the status of women, than of men.

Marital Status and Age at Marriage

Marriage and fertility are two closely related aspects of a Pakistani woman's life. The religious beliefs define marriage to be an obligation for every Muslim male and female. Also, the historical trends have led to the institution of an early age at marriage following soon after puberty, and thus ensuring a long reproductive span to the female. Over the last three decades, the age at marriage has been rising, but marriage still remains nearly universal in Pakistan.

According to the 1981 census, close to three-fourths of the women aged 20–24 were already in a marital union. The sharp difference in the percentage of never-married women in rural vs. urban areas is worth noting. About 53.7 per cent of the women in urban areas were still unmarried in the age group 20–24 compared with only 23.2 per cent of the rural women. Also, the percentage of never-married women in the age group 35–39 was much higher in the urban than the rural areas, being 4.1 and 1.7, respectively (Table 1). This indicates that the status of urban women is changing much faster than that of the rural women. Previous analyses of these phenomena indicate that urban residence, school attendance above the primary level, and employment prior to marriage, especially for cash income, are important factors in delaying marriage (Alam and Karim 1986). Women were found to be marrying about two years later in 1972 than in 1951. In 1981, the singulate mean age at marriage (SMAM) was 20.8 years compared with 17.9 years in 1951 and 19.8 years in 1975 (Alam and Karim 1986).

What is also worth noting is the highly permanent nature of marriage. Only a negligible proportion (less than half a per cent) of all marital unions get severed on account of divorce (Table 1). Almost all broken marital unions result from the death of the spouse. The low rate of divorce can be traced back to the cultural traditions prevalent in pre-partition India which held divorce in great contempt, even though divorce is permitted, but not encouraged, in Islam.

TOWARDS CHANGE

In order to understand the factors that are likely to be important in bringing about a change in the status of Pakistani women, two elements may be considered: (a) the institutional level approaches, plans, and actions, particularly by the government, and (b) community responses to the felt need for generating a change, particularly by women's groups.

Among the institutional level changes brought about by the government, the establishment of a Women's Division within the Cabinet Secretariat in January 1979, is a major one. The main functions of the Women's Division include the following (Women's Division 1979):

1. To formulate public policies and laws to meet the special needs of women.
2. To register and assist women's organizations.

3. To undertake and promote projects for providing special facilities for women.

4. To undertake and promote research on the conditions and problems of women.

5. To represent the country in international organizations dealing with problems of women and in bilateral contacts with other countries.

6. To ensure that women's interests and needs are adequately represented in public policy formulation by various organs of government.

7. To ensure equality of opportunity in education and employment and the full participation of women in all spheres of national life.

The Women's Division has sponsored more than 4,000 literacy centres in rural areas all over the country. It has established several vocational and skill-development centres, and provides assistance to other agencies (such as voluntary agencies) involved in women's programmes. The Division has a research wing and during 1979–80 contracted out about 25 research projects to gather information on particular aspects of women's lives, such as female crime in urban and rural areas, and sex role images in textbooks.

In addition to the Women's Division, the government has also appointed an Advisory Commission composed of thirteen females and three honorary male members. The duties of the Commission are as follows:

1. To ascertain the rights and responsibilities of women in an Islamic society and to make recommendations to the federal government for effective safeguards of women's rights.

2. To advise the federal government on measures to provide educational, health, and employment opportunities for women.

3. To determine the services that women can render in eradicating ignorance, social evils, poverty, and disease in the country.

4. To suggest measures to integrate women of minority communities into the national life.

The above guidelines on which the government is seeking advice re-emphasize the fact that no clear concept about the appropriate roles of women exists as yet within the country.

Yet another noticeable change in the government emphasis on

women's status is the overt recognition given to the subject in the latest development plan, the sixth Plan, covering the period 1983–1988. Specific targets in the areas of education, employment, mortality, and fertility were set up in order to 'eliminate three crippling handicaps: illiteracy, constant motherhood, and the primitive organization of work' (Planning Commission 1983: 348). The framework of the Plan emphasizes equality of opportunity. It states that women's development is a prerequisite for overall national development and no society can develop 'half liberated and half shackled.'

Table 2 shows the quantitative targets that the sixth Plan hopes to accomplish by 1988. While an evaluation of the targets or their achievements is beyond the scope of the present paper, it appears from a cursory comparison of the benchmark data and the targets that the latter are highly ambitious—or even unrealistic. It would take no less than a miracle to increase the enrolment of primary school age (10–14) girls from 7.3 per cent in 1981 to 50 per cent in 1988; or reduce infant mortality from above 100 in the 1970s to only 50 per thousand live births in 1988. Even though the targets seem unrealistic, the focussed attention towards women's development is nevertheless a welcome sign.

Among the community efforts aimed at achieving an improvement in the status of women, the activities of several non-governmental organizations are worth mentioning. Some of the notable ones among the organizations are the All Pakistan Women's Association (APWA), an organization that dates back to 1949; the Pakistan Women's Institute (PWI) at Kinnaird College, Lahore; Behbud, and a few other voluntary organizations (see Shah 1986a for details).

Among the more recent community efforts at addressing the issue, the Women's Action Forum (WAF) is probably the most vocal, visible, and action-oriented. It is a non-political, non-hierarchical, and non-governmental lobby-cum-pressure group that was first organized in Karachi in September 1981. It has received endorsement and support from several women's organizations such as APWA and Behbud. WAF is 'committed to protecting and promoting the fundamental human rights of women by resisting and fighting all forms of oppression and by educating women regarding their rights' (WAF 1983). The WAF charter holds that women are equal partners in the development of the nation. As such, they have a right to equal opportunities in all walks of life and are entitled to equal pay. It also states that women have a right to determine their lives according to their own aspirations

TABLE 2
Government Targets Aimed at Changing Selected Quantitative Aspects of Women's Roles in Pakistan

	Target for 1988[a]	Approximate value for latest available years
EDUCATION		
Enrolment of girls at primary level		
Rural areas (%)	50	7.3 (1981, Census, females age 10-14 in school)
Urban areas (%)	90	41.1 (1981, Census, females age 10-14 in school)
Number literate adult females	Additional 10 million	4.2 million age 10+ (1981, Census)
EMPLOYMENT		
% females in govt. service	10-15 through quota	3 (1983 plan)[c]
HEALTH & MORTALITY		
Reduction in infant mortality to:	50 per 1000 live births	143 (1970–75, PFS)[d]
Increase in life expectancy to:	60+ years	52.9 for males/1968–71 51.8 for males, PGS[e]
Health care	Provision of one trained dai per village i.e. 45,000	10,000 dais (1983 Plan)
Immunization	5-6 million children to be immunized every year	—
FERTILITY LEVEL AND CONTROL		
Total fertility rate women 15-49	5.4	6.5 (1979–80, PLM)[b]
% acceptors among married couples, wife aged, 15-44	18.6	3.3 (1979–80, PLM)[b]

Note: — Not available.
Sources: a. Based on the Sixth Five Year Plan (Planning Commission 1983)
    b. Population, Labor Force and Manpower Survey, 1979–80.
    c. Planning Commission 1983: 350.
    d. Pakistan Fertility Survey (Alam and Shah in Nasra M. Shah (ed.)), *Pakistani Women: A Socioeconomic and Demographic Profile*, 1986
    e. 1968–71 Population Growth Survey (in ibid.).

and must be provided the opportunities to facilitate the realization of their potential, whether it is in the intellectual, physical, or spiritual field. It believes that women and men are governed by the same moral code. WAF therefore opposes any action or speech based on the assumption that women qua women provoke men and are thus to be kept wrapped in Chaddars or Char-divaris (four walls of the house). The WAF charter advocates purity of mind through proper education of women and men rather than by segregation, and it upholds the fundamental human rights for women and men as laid down by the United Nations (WAF 1983).

No firm figures on the membership of WAF are available at this time. It is clear, however, that the group has become highly visible in the press and gets a fair amount of coverage in the news. It has passed several resolutions protesting certain government decisions regarding the activities and status of Pakistani women. For example, it has protested the recent government ban on women's participation in national and international sports. WAF also opposes the idea of a separate university for women on the grounds that the curricula proposed for this university are limited and the quality of education is likely to be poor given the shortage of resources.

CONCLUDING OBSERVATIONS

An objective analysis of data from several censuses and surveys indicates that only minor changes have occurred in most of the quantifiable indicators of female status over the last two to three decades. About 85 per cent of all Pakistani women aged 10-plus are illiterate; less than 1 per cent have college education; and only a small percentage are reported to participate in the labour force. An average Pakistani woman marries young, bears 6.7 children, and only about one-tenth are making any efforts to control their fertility. Roughly 6.8 women (per thousand) die annually in childbirth. Finally, females still have a lower expectation of life at birth than males. All of the above indicators lead to one conclusion; the status of women leaves a lot to be desired, and has a long way to go in Pakistan.

In terms of the directions towards change the various institutional arrangements (e.g. the Women's Division) and the planning documents suggest a high governmental commitment towards improving the situation of women, particularly in terms of literacy, health and nutrition, and equality of job opportunities (for the urban, educated women).

Yet, certain other governmental efforts suggest that a clear concept about the appropriate roles of women in society is still lacking, and the answers are yet being sought. The community response to the felt need for change also falls within a wide spectrum, ranging from the activities of the Women's Action Forum advocating wide-ranging changes to the highly traditional orientations of certain religious organizations. A consensus on how female roles should be redefined within the Pakistani society does not exist as yet, mainly because different community groups have different interests, orientations and concepts about such redefinition. The situation is potentially rife with conflict and requires a concerted, well coordinated change that would improve the situation of women as members of a healthy, affluent, and productive society.

REFERENCES

Abbasi, Nasreen, 1982. *Problems of Conceptualisation and Measurement of Rural Women's Work in Pakistan* (The Hague: Institute of Social Studies) (unpublished).

Alam, Iqbal and Mehtab Karim, 1986. 'Marriage Patterns, Marital Dissolution, and Remarriage' in Nasra M. Shah (ed.), *Pakistani Women: A Socioeconomic and Demographic Profile* (Islamabad and Honolulu: Pakistan Institute of Development Economics and East-West Center).

Alam, Iqbal and Nasra M. Shah, 1986. 'Population Composition, Mortality and Fertility' in Nasra M. Shah (ed.), *Pakistani Women: A Socioeconomic and Demographic Profile* (Islamabad and Honolulu: Pakistan Institute of Development Economics and East-West Center).

Alauddin, Talat, n.d. 'Contribution of Housewives to GNP: A Case Study of Pakistan' (Islamabad: Pakistan Institute of Development Economics and East-West Center).

Chen, Lincoln, Emdadul Huda, and Stan D'Souza, 1981. 'Sex Biases in the Family Allocation of Food and Health Care in Rural Bangladesh,' *Population and Development Review* 7(1).

Dixon, Ruth, 1978. *Rural Women at Work* (Baltimore: The Johns Hopkins University Press).

Farooq, Ghazi M. 1975. *Discussions and Structure of Labour Force in Pakistan in Relation to Economic Development: A Comparative Study of Pakistan and Bangladesh* (Islamabad: Pakistan Institute of Development Economics).

Jillani, M.S., 1964. Changes in Levels of Educational Attainment in Pakistan 1951–61, *Pakistan Development Review* 4(1): 69–92.

Oppong, Christine and Katherine Abu, 1985. *A Handbook for Data Collection and Analysis on Seven Roles and Statuses of Women* (Geneva: International Labour Office).

Oppong, Christine, 1980. *A Synopsis of Seven Roles and Status of Women. An Outline of a Conceptual and Methodological Approach.* World Employment Programme Working Paper No. 94, (Geneva: International Labour Office).

Papanek, Hanna, 1973. 'Purdah: Separate Worlds and Symbolic Shelter,' *Comparative Studies in Society and History* 15(3).

Pastner, Carrol McC, 1974. 'Accommodations to Purdah: A Female Perspective,' *Journal of Marriage and the Family*, 36(2).

Planning Commission, 1983. *The Sixth Five Year Plan 1983–88* (Islamabad: Government of Pakistan).

Retherford, Robert D., G. Mujtaba Mirza, Mohammed Irfan and Iqbal Alam, 1987. 'Fertility Trends in Pakistan—The Decline that Wasn't,' *Asian and Pacific Population Forum*, 1(2): 1–10.

Rukanuddin, A.R., 1967. 'A Study of the Sex Ratio in Pakistan' in W.C. Robinson (ed.), *Studies in the Demography of Pakistan* (Karachi: Pakistan Institute of Development Economics).

Shah, Shah and Ahmed, 1977. 'Labour Force, Employment and Unemployment Statistics in Pakistan' in *Manpower and Employment Statistics in Pakistan* (Islamabad: Pakistan Manpower Institute).

Shah, Nasra M. (ed.), 1986a. *Pakistani Women. A Socioeconomic and Demographic Profile* (Islamabad and Honolulu: Pakistan Institute of Development Economics and East-West Center).

————, 1986b. 'Changes in Female Roles in Pakistan: Are the Volume and Pace Adequate? *The Pakistan Development Review*, 25(3): 339–363.

————, M. 1986c. The Transition in Female Status in Kuwait: Issues and Likely Impacts,' in Cairo Demographic Centre *Population and Development Symposium, 1985*, (Special Issue) Research Monograph Series No. 14: 269–288.

Statistics Division, 1984. *1981 Census Report of Pakistan*. Islamabad: Population Census Organization, Government of Pakistan.

United Nations, 1980. *Sex-based Stereo Types, Sex Biases, and National Data Systems* (New York: United Nations Secretariat (ST/ESA/STAT/99).

Women's Action Forum (WAF), 1983. Charter of Women's Action Forum. (Islamabad: Working Committee of WAF) (mimeo).

Women's Division, 1979. 'Working Paper for Annual Development Programme 1979–80 (Islamabad: Cabinet Secretariat, Government of Pakistan) (mimeo).

Zurayk, Huda, 1985. 'Women's Economic Participation' in Frederic C. Shorter and Huda Zurayk (eds.), *Population Factors in Development Planning in the Middle East* (New York: The Population Council).

The Status of Women in Iran

Akbar Aghajanian

The concept of the status of women is multi-dimensional and its measurement varies according to the definition and the context of society (Mason 1986). The three general dimensions of the status of women recognized are: (a) the ability to control important events in life or relative freedom from control by others, autonomy (Dyson and Moore 1983); (b) wealth and prestige (Blumberg 1984); (c) access to valued resources such as education, health and paid employment (Safillios-Rothschild 1985). These dimensions of the status of women which relate to the objective and actual behaviour must be distinguished from women's 'rights and duties,' or legal status.

Among the three general dimensions of the status of women, autonomy and prestige need to be studied and measured at micro-level using household data. but access to resources, such as health and education in the community, could be readily measured through aggregate data which are available in the censuses and surveys. It is also possible to study the legal position of women by considering the laws and regulations specifying the right and duties of women, particularly the family laws.

This paper is about the status of women, as measured by their access to valued resources of education and paid employment, and the legal status of women in Iran. The latest available national data will be used to explore this dimension of the status of women and its changes through time. Also the legal status of women will be considered in relation to legal and social changes in the Iranian society in the recent decades. But we first provide a profile of the demographic situation of women.

DEMOGRAPHIC PROFILE

The population of Iran was about 34 million in 1976, about 16.3 million of it women. The sex ratio was 106.1. In 1966, 48.2 per cent of the total population was female. This increased by 1976 to 48.5 per cent as female longevity improved and the number of women surviving after age 65 increased (Table 1).

TABLE 1

Proportion of Women by Age Group of Population, 1966, 1976

Age group	1966	1976
0-14	47.8	47.9
15-64	48.7	49.9
65 and above	46.6	47.3
All ages	48.2	48.5

Source: Iran Statistical Center, 1967, 1980.

Iranian women married, on an average, at age 18.4 in 1966 and 19.7 in 1976. An urban woman marries, on an average, one year later than a rural woman. Husband-wife age differential was 6.6 years in 1966; it declined to about 4.4 years for all women, to 4.9 years for urban women, and to 3.6 years for rural women (Table 2). The decline in rural areas was not because of the increase in female age of marriage; rather, it was due to decline in the male age at first marriage.

TABLE 2

Singulate Mean Age at Marriage for Men and Women

Year	Total		Urban		Rural	
	M	F	M	F	M	F
1966	25.0	18.4	25.6	19.0	24.4	17.9
1976	24.1	19.7	25.1	20.2	22.7	19.1

Source: Iran Statistical Center, 1984.

The marital status of women is reported in Table 3. The proportion of never-married among women 10 years and above has increased from 26.8 per cent in 1966 to 32.7 per cent in 1976. This is consistent with the slight change toward increase in age at first marriage. The proportion of both the widowed and the divorced among women declined during the 1966–1976 period. Widowhood decreased on account of improvement in the health and longevity of men. The decrease in divorce could be related to the legal changes about the family, which will be discussed in the section on legal status of women.

TABLE 3
Marital Status of Female Population 10 years and older,
1966, 1976

Marital Status	1966	1976
Married	61.0%	58.5%
Widowed	10.8	8.1
Divorced	0.9	0.7
Never-married	26.8	32.7
Not reported	0.5	—
Total	100.0	100.0

Source: Iran Statistical Center, 1967, 1980.

Fertility Patterns of Women

Fertility was first estimated in Iran from the 1956 census data. Age-specific rate of fertility estimated from the 1956 and 1966 censuses of population of Iran is reported in Table 4. By 1966, there seems to be a slight increase in fertility as a result of significant socio-economic improvement influencing nutrition and fecundity. Age-specific fertility rate had declined at all ages during the 1970s. Total fertility rate declined from 7.7 to 6.6 during the 1966–1976 period. This decline is related to the modest increase in age at first marriage for women and reduction of proportion of ever-married women on the one hand, and a decade of family planning campaign affecting marital fertility.

TABLE 4
Age-specific Fertility Rates for Iranian Women

Age Group	Age-specific fertility rates		
	1956	1966	1976
15-19	42	45	146
20-24	352	375	327
25-29	371	394	303
30-34	362	355	230
35-39	277	291	186
40-44	81	82	95
Total Fertility Rate:	7.3	7.7	6.6

Source: For 1956 and 1966 M. Amani, 1974 *The Population of Iran* (Paris: CIRED series); for 1976, Iran Statistical Center, 1977.

The crude birth rate registered for different years since 1976 suggests that, with the exception of a drop in birth rate in 1978, the year of revolutionary upheavals, there is an increasing trend in crude birth rate during the post-revolution era. Registered birth rate increased from 45 births per thousand population to 63.0 in 1980 and it has been maintained at the level of 50 since 1982. Lowering minimum legal age of marriage, promotion of Islamic values of marriage and procreation, and lack of a family planning programme and no policy of birth control, have contributed to the increasing birth rate in post-revolution Iran.

Family Planning

While traditional methods of contraception including 'coitus interruptus' have been known and practised in Iran from the earliest times (Moore et al. 1972) modern contraceptives were first introduced in 1960 and family planning services were established in 1967. At the time of establishing the programme, a figure of 10 thousand acceptors was reported (Table 5). By 1968, a year after the programme was introduced, the number of acceptors increased to 124 thousand. The rate of increase in the number of acceptors accelerated during the following years. The proportion of acceptors to eligible women in the reproductive ages, 15–44, increased from 3 per cent in 1967 to 11 per cent in 1977. Estimates suggest that currently about 22 per cent of married women use contraceptives (Aghajanian 1986). Most of these women are high parity women with four or more children, they are above age 35 and mostly live in urban areas. Since there has not been a public population policy in Iran and there has not been any campaign in recent years for accepting family planning, it is less likely that the number of acceptors has increased much.

Mortality Among Women and Children

In the 1960s and 1970s, mortality in general and infant mortality in particular declined in Iran. For example, infant mortality declined from a high rate of 184 per thousand live births to 112 in 1976 (Iran Statistical Centre 1982). This decline was due both to socio-economic changes and rising level of standard of living, on the one hand, and also improvement and importation of medical technology and education. The expansion of vaccination and aggressive programmes for malaria eradication contributed to the significant decline in mortality.

TABLE 5
Number and per cent of Family Planning Acceptors in Iran, 1967–77

Year	No. of Acceptors (0'000)	Annual Growth Rate	Per cent to women 15-44
1967	10.4		0.02
1968	124.3	10.4	2.8
1969	212.3	53.6	4.8
1970	299.0	24.2	6.8
1971	385.0	25.2	8.3
1972	445.0	14.5	9.6
1973	470.0	5.4	9.4
1974	481.0	2.3	9.3
1975	506.0	5.5	9.2
1976	572.0	12.0	10.4
1977	621.0	8.0	11.0

TABLE 6
Mortality of Women and Children in Iran

Measure		Rural	Urban
Infant Mortality:			
	Male	113.3	58.8
	Female	127.0	64.7
Life expectancy at birth:			
	Male	55.8	
	Female	55.0	

Source: Iran Statistical Center, 1983.

Women's health situation improved along with the improvement in the health of the general population. But relative to men, women are still behind. For example, female infant mortality in rural areas is about 11 per cent higher than male infant mortality and about 9 per cent higher in urban areas. Men have also higher life expectancy at birth.

While mortality has declined in general, maternal mortality still remains high because many women in small cities and rural villages have home deliveries and are attended only by traditional midwives. A very recent study shows that for every thousand live births in rural areas twelve women will die; in urban areas seven women will die per thousand births (Afzali and Rezai 1986). Clearly, there is much room for further decrease in female infant mortality rate and maternal mortality rate.

WOMEN AND EDUCATION

Education is an important step in improving the status of women specially because it is a prerequisite for paid employment in the modern sector of the economy. There are two important factors in the educational attainment of women: (a) availability of the educational opportunity, and (b) the attitude of parents and public about educating daughters. In the recent decades educational opportunities have been expanded in Iran. The general attitude has also changed toward the education of women favourably.

Female literacy lags behind male literacy, though in absolute terms female literacy has gone up (Table 7). In 1966, male literacy was more than double that of female literacy. In 1976, the male-female literacy gap shows an increase, though female literacy in both rural and urban areas has increased substantially. While the urban women have narrowed the literacy gap vis-a-vis the males, in the rural areas the gap has widened by more than 6 per cent.

TABLE 7
Literacy Rate for Population 7 Years and Older

Region	1966			1976		
	M	F	Diff.	M	F	Diff.
All country	39.2	17.4	−21.8	58.6	35.0	−23.6
Urban areas	61.4	38.3	−23.1	74.4	55.1	−19.3
Rural areas	24.5	4.1	−20.4	42.9	16.6	−26.4

Source: Iran Statistical Center, 1967, 1980.

School enrolment rate of the eligible population has also increased between the years 1966 and 1976, but the lower relative position of women on this index is evident from Table 8. From the lower secondary level to higher levels of education, when girls enter teenage, their school retention rate progressively declines. While 76.0 per cent of the eligible males are enrolled at the lower secondary level, only 49.4 per cent of the eligible females are enrolled. Note that about 30 per cent of the female population eligible for secondary school enrolment are married by this age.

TABLE 8
School Enrolment of Population 7–24 by Sex

Level	1966		1976	
	Male	Female	Male	Female
Primary	69.5	35.0	86.4	63.9
Lower secondary	55.5	30.0	76.0	49.4
Higher secondary	31.5	13.5	46.9	25.8
College	10.4	3.2	14.0	6.3

Source: Iran Statistical Center, 1967, 1980.

WOMEN AND EMPLOYMENT

Iranian women and specially those in the rural area have always made valuable contribution to the economy of the household by providing their labour to agricultural activity, animal husbandry and carpet weaving. But their contribution has not been counted as separate from the usual family roles and it has not improved their position. It is only employment outside the home, which is paid for and creates roles separate from the familial roles of mother and wife, that improves the status of women and their economic independence.

Table 9 shows the activity rate of population in the 15–64 age group in 1966 and 1976. In 1966, 15.6 per cent of the women reported active economic participation in comparison to 89 per cent males. This

TABLE 9
Age Specific Activity Rate of Population 15-64

Sex	1966			1976		
	Total	Urban	Rural	Total	Urban	Rural
Male	89.0	83.0	91.0	85.0	78.0	90.0
Female	15.6	6.4	14.2	14.0	10.6	17.0

Note: The denominator in calculating the rates is population of each sex in age group 15-64. The male female rate does add up to 100.
Source: Iran Statistical Center, 1967; 1980.

figure decreased to 14.0 per cent in 1978 due to increased female enrolment in school in the 15–19 age group. The combined data from rural and urban areas however obscure the real nature of the labour force behaviour of women. This is because of the differences in the nature and organization of the economy and family in rural and urban society. The dominant economy in the rural areas is the household economy with the household as a unit of production: working roles are not separated from the family roles. In urban society, the organization of work is distinct from family organization. Hence, working roles are mostly out of the household; not only are they separated from family roles but sometimes clash with them.

The percentage of women working in the urban areas increased to 10.6 per cent in 1976 compared to 6.4 per cent in 1966, but the figure is too far away from male employment and compares poorly with some other Asian countries. Also, among the 17 per cent rural women reported to be working in 1976, about 40 per cent did unpaid family work. In general, there is much room for expansion of paid employment for women, which would increase their economic independence and status.

WOMEN'S LEGAL STATUS

The legal system provides protection of the rights and duties of women in society. Both sexes are equal before law, but in application to certain affairs of life, there may be a difference. This is why family laws are considered and studied as an index of the legal status of women in relation to men. In Iranian society, traditional family laws have been dominated by the rules of Islam and Sharia. A woman could be married off at age 9 unless there was a physical barrier and a man could marry at 14. The husband is responsible for supporting his wife and children, providing them food, clothing, shelter, and any comforts to which the wife has been accustomed in her father's house. In turn, the husband is the boss and the duties of a wife are providing services such as cooking, sewing, cleaning and sex availability. A man could have four legal wives by contract and also temporary wives. He could divorce any of them at will merely by saying 'Talagh' (I divorce you) in the presence of two witnesses.

The 1967 Family Protection Law was designed for family protection and introduced as part of social reform by Mohammad Reza Shah. It increased the legal minimum age of marriage for women to 15 and later to 16. The act prohibited men from exercising their former absolute right of divorcing a wife or marrying a second women without permission of the first wife. Polygyny was not widespread in Iran, and in 1976 there were only eleven men married to more than one women per thousand men. But divorce was widespread, and the new law made a significant improvement in the state of affairs. It required a court order for divorce, and this was granted only when the divorce case was proved irreconcilable in the court. The new law gave the woman the right to ask for divorce and restricted the man's previously unlimited freedom.

But the picture has changed in post-revolution Iran. The 1967 Family Protection Law was suspended in 1979 and replaced by the Special Civil Law drawn purely from Islamic Sharia—Islamic laws based on the Koran and the teachings of Mohammad as interpreted and introduced over the years by Islamic scholars and jurists. The legal minimum age of marriage was lowered to 13; divorce was again granted to men on demand, and to women only under certain circumstances. Polygyny was declared legal without the first wife's consent.

According to the new law, a woman can still petition the court for a divorce on the grounds of her husband's non-support, desertion, or maltreatment. More importantly, a woman can protect her rights in marriage by inserting clauses specifying conditions of divorce into the marriage contract drawn specifically for the couple. A woman thereby secures her right to divorce should her husband violate the conditions in the contract. While there is no data currently available, it seems that many women are using this privilege to enhance their power in relation to men.

The constitution of the Islamic Republic states that 'all citizens of the nation, both men and women, equally enjoy the protection of law and enjoy all human, political, economic, social, and cultural rights in conformity with Islamic criteria.' According to the law, women like men could and should have as much education as they want and they are not legally barred from employment outside the home. Women have the right to vote and serve in most offices other than those of judge or president. Specific rights are also emphasized for women as mothers and wives.

SUMMARY AND CONCLUSION

Historically, women have been praised as good wives and mothers in the Iranian society and culture. From the point of view of Islam, which has influenced the Iranian culture for a long time, women have been given the highest respect for they bear and raise the next generations of committed Muslims. In this cultural context, women's worth has been derived from their ability to produce and raise children and their roles limited to those of housewife and mother. Associated with this has been early marriage, early child bearing, large number of children, life-time dependency on a male, and low social participation in the society at large.

In the recent decades this pattern has changed. Legal changes have improved the ability of women to make decisions regarding various aspects of their life. Relative to the past, women's educational attainment and their participation in paid employment has increased and this has resulted in lowering their economic dependency. Non-familial roles for women have been publicly promoted and women have found a new place in society. In the Islamic revolution, women played a significant role out of home and as a major political force. However, there is much room for improvement of women's status relative to men in the current Iranian society, specially of those 50 per cent who live in the villages.

REFERENCES

Aghajanian, Akbar, 1986. 'Fertility and Value of Children in Iran,' Research Report No. 1, Department of Sociology and Regional Planning, Shiraz University.

Amani, M. 1974. *The Population of Iran* (Paris: CIRED series).

Dyson, Tim and Mick Moore, 1983. 'On Kinship Structure, Female Autonomy, and Demographic Behavior in India,' *Population and Development Review* 9 (1): 35–60.

Iran Statistical Center, 1967. *Results of the Census of Population and Housing of Iran, 1966.* Tehran.

Iran Statistical Center, 1977. *Population Growth of Iran, 1974–75.* Tehran.

Iran Statistical Center, 1980. *Results of the Census of Population and Housing of Iran, 1976.* Tehran.

Iran Statistical Center, 1987. *Statistical Selections,* 2 (13) Tehran.

Mason, Karen Oppenheim, 1984. 'The Status of Women, Fertility, and Mortality: A review of Interrelationships,' Research Report (Ann Arbor: Population Studies Center, University of Michigan).

Mason, Karen Oppenheim, 1986. 'Status of Women and Fertility,' *Sociological Forum*, 1 (3).

Safilios-Rothschild, Constantina, 1985. 'Socioeconomic Development and Status of Women in the Third World,' Working Paper No. 112, Center for Policy Studies, The Population Council.

Status of Women in Kuwait

Mohammed A. Al-Sharnoubi

In terms of their social and demographic characteristics, Kuwaiti women have many things in common with their sisters in the developing countries particularly in the West Asian region, who belong to traditional Islamic societies. In this paper, an effort is made to focus on their educational background, participation in labour force and other economic activities in this state, whose standard of living is among the highest in the world.

Women's participation in economic activities is inherently related to their education. In turn, their nuptiality status is closely related to their participation in economic activities. Both these relationships reflect the present level of development and the family size in future. The three criteria of women's education, participation in economic activities and nuptial status are crucial indicators to the need of the future labour force in Kuwait. Migrants constitute more than 60 per cent of the total population of this tiny state. Is it possible for Kuwaiti women to replace some of them and lend a hand to the wheel of development? This is the major question before the planners and administrators.

Development of Education

The first school for boys was built in Kuwait in 1921. In 1927 the first school for girls was built for teaching the Arabic language, Holy Koran and household work. Till 1932 there were four primary schools. Since 1956 the state has set up an integrated educational structure for primary education. Education was made compulsory for children between six and fourteen years in 1965. The University of Kuwait was established in 1966. There are also a number of other educational and technical institutions but the women generally attend only the academic institutions to graduate as teachers.

In the period 1965–1983, the male-female gap in educational enrolment has consistently narrowed at all stages. The girls accounted for

47 per cent of the total enrolment at the secondary stage in 1982–83, compared to 35 per cent in 1965. Educational enrolment as a percentage of the relevant female population (6–22 years) also increased from 49 per cent in 1970 to 66 per cent in 1980. The increase in the percentage of girls enrolled in the period 1970–1980 was 45 per cent as compared to 27 per cent for males. The rate of males joining the schools as compared to university by 1980 increased to three-fold from 1970. The corresponding rate for females was four-fold.

Besides the university, there are many other institutions for women's learning in various fields. Among these, five deserve special mention: (*a*) The Institute for Girl Teachers imparts education to girls upto general secondary certificate level after which they are eligible to teach at the kindergarten and primary level. (*b*) The Commercial Institute for Girls trains girls with secondary education in commercial and secretarial jobs. This institute graduates technical assistants in Statistics, computer jobs and other office work. (*c*) The Health Institute for Nurses trains girls for serving in government hospitals and public health offices. (*d*) The Institute for Fine Arts offers a graduate programme in fine arts like music and theatre. This institute is co-educational. (*e*) The Institute for the Handicapped offers valuable opportunity to a section which would otherwise be neglected. The University has a special faculty for girls with specialization in human studies and sciences. Girls completing this course are eligible to join the faculties of medicine, law and commerce and other faculties with their male counterparts.

The mean rate of annual growth in university education for both males and females fluctuates. This differential growth was the maximum during the period 1966–1971, 35.6 per cent for males, and 50.2 per cent for females. Females invariably got distinction in these courses. However, this growth severely declined in the period 1971–1976. The sex ratio in university education has been reversed from the male predominance of the 1960s. There were 139 boys per 100 girls in 1966. After introducing university education these numbers amounted to 87 boys per 100 girls in 1983–84. This phenomenon is obvious, if we take into consideration the Kuwaiti girls only. The total number of enrolled students in 1983–84 was 16,163, 10,411 of them Kuwaiti boys (64.4 per cent) and 5,752 girls. Most girls were enrolled in humanities. In the faculties of medicine and science they constituted the majority.

The trend and variances in the educational status show clear differentiations between girls and boys beyond the age of 10 years from 1957 onwards. However, till 1957 the illiterate girls' ratio was higher than that of boys. Subsequently over the next decade illiterate girls' ratio decreased substantially. In 1957 this ratio was only 24 per cent.

Before 1937, only 1.8 per cent of females (aged 10-plus) received primary certificate. This percentage increased to 18.4 in 1980. The ratio of girls who received the general secondary certificate (or plus the secondary and minus the university) increased to 52.9 per cent in 1980 as compared to 12.5 per cent in 1957. The percentage of girls who had acquired university certificate multiplied by 11-fold in 1980, from 0.4 per cent in 1957 to 4.6 per cent. The net result of this educational development was a great decline in the ratio of illiterate girls from 76 per cent in 1957 to 35.7 per cent in 1980 (50 per cent for Kuwaiti women and 23 per cent for non-Kuwaiti women).

Adoption of compulsory education and its continuous development by the Government was the main factor that led to this decline in illiteracy. The large-scale expansion of technical and applied institutions and the university have also raised the participation of women in different labour forces. Another landmark in this field is the establishment of adult education centres, which also helped to reduce illiteracy of adult female population.

LABOUR FORCE PARTICIPATION OF WOMEN

The 1980 census has shown the extent of economic activity of the Kuwaiti women and their participation in the economic development of Kuwait. The female labour force in the total population was 59 per cent. The female ratio in the total economic activity or labour force was 79.8 per cent. The female distribution differs from male distribution for the same avocations in different age groups, except in the 15–19 age group. About 60 per cent of this age group are non-working pupils, about the same as males. The ratio declines to 27 per cent for females in the age group 20–24 (students only); the rest of them work at home. In the 25-plus age group 93 per cent of the women labour force are working only at home. There are marked differences in the participation of Kuwaiti and non-Kuwaiti women in the labour market and economic activity.

More non-Kuwaitis are taking part in the economic activity because of the decline in the Kuwaiti women's participation in economic activity and the shortage in Kuwait of skilled labour in the face of mounting demands for trained labour. There is a wide differentiation in male-female participation in economic activity between Kuwaiti and non-Kuwaiti labour force. The economic activity rate of the Kuwaiti males was seven times that of the females in 1980. The labour force participation rate of non-Kuwaiti men during the same period was 3.5 times that of non-Kuwaiti women.

The highest economic activity rate for Kuwaiti women is in the age group 25–29 at 23.3 per cent. In the younger age groups there is a decrease in labour force participation due to their involvement for a long time in setting up a family followed by the birth of the first child. The low level of women's participation in economic activity is also due to their low educational level besides their habits, traditions and dogmas.

The general rate of the economic activity of non-Kuwaiti women in Kuwait amounted to 16.6 per cent, three times that of Kuwaiti women. The former's economic activity rate increased gradually for the age group 15–24 and reached the peak for the age group 40–49. Some non-Kuwaiti women in Kuwait entered the labour force for the first time in their thirties and forties or even later, which may explain the increasing participation of the non-Kuwaiti women in the older age groups upto fifty. Also, the activity rate of non-Kuwaiti women in Kuwait has increased more than in other similar Arab countries. In general the migrant women in Kuwait desire to work because most of them are wives of highly educated men or they are in technical and scientific professions like teachers or physicians or work as domestic servants.

Marriage greatly influences the economic activity rates of women in Kuwait, the married women being normally less inclined to work than the single ones. The divorced women and the widows work by force of circumstances. In 1980, the married women's participation rate in economic activity was less than that of single women. The highest rates were among the divorced both among the Kuwaiti and non-Kuwaiti women. The Kuwaiti widows' participation in economic activity has declined because they enjoy social security ensured by the state.

The married women's participation rate in economic activity is less than among single women both among the Kuwaiti and migrant women. The difference in rates for the Kuwaiti women increased with the age groups, reaching the peak for the 25-29 age group, and declined thereafter. The economic activity rates for both married and divorced Kuwaiti women reached the peak at the age of 25–29 and then declined. Participation of widows was the highest at the ages of 20–24 and then it fell. In general the economic activity rate of non-

Kuwaiti women-reached the top in the age group of 40–44 years, except the single women. Generally, the economic activity rate has increased during the recent past for all the age groups of women in Kuwait.

The economic activity rate shows a clear correlation with educational levels. The economic activity rate of illiterate women was only 1 per cent in 1980 but this rate has steadily been increasing during the recent past to reach 4 per cent which is closer to that of literate women who can read and write. Participation rate of women with intermediate level certificates was 5.6 per cent, 43.6 per cent for those with secondary grade certificates (less than the university certificate), and 82.2 per cent for those with university certificates respectively.

Among non-Kuwaiti women in Kuwait, participation in economic activity for women with secondary grade certificate was 40.3 per cent in 1980 and 66.8 per cent for those with higher education. Participation rate for illiterate women increased to 30.7 per cent during the 1980 census period, many of them working as domestic servants. The proportion of educated women among the migrants has increased considerably. Women who can read and write accounted for 32.2 per cent of the migrant working women, those with primary certificates only for 7.6 per cent and intermediate certificate holders for only 6.1 per cent. Better educated women participate more actively in the labour force on account of postponement of marriage, late childbirth and desire to study further. The burden of dependency among the Kuwaiti population has increased due partially to the noticeable decrease in the economic activity of their women.

Among the Kuwaiti population, 90.9 per cent of the working women are in the service sector as against 70.2 per cent of the working men. Those in the transport, storage and communication sectors account for 4.7 per cent, in financial and properties sector and other services 2.5 per cent, and in the remaining sectors of economic activity less than 1 per cent. Among the non-Kuwaiti women, 88.5 per cent work in the services sector and 3.8 per cent in commerce and hotels sectors.

POPULATION PROFILE

Nuptiality Status

Marriage and other related matters such as age at marriage, polygamy and divorce are important social events that must be given special care in the planning of population policy. Vital statistics for Kuwait are available since 1957 and subsequently from 1963 onwards. Population characteristics have a clear duality between Kuwaitis and non-Kuwaitis. Among Kuwaitis, in 1980, 28 per cent of Kuwaiti women of marriageable age were single as against 24 per cent unmarried adult men.

According to the 1965 census the ratio of women in the 15-plus age group who married once was about 84 per cent which came down to 72 per cent by 1980. Among non-Kuwaiti women too, the ratio of single women to married women similarly went up during the period. This may be partially due to the change in the age structure of the migrant women.

A general decline in mortality has brought down the incidence of widowhood for both males and females. In 1980 the ratio of the widowerhood between males and females was 1:10 among the Kuwaiti population. The higher incidence of widowhood among women can be explained by such factors as their younger age compared to that of their husbands by an average of five years and higher incidence of remarriage among widowers.

There is an increasing tendency towards postponement of marriage. In 1965 the ratio of single women was about 58 per cent for age groups 15–19 and about 16 per cent for the age group 20–24. By 1980 this ratio had increased to 80 per cent and 39 per cent respectively. On-going social change in terms of increased female education and labour force participation has brought down the ratio of married women for all age groups upto 30–40 years.

The crude marriage rate for Kuwaitis was 11 per cent in 1981 as against only 4.6 per cent in 1965. There has not been much change in the crude marriage rate for non-Kuwaitis: it was 3.3 per cent in 1965 and 3 per cent in 1981. The decrease is little because most migrants come to Kuwait without families. This was also the reason why the sex ratio was large for males for some time. Later on, the single migrant males married in their home countries and brought their spouses to Kuwait. Because such marriages would not be registered in Kuwait, the comparison of marriage indicators of migrants must be dealt with care.

The crude marriage rate does not give as true a picture as can the general marriage rate. The crude marriage rate among the Kuwaitis, who represent about half the population, increased two-fold. However, the general marriage rate for the migrants has begun to decrease gradually in the last few years.

Intermarriage between Kuwaitis and non-Kuwaitis shows a mixed trend. In 1976 about 28 per cent of Kuwaiti women had non-Kuwaiti husbands; in 1981 the figure decreased to 10 per cent. On the contrary, marriages between Kuwaitian men and foreign women have increased from 7.8 per cent in 1976 to 15 per cent in 1981. Most of these foreign wives come from Iraq. The rest are generally from Egypt, followed by Saudis, Jordanians and lastly Palestinians. Monogamy is more common. Incidence of polygyny increases with increase in the age of the males until the age group 40–49 years, after which it falls. Ninety-three per cent of the married men were monogamous. Among the migrants, polygyny is much less common because of their low income and non-Islamic faith. Polygyny is found more among the less educated men. According to the 1980 census 7 per cent of the married, divorced and widowed women married more than once and 1 per cent of them married three times and more. More widowers remarry than widows. The Islamic Law (Shariat) allows polygyny but not polyandry.

The minimum age at marriage is part of Kuwaiti law. Most girls marry between the ages of 15 and 20 and most men between 20 and 30. The mean age at marriage of the Kuwaitis was 19.1 years in 1968, and 20.7 years by 1980. Clearly, there is a general trend towards increasing age at marriage. The Kuwaiti women's mean age at marriage increased from 18.9 years in 1965 to 19.8 years by 1970, and further to 22 years in 1980. For non-Kuwaiti women the mean age at marriage increased from 18.9 years in 1965 to 20 years in 1975 and to 21.3 years in 1980. This increase is due to the increase in the number of such women, census after census, who remain single.

Sex Ratio

Females accounted for 26.3 per cent of the total population in 1957, 24.1 per cent in 1961, 23 per cent in 1965, 23.3 per cent in 1970, 23.7 per cent in 1975 and 21 per cent in 1980. At last it became 20.2 per cent in 1985 when the population increased from 206,473 persons in 1957 to 1,695,128 persons in 1985. Migrants constituted less than half of the society during this period, but are now more than 60 per cent of the total population. There is a large difference between the sex ratio (the number of females per 100 males) of locals and the migrants. This is reflected in the general sex ratio which amounted to 177.5 in 1957 and 161.6 in 1985. The sex ratio of the locals during the various censuses was 108.6, 109.1, 104.7, 102.1, 100.5, 98.5 and 98.5 during the 1957–1985 period. The stability noticed in the sex ratio at 98.5 in the period 1980–1985 will lead to many social and economic problems in the near future.

Kuwait like many other developing countries has a high birth rate but the study of fertility has not been related properly to the social characteristics of women. The crude birth rates of the local people and immigrants are similar because of the several common characteristics between Kuwaiti and non-Kuwaiti women notwithstanding the differences in the socio-economic conditions of Kuwaiti and immigrant women.

REFERENCES

Al-Mousa, Ali. 'Technological Development and Human Resources in Kuwait,' presented at Kuwait National Symposium on *Science and Technology for Development*, 1978.

Briks, J.S. and Sinclair, C.A. *International Migration and Development in the Arab Region*, (Geneva: ILO), 1980.

Central Statistical Office (CSO), *Vital Statistics: 1967–79* Kuwait.

Durch, J.S. *Nuptiality Patterns in Developing Countries: Implications of Fertility.* (Washington, D.C.: Population Reference Bureau), December 1980.

Demographic Estimation: A Manual on Indirect Techniques, National Academy of Sciences, May 1979.

Hill, Allan, G. *Mortality and Fertility Levels and Trends in Kuwait*, Centre for Population Studies, London School of Hygiene and Tropical Medicine, 1980 (mimeo).

Ministry of Planning, Central Statistical Office, *Annual Statistical Abstract, 1970, 1975, 1980, 1984.*

Ministry of Planning, Central Statistical Office, *The Seasons of Years, 1957, 1965, 1970, 1975, 1980, 1985.*

Seetharam, K.S. and Al-Omaim, Musa'ad H. 'Migration and Population Growth in Kuwait, 1957–70' in *Urbanization and Migration in some Arab and African Countries*, Research Monograph Series, Cairo Demographic Centre, 1973.

United Nations—ECWA, 'International Migration in the Arab World' Vols. I and II, Proceedings of an ECWA Population Conference, Cyprus, 1981.

United Nations, *Manual X, Indirect Techniques for Demographic Estimation*, 1983.

United Nations, 'Method of Analysing Census Data on Economic Activities of the Population,' *Population Studies*, No. 43, 1968.

United Nations, 'National Programme of Analysis as an Aid to Planning and Policy-making,' *Population Studies*, No. 36, 1964.

II

WOMEN IN INDIAN SOCIETY

Status of Women and Population in India

K. Mahadevan, G. Radhamani, N. Audinarayana, R. Jayasree and Dominic E. Azuh

In size and population, India is the second largest nation in Asia next only to the People's Republic of China. It has a land area of 3,287,782 square kilometres, which is 2.4 per cent of the earth's land surface. India is the seventh largest country of the world, but it is less than half the size of Australia, the sixth largest country, and only one-seventh of the USSR, the world's largest. It is divided into twenty four states of varying sizes and seven union territories. According to the 1981 census the total population of India was 685 million (331 million female, 354 million male). Out of them 525 million live in rural areas and 160 million in urban areas (23.3 per cent). The density of population per square kilometre numbered 216. India has several religious groups, the largest being the Hindus (82.4 per cent) followed by Muslims (11.4 per cent) and Christians (2.4 per cent). There are also Sikhs, Buddhists, Jains and Zoroastrians.

India is one of the most ancient civilizations of the world. The Indian subcontinent was the abode of the ancient culture of Harappa and Mohen Jodaro. One of the most ancient and rich languages of the world, Sanskrit, flourished in this land. It is the vehicle and treasure-house of Hindu culture and is rich with several works of classical literature, religion and philosophy. Sanskrit has also influenced the growth of several languages in South and South-east Asian countries and also their culture. Sanskrit, Hindi and other languages of the Indo-Aryan family have feminine and masculine genders in their common usage. Even the present-day population of this continent manifests great diversity of culture which is ancient, transitional and modern. There are several hundreds of isolated tribal communities with a distinct culture of their own and many castes and sub-castes. There are also seven major religious groups. India has also the distinction of being the birth-place of Hinduism, Buddhism, Jainism and

Sikhism. The subcontinent itself has been symbolized in the form of a mother figure, Bharat Mata. Among the several gods and goddesses worshipped throughout India, the most famous is the goddess Durga or Bhadrakali. Very benevolent goddesses are also worshipped as symbols of education (Saraswati) and of wealth (Mahalakshmi). The consorts of the principal gods have been accorded equal status indicating the importance given to them in the past.

SOCIETY AND WOMEN

In Hindu society the status of women underwent changes during the different stages of development of Hinduism and its offshoots. Some scholars claim that in Hindu society, particularly in India, women had a better status in ancient times than in the medieval and the modern times (Kane 1974: 365). According to the Shaivite school of the Hindu pantheon, 'a woman is one half of a man' (Ardhanariswara). It is one of the earliest depictions of woman as an integral part of man. However, an analysis of certain aspects of ancient Hindu philosophy and other customs confirms that women did not enjoy equal status with men. For instance, Hinduism prescribed four major Asramas (stages in life) for men, which were not enforced on women. The Asramas according to Manu, a Hindu philosopher, begin with Brahmacharya during which stage a man completes his education while residing at his teacher's house. After the period of study, during the second stage of his life (Grahastashrama) he marries and becomes a householder, discharging his duties to his ancestors by begetting sons and to the gods by performing Yajnas (Poojas). When he has reached the middle age he leaves for the forest to assume the next Asrama, Vanaprastha. After spending the third stage of his life in the forest, he renounces the world and spends the rest of his life as a Sanyasin (Kane, 1947: 417). These stages of life were, by and large, followed by men in the past, but women continued to be at home with limited roles and opportunities. This supports the assumption that women had a low status in Hindu society in the past. Manu also prescribed a perennial dependent role for a woman throughout her life starting with the father, continuing with her husband and ending with the son. In many regions of India, she did not enjoy property rights. All this further supports the above assumption. Therefore, it is difficult to accept Kane's view that women in ancient India enjoyed a relatively better status than at present.

Another major religion in India, Islam, prescribes a Dean or a complete way of life for Muslims, both men and women, who are defined as different but complementary. In several aspects the two sexes are accorded equal status. Islam teaches that men and women are equal as human beings; children of both sexes should be treated equally, both should be provided with education, love and affection, both men and women have the right to express their opinions in the selection of their mates; both have the right to own property, etc. In certain other aspects role expectations for men and women are different, e.g., with regard to Purdah. While both men and women are expected to be modest in dress and behaviour, the restriction on women is greater. Most Islamic scholars agree that women should cover their bodies from head to toe; others believe that they should cover their faces also (Shah 1981; Makhdoom Shah, 1981: 3).

Many religions, while they eulogize women as equal to goddesses, assign to them an inferior position in society. This is true of many Asian, African and Latin American countries. However a woman's status is much better in Christian societies, both in the developed and the developing countries and certain African Muslim countries, where bride price is given and/or children are taken care of by the father in the event of a divorce.

Children are generally valued in present-day India, but sons are preferred over daughters everywhere, except among the matrilineal communities in Kerala, like Nairs, Izawas, Kurichiyans, artisans etc., and the Khasis in Assam. Among matrilineal communities the status of women is high in all spheres of life. A number of studies carried out in the recent past on the value of children have confirmed that this concept is the principal determinant of high fertility in most regions of India (Mahadevan 1989, 1987 and 1979; Vlassoff and Vlassoff 1980; Cain 1981). The greater value attached to sons is based on the several roles they perform in the family and also on their right to inherit. Girls did not have property rights till recently. Today despite the existence of equal legal sanction it has rarely been followed in practice. In several states, even today, girls are given only dowry and no share of parental property. The absence of property rights tends to lower the status of girls in society. This reality explains the existing low status of women in most parts of the country, particularly in the rural areas.

Adult women also face discrimination and injustice in the name of several customs pursued in different cultural groups throughout India. Sati, which was practised widely in the past and now to a smaller degree in northern India, minimized the importance of married women during the men's lifetime and ruled out their survival after their men's death. According to this custom, a loyal wife should immolate herself on the pyre of her husband in order to attain salvation. Widows are discriminated against, isolated and restricted. Among Brahmins, Gounders, Vellalas and several other upper castes in India they can wear only plain white, and cannot remarry. Participation in auspicious social functions like marriages, Pujas, birthday celebration and so on are taboo for widows. The mere sight of a widow is believed to be inauspicious when commencing any function or a journey. Exceptions to this degradation of widows are, however, found in certain communities and in the urban areas. The late M.G. Ramachandran, former Chief Minister of Tamil Nadu appointed over 20,000 widows as paid assistants in the mid-day meal programme launched extensively in the state during the 1980s, which enhanced their status in this part of the country.

EDUCATION OF WOMEN

Education underwent radical changes ever since the British came to India in the sixteenth century. The traditional form of education (the Gurukula system) was largely aimed at imparting literacy to boys under a single teacher. Girls were taught by their mothers and in single-teacher schools upto the primary school level. But English education institutionalized coeducation in the premises of the former schools. Even today in the rural areas, Muslims and backward caste Hindus neglect the education of their girls because of the women's low profile and limited roles assigned to them in these communities. The loss of chastity is feared, when they are exposed to wider society. Nevertheless the establishment of modern schools in rural and remote areas throughout India has created the scope for education among girls, even in the traditional communities.

Educationally, women lag far behind men throughout India except in Kerala and the four metropolitan cities of Delhi, Bombay, Calcutta and Madras. As per the 1981 census only 25 per cent of women are educated as against 47 per cent men. The projected national targets of universal primary education by 1990 and universal elementary education by 1995 do not give any satisfactory answer to the ever growing proportion of illiterates in India. It is estimated that by 2000 A.D., India will account for nearly 55 per cent of the world's illiterate population in the age group 15–59, and the majority of them may be women (Government of India 1988: 36). Educational differentials are noticed on the basis of rural, urban, sex, caste, religious groups and states throughout India. For example, the enrolment rate of scheduled caste girls in school is even lower than that of the general female population. Female literacy among tribals is almost negligible, that among Muslims being slightly better. Among the states in India, female literacy is highest in Kerala (65.7 per cent). Only in three union territories female literacy has crossed 50 per cent. In six states female literacy falls as low as 20 per cent.

The growth in female literacy in Indian history however is encouraging. Female literacy has gone up from 13 per cent in 1961 to 25 per cent by 1981, indicating a doubling of literacy level in two decades. The trend is consistent for both rural and urban areas (Table 1).

TABLE 1
Literacy Rate of Women and Total Persons in India by Place of Residence and Census Decades

Census year	Literacy Rate					
	Female			Total		
	Total	Rural	Urban	Total	Rural	Urban
1961	12.96	8.55	34.51	24.04	19.01	46.97
1971	18.70	13.08	42.05	29.48	23.69	52.37
1981	24.82	17.96	47.82	36.23	29.65	57.40

Sources: Calculated from Socio-cultural table of *Census of India 1961* Vol. I, Part II C(i) India; *Census of India 1971* Series I, India 42(i); and *Census of India 1981* Series I, India, Part IV.A.

At all levels of education in the last three census decades proportionately less girls were enrolled than boys. While 95.8 per cent of boys enrolled in primary school by 1981 the rate was only 64 per cent for girls. At the middle school level, 54 per cent of the boys as against 29 per cent of girls continued their education. At the high school level, only 15 per cent of girls continued their studies as against 34 per cent of boys. The trend was consistent during the preceding decades also (Table 2).

At the primary level, the enrolment ratio of girls to boys improved from 61 girls per 100 boys before the 1970s to 65 during 1971–1981, but this achievement was neutralized by large-scale dropout of girls at

TABLE 2
Gross Enrolment Ratios of Boys and Girls in India by Three Census Decades

| Level of Education | Gross Enrolment Ratios, India | | | | | |
| | Boys | | | Girls | | |
	1960–61	1970–71	1980–81	1960–61	1970–71	1980–81
Primary classes I–V (6–11 yrs.)	82.6	92.6	95.8	41.4	59.1	64.1
Middle classes VI–VIII (11–14 yrs.)	33.2	46.5	54.3	11.3	20.8	28.6
High/Higher Sec. class X–XI/XII (14–17 yrs.)	16.7	27.1	34.2	4.1	10.2	15.4

Source: Government of India 1987, A Hand Book of Educational and Allied Statistics, Ministry of Human Resources Development, New Delhi.

different stages of school education. While 63 per cent of them drop out at the primary level, almost 77 per cent discontinue at the early elementary stage.

EMPLOYMENT STATUS

Women's employment at home and outside has been perceived differentially based on the concept of work adopted by the census, sample registration scheme, research planners and administrators. Even the general concept of work was redefined during the 1971 census leading to more confusion. Therefore it is necessary to define the work relating to production at home and outside. Without the long hours of work that women put in at home all other production would come to a halt. Regardless of whether they are paid or not, the work they do in the family has productive value, obviously more indirect than direct. A time motion study would throw light on the magnitude of energy expended by women in managing the affairs of the family. Women's employment status may have to be viewed in the light of this reality.

Work participation of women in India is very poor (14 per cent) according to the 1981 census, and almost double in the rural areas than in the urban. On the other hand, men work extensively (52 per cent), and do not show substantial differences in rural-urban comparison. Women's work participation fluctuated considerably from a relative high in 1961 to the lowest in 1971. Such differences are not

noticed with regard to men. The dip in women's labour force participation during the 1971 census period might be due to the confusion
created by the redefinition of work participation at that time (Table 3).

TABLE 3

*Work Participation Rates of Males and Females by Place of Residence and Age
Groups in India during 1961, 1971 and 1981 Census Periods*

Area/Age group	Female Work Participation Rate			Male Work Participation Rate		
	1961	1971	1981	1961	1971	1981
Work participation rate:						
Total	27.96	11.87	13.99	57.12	52.51	51.62
Rural	31.42	13.10	16.00	58.22	53.47	52.62
Urban	11.09	6.61	7.28	52.40	48.82	48.54
Age group:						
5-14	10.58	3.97	3.98	14.64	10.13	7.25
15-59	45.87	19.60	22.61	91.60	86.89	83.87
60+	22.38	10.50	10.15	76.61	73.78	63.88

Sources: Calculated from the General Economic Tables of *Census of India, 1961,*
Vol. I, India, Part II B(i); *Census of India, 1971*, Series I—India, Part II B(i);
and *Census of India, 1981*, Series I—India, Part III A(i).

In the all-India government services there are currently 994 women
officers as compared to 15,993 men officers (5.8 per cent of the total).
The Indian Administrative Service has 339 women officers (7.5 per
cent of the total). Job stereotyping exists in the services as well: the
Indian Forest Service has only ten women officers (0.6 per cent)
followed by the Indian Police Service with only twenty-one women
officers (0.9 per cent). There are eight women Vice-Chancellors in the
total number of 158 universities in India. While there is no woman
Supreme Court Judge, there are eleven women High Court Judges as
against 380 men judges (Government of India 1988).

Work participation of women in different age cohorts revealed
significant differences in the 1981 census. Nearly a quarter of the
women were employed when they were adults and not old. The young
and old cohorts of women participated much less in gainful employment. The trend is consistent with that in the preceding two decades.
Male participation in gainful employment was very high for the adult
population (84 per cent) as well as the older population (64 per cent)
according to the 1981 census. A similar trend was noticed during the
1971 census with the exception that slightly more older men were

working at that time. The overall findings of Table 3 confirm that massive creation of appropriate employment opportunities is needed for providing income generating activities among women to improve their living conditions and their status in society.

Women's sector-wise employment shows conspicuous differences among the primary, secondary and tertiary sectors during the 1971 and 1981 periods, their employment in the primary sector being the highest. Though the employment of men is also the highest in the primary sector, significantly more of them were cultivators and not agricultural labourers. Also, proportionately more men worked in non-household industry in the secondary sector and in trade and commerce in the tertiary sector. Even so, men's participation in the non-agricultural sector is meagre. Considering the industrialization and urbanization that have taken place in India since independence, this reveals that industrialization in India has not been labour-intensive and transfer of people from agricultural to non-agricultural areas still remains a distant goal. Without a revolutionary transformation in this regard benefiting both men and women, their standard of living and status will remain very low.

Wages of women across all communities remain very low; they receive perhaps only half the wages that men get. There is discrimination in the quantum of wages received by women belonging to the scheduled castes (Rs 1.60) as against the upper castes (Rs 1.88). The same trend existed for men as well. The gross differences and disparities noticed in the lower wages received by women in general and still lower rates received by those belonging to the scheduled castes and scheduled tribes as against others need to be set right in order to emancipate women and improve the quality of their life in general.

POPULATION PROFILE

The proportion of the female population in different age cohorts remained more or less constant during the last three decades (1961–1981). While 39.6 per cent of females in the 1981 census were children below the age of 14 years, 53.8 per cent were adults and only 6.6 per cent were older. The trend was similar in the case of men. Among both men and women there was a slight increase in the proportion of children and old people between the two censuses of 1961 and 1971 (Table 5).

TABLE 4
*Percentage Distribution of Women Workers by Industrial Categories during
1961 to 1981 Periods*

Industrial Category	Females			Males		
	1961*	1971	1981	1961*	1971	1981
Cultivator		29.7	33.2		46.2	43.7
Agricultural labourer		50.4	46.1		21.2	19.5
Livestock, forestry, fishing etc. and Mining and quarrying		2.9	2.2		2.9	3.0
Primary sector		83.0	81.5		70.3	66.2
Manufacturing, processing servicing and repairs						
Household industry		4.2	4.6		3.4	3.2
Other than household industry		2.8	3.6		6.6	8.9
Construction		0.6	0.9		1.3	1.9
Secondary sector		7.6	9.1		11.3	14.0
Trade and commerce		1.8	2.0		6.4	7.4
Transport, storage and Communication		0.5	0.4		2.9	3.4
Other services		7.1	7.0		9.1	9.0
Tertiary sector		9.4	9.4		18.4	19.8

Note: * Data not available.

TABLE 5
Population of India by Age and Sex during 1961, 1971 and 1981 census periods

Age Group	Females			Males			All		
	1961	1971	1981	1961	1971	1981	1961	1971	1981
0-14	41.2	42.1	39.6	40.9	41.9	39.5	41.0	42.0	39.5
15-59	53.0	51.8	53.8	53.6	52.2	54.1	53.3	52.0	53.9
60+	5.8	6.0	6.6	5.5	5.9	6.4	5.6	6.0	6.5

Source: *Census of India 1961*, Vol. I, Part II C(i); *Census of India 1971*, Series I, India 42 C(i); and *Census of India 1981*, Series I, India, Part IV-A.

In all the three decades of the recent past, the sex ratio was not in favour of women either in the rural or the urban areas. It declined from 941 in 1961 to 933 by 1971, on account of a decline in the rural areas (963 to 952). In the urban areas, the sex ratio increased significantly from 845 in 1961 to 880 by 1981. This reveals that the risk to women's lives is much higher in the rural areas than in the urban areas where also they are not very safe. There may be other reasons for this unbalanced sex ratio which may need further investigation (Table not given).

Nuptiality

Marriage is almost universal in India. Child marriage was the norm in the past, but today it is found only in some northern states like UP, Bihar, Rajasthan and MP. Marriages are held at later ages in most of the southern states. Kerala has the highest age at marriage for both girls (22 years) and boys (27 years), according to the 1981 census. The mean age at marriage of girls has gone up to 18.3 years as against 16 in 1961. For the boys it was 23.3 years in 1981 as against 21.1 years in 1961. The legally prescribed minimum age for girls is 18 years and for boys 21 years.

The 1981 census reveals that almost 6.5 per cent of children got married at the young age of 14 or even earlier. The figure in 1961 was 19 per cent. Child marriages in the urban areas accounted for 2.4 per cent of marriages in 1981 as against 7.7 per cent in the rural society. The proportion of youth marrying in the age group of 15–19 years was also high at 43 per cent in 1981, though much lower than the 70 per cent recorded in 1961. Such marriages were significantly more in the rural areas (48.8 per cent) as against only 28.21 per cent in the urban areas by 1981. Since most of such marriages would have concerned girls, rigorous efforts need to be made to postpone their marriages. This is a social necessity and a demographic imperative for improving the quality of their life and status in general (Table 6).

Fertility

The fertility measures considered here include the child-woman ratio and the crude birth rate. Birth rate in India has come down from the high figure of 41.7 in 1961 to 33.9 in 1981, which figure is still on the high side, considering the inputs to family planning made in India.

TABLE 6
Nuptiality Indicators during 1961, 1971 and 1981

Nuptiality Measure	India		
	1961	*1971*	*1981*
Sigulate Mean Age at Marriage			
Females	16.1	17.2	18.3
Males	21.1	22.4	23.3
Females married in 0-14 age group			
Total	19.22	11.53	6.48
Rural	22.00	13.47	7.70
Urban	6.79	3.73	2.35
in 15-19 years			
Total	70.61	55.41	43.44
Rural	73.65	61.03	48.80
Urban	51.60	35.91	28.88

Sources: Agarwala, S.N., 1972. *India's Population Problem* (New Delhi, Tata McGraw Hill) and *Census of India 1981* Series I, India Part II Special.

Birth rate declined more during the 1961–1971 period (12.1 per cent) than in the 1971–1981 period (9.7 per cent). This again is a discouraging feature because the intensive family planning programme came into being in the 1970s. The child-woman ratio also showed a steady decline from 1961 (659) through 1981 (546). The percentage of decline was negligible during the 1961–1971 period (0.61 per cent) as compared to the 1971–1981 period (16.64 per cent). All these findings do not show an encouraging decline in birth rate commensurate with efforts made to bring down the birth rate (Table 7).

TABLE 7
Fertility Measures during 1961 to 1981 Period in India

Fertility measure	Year			Percentage decrease	
	1961	*1971*	*1981*	*1961–71*	*1971–81*
Child-woman Ratio					
(0-4/15-48)	659	655	546	0.61	16.64
Crude Birth Rate	41.7	37.2	33.9	12.10	9.73

Sources: *Census of India 1981*, Series 20, Tamil Nadu Part II Special and *Family Welfare Year Book* 1972–73 and 1982–83.

Mortality

The measures of mortality considered here include infant mortality, crude death rate and expectation of life at birth. They have been analysed on the basis of sex and rural-urban background during the last three census periods (1961–1981). According to the census findings the infant mortality rate (males) was 132 in 1971 and declined to 110 by 1981. The trend of decline is very slow. But the decline in female infant mortality was more encouraging, from 148 to 111 during the same period. The decline in the urban areas was more or less uniform for both girls and boys. Crude death rate has been reduced to almost half (12.5 in 1981 from 22.8 in 1961), which is a remarkable achievement compared to the slow decline of exclusive infant mortality. But the expectation of life at birth has increased very slowly for both males and females. During all the three decades the figure was slightly more for men than women. The latest figure is around 55 years for both the sexes (Table 8).

TABLE 8
Health and Mortality Measures During 1961, 1971 and 1981 Census Periods

Mortality Measure/Sex		India		
		1961	1971	1981
Expectation of Life at Birth:				
	Male	41.9	46.4	50.9
	Female	40.6	44.7	50.0
Infant Mortality Rate (All areas)				
	Total = 139 Male		132.0*	110.0
	Female		148.0	111.0
Rural:	Male		141,0	119.0
	Female		161.0	119.0
Urban:	Male		85.0	63.0
	Female		85.0	62.0
CDR		22.8	15.1	12.5

Note: * Data refers to 1972
Source: Government of India, Family Welfare Year Book 1985–1986.

Family Planning

Though the national family planning programme was officially launched in India as early as in 1952, it was properly organized only in 1966, when a full-fledged Department of Family Planning was instituted in the Central Health Ministry. During the first three five-year plan periods beginning from 1951, the programme received less priority. It received a boost during the Emergency period in 1977–78, but this boomeranged during a couple of the following years because of the excesses committed in cases of sterilization during this period. The programme recovered once again during the early 1980s and had a very high priority in the allocation of funds. During the seventh Plan it was given the highest priority by the Planning Commission. Rs 35,000 million were allocated but the implementation lacked dynamism and seriousness. As a result, only 38.70 per cent of the eligible couples have been protected with one or another contraceptive method (1986). This has risen significantly from 15 per cent in 1973 to 25.7 per cent in 1982 to the present level. Currently it is estimated to be around 40 per cent in 1988. Considering the inputs that have gone into this programme during the last thirty-six years the achievement is not encouraging. However, more and more women are enthusiastic about this programme and their numbers are increasing by leaps and bounds. Since 1961, the percentage share of sterilized women as against men has increased from 38.9 per cent in 1951 to 78.6 per cent by 1980–81 and to 81 per cent by 1986. It is a tremendous success and beneficial for improving the quality of life of women and their status alike. The progressive and significant increase in the acceptance of family planning by women in India indicates the possibility of liberating them from their traditional major role of procreation and to elevate them to the status of partners in development (Table 9). The general demographic profile for the country is given in Table 10.

IMPLICATIONS FOR DEVELOPMENT

Although ancient Indian literature provides references about the better status given to women, today they do not enjoy that status. Exceptions exist, such as the matrilineal communities of Nairs and Khasis and even among certain patrilineal communities, namely Koorgis in Mysore, the Parsis in Maharashtra, and certain communities of Punjab, Christians etc., where the women have better status than their counterparts in other communities. However, most of the major communities lag far behind in this matter. The dimensions of women's status which require improvement are many. In the lines that follow, certain crucial aspects of the status of women and the policy and programme implications needed for their improvement are highlighted.

TABLE 9
Indicators of Family Planning Performance in India during the last Three Decades

Family Planning Measures

1 Percentage of Couples currently protected		
	Up to March 1973	15.0
	Up to March 1982	25.7
	Up to March 1986	38.7
2 Percentage Share of Tubectomies to Total Number of Sterilizations		
	1961	38.92
	1970–1971	33.92
	1980–1981	78.62
	1985–1986	80.98

Sources: *Family Welfare Year Book* 1972–73; 1980–81; 1981–82 and 1985–86 and Government of India *Pocket Book on Family Welfare Information*, 1987.

First of all, urgent and all round efforts need to be made to make the vast majority of illiterate women (65 per cent) literate and to enable them through education to change for the better in most aspects of their life. Even the literates are backward in many aspects, which also need selective and special attention. Since the level of their education is very low most women are employed in the primary sector and get very low wages. There is an urgent need to revise the wages of women working in low-paid categories of jobs. Further, the disparity of wages paid to women may also have to be reduced, if not removed altogether now. Certain suitable categories of employment, where women work efficiently may be reserved for them. Teaching up to the high school level, sales, reservation, medicine, etc., constitute a few priority areas.

The health status of women in general deteriorates when they remain illiterate and give birth to large numbers of children. Their health also is affected by frequent abortions and poor intake of balanced and nutritious food. A wrong life style, poor hygiene, unhealthy superstitions and other cultural practices also cause many hazards to their health. This confirms the urgent need for regular health, nutrition and population education among all sections of women. Such education may form a part of the school curriculum right from the third standard in view of the large-scale dropout of girls

TABLE 10
General Demographic Profile

Census year	Total Population (in lakhs)			Decennial change (per cent)	Growth of female population (per cent)	Sex ratio	Density	Percentage of urban population
	Persons	Males	Females					
1901	2384.0*	1207.9@	1173.6	—	—	972$	77	10.84
1911	2520.9	1283.8	1237.1	5.75	5.41	964	82	10.29
1921	2513.2	1285.5	1227.7	(—)0.31	–0.76	955	81	11.18
1931	2789.8*	1429.3	1357.9	11.00	10.61	950$	90	11.99
1941	3186.6*	1636.8	1546.9	14.22	13.92	945$	103	13.86
1951	3610.9	1855.3	1755.6	13.31	13.49	946	117	17.29
1961	4392.3	2262.9	2129.4	21.64	21.29	941	142	17.97
1971	5481.6	2840.5	2649.1	24.80	24.41	930	177**	19.91
1981@@	6851.8	3544.0	3307.8	25.00	24.87	933	216+	23.31

Notes:
* The distribution of population by sex for Pondicherry for 1901 (246,354), 1931 (258,628) and 1941 (285,011) is not available. The figures of these years are, therefore, exclusive of these populations so far as distribution by sex is concerned.

@ Sex-wise distribution of Chandranagar (26,831) of West Bengal and Gonda (18,810) of Uttar Pradesh is not available.

$ Excludes Pondicherry

** Excludes Jammu and Kashmir.

@@ Includes projected population of Assam where the 1981 census could not be conducted owing to disturbed conditions prevailing in that state, then.

+ The density has been worked out on comparable data.

Source: Government of India, *Family Welfare Year Book, 1985–86*, p. 41.

from schools. Several other policy and programme interventions are also needed.

Urgently Needed Policy and Intervention

Though the National Perspective Plan drafted for women during A.D. 1988–2000 has certain good policies, it gives more emphasis to legal changes and does not concentrate on daily issues that affect the status of women. The following issues deserve attention:

1. Suitable household appliances may be manufactured on a large scale to simplify household work and to save time so that women may divert their attention to education, skill development and organized social activities through mothers' clubs.

2. Healthy and attractive pre-school education may be institutionalized in rural areas to liberate women from the full-time drudgery of child care.

3. Compulsory free education for girls up to graduation should be promoted throughout the country without any loss of time. The content of such education should have relevance to enhance their status and improve their health. For making education acceptable to parents more girls' schools may be opened. Since there is very great demand for nurses, female health assistants and teachers for kindergartens, avenues in these areas may be expanded expeditiously. Residential hostels for working women also may be opened in all the necessary areas.

4. Mechanization of agriculture and manual work may be given high priority to reduce the health hazards of women labourers.

5. Special efforts may be made to provide water and fuel at close quarters to women in general. These two basic necessities take up a lot of their energy and time, due to the drudgery and frustration involved.

6. Entertainment-cum-non-formal education may be suitably arranged through television and radio by providing a separate facility for women in all villages. The cost of a television set may be reduced by producing small sets at reasonable prices for the benefit of women in the rural areas.

7. For changing laws unsuitably affecting women a commission may be appointed soon. For actively implementing the recommendations of such a commission, at least 30 per cent of

the seats in state assemblies and parliament may be reserved for women.

8. For minimizing health hazards and risks involved during child birth and maternity care of women, one trained nurse/midwife may be made available for every one thousand women in a village.

9. Processed, nutritious and reasonably priced food items may be marketed on a large scale to reduce the perennial drudgery involved in cooking by women in general.

10. Voluntary agencies may be given enough financial support to take up suitable projects for improving the civic amenities, providing security for destitute and old women, and divorced, separated and widowed women as well.

11. The cost of marriage may be reduced by providing free facilities to arrange marriages and loans for marriages, strictly reducing if not abolishing dowry etc., to overcome the dislike for daughters and also to improve their chances of survival and proper development.

12. Under all the suitable institutions and departments, research and action programmes related to development of women may be encouraged.

13. Eve teasing, rape, prostitution etc., should be severely punished. More police women may be appointed for this purpose.

14. Exploitation and harassment of women in business, advertisement and entertainment may be banned.

15. A Department for Development of Women may be instituted directly under the control of the Prime Minister, Chief Ministers and Collectors to give high priority to their development and for expediting the process of justice to them.

These are only a few policies but many more may be identified through further research and experience.

REFERENCES

Cain, M., 1981. 'Risk and Fertility in India and Bangladesh,' *Population and Development Review*, Vol. 7, No. 3.

Government of India, 1988. *Draft National Perspective Plan for Women, 1988–2000 A.D.*, pp. 1–81.

Kane, P.V., 1974. *History of Dharma Sastra*, Vol. II, Part I (Poona: Bhandarkar Oriental Research Institute), Chapters VII to IX.

Mahadevan, K., 1989. *Population Dynamics in the Indian States* (New Delhi: Mittal).

————, 1987. *Social Development, Cultural Change and Fertility Decline* (Sage: New Delhi).

————, 1979: *Sociology of Fertility: Determinants of Fertility Differentials in South India* (New Delhi: Sterling).

Shah, Nasra, M. 1981. 'Redefinition of Female Roles and Status in Pakistan, Issues and suggestions,' paper contributed to session F. 29, 'Demographic Consequences of Change in the Roles of Women,' XIX, General Conference of the IUSSP, Manila, 9–16 December 1981, p. 3.

Shah, Makhdoom A., 1981. 'Role and status of women in Pakistan: Perception and Reality,' in Nasra M. Shah (ed.), *Pakistani women: A Socio-economic and Demographic Profile* (Islamabad: Pakistan Institute of Development Economics).

Vlassoff, M. and C. Vlassoff, 1980. 'Old age Security and the Utility of Children in Rural India,' *Population Studies*, Vol. 34: pp. 487–499.

Kerala Women in Historical and Contemporary Perspective

P.K.B. NAYAR

An outstanding characteristic of the women of Kerala which contrasts them from their counterparts elsewhere in India is the higher status they enjoy in society. This is not only reflected in education and in the large proportion of women in employment but also in the higher age at marriage, in the initiative taken in family planning and in pioneering and promoting a number of women's organizations which give women a significant role in social work activities. These achievements were not made overnight or even in a few years. Women's high status in Kerala has a long historical past. It is founded on ecological and sociological factors.

KERALA'S ECOLOGY

The unique feature of Kerala's ecology is the absence of the village system of the all-India type with clustered habitats. In Kerala, houses are scattered far and wide. A comparatively fertile land, abundant supply of water during most part of the year and the natural protection offered by the Arabian Sea in the west and the Western Ghats in the east, enabled the Keralite to dispense with the village community life and to settle down anywhere he liked. The individual Keralite did not feel the need for protection by the community with its security system for combating internal and external threats to life and property as much as was felt by his other Indian counterparts. As a result, the village community mediating on all matters concerning the individual did not develop in Kerala in the form in which it developed in other places. Naturally, the individual felt free to act in his own best interest without much concern for or pressure from the community. This contributed to the rise and growth of individualism and competition in the social and economic spheres. It is inevitable that the spirit of individualism should pervade not only the male sex but the female sex as well.

DEMOGRAPHIC COMPOSITION

Kerala's population has a unique religious composition with 59.4 per cent Hindus, 21 per cent Christians and 19.5 per cent Muslims. The religions of Christianity and Islam came to Kerala in the very first century of their founders and were warmly received. Kerala has the highest Christian population among major Indian states and next to Kashmir, it has also the highest Muslim population. The element of cosmopolitanism that the peaceful and harmonious coexistence of fundamentally different religions generated and supplied a certain element of tolerance among the Keralites and this indirectly influenced the male attitude towards the female to some extent.

However, ecology and religious pluralism should be taken more as contextual than as contributory factors in the rise and growth of status among women in the state. Historical factors (which were of course influenced by the above two elements) offer a better explanation of the important role of women in society.

The Vedic period had accorded a very high position to women. There were women composers of Vedic hymns and women were invariably associated with all important religious and social functions. In fact, a woman was treated as man's partner on equal terms. It was only during the later period, when the caste system became crystallized, that women were subordinated to men and Manu's dictum that 'at no stage in life does woman deserve to be free' became generally accepted. However, in Kerala, Aryan influence came very late, possibly during the seventh or eighth century A.D. and gathered strength in the tenth century. Before this period, Kerala life was mainly dominated by Dravidian culture. The most vivid description of the life of early Keralites is given in the Sangam literature.

WOMEN IN THE SANGAM AGE

The exact period of the Sangam literature is a matter of dispute among scholars. Some attribute it to the centuries before Christ. The generally accepted view is that the Sangam works were composed during the first five centuries of the Christian era.

The Sangam age was characterized not only by the absence of caste system with its invidious distinction between different castes but by the high status accorded to women in society. Communities such as Panans, Parayas, Kuravas and Vetas who were later accorded an inferior (and even degrading) status had high status in the Sangam age and were noted for their literary achievements.

Throughout the Sangam age women enjoyed a high status in society. Women were trained not only in the three Rs but in music (including instrumental music) and dancing. The emphasis was on the enrichment of life by acquiring proficiency in arts, letters, philosophy and above all high morals. The story of Kannaki immortalized in the *Chilappadikaram* by Elengo Adigal was held out as an example of supreme female virtue. The fact that women's education received great patronage during the Sangam age is evidenced by the *Purananuru* which mentions as many as fifteen poetesses by name.

During the early post-Sangam age also, the position of women was more or less unaffected. Both Buddhism and Jainism, which became popular during this period in Kerala, had accorded high status to women. Education was part of the requirement of Buddhist nuns and schools were run by the nunneries. However, the coming of the Aryans to Kerala in large numbers in the subsequent centuries (eighth century and later) tilted the scale against women. The domination of the Aryans in Kerala was a blow not only to Buddhism and Jainism but also to many existing social institutions. Aryan gods and goddesses were planted in the local temples and Sanskrit replaced the vernacular in education and literary composition. Since Brahmins did not accord to their women any significant status in society, women were relegated to the position that Manu had prescribed for them in his treatise (quoted earlier). The Brahmins introduced the system of child marriage, prohibition of widow remarriage, and a host of other practices the effects of which were to push womanhood to a lower position in the household and in society.

Nonetheless there was one redeeming feature. The Brahmin hold over Kerala was never complete. The Nair community had established itself powerfully in Kerala during this period and the Aryan Brahmins found it very difficult to dislodge them. In most cases, compromises had been arrived at on the basis of a policy of give and take on both sides. The Nairs were given a dominant position in the caste hierarchy and were functionally equated with the Kshatriyas.

MARUMAKKATHAYAM

An institution which protected the rights and position of women in society during the period of the Nambudiri (Kerala name for Brahmin) dominance over Kerala and throughout the later period was Marumakkathayam, the law of inheritance through the female line. The Tharaward was the repository of this system and it was a big joint family. It is very difficult to establish the exact date of origin of this system. Scholars believe that it existed in a rudimentary form earlier but became more popular and widespread during the eleventh century which witnessed a long-drawn-out war between the Chera and Chola kingdoms. The vicissitudes of this war were also followed by the destruction of long established institutions and the security provided by them. Marumakkathayam came in the wake of these. It was not confined to the Nair community alone. The Kshatriyas, some of the Moppila Muslims of Malabar and many of the Ezhavas families also followed this system.

The full impact of Marumakkathayam on women's status has not been fully appreciated. According to Woodcock (1967)

> probably the most important effect of the matrilineal (Marumak-kathaya) system is that it had left Malayali women with an influence and an independent outlook which one will not find anywhere else in India. By maintaining a position for the woman within the family, it had prevented widowhood from becoming the sordid tragedy which it was—to a great extent still is—in other Hindu societies.

THE PALLI

A major index in the status enjoyed by women in Kerala during the medieval and modern period was the amount of education attained by them. Even as the Brahmins had introduced Sanskrit schools and had restricted admission to only members of their community, the traditional system of education was allowed to continue intact. Under this system, education was offered in vernacular with Sanskrit coming into use only in the later years. Each Kara (village) had a school called Ezhuthupalli under an Ezhuthachan or Asan. The village school was supported by donations in kind from the pupils. Both boys and girls were admitted. The Palli offered instruction to pupils from five to ten years. All children were taught the three Rs, the Kavyas and rudiments of astronomy and astrology. Advanced courses included the detailed study of Kavyas, Alankars, Natakas, Logic, Grammar and Ayurveda. The girls had also to specialize in recital of verses from Ramayana, Mahabharata and the Puranas as also in dancing (Thiruvathiga Kali). The system of education aimed at the moral, intellectual and physical development of the pupil.

THE KALARI

This is a unique institution peculiar to Kerala and was intended to train the martial communities in physical fitness and warfare. The chief instructor in the Kalari was the Kurup or Panicker. Both boys and girls were admitted to the Kalari; usually training stated at the age of 8; one would go to Kalari after completing education in the village school. Courses included instructions in the use of weapons, physical feats such as fencing, boxing and wrestling as also training in self-defence. The objective was to enable one to keep the body supple and agile. Advanced forms of training included archery and knowledge of the 'eighteen techniques' used in Ankam—a duel fought by nobles to keep their word of honour. The Kalari became prominent during the Chera-Chola war of the eleventh century.

Though a predominantly Nair-Ezhava institution, the Kalari seems to have attracted the Muslims, Christians and even the Namboodiris. Aristocratic Nair and Ezhava families considered that no education of their girls was complete without a course in advanced techniques taught in the Kalari. We have the exploits of heroines like Unni Archa and Ponni vividly described in the *Vadakkan Pattukal* (Ballads of Malabar). The fact that ladies in Kerala received training in warfare is endorsed by the fact that one of the queens of South Travancore (the Rani of Desiganad) had her body guard of 500 persons entirely consisting of women. The martial exploits of women in driving out the army of the Raja of Kongu Nadu may also be mentioned in this connection. Several similar adventures of women of Malabar are narrated by the historians of this period.

STATE AND EDUCATION

Direct activity of the state in the field of education began only in 1917 when Rani Gouri Parvathi Bhai, the ruler of Travancore, with the assistance of Dewan Munro, introduced free and compulsory education in Travancore for all children. Under state control and supervision, primary schools were opened in all villages and guardians of children in the age group 5–10 were enjoined under law to send them to school. A similar step was taken in the State of Cochin in 1918. In 1834, Travancore government started the first free school in Trivandrum with English medium (then known as the Raja's Free School). In 1966, it became a college—the forerunner of the present University College at Trivandrum. In Cochin, an English medium high school was started in 1845 and in 1875 it was raised to the level of a college (the present Maharaja's College at Ernakulam). In Calicut, a private English school for young princes of the Zamorin's family was started in 1877; it was later thrown open to all caste Hindus. In 1879 it was raised to a college (the present Guruvayoorappan College).

However, the popularization of women's education in the nineteenth century was largely the work of missionaries who opened schools for girls in different parts of Kerala, especially Travancore. Mention may be made of the boarding schools for girls at Nagercoil (1819), Alleppey (1820) and Kottàyam (1822). The first English medium school for girls was started by the State of Travancore in 1864 at Trivandrum. It was later raised to a college (the present Women's College).

As a result of all this, education of girls in Kerala, especially of Travancore, had already crossed the threshold. A breakdown of the literacy rate by communities for the year 1891 showed that Nair women topped the list (Aiya 1906) (Table 1). The 1901 census of India showed that Travancore stood first in female literacy among Indian states. The picture that emerges of the Kerala women at the beginning of the twentieth century is that there were ample opportunities available to them to get free education at all levels in the schools and that at the higher level, a few colleges existed and were, indeed, used by them liberally. The Nairs were the largest number of those who availed of the educational facilities. According to Nagam Aiya (1906: 474)

no (Nair) girl is permitted to grow up to womanhood without a fair knowledge of reading and writing. Education is a sine qua non of every (Nair) household. Curriculum for the well-to-do go beyond the three Rs, to Sanskrit for reciting Kavyas, Natakas, etc., and to the practice of musical instruments and of music and dancing.

When Lord Curzon visited Travancore in the early part of the twentieth century,

TABLE 1
Female Literates in Kerala, 1891

Community	Number
Nair	16,673
Christian	8,454
Muslim	358
Brahmin	1,469
Ezhava	1,089
Others	6,096
Total	34,139

the sight that pleased him most was the vast array of bright-eyed student girls who were called upon together to receive him; and of the several acts of administration which he commended much, one was the generous help given by His Highness in the cause of female education (Aiyer, 1923: 235).

EDUCATION OF WOMEN IN THE TWENTIETH CENTURY

The lead thus established for female education in the nineteenth century gathered momentum in the twentieth century. Government and missionary activities in education resulted not only in the establishment of a number of separate schools for women but in large enrolment of girls in mixed schools. The state gave 50 per cent concession in fees to women students in English medium schools besides other special facilities. As a result, the number of girls attending schools in Travancore rose from 14,139 at the end of the nineteenth century (1891) to 5,29,422 in 1948–49 and 22,57,888 in 1970–71. The post-independence period witnessed not only a big spurt in education in general, but government's efforts at extending education to the weaker sections resulted in women from the backward classes also being enrolled on a massive scale. This period also witnessed the starting of a number of professional institutions at undergraduate and graduate levels and women's enrolment in them.

EDUCATION OF BACKWARD CLASS GIRLS

The states of Travancore and Cochin took special interest in enrolling girls from the backward classes and especially the scheduled castes. Throughout the nineteenth century restrictions existed in the admission of these communities to even state-supported schools. In 1904, however, the schools were opened to all classes in Travancore and in 1919 in Cochin. A large number of institutions for backward classes received government grants and the minimum strength of backward community students in schools for eligibility for grants was lowered in 1930. These children got complete exemption from tuition fees as also from examination fees. Special officers were appointed to supervise the progress of education of these communities. As a result of all this, the number of pupils from backward and depressed classes reached the strength of 112,314 in 1950 and of these, 31,660 were girls. After independence, these communities received further encouragement from the state. By 1975–76 there was a more than six-fold increase in the enrolment of backward class children in schools.

A characteristic feature of the educational system prevailing in the state is that all schools upto SSLC (Secondary School Leaving Certificate) are state-supported. The salary of the staff of these schools is provided by the state. During 1979–80, there were a total of 6,970 lower primary schools, 2,739 upper primary schools and 1,680 high schools in the state. Altogether 5,596,251 students were enrolled in them. Of these, 48 per cent students were girls. More than 50 per cent of the 175,757 teachers in these schools were women. Nearly two-thirds of the schools are owned by private agencies though they are fully supported by the state. Education in Kerala upto SSLC is free.

The educational picture of Kerala will not be complete without a mention about the pre-primary educational facilities and the efforts at continuing education for the illiterate and dropout. Both programmes have been taken up in a large way and women have been the beneficiaries in these as much as men. Enrolment in pre-primary schools is equally shared by the two sexes.

A few interesting features of the Kerala educational scene will reveal the inner dynamics of the state's education.

As per the 1981 census, female literacy is 64.48 per cent, male literacy 74.03 per cent and general literacy 70.42 per cent.

The percentage of pass in examinations secured by girls is almost equal to that of boys. In 1974–75, girls secured 49.25 per cent pass in the SSLC examination. In 1961–62, the figure was only 35.62 per cent. The trend indicates that girls would even excel boys in studies in the years to come.

Sex-wise enrolment in the different classes (Standard I to X) is near equal and varies only within 5 per cent.

·In the matter of wastage and stagnation, the index shows only 16 points of difference between the boys and girls (boys 56.0; girls 54.4). In 1973–74, the number of girls to 100 boys in the age group 5–11 was 92.83; 11–14 was 88.87 and 14–16 was 93.03. For 1978–79, these figures were 96.51, 87.32 and 90.3 respectively. There is not much room for concern in this area.

In admission to professional (degree) colleges, girls are racing fast to catch up with the boys. In 1976–77, out of the total of 3,885 students for BSc Engineering, 373 were girls. In the same year, in BSc Agriculture out of 73 students, 29 were girls. Similarly, 240 out of 572 MBBS students were girls.

A fairly large proportion of teachers in schools are women. In the lower primary school, they constituted 52.8 per cent; upper primary school 48.6 per cent; and high school 46.7 per cent as per statistics relating to government schools for the period 1976–77. In the colleges also the percentage of lady teachers was 45.2.

WOMEN IN EMPLOYMENT

In traditional Kerala society, by and large, only women in the lower strata went for employment and, mostly in agriculture. Women of well-to-do families and noble families seldom worked. Indeed no meaningful employment was available to them. It was only with the spread of modern education and the modernization of society that new jobs came up largely due to the needs of government and industry consequent on their expansion. New jobs came up but the tendency was for men to seize them. This was for several reasons: (*a*) the job market was monopolized by men; (*b*) many jobs required some education or training; (*c*) men were considered breadwinners; and (*d*) women's proper place was considered to be the home. However, in Kerala, the advantage enjoyed by women enabled them to successfully compete with men in the employment market. Even so, sizeable entry of women in modern employment was a post-independence phenomenon.

The percentages of work participation rates of women in Kerala and India for the past three census decades are given in Table 2. One significant feature of these figures is that work participation of women in both India and Kerala has decreased over the decades. The low figure for Kerala compared to India is because of the severe unemployment in the state and the fact that women will be the first to be

TABLE 2
Work Participation Rates of Women (per cent)

| | Kerala | | | India | | |
	Women	Men	Total	Women	Men	Total
1961	19.71	47.20	33.31	27.93	57.16	42.97
1971	14.60	45.22	29.74	14.22	52.75	34.19
1981	17.02	45.25	30.90	20.85	53.19	37.55

pushed out of the market in such an event. The decline in participation rate is also attributed to higher attendance at school by the backward class children due to extensive encouragement for education. In Kerala this phenomenon happened earlier than in the rest of India and consequently swelled the number of unemployed in the white-collar labour market. It may also be noted that the working population (both men and women) as a proportion of general population has fallen over the last twenty years (1961–1981).

The distribution of work force among the different (primary, secondary and tertiary) sectors by sex shows that a comparatively larger proportion of women workers is engaged in secondary and tertiary sectors in Kerala (which together absorb more than 45 per cent against the all-India figure of 20 per cent).

Table 3 gives the percentage of female workers in the different sectors in 1971. More women in Kerala go for service sector jobs (46.30 per cent) whereas agricultural work continues to provide employment to 80 per cent of the women in India. It may, however, be pointed out that the majority of the work force (54 per cent) among Kerala women is engaged in agriculture where there are more women labourers than men.

TABLE 3
Sector-wise Employment of Women, 1971 (per cent)

Sector	Kerala	India
Primary sector	53.70	80.18
Secondary sector	26.31	10.55
Tertiary sector	19.99	9.27

Factory Employment

Kerala has a high percentage of women labour in the factory sector—38 per cent as per the 1971 census against 9 per cent for all India. However, the majority of them are in depressed industries like cashew, coir and handloom. Women account for 90 per cent of cashew workers, 76 per cent of coir workers and 42 per cent of handloom workers. The pattern of employment of women in factories is given in Table 4. Of late, the tendency on the part of factories has been to hire more women especially in such industries where women could handle things better and more dexterously. A publication by the State Bureau of Economics and Statistics (*Growth of Factory Employment in Kerala*) shows that more than 50 per cent of the employees in registered factories are women. However, the income of these women workers is generally low because of the low-technology and high labour-intensive character of these factories. In some industries like cashew and coir, there is even considerable under- and unemployment. Coir workers get only one hundred days' work.

TABLE 4
Women's Employment by Industry, Kerala, 1971

Industry	Percentage share of women
Cashew, coffee, matches, fruit canning and coir	More than 50
Electronic instruments, fish canning, plywood and veneer, cotton mills	40 to 50
Manufacture of allopathic medicines	30 to 40
Weaving, book binding, flour mills, polythene bags, embroidery, tiles	20 to 30
Ceramics, paper, pencil, rubber sheets, children's play equipment	10 to 20

The Service Sector

The high level of education of women of Kerala has enabled them not only to aspire for white-collar and similar more respectable jobs but also to secure them advantageously. A good number of women find jobs in other services where they have an edge over men. The proportion of employment of women in the service sector is given in Table 5.

TABLE 5
Women in the Service Sector, Kerala, 1971

Occupation	Per cent
Professional, technical and related workers	33.7
Administrative, Executive and Managerial workers	1.5
Clerical and related workers	10.5
Sales workers	5.1
Service workers	30.4

In the first three categories, government is the biggest employer of women, closely followed by banks. Women find the largest proportion of jobs in education and in health departments. We have noted earlier that more than 50 per cent of school teachers in Kerala are women. Nursing is a profession where the staff are almost entirely women. All the staff nurses (3,057) and 607 out of 639 head nurses in Kerala in 1978 were women. To this number should be added the 2,971 ANMS and midwives. Private hospitals and nursing homes employed over 2,500 nurses during this period. Because of the large number of women nurses the Health Services Department in Kerala has 4,357 women employees out of a total of 6,708 employees.

Next to Education and Health, the Government Secretariat and Accountant General's office at Trivandrum have the largest proportion of women employees. In the Government Secretariat they form 26 per cent (768 out of 2,964) and in the Accountant General's office they constitute 25 per cent (580 out of 2,327).

Considerable number of women are holding administrative/executive positions in the services though their proportion compared to men is very low. The proportion of women gazetted officers in 1978 was 17 per cent (2,136 out of 12,874). Eight per cent of the IAS officers were women. Fourteen per cent of the Deputy Secretaries also were women. The higher level women officers are concentrated in a few departments—Health Services (645), Collegiate Education (420), General Education (263), Medical Colleges (108). Together they constitute 66 per cent of the women gazetted officers. In the General Education Department, out of 523 heads of high schools, 219 (43 per cent) are women.

A fact worth mentioning in the employment of women is that when jobs require confidentiality or trust, women are preferred to men. For example, in the Government Secretariat, out of 162 confidential

assistants 105 are women. This is indicative of the fact that even men admit the superior qualities of women in some of the very delicate areas of human behaviour.

One reason for the lower number of senior posts available to women in services seems to be that in government service, length of service is a criterion for promotion and the women incumbents have not been in their posts long enough to become eligible for promotion. Large-scale entry into government service has been a recent phenomenon. Another equally plausible reason is that some of the jobs—like engineering and police—have not been attractive to women and so they kept away from them. However, in Kerala, women are progressively moving into the engineering professions as is shown by the increasing interest in engineering education shown by girls in recent years.

The bulk of the women employed in services in Kerala come under the category of domestic servants, cleaners, sweepers and so on. It has been noted earlier that women service workers constitute 30 per cent of women in the service sector. Employment in this sector is irregular (domestic servants are mostly part-time) and wages are very low.

Unemployment and Women

The large-scale unemployment prevailing in Kerala has affected women in the labour force as much as it has affected men. According to the Unemployment Survey conducted by the State Bureau of Economics and Statistics, 4.86 per cent of the labour force in 1977–78 was unemployed, of which men's share was 6.1 per cent and women's share 3.2 per cent. It is natural to expect that in the days to come, as economic problems are bound to grow, more and more women will be compelled to seek jobs and to swell the number of the unemployed. The survey quoted above showed that in absolute numbers, out of the 1,550,000 unemployed, 580,000 were women. Their breakdown in terms of education is given in Table 6. The provision of meaningful roles for women in the economy should certainly form an important aspect of the socio-economic planning in the years ahead.

WOMEN IN SOCIETY

Traditionally women in Kerala had an advantage in several fields compared to women in other parts of the country. They were

TABLE 6
Unemployment among Women in Kerala

Educational level		Number	Per cent
Illiterate		92,000	15.9
Literate but below matric		272,000	46.9
Matric and above		216,000	37.2
	Total	580,000	100.0

economically secure and emotionally integrated with the Tharavad through the Marumakkathayam system; the problem of dowry and widowhood did not bother them; education kept them in schools for several years and prevented them from marrying early; it also gave them a broader perspective towards society and their role in it. All this enabled them to enjoy a high status in society. The position of women in Travancore before independence is best described by Her Highness Sethu Parvathi Bhai, Maharani of Travancore, in her Presidential Address to the tenth All India Women's Conference in Trivandrum in 1935:

> The woman is here recognised as the head of the family and succession is traced through her. No restriction on the holding and disposition of property and no inequalities regarding education, social life and cultural growth have hampered our sex. Not only has our history afforded instances of queens who have stamped their individuality on the chronicles of their country but in the fine arts and philosophy women have played a notable part. The equality of women with men in the matter of political as well as property rights is today an established fact. Female literacy in Travancore has attained high standards (Velu Pillai 1936: 43).

This was the foundation on which the present status of women has been built. One should not, however, think that all classes and castes enjoyed the position described by the Maharani. The picture applied most appropriately to the Nairs and other well-to-do communities. By and large, society was more liberal towards women and this was strengthened by structural and processual factors. Women of all castes and economic levels enjoyed considerable freedom and commanded a good amount of respect.

A major bane of Indian society and one which kept women at a low ebb was child marriage. Baden Powell noted that in India girls were married even before they attained the age of five and there were widows even among those children who had not reached their first birthday. In Kerala there is a happy contrast. Here, women married late and widowhood was never a curse as widows could remarry without any social opprobrium. The data given in Table 7 on age at marriage in Kerala and India for the present century make interesting reading.

TABLE 7
Mean Age at Marriage of Females in Kerala and India

Period	Kerala	India
1901	17.13	13.2
1911	17.35	13.6
1921	17.80	12.6
193¹	19.66	15.0
1941	19.35	15.4
1951	19.85	16.1
1961	20.64	17.2
1971	20.88	18.0

Marrying late enabled women to have better choice of husbands, better understanding of family responsibilities, family planning, and child care. These coupled with education, which women of the state enjoyed, contributed to more sober decisions on the number of children to be given birth to and greater ability to implement these decisions. This has been a key factor in the steep fertility decline of Kerala women in recent years (Nayar 1981). Education and late marriage also made women more health and hygiene conscious, better equipped for pre-natal and post-natal care including child rearing and associated problems, and this in turn reduced infant and child mortality (Nayar 1983). Today, Kerala leads India in the reduction of birth rate (26.8), death rate (7.0) and infant mortality rate (42). The corresponding figures for India are 33.3, 12.4 and 127 respectively.

Another area where women have been able to make an impact on society in Kerala is in social welfare activities. A study conducted by the Sociology Department of Kerala University (Nayar 1975) showed that the largest number of voluntary social service agencies (in terms of population size) existed in Kerala (754 active societies) and a sizeable

number of them (279) were run by women. The beneficiaries of 188 of them also have been largely women. Self-employment programmes for women in Kerala also have caught up in a big way as is indicated by the over 2,000 women's industrial units functioning efficiently in the state.

REFERENCES

Aiya, V. Nigam, 1906. *Travancore State Manual*, Vol. II (Trivandrum).

————, 1891. *Report of the Census of Travancore*, Vol. I (Trivandrum).

Aiyer, S. Ranganatha, 1923. *Progressive Travancore* (Trivandrum).

Government of Kerala. *Statistical Handbook of Kerala* (for different years) (Trivandrum: Bureau of Economics and Statistics).

————, 1978. *Women in Kerala* (Trivandrum: Bureau of Economics and Statistics).

Menon, A. Sreedhara, 1979. *Social and Cultural History of India—Kerala* (New Delhi: Sterling).

Nayar, P.K.B., 1975, *Study of Social Welfare Agencies in Kerala*, monograph prepared for the Central Social Welfare Board, New Delhi.

————, 1981, 'Factors in Fertility Decline in Kerala 1951–81,' Paper presented at the International Population Conference, Manila.

————, 1983, 'Impact of Welfare Measures on Mortality—A Study in Kerala, India,' Paper presented at the International Seminar on Social Policy, Health Policy and Mortality Prospects, Paris.

Pillai, Kunjan, 1970. *Studies in Kerala History* (Trivandrum).

Pillai, T.K. Velu, 1936. *Travancore State Manual*, Vol. II (Trivandrum).

Woodcock, George, 1967. *Kerala: A Portrait of the Malabar Coast* (London, Faber and Faber).

Status of Women in West Bengal

SABITA GUHA AND PRANATI DATTA

The greatest revolution in a country is the one that affects the
status and living conditions of its women.

Jawaharlal Nehru, *Discovery of India.*

A HISTORICAL PERSPECTIVE

To define the status of a human being in relation to his or her
environment is difficult indeed. To think in terms of the status of an
entire section of population is harder still. But the international decade
of women appears to have inculcated an urge towards defining the
status of women in each particular society with a view to improving
upon the socio-economic condition of the 'weaker sex'. It is generally
felt that since women are physically and emotionally weaker than
menfolk they are likely to be exploited in a male-dominated society.
This is but a simplistic version of the main issue. Women do not form
a homogenous group in any society, not to speak of Indian society.
The position and problem of women differ due to differences in social
status, educational standard, economic ability, religious belief and so
on and so forth. Moreover, human society is dynamic. With the
passage of time, ideological changes take place resulting in social
transformation. Still the present cannot be entirely dissociated from
the past and the future prospect does not lie in preserving the present
status quo, but in accepting changes for the better.

With this in mind we may now make an attempt to find out how
women are faring in West Bengal, the leading state of eastern India.
Even in this particular region conditions are not alike everywhere.
There is apparently nothing in common between a Manipuri girl
selling her handicrafts in a Hat (weekly market) and a sophisticated

Note: The authors are thankful to Dr Phula Renu Guha, MP and Mrs Gita Basu of
AIWC for their helpful suggestions and information.

Bengali lady running a fashionable boutique. Language, religion, social customs differ. The hill tribes in the north-east region, the Garos and the Khasis, practise matrilinear heritage and the women have more social freedom but at the same time share greater economic responsibility. The condition of women in the remote villages of Bihar is more deplorable than that of women in rural areas of West Bengal and Orissa. Economic condition is a crucial factor in determining the status of women. Herein the best all-India classification so far has perhaps been provided by the Committee on Status of Women 1974 which lays down three broad categories namely, (*a*) women below the subsistence line, (*b*) women who move continuously between security and subsistence, and (*c*) women firmly above the security line.

While categorization may be possible in the present context, the past is a conglomeration of facts and ideas about women in general. Whenever we think of ancient India, it is customary to refer to the Vedic period—the glorious era of Indian society. It is generally held that at that time the status of women left nothing to be desired. We are familiar with the names of lady scholars like Lilavati, Mayetreyi, Gargi, to name a few, though we do not know to which economic class they belonged.

Coming to more factual statements for the recent past, we find that *Manusmriti* influenced Bengali Hindu society. It is not at all a liberal document so far as women are concerned. The whole injunction of the Sastra runs thus: 'Father protects a woman during childhood, husband during youth, sons during old age, so a woman deserves not freedom forsooth' (*Manusmriti*, 9.148). Thus women will always have a subordinate role in family and in society; at the same time she will always be under protective care. But it may appear strange that the male-dominated society seemed to have a great respect for womanhood.

In the Hindu pantheon there are numerous gods and goddesses, each one having a special role in the welfare of human beings. In Bengal, Kali—the goddess of powers is a unique conception. A number of devotees like Kamalakanta, Bamakhepa and the notable Sri Rama-krishna worshipped the goddess Kali for emancipation with single-minded devotion. In Bengal, goddesses like Durga, Lakshmi, Anna-purna are more popular than their male counterparts. While in day-to-day life, women had to face humiliation, society was in general respectful to the concept of womanhood. The Bengali mother was revered and she held sway over the entire family. To quote from the same

Manusmriti, 'A mother excels a father, ever thousand times in glory great' (9.26). The idea seems to be, while women are to be protected from the rough and tumble of daily life, the struggling menfolk may turn to them for solace and comfort from time to time.

The Muslims reigned over the plains of eastern India for many centuries prior to the coming of the British. In Muslim society women occupied a subordinate position. Bengali society became conservative under Muslim influence. The purdah system which kept women confined strictly within the four walls of the house led to the alienation of women from the mainstream of society. The high caste Hindus did not convert to Islam. But they confined their women indoors imitating the practice of the ruling classes. The poor low-caste people adopted the Muslim religion and the womenfolk lost much of their freedom under the influence of new religious strictures.

During the second half of the eighteenth century, the British rule gradually extended over Bengal, Bihar and Orissa. Society became dormant and exploitative under this alien rule in which the 'weaker sex' suffered the worst. The birth of a female child was decried in each and every stratum of society. Among the poor Hindu and Muslim families women were mere family drudges. Even within the rich and middle class Hindu families who might be deemed to be more enlightened, there were all sorts of queer restrictions. Women were denied education because of a general belief that literacy would lead to the early death of one's husband. Women were mortally afraid of widowhood, because either a widow would have to burn herself on the same pyre along with her husband to become a Sati or she would have to accept a barren life being cut off from all outlets of family and social life. Childbirth was regarded as a dirty affair and it used to take place in the most unhealthy surroundings at a distance from the main residence exposing both mother and child to health hazards. On grounds of prudery, doctors were not allowed to examine a woman patient. Thus women had no education, no health care, no cultural life. Naturally they were easy victims of superstition.

While marriage appeared to be the only succour of the womenfolk, they were not assured of a happy married life always. The rich Babus were often eccentric and maintained extra-marital relations. The wife was not a companion but a possession, to be maintained mainly for the birth of a male child which would ensure continuance of lineage. If one wife failed to deliver the goods, another might be tried and more would not be discouraged at all. Among the high caste Brahmins the

Kulin system made polygamy an accepted convention. A Kulin would marry a number of girls within his own sect on religious grounds. He would get dowry for this sacred act of saving the society, but did not have to take any responsibility for the wives whatsoever. Polygamy was also quite common among Muslims. Wives provided cheap labour at home and in the farm and would supply children. More wives brought more social prestige. Relinquishing wives on flimsy grounds was quite common and not disapproved among Muslims and Hindus. Thus the coveted institution of marriage also failed to ensure the desired security for women. But for the undercurrent of respect for womanhood noted earlier, the Bengali women would have faced many more hardships in such a social environment. The family tie which fostered such feelings saved the society as well as its women from grievous misfortune.

Under the western influence, a wave of modernization swept the Bengali middle class Hindu society in the early nineteenth century. A few social reformers did outstanding work to remove injustice to women and popularize female education. Notable among them were Raja Rammohun Roy, Pandit Iswar Chandra Vidyasagar, Pandit Sibnath Sastri, to name a few. It was Raja's untiring effort which led to the abolition of Sati Daha in 1829, and the practice was declared illegal and punishable by criminal courts. Next, the great humanitarian Vidyasagar made possible passage of the Widow Remarriage Act in 1856. Moved by the condition of child widows, he struggled all his life to make widow remarriage socially acceptable. The Muslim elite, however, suspicious of western influence, kept themselves aloof from it.

The status of women continued to change for the better throughout the nineteenth century. The spread of education among women had a salutary effect. The first two women graduates, Chandramukhi Basu and Kadambini Basu were from a Christian and Brahmo family respectively. The Tagore family, both its male and female members, ably took up the women's cause. In this they received full support from the Chowdhury and Roy families of Calcutta.

The litterateurs, political leaders, social reformers of the day, in fact, eminent persons from all walks of life felt that a society could hardly move forward if half of its members were neglected. So the crusade against social evils started in right earnest. Bankim Chandra depicted powerful characters of ideal womanhood in his novels. The heroines in Rabindranath's novels had enough female attractions: they were dignified and displayed an independent spirit. Sarat Chandra went a step

further and showed that a woman preserved her loving nature and self-respect even when she became a fallen woman under the pressure of circumstances.

In politics both the Indian National Congress and the revolutionary parties cast their spell on Bengali women as they felt themselves free from the shackles of social taboos. The all-pervading influence of Swami Vivekananda also contributed a great deal towards women's emancipation. His disciple, Sister Nivedita left her mark in almost every sphere of Bengali life, revolutionary politics, scientific discourse, artistic exploration and, above all, women's education.

While social transformation was thus taking place bringing in a revolutionary change in the society's attitude to women, the women themselves were not sitting idle. A handful of women, from time to time, proved their worth in different spheres of life even before real progress started. Rani Bhavani and Rani Rashmoni belonged to this old school.

Bengal is proud of her daughters—Sarojini Naidu, Sucheta Kripalani and Aruna Asaf Ali played important roles in all-India politics. Bengal was the first to send two women Swarnakumari Ghosal and Kadambini Ganguli as delegates to the Congress session held in Bombay in 1889. Bengali women's association with the Congress continued uninterrupted. Women went to jail, faced hardships and proved themselves worthy partners in the struggle for freedom. Matagini Hasra, an old traditional woman, laid down her life in Midnapore while leading a peaceful Satyagraha. Young girls with revolutionary zeal made attempts on the lives of British officials. Pritilata Waddedar participated in the armoury raid at Chittagong. The participation of poor peasant women in the Tabhaga movement[1] was a unique phenomenon.

Some of the Bengali women simultaneously pursued political and literary careers. Apart from being an able lieutenant of Mahatma Gandhi, Sarojini Naidu was famous for her lyrical poems in English. Sarala Devi, a niece of Rabindranath Tagore, was a prolific writer and a committed political activist. She composed Swadeshi (nationalistic) songs, wrote inspiring articles and edited journals. Her untiring effort to enliven and embolden Bengali youth was noteworthy. She was the founder of the Bharat Stri Mahamandal, the first women's organization in India.

There were other Bengali women, not as educated and liberated as Sarojini Naidu or Sarala Devi, who quietly pursued their literary careers. The contribution of some of the women of the Tagore family to literature and the other arts is noteworthy. The Hindu Female School, the first girls' school, was started in 1849 in Calcutta and for a long time remained the only such school. Women mostly depended on what they were able to learn at home. Widows living in their parents' houses often took up literary pursuits seriously. A number of middle grade writers appeared on the scene and dealt with the tyranny of the household and social injustice towards women, especially in their memoirs. Their efforts indirectly helped the cause of women. The transformation and modernization of Bengali women that gathered speed in the middle twentieth century had its roots in the efforts of the liberal minded, half educated, idealist Bengali women of the late nineteenth and early twentieth centuries. During this period, Bengal watched the advent of Sarada Devi, wife of Ramakrishna in the religious world. She is the personification of ideal womanhood and her influence still persists among modern women striving for emancipation.

DEMOGRAPHIC PROFILE

It is very difficult to define the status of a whole section of population comprehensively. However, to start with, we may indicate a few demographic features to suggest that the condition of women in West Bengal is on the whole improving. Almost all over the world, barring the Indian subcontinent, the sex ratio is in favour of the female. In India ever since the first recorded census in 1901 the sex ratio has been adverse for the female, a major indicator of the low status of women. The sex ratio has in fact been declining continuously, and the trend seems to have been checked only recently (see Table 1). In Bihar and Orissa the sex ratio has been continuously falling. In West Bengal and Assam, the sex ratio is much lower than the all-India figure but it is improving. In the 1981 census, the sex ratio shows considerable improvement in West Bengal, indicating a change in the status of women for the better. (It may be noted that in Bangladesh, which was part of Bengal before partition, the sex ratio in 1951 was 910 and 939 in 1981.)[2]

The sex ratio as an indicator of the status of women may not give the total picture because one does not know for certain the sex composition of live births. However, it is general knowledge that men on the whole get better food and greater attention in Indian families. Female babies and girls are often neglected and discriminated against in

TABLE 1

Trend in Sex Ratio in the Twentieth Century

Year/State	1901	1921	1941	1951	1961	1971	1981
Assam	919	896	875	868	869	896	901
Bihar	1054	1016	996	990	994	954	946
Orissa	1037	1086	1053	1022	1001	988	981
West Bengal	945	905	852	865	878	891	911
India	972	955	945	946	941	930	933

Source: *Census of India 1981*, Series 1, Primary Census Abstract Part II B(i).

respect of food, education and health care. The two estimates presented in Table 2 speak for themselves.

TABLE 2

Estimated Death Rate and Infant Mortality Rate by sex—1981

State	Death Rate		IMR	
	M	F	M	F
Assam	12.5	10.6	105	106
Bihar	12.6	15.3	112	124
Orissa	13.1	13.0	139	130
West Bengal	11.2	10.7	94	89
India	12.4	12.7	110	111

Source: Sample Registration System 1981, Vital Statistical Division, Office of the Registrar General of India, Ministry of Home Affairs.

In spite of women being biologically sturdier, the incidence of mortality is higher among women in India. The case of Bihar is quite discouraging. However, West Bengal conforms mostly to the biological law.

The expectation of life at birth is an accepted indicator of the mortality trend. Like sex ratio female life expectancy has shown a slight improvement in recent years at the all-India level. However, the present euphoria regarding improvement in female life expectancy needs to be examined in greater detail. While at the all-India level in 1961 life expectancy was 41.89 years for male and 40.55 years for female, these were considerably improved and were estimated at 54.1 and 54.7 years respectively in 1980. Thus for the first time female life expectancy marched ahead of male life expectancy.[3] The sex-wise life expectancy for the quinquennial 1970–1975 for India and eastern states is presented in Table 3.

TABLE 3
Sex-wise Expectation of Life at Birth

State	Period	Life expectancy (years)	
		M	F
Assam	1970–1975	46.2	44.8
Bihar	1970–1975	54.5	54.9
Orissa	1970–1975	46.0	45.3
West Bengal	1971–1975	57.7	48.1
India	1970–1975	50.5	49.0
	1971–1975	57.3	56.0

Sources: (1970–75) *Census of India Occasional Paper No. 1*, 1984 and (1971–75) Projected values quoted in A synopsis report of Committee on Status of Women in India 1974, ICSSR.

Thus barring projected values for Bihar and West Bengal, life expectancy was lower for females in 1970–1975 in the other two states as well as in India. Projected values at the all-India level for 1971–1975 were on the high side 57.3 (M) and 56.0 (F), compared to SRS 1971–1975 estimates, though female life expectancy was lower. Thus we may conclude that West Bengal achieved higher life expectancy for females in 1971–1975, even if the projection is on the higher side.

Women and Marriage

The improvement in sex ratio and female life expectancy augurs well for the socio-economic status of women in general. Perhaps the huge amount spent on family welfare—specially maternal and child welfare schemes—is showing results. The trend needs to be watched in the next decade and improved upon. However cases of dowry deaths and other harassment of women speak ill of their social status. At one time Bengali women had to suffer considerably on account of the practice of Satidaha and Koolin marriage, which were the worst manifestations of male chauvinism. Fortunately, such institutions are things of the past and the dowry system is not such a menace in Bengali society as it is elsewhere. Enlightened middle class families are mostly in favour of repudiating the system. However, marriage as an institution is highly respected all over India and parents are always in favour of marrying off their children early. From a sociological and demographic point of view, this institution is very important since it leads to reproduction.

Table 4 gives the singulate mean age at marriage. Compared to other eastern states as well as India as a whole, the mean age at marriage is higher in West Bengal both for men and women. Over the decade 1971–1981, the mean age at marriage of women has enhanced by 1.34 points reaching near 20, a biologically sound age for reproduction. The statutory minimum ages at marriage as laid down under the Special Marriage Act, 1954 are 21 years and 18 years for males and females respectively.

TABLE 4
Singulate Mean Age at Marriage by Sex (Hajnal's Method)

State	Year			
	1971		1981	
	M	F	M	F
Bihar	19.84	15.27	21.47	16.53
Orissa	22.57	17.29	24.17	19.04
West Bengal	24.28	17.92	25.66	19.26
India (excludes Assam)	22.36	17.16	23.27	18.32

Source: *Census of India 1981*, Series 1 Part II (Special) Reports and Tables based on 5 per cent data.

The child-woman ratio, which is closely related to incidence of marriage as well as age at marriage in India indicates the trend of population growth and the status of women. A small family size and a low child-woman ratio contribute a great deal to the improvement of the status of women. The child-woman ratio is encouraging for West Bengal (Table 5).

While CWR in West Bengal was slightly higher in 1971 than in 1961, it recorded a sharp fall in 1981 resulting in nearly 30 per cent movement downwards. While it is on the decline in two other states as also in India the sharp decline in West Bengal is noteworthy.

The crude birth rate in India was estimated to be 33.9 in 1981. In the same year the crude birth rates for the eastern states—Assam, Orissa and West Bengal are 33.0, 33.1 and 33.2 respectively, while it was 39.1 for Bihar. In urban areas of West Bengal, the CBR was only 20.0, the lowest among the eastern states.[4] Of the major

TABLE 5
Child-woman Ratio and its Percentage Variation

State	Ratios in year			Per cent change	
	1961	1971	1981	1961–71	1971–81
Bihar	661	643	597	2.72	7.15
Orissa	588	636	507	−8.16	20.28
West Bengal	697	700	493	−0.43	29.57
India	659	655	546*	0.61	16.64*

Note: * excludes Assam.

$$CWR = \frac{\text{Children in 0–4 age group}}{\text{Women in 15–49 age group}} \times 1000$$

$$\text{Rates of change} = \frac{CWR\ 1961 - CWR\ 1971}{CWR\ 1971} \times 100$$

$$\frac{CWR\ 1971 - CWR\ 1981}{CWR\ 1971} \times 100$$

Source: *Census of India 1981*, Series 1, Part II Special Reports and Tables based on 5 per cent sample data.

eastern states, the indicators for the status of women appear to be always unfavourable for Bihar and most favourable for West Bengal.

Women and Family Planning

The small family norm seems to be catching the imagination of West Bengal. Not only the elite class, but the economically weaker section and traditional rural families are gradually beginning to appreciate the need for holding family size in check. This is indicated by the gross fertility rate (number of live births per thousand women in reproductive age group 15–49 years) presented in Table 6. Of the four states GRR is lowest for Assam. Excepting Bihar, the two other states have GRRs lower than the all-India level. The GRR for urban Bengal is as low as 77.2, which speaks for a general acceptance of the small family norm.

Among the family planning measures, while the effective protection rate is higher than the all-India average in Orissa and West Bengal, it is lower for the other two states (Table 7).

The most effective method of family planning is sterilization. Medical termination of pregnancy, which is legalized now, also con-

TABLE 6
Areawise Gross Fertility Rate

State	GRR 1981		
	Rural	Urban	Total
Assam	133.0	88.3	129.4
Bihar	174.5	145.7	171.2
Orissa	132.4	116.4	131.2
West Bengal	157.8	77.2	138.4
India	149.4	107.2	140.3

Source: Sample Registration System, 1981, Vital Statistics Division, Office of the Registrar General, India.

TABLE 7
Couples Effectively Protected by Various Methods, March 1982

State	Estimated No. of Eligible Couples (in '000)	Per cent Effectively Protected (All methods)
Assam	3,010	18.3
Bihar	13,332	12.2
Orissa	4,680	26.1
West Bengal	8,450	24.4
India	1,18,767	23.7

Source: *Year Book 1981–82*, Family Welfare Programme, Government of India.

tributes a great deal towards lowering birth rate. Since women have to bear the major brunt of reproduction in the form of child bearing and child rearing, their eagerness for limiting the family size should normally be greater. Though vasectomy is a much easier method than tubectomy, tubectomy cases form a major portion of sterilization (Table 8). Assam is an exception, while West Bengal also has a lower tubectomy rate compared to others. Whether this is due to women having a more favourable social status and greater awareness on the part of people of women's well being, one cannot say definitely.

With reference to abortions, West Bengal takes the lead (Table 9). In India, socially, abortion is often unacceptable. The attitude is gradually changing among the educated, specially with the spread of female education. The higher abortion rate in West Bengal of course does not indicate a better social status of Bengali women. For abortion

TABLE 8
Sterilizations done in 1980–81, 1981–82

State	No. of sterilization cases		Per cent of tubectomy	
	1980–81	1981–82	1980–81	1981–82
Assam	23923	34116	36.7	37.2
Bihar	96422	159304	78.8	75.8
Orissa	92939	110130	83.1	85.8
West Bengal	209940	217329	61.3	69.6
India	2052770	2791579	78.6	79.5

Source: Same as Table 7

TABLE 9
Medical Termination of Pregnancies performed during 1980–81 and 1981–82

State	No. of terminations	
	1980–81	1981–82
Assam	8,055 (2.1)	9,426 (2.2)
Bihar	9,642 (2.5)	9,955 (2.3)
Orissa	15,961 (4.1)	19,566 (4.6)
West Bengal	20,293 (5.2)	31,225 (7.3)
India	388,405	426,551

Note: Figures in parentheses indicate percentage of all-India figure.
Source: Same as Table 7.

is most often resorted to when pregnancies take place outside wedlock. Nonetheless, it is generally accepted that the spread of female education is the most effective method of lowering birth rate. Enlightened women are a great social asset.

WOMEN AND EDUCATION

We have noted that in the early nineteenth century female education was tabooed. According to the 1901 census literacy rate was 17.16 for males and only 1.18 for females. Still, enterprising women used to learn to read and write at home with the help of their husbands or brothers. There was little spread of formal education even after the opening of a girls' school in 1849. Things gradually began to look up since the middle of the twentieth century. But sex disparity in literacy is still conspicuous and persistent (Table 10).

TABLE 10
Sex-wise Literacy Rate 1941–1981

Year	1941	1951	1961	1971	1981
Female	8.93	12.34	17.0	22.4	30.25
Male	29.39	34.06	40.1	42.8	50.67

Sources: *Statistical Abstract*, West Bengal 1976–77 and *Economic Review 1985–86* (for 1981) Bureau of Applied Economics and Statistics, Government of West Bengal.

West Bengal stands tenth among eighteen states in female literacy according to the 1981 census. Among the eastern states West Bengal stands first (Table 11). In the 1971 census, West Bengal was placed thirteenth, and its slow progress upwards in rank indicates that its pace in this sphere is slower than that of some other advanced states of India.

TABLE 11
Female Literacy Rates in Eastern States 1971, 1981

State	Literacy rates	
	1971	1981
Assam	19.27	—
Bihar	8.72	13.62
Orissa	13.92	21.12
West Bengal	22.42	30.25
India	18.70	24.82

Sources: *Census of India 1981*, Series 1, Primary Census Abstract Part II B(i) and *Census of India 1971*, same part II A(ii).

According to the fourth all-India Education Survey, the percentages of enrolment of children (6–11 years) at the primary level were 60.90 and 39.10 for boys and girls respectively, showing a large gap. Enrolment at different school levels is slightly better of late, though the disparity is larger at the higher level. Figures for West Bengal are given in Table 12.

TABLE 12
Female Enrolment in Schools in West Bengal in 1985–86

Classes	Total enrolment	Per cent of female students
Class I to V	8,040,000	42.56
Class VI to VIII	2,837,000	42.90
Class IX and X	1,017,000	31.96

Source: Education Department, Government of West Bengal.

The sex ratio is not at all encouraging for different levels of education. In West Bengal, it is extremely low for technical education, but favourable in general education compared to the all-India level, and especially so at the higher education level (graduate and above; Table 13). It is encouraging to note that the state government received an award in 1987 at the all-India level for its commendable work in female education.

TABLE 13
Sex Ratio at Different Levels of Education 1981

Level of education	West Bengal	India
Primary	622	555
Middle	491	461
Matric/Secondary	368	370
Higher Secondary/Pre-University	365	322
Non-technical diploma holder	221	536
Technical diploma/Certificate holder	82	251
Graduate and above	350	31

Source: Calculated from the figures presented in special reports and tables based on 5 per cent sample data in Series 23 West Bengal, *Census of India 1981* and Series I, India, Part II, Special *Census of India 1981*.

The spread of female education is absolutely necessary at this stage. A woman's role is traditionally assigned to home making. She is expected to discharge her duties competently when she is more enlightened. An educated woman no doubt performs her household chores more efficiently and a professional career enables her to enjoy economic freedom as well. Moreover she becomes a more likable and reasonable partner in family life and a more responsible mother of children.

WOMEN AND EMPLOYMENT

Education and health care open a vista of better living before women. The social status of women has been greatly enhanced as equal partnership in married life is more or less an accepted norm among the educated people in West Bengal. Women also have a say on the size of the family. They are no longer machines for child bearing and child rearing. Their entry into the labour market has enabled women to taste economic freedom. Women's employment has brought two congenial effects in society—it has raised the level of living and has exerted an effective control on family size.

Much of the difference in social status, educational standard, attitude to women's role in family life, and so on stems from the economic status of women in a society. Women's employment is therefore important. In India, even now, there is a basic difference between men's work and women's work. While women mostly work indoors, men spend a substantial portion of their working time in outdoor work. Even a working woman spends a lot of time attending to household chores, while a man's household work is mostly limited to shopping, gardening and such other outdoor activities.

Whatever may be the modern outcry for valuation of household work, in economics employment and work generally refer to those categories which generate income: work here means marketed work. Hence to have an insight into the economic status of women, we have to refer to labour force participation rate (LFPR) and more generally work participation rate (WPR).

WPR for females is low indeed in West Bengal compared to India as well as the two other eastern states (see Table 14). Punjab and Haryana,

TABLE 14
Female Work Participation Rate 1971–1981

State	Female WPR	
	1971	1981
Assam	4.66	—
Bihar	8.88	9.06
Orissa	6.81	10.70
West Bengal	4.43	5.58
India	12.06	13.99

Source: *Census of India 1981*, Series 1, Part II B(I) Primary Census Abstract.

TABLE 15

Sex Ratio among Total Population, Total Workers and Three Categories of Workers 1971, 1981

State	Sex Ratio									
	Total population		Total workers		Cultivators		Agricultural labourer		Household industry	
	1971	1981	1971	1981	1971	1981	1971	1981	1971	1981
Assam	897	—	100	—	48	—	54	—	335	—
Bihar	954	975	162	567	59	298	359	1028	160	527
Orissa	988	981	122	348	46	92	252	462	317	387
West Bengal	891	911	81	146	29	51	144	181	150	264
India	930	934	210	351	134	192	498	598	265	365

Source: *Census of India* 1981 Series, 1, Part II B(i), Primary Census Abstract and *Census of India* 1971 Series 1, Part IIA(ii), Union Primary Census Abstract.

two progressive states in India also have a quite low WPR, and the social status of women there leaves much to be desired. But WPR is not the only indicator of socio-economic status. We cannot conclude from the figures in Table 14 that the women of Bihar enjoy a better socio-economic status because of a higher female WPR.

TABLE 16

Percentage Distribution of Main Workers (Female) into Broad Industrial Categories, 1981

State	Total main workers	Cultivator	Agri. labourer	H.H. ind., manufacturing processing etc.	Other workers
Bihar	100	25.54	63.33	2.76	8.37
Orissa	100	24.50	54.24	5.69	15.57
West Bengal	100	14.67	39.43	7.50	38.40
India	100	33.20	46.18	4.59	16.03

Source: *Census of India 1981*, Series 1, Part II B(i), Primary Census Abstract.

According to the 1981 census in Bihar there was a dramatic increase of women's participation in labour force in 1981, and the sex ratio in agricultural labour force was extremely high (see Table 15). This does not speak very well of women's social status. Sex ratio in total workers is the lowest in West Bengal indicating a low level of female employment. Among different occupations, sex ratio is highest for household industry.

In two states, more than half of the female workers are employed as agricultural labourers (see Table 16). In India the percentage of female workers in this category is 46.18 whereas in West Bengal it is much lower, 39.43. Moreover, in 'other workers' group the percentage is almost identical (38.40) in West Bengal. This indicates occupational diversity among women in West Bengal.

The percentage of women workers in the total working force was only 7.49 according to the 1971 census and it showed a marginal increase in 1981 reaching nearly 9.81 per cent. The percentage distribution of female workers among nine occupational classes is given in Table 17. Comparing the two sets of data in Table 17 we find that the percentage share of women workers has dropped by a little more than five points (from 68.39 per cent to 63.24 per cent) in the first three categories (agriculture and allied services) taken together in ten years. Within these categories themselves the 'agriculture labour' group

TABLE 17

Percentage Distribution of Female Workers among Broad Industrial Categories 1971, 1981

Industrial category	Percentage of workers	
	1971	1981
Total workers	100	100
Cultivators	12.19	14.67
Agricultural labourers	44.44	39.39
Livestock, hunting, plantation, forest, fishery	11.76	9.18
Mining and quarrying	.65	.74
Manufacturing industry (including household)	9.49	15.27
Construction	.44	.46
Trade and Commerce	2.26	2.51
Transport, storage and communication	1.18	.79
Other services	17.58	16.99

Source: Calculated on the basis of tables given in *Census of India 1971* Series 22, Part II B(i) 1971 and Series 1, Paper 2 of 1981.

shows a comparatively sharper decline. As against that, women's participation in the industry group has increased. Thus, it appears that women are moving towards more remunerative occupations.

Finally, a few measures calculated from three rounds of NSS (National Statistical Survey) estimates as presented in Table 18 reveal the general trend in female labour participation and the rate of growth of female workers in the economy. While the sex ratio has increased considerably in ten years, the rate of increase of female labour is higher for the first quinquennium. In the second phase the rate of growth in the urban sector is much higher than that in the rural sector. Since better jobs are available in urban areas, this is a favourable trend.

TABLE 18

Sex Ratio and Rate of Growth of Female Labour Force from 1972–73 to 1983

NSS round	Ratio	Rural	Urban	Total
27th (1972–73)	218			
32nd (1977–78)	291	52.46	37.87	57.08
38th (1983)	309	8.92	27.59	12.15

All this discussion reveals that women in West Bengal are marching ahead. Starting from a low sex ratio and an abominably low literacy rate at the beginning of the century, they have considerably improved their position. Their performance in higher education is not unsatisfactory. They are also trying to attain economic independence and have achieved a respectable marital status. The misgivings about family planning are gradually disappearing even among the poor uneducated class. In fact, excepting work participation rate, all other indicators of the status of women are more favourable for West Bengal than her sister states, though admittedly the census 1981 data are not available for Assam. But work opportunities are not identical for the two sexes in higher and responsible occupations. Moreover, working women still have to take up a lot of responsibility at the family level, which makes life quite strenuous for them. The menfolk should come forward to help their partners in household work in a big way.

WOMEN AND EMANCIPATION

One of the redeeming features in India since independence is the Indian state's active interest in women's welfare. Indian women had been asking for franchise during the British rule and the constitution of free India gave it to them. Pandit Nehru even involved women in the framing of the constitution by including fourteen women as members of the Constituent Assembly of India.

The constitution of India guarantees equality of status to both men and women through Articles 14, 15 and 16, which lay down that the State shall not discriminate on grounds of sex, religion, race, caste or place of birth. India has also signed the UN convention granting political rights to women. Formally, the legal status of women under civil law is high. But in real life women are not always treated equally in every region. We have already noted the differences prevailing among the eastern states which have close socio-cultural ties. As commented in the report of the Committee on the Status of Women in India, 1979, 'large masses of women in this country have remained unaffected by the rights granted to them by the constitution and the laws enacted since independence.' The chairperson of the committee was Dr Phularenu Guha from Bengal who is carrying on an indomitable fight for the cause of women even in lowest strata of society.

Women are on the whole socially better off in West Bengal than in many other states of India. Gone are the days of Sati Dah or burning of women in the pyres of dead husbands with an eye to grabbing the widows' property, of Kulin Pratha or the ignoble custom of polygamously marrying innumerable women at a time for money, apparently on religious ground. There was even the custom, though not very popular, of Ganga Sagare Kanya Visarjana (throwing baby daughters at the confluence of the Ganges and the Bay of Bengal). Gone also are the days of Gouridan where daughters were given in marriage at the tender age of eight. The young girls were often victims of the lust of men much older than themselves which caused them immense health injury.

Bengal is thankfully rid of such oppressive practices. Even the menace of 'bride burning' does not haunt this state, except for isolated cases of dowry incidents. Women have successfully fought their case to establish an honourable status for themselves within the family. Women move freely in all walks of life, which they could not even two decades earlier. We have referred to a three-fold classification of women according to their economic status. Women belonging to the second category carried the struggle at home and within the middle class society. The ladies from the elite class belonging to the third category involved themselves in social work mainly to do something for the women in the lowest rung of society. These voluntary organizations have also contributed to women's emancipation.

The spread of education is a definitive step toward modernization. After the establishment of the first female school there was a lull. Then women from the elite class came forward. Sarala Roy and Abala Bose, themselves wives of great scholars, established two model schools for girls at Calcutta. Hemalata Sircar, daughter of Pandit Sibnath Sastri, a social reformer, started a model school in the hill areas of Darjeeling. Female education thus spread to remote corners. It has been a long way from the times when a special committee was constituted for deciding whether women should be allowed to appear in graduate or post-graduate examinations of the Calcutta University or take admission in a medical college. Now all courses are open to men and women alike. Bengali girls are exploring new fields. Bengal produced the first woman commercial pilot in India, Durba Banerjee. In sports, Bengali girls are doing exceptionally well in swimming. Law and medicine can boast of many competent female professionals. In the technical field, Bengali women are still somewhat shy, their preference being the practice of art in all forms. Sudipta Sen was among the scientific team in the recent Antarctica expedition. Thus Bengali women have achieved success in various fields of activity.

Both state and voluntary organizations are doing their bit to bring about an overall improvement of women irrespective of socio-economic status. The Central Government has made a number of enactments like Suppression of Immoral Traffic Act, 1956, Dowry Prohibition Act, 1961, Maternity Benefit Act, 1961, Medical Termination of Pregnancy Act, 1973, all for the benefit of women. Much depends on their successful implementation. Recently a separate department for looking after development of women has been created at the Centre. The Central Social Welfare Board also helps mainly women and children. The Left Front Government of West Bengal is disposed towards striking at the root of all sorts of exploitation. Women being at a disadvantage in a male-dominated society naturally deserve protection. Chaya Bera, the Minister of State feels that the marxist philosophy stands for equality of status for both sexes and since a large section of Bengali society accepts this creed, the society has acquired a progressive outlook. This is likely to enhance the status of women in society.

Among voluntary organizations, the West Bengal unit of the All India Women's Conference has rendered manifold services since its inception in 1926 under the guidance of Sarojini Naidu and Margaret Cousins. The organization fosters a threefold objective to look after the general welfare of women and children, to press for social reform and to establish equal rights for women. Rabindranath Tagore, in his address to its annual conference held at Calcutta in 1934, said, 'The cadence of human civilization is out of step and disjoined and harmony can only be restored when men and women contribute in equal measure." A healthy society can develop only when there is perfect harmony between man and woman.

Voluntary organizations have multiplied in number and in objectives since the early twentieth century. Some of them try to provide economic security to the needy. Others look after maternity/child welfare and family planning. Some units arrange for legal aid in divorce cases or property matters. A state women's coordination council has been set up to coordinate the work of eighty-two voluntary organizations working for women's welfare and to prevent overlap in their activities.

In the ultimate analysis, emancipation can come only when the average woman becomes conscious of her rights and duties. A modern enlightened woman, if she becomes self-centred and vain, disrupts family life. Divorce and extra-marital relations harm children. Delinquency among the young is on the increase, which is not a good sign. An enlightened woman is one who can take her own responsibility in all spheres of life—within the family, in the external world of economic activity and in her social environment—while retaining her presence of mind and gracefulness. Tagore in his poem on the 'Bold Woman' sang of the woman who challenges God to confer upon her the courage to build her own destiny. She selects her partner herself amidst the rough and tumble of everyday life. Modern Bengali women are on the path of conquering their destiny, but they would do well to follow a path of reason and avoid unnecessary aggressiveness.

NOTES

1. The Tebhaga movement was a militant movement of Bengali peasants, launched in 1946, for a two-thirds share in the harvest. The women formed a fighting troop called Nari Bahini which came to the forefront.
2. *Monthly Statistical Bulletin of Bangladesh*, August 1986.
3. *Statistical Abstract for India*, 1984, Central Statistical Office, Government of India.
4. *Sample Registration System 1981*, Vital Statistics Division, Office of the Registrar General, India.
5. Quoted in the Souvenir published on the occasion of Annual Conference of AIWC, Calcutta, 1978.

Status of Women in
Punjab and Haryana

K.P. SINGH

The subject of the status of women in any given society or region is very vast and complex. It has many facets, therefore, generalization is difficult because of the existence of considerable variations within any region in terms of rural-urban, caste and religious groups. The present chapter, therefore, presents a broad picture of the status of women in the states of Punjab and Haryana.

In 1966, Punjab was divided into two states of Punjab and Haryana on the basis of language. Since the present state of Haryana was carved out of Punjab, both the states have great similarity in their social and cultural values and their economy is by and large based on agriculture.

As per the 1981 census, Punjab comprised 16.79 million persons out of whom 8.94 million (53.24 per cent) were males and 7.85 million (46.75 per cent) females, whereas Haryana consisted of 12.92 million persons, of whom 6.91 million (53.48 per cent) were males and 60.1 million (46.51 per cent) females. In both Punjab and Haryana agriculture is the main occupation of the people. The dominant religion in Punjab is Sikhism while in Haryana Hinduism comes first and Sikhism comes next.

Historically, both states in the past had always attracted foreign invaders. Alexander the Great conquered Punjab in the fourth century B.C. After him, the Greeks, Sakas, Kushans and Huns invaded Punjab. The Mughals also came through Punjab and after them came the Britishers who conquered Punjab in 1850. After almost a hundred years of struggle Punjab attained freedom along with India in 1947. Thus throughout history the first aggressive onslaught and fury of the invaders was borne by the people of Punjab. As a consequence of countless and repeated invasions, the women of this territory were mostly confined to the inner parts of their homes. This gave rise to child marriages, the Purdah system and a variety of other practices prejudicial to women.

At first these practices were adopted to provide protection to women but later on they led to their subordination which became the rule of the day. Historical evidence indicates that with the decline of the Vedic era and the influx of foreign invaders, the status of women deteriorated further. It is said that the status of women was miserable and was at its lowest ebb before the advent of the Sikh religion in the sixteenth century.

Sikhism is a revolutionary religion in several ways and one of them is the position and status it gives women in society as well as in politics. The Sikh Gurus expressed great concern regarding the status of women in society and felt the need to give a place of honour to women. Guru Nanak, the first Sikh Guru, proclaimed unequivocally that woman was equal to man in all aspects, political, social, religious, economic, cultural and martial and was limited only by biological considerations. In *Asa di Var*, he asks, 'why then revile woman who giveth birth to great heroes? (Singh 1983). The Sikh Gurus were the first to protest against the evil of Sati. Guru Amar Das (the third Guru) said, 'Blessed are those Satis, who lead a life of contentment and chastity.' Thus among the followers of Sikhism widow remarriage was encouraged, the Purdah was discarded and women stepped out of their homes to assist menfolk whenever and wherever necessary. Even the Sikh baptism was made equally available to men and women.

In Sikhism, in brief, women have not only been considered equal to men but they have played a positive and significant role in Sikh history. They have stood shoulder to shoulder with men in war and peace, in religious, social and political service and in other walks of life. Darling (1929) while writing about Sikh women, stated that in central Punjab, the Sikh woman had a better position than any other of her counterparts. Among Muslims women do not go to the mosque but a Sikh wife accompanies her husband to the Gurdwara, and men and women worship there on an equal footing.

However, in spite of the positive role played by the Sikh religion in improving the status of women, the vast majority of women continued to be regarded as inferior to men, and suffered from various disabilities like the Purdah, child marriage and the practice of Sati etc.

With the advent of British rule, the process of emancipation of women became more rapid as the Britishers took various steps to improve the status of women and made special efforts to spread education among them. The result of educational changes, in the words of Yogindra Singh (1973), was two-fold: 'first the interjection of the western values and ideologies among the members of the new educated classes and secondly the rise of social and cultural reformation movement.' Various social movements like the Arya Samaj, Dev Samaj, Kuka and Akali movements also played a very important role in improving the status of women. Thereafter, the women of Punjab played a commendable role in the freedom struggle against the British rule. Raj Kumari Amrit Kaur, a princes of the Kapurthala ruling family gave up the pleasures of a princely home to fight for the independence of India and later on became the first Health Minister of independent India. Noor Jahan, Amrita Shergill and Amrita Pritam hold a place of pride in music, painting and literature.

Real changes in the status of women have been observed after India's independence. The influx of refugees from West Pakistan as a result of India's partition in 1947 accelerated the pace of change. Randhawa (1960) remarked that 'Society is undergoing radical change and new values are emerging.' According to him women in East Punjab before partition were socially backward and Purdah-ridden but after partition West Punjab refugees had a liberalizing influence on the women of East Punjab.

In recent years, due to the green revolution, education and social mobility, social life in these two states is in transition and the direction of change is from tradition to modernity. Education is spreading fast among women, especially in urban areas and educated women are increasingly taking to gainful employment. There is a marked change in the occupational pattern and now besides the traditional occupations of teachers, doctors and nurses, more and more women are going for non-traditional occupations. In the family too the trend is towards more equalitarian attitude and the norm of male superiority is meeting with resistance and the customary practice of Purdah has largely disappeared from the urban areas.

The changes are more prominent and rapid in urban areas, whereas in rural areas the life of a woman still centres round her farm, cattle and home. She is the first to get up and the last to go to bed. She milks the cow, churns butter, scrubs utensils and in the scorching heat of May and June she bakes hundreds of chapatis not only for the family but also for labourers hired for harvesting. She still observes Purdah (more so in Haryana) and remains confined to the four walls of the house.

In recent years the governments of Punjab and Haryana have taken various steps to improve the status of women in their respective states. They have opened women and children development and welfare corporations for the promotion of the economic welfare of women, particularly those from the weaker sections of society.

DEMOGRAPHIC PERSPECTIVE

Sex Ratio

In Punjab and Haryana the population is highly masculine as there are 886 and 870 females respectively for every 1,000 males. This is the second and third lowest in the country after Sikkim. In Punjab sex disparity was much higher in 1901 (832 females per 1,000 males) but during the past eighty years it has improved. Various reasons like higher female mortality, higher under-enumeration of females, greater preference for sons, neglect of female babies and general neglect of women are attributed to it.

The census data reveal that female infants are subject to greater risks of mortality than males in the Northern states of Punjab, Haryana, Rajasthan and Uttar Pradesh. In Punjab, girls are considered another man's wealth (Begana Dhan) while sons are one's own. Griffin (1909) in the earlier years of this century mentioned that 'the girls are sacrificed in order that loans for their marriage expenses may not encumber the land descending to the sons. The birth of a daughter is regarded as the equivalent of decree for Rs 2000 against the father.' He further says that Maharaja Ranjit Singh's own mother, as an infant, had a narrow escape from the custom of female infanticide and there are numerous reports and surveys that bear out the fact that there is a gross neglect of female infants and babies. Girls and women suffer from many disadvantages that shorten their lives. This is supported by the Khanna study (1971) which shows that the death rate at every age is higher for females (Table 1). This fact can be further substantiated from the sex differentials in the life expectation of males and females in these states (Table 2).

Regarding sex differentials in under-enumeration of females in the census, the results of the post-enumeration check for the 1971 census (Table 3) reveal that among the four groups of status, group A comprising the four southern states shows the lowest net omission for

TABLE 1
Sex-wise Death Rate in Different Age Groups (Khanna study)

Age group	Males	Females
1-14	19.2	28.8
15-44	1.9	5.2
45+	30.7	31.9
All age groups	14.6	19.1

TABLE 2
Life Expectation at Birth for Males and Females

State	Males	Females	Total
Punjab	59.0	56.8	57.9
Haryana	59.0	55.6	57.5

Source: *SRS Bulletin*, 1984 Vol. XVIII.

TABLE 3
Net Omission Rate per 1000 Enumerated Persons by Sex and Groups of States, 1971

Sex	Group of States			
	A	B	C	D
Male	11.4	14.6	18.1	16.9
Female	12.9	16.6	19.2	25.9

Source: Post enumeration checks—Preliminary results 1971 census.

both males and females. The highest omission of females is observed in group D (Haryana, Punjab, Delhi and Uttar Pradesh). Further the sex differential in undercount is most marked in the northern group which is more deficit in females compared to other groups. Thus sex differentials in undercount vary between regions and female undercount is comparatively higher in the northern region compared to other regions mainly because girls are considered another man's property and hence not counted whereas sons are one's own.

An important consequence of fewer women than men in Punjab is that a number of peasants especially the Jat Sikhs have to stay either unmarried or practise polyandry. Virk (1963) mentions that it is a nightmare for the mother and father and hell on earth for the old bachelor. In the midst of a civilization that has a long known history and limitless future, the unmarried man in Punjab looks ephemeral. As soon as he dies, his land will be divided among his brothers or their sons and his line will come to an end. A tremendous lot of folklore has grown up around this tragic figure who is called Chara (single).

Age at Marriage

The census data indicate that the mean age at marriage for females is on the increase in both the states. The mean age at marriage for females in Punjab and Haryana works out to be 21.12 and 18.22 respectively. In 1981, of the fourteen major states, Punjab occupied the second position in age at marriage, Kerala being the first, whereas Haryana occupied the tenth position. It has been further observed that age at marriage is higher in urban than rural areas. Communitywise, in both the states the Sikhs have a higher age at marriage than other religious groups. There is no direct evidence of child marriage in these states but the census data of 1981 show that 6.97 per cent of the women in Haryana were married in the age group of 10–14 years but this percentage was only 1.33 in Punjab. This indicates that early marriage still persists and its incidence is more in Haryana than in Punjab.

Thus Punjab is ahead of Haryana in terms of female age at marriage and this might be due to comparatively higher female literacy rates in Punjab. Minkler (1970) while pointing out the impact of the Green Revolution states that the intensification of agriculture in rural Punjab has considerably increased the work load of farming families both at home and in the fields. Since there is considerable demand for agricultural labour particularly during the peak agriculture seasons, girls from the families of landless labourers too, are in a position to earn wages to provide not only additional income for their families but also earn a part of their dowries. They are therefore, kept unmarried for a longer time.

Migration

Migration is an important factor as it can affect several aspects of a woman's life. Migrating women may be pushed into the labour force if they are heads of households. They may also have greater freedom and opportunities for education in some cases. A closer look at the 1981 census shows that in Punjab migrants constituted 35.16 per cent of the total population of which 22.13 per cent were males and almost 50 per cent were females. Similarly in Haryana, migrants constituted 32.5 per cent of the total population, out of which 17.97 per cent were males and almost 50 per cent were females. Another important fact is that among female migrants within the state nearly 80 per cent in both the states are rural-to-rural migrants, and a very small proportion of them are rural-to-urban migrants. This short-distance migration is mostly due to marriage. This has been further substantiated from the reasons for migration (which have been analysed in the 1981 census). In both the states marriage is the main reason for female migration. The proportion of women who have moved to other places because of employment or education is very small in Punjab and much smaller in Haryana indicating thereby that in these states women still do not usually move autonomously for the sake of employment or education.

SOCIO-ECONOMIC AND FAMILIAL PERSPECTIVE

Literacy and Educational Level

The position of women's education was rather disappointing in the past. The custom of early marriage and the conservatism of the people were the main reasons for the slow growth of education among women. Moreover, there was a dearth of women teachers and separate schools for girls. Still, before India's independence various socio-religious organizations like the Arya Samaj, the Dev Samaj, the Singh Sabha and the Chief Khalsa Diwan and the Muslim Anjumans played a significant role in the spread of women's education. The British government also took interest in the education of women. The report on the progress of women in the Punjab for the year 1938–39 remarked that 'the limiting factor has usually been a matter of finance and not the apathy of the people' (Proceedings of the Dept. of Education, Punjab 1938–39). Since India's independence rapid changes have been taking place in improving women's education. There has been a significant increase in the number and percentage of institutions as well as women scholars in both the states.

According to the 1981 census, the female literacy rate in Punjab and Haryana is 34.14 and 22.23 per cent respectively as against 24.88 per cent for the country as a whole (Table 4).

TABLE 4
Area and Sex-wise Literacy Rates in Punjab and Haryana in 1981

| | Punjab | | Haryana | | India | |
	M	F	M	F	M	F
Total	46.59	34.14	47.18	22.23	46.72	24.81
Rural	40.91	28.35	42.87	15.34	40.62	17.99
Urban	61.12	49.57	64.89	47.23	65.58	47.65

Source: *Census of India*, Series I Paper 3 of 1981.

The data show that the female literacy rates in Punjab are fairly above the national level whereas in Haryana they are lower in the total as well as in rural-urban areas. Another important fact is that the gap between male and female literacy is comparatively much wider in Haryana, especially in rural areas. It further shows that the gap between rural and urban female literacy is also much wider indicating thereby that, firstly, female literacy in general in Haryana is less than half of the male literacy and secondly, rural female literacy is much lower than male literacy in the state.

Apart from the rural-urban variations, the level of female literacy also varies with the level of socio-economic development of the district; for example, in Punjab, female literacy rates are fairly high in Majha and Doaba (Amritsar, Jullunder, Kapurthala, Hoshiarpur, Ropar, Ludhiana etc.) but significantly low in Malwa (Sangrur, Bhatinda, Faridkot and Ferozepur) as these districts are comparatively less developed. Similar variations exist in Haryana and female literacy rates are much lower in comparatively less developed districts of Jind, Bhiwani, Hissar and Sirsa.

Literacy rates also varied between the Sikhs and the Hindus. The Singh Sabha and Akali Movement laid great emphasis on female literacy and opened various schools for women. Darling (1934) states that 'it is typical of the Sikh that he is almost as eager for the education of his daughter as his son, for the double reason that she may be able to read the Granth Sahib and be an economical wife.' Kapur (1986) also states that the 'Singh Sabha emphasis on female education among Sikhs ensured an even higher proportion of females literate among the Sikhs than among the other communities in Punjab.'

A more realistic character of the progress of female education is the female enrolment in schools. In Punjab the total female enrolment is 43.6 per cent of the total enrolment whereas in Haryana it is 39 per cent. On the whole in both the states the percentage increase in women's enrolment, relatively speaking, is much more in the primary stage indicating thereby a higher dropout rate at higher age groups. Although on the whole in both the states there has been a phenomenal increase in women's education, still Haryana lags behind Punjab as one of the major fourteen states. Punjab occupies the third place whereas Haryana occupies the eighth position in terms of female literacy.

Employment

An important variable that is closely related to the status of women is their work role, particularly their employment outside the home. The census data indicate that female labour force participation rates are the lowest in the country in these two states. Punjab in fact has the lowest proportion of female workers and Haryana has the second lowest. Various reasons have been attributed to it. Throughout the past, this part of India was the scene of frequent invasions from the west by the Aryans, the Greeks, the Huns and the Mughals etc. The recurrent wars here necessitated a closed society for the females in which they were to remain in Chardwari (the four walls of the house) and Purdah. Chandna (1967) also points out that in Punjab women belonging to the upper castes do not participate in agricultural activities at all, because of cultural taboos. The cultural history of the region does not allow much freedom and mobility to females and discourages their participation in outdoor activities. D'Souza (1975) argues that in Punjab women usually work only when there are economic compulsions; when it becomes unavoidable due to some other reason, men allow their women to enter the labour force and they like to withdraw them as soon as their status has improved.

There are significant variations within each state in the proportion of female workers to total female population. In Punjab the proportion of female workers is comparatively low in the Malwa area (Sangrur, Bhatinda and Faridkot). These are comparatively less developed areas and the proportion of scheduled caste population is also low in them. In Haryana the areas lying south of the Ghaggar river (Bhiwani, Sonepat, Rohtak, Hissar and Jind) have moderate to relatively high female participation in work. Even before Punjab's reorganization these areas had much higher (30 per cent) proportion of females in the working force. As mentioned by Chandna (1967) the cultural background of the people of this part of Haryana approves of female participation and the economic hardship forces females to join with males in the economic field. The predominantly agrarian economy, the social backwardness of the people and poor literacy standards, are some of the factors associated with high female participation in work in this part of Haryana.

An analysis of the data on occupational structure for India as a whole reveals that the bulk of the female labour force is concentrated in rural areas and absorbed in agriculture-related activities. But the situation is just the reverse in Punjab (Table 5) where the proportion of female workers is more in urban areas. In Haryana too, it was so till 1971 but since 1981 the proportion of rural female workers has increased.

TABLE 5

Percentage of Female Workers in Agriculture, Household Industry and other Workers in 1971 and 1981

State	Cultivators		Agricultural Labour		Household industry		Other workers	
	1971	1981	1971	1981	1971	1981	1971	1981
Punjab	5.58	10.42	10.92	26.95	7.21	6.53	76.29	56.00
Haryana	36.96	49.30	25.96	22.20	3.97	2.85	33.11	25.00

Another important aspect of the occupational structure of these states is that in Punjab 37 per cent of females are involved in agriculture-related activities and 56 per cent are other workers and this means that more women in the state are engaged in manufacturing processes and other services than the two main agricultural occupations of cultivators and agricultural labourers. However, in Haryana nearly 50 per cent of the females are cultivators and another 22 per cent are agricultural workers. In Haryana the proportion of female workers engaged in agriculture-related activities is even more than that of men. This is why it is said that in contrast to a Sikh Jat farmer who considers it below his dignity to allow females to work outdoors a Hindu Jat farmer has no such inhibitions. Women in Haryana are actively involved in agriculture and they even plough the fields.

However, the 1981 census has revealed a significant increase in female workers in both the states. In Punjab, the green revolution has resulted in rapid increase in agricultural productivity, which in turn has created a new demand for labour supply. This is evident from the fact that Punjab has attracted a large number of migrant workers from the other states (Sethi 1984). There has also been a change in the cropping pattern in Punjab during the last decade because of which rice and vegetables have become important new crops. The growth of these crops is associated with the requirement of female labour (Garewal 1980). In Haryana too the increase in women's activity rate may be partly due to agricultural and industrial development and partly due to the rapid development of industrial centres at Faridabad, Sonepat and Bahadurgarh.

Marriage and Family

Monogamy is the most widely practised form of marriage in Punjab and Haryana but in the past a second wife was sometimes taken if the first wife was barren or gave birth only to female children (Reed 1908). Polygamous unions are however not altogether unknown. Several writers have reported the existence of polyandry among Jat Sikhs and other low castes where two or three brothers sometimes share a wife (Westermarck 1926, Singh 1976).

The incidence of dowry is fairly common and high in both the states although there are some intra-regional variations. For instance, in Punjab the incidence of dowry is found to be much more in Majha and Malwa than in Doaba. In Majha it is more because of the prosperous farm economy of the region while in Malwa it remains a legacy of the erstwhile feudal order. Doaba is a region of small land holdings and a substantial portion of displaced persons.

Although divorce did not exist as a recognized institution in the past, a person was at liberty to sever all connections with his wife if she did not give birth to a male child or was unchaste. Widow remarriage was also generally not allowed. The relation between husband and wife was a sacrament indissoluble save by death. But widow remarriage was common among the Jats and other agricultural castes, artisans and menial classes (Census 1911).

Both the states have a patriarchal society and follow patrilineal mode of descent. The male is the perpetuator of the line and the family name. The common mode of family organization among land-owning people is the joint family though this pattern has been undergoing considerable change due to urbanization, modernization and social mobility.

As indicated by Karve (1968) in the family there are two sets of women. In the first set are women who are brought to the house as brides, wives and daughters-in-law and to the second belong women who are born in the family, i.e., sister or daughter. Different codes of behaviour for daughter and daughter-in-law are prescribed. A daughter-in-law is expected to adjust herself to her in-laws' household and she is usually placed under several restrictions particularly in rural areas, and she has little say in decision making and is subordinate to her mother-in-law. She has to show deferential manners to all elders in the household. Her status in the family depends partly on her husband's contribution to the family economy and the amount of dowry she brings and partly on the number of sons she produces. On the other hand a daughter has great freedom at her father's place and uses it even when she comes back. Leaf (1972) in his study of a Sikh village says that when a girl approaches the marriageable age, the sense of future parting becomes prominent and the girl is treated with the greatest solicitude. She is given lighter work and better clothes, not only to make herself happy, but also to make her more desirable as a wife through showing her person and her family in a good light.

In the family there is a strong desire for male children. The birth of a male child is considered auspicious and celebrated jubilantly, whereas the birth of a female is a matter of great misfortune. That is why Darling (1934) says: 'Feed son and bullock well: both are bread winners.' The social status of a woman who gives birth to more female children is lowered in society. From the very beginning girls are reared in a different manner.

The practice of Purdah still exists in rural areas especially in the presence of the father-in-law and the elder brother of the husband. In villages it is mainly confined to the higher castes and the gentry or to those who would pass as such. It is typified by the veil which is drawn across the face. The rigour of full Purdah according to Darling (1934) derives from the terrors of past invasions but the veil owes its origin to the rules and restrictions of the joint family system. A woman must veil herself in the presence of an elder, superior or stranger. They also forbid all communication between a daughter-in-law and a father-in-law and even between a wife and her husband's elder brother. The Purdah is much more widely prevalent in Haryana than in Punjab. The report of the National Committee on the Status of Women (1974) pointed out that the highest percentage (72.61 per cent) of women in Haryana observed Purdah before the father-in-law whereas this percentage was 44.6 per cent in Punjab.

Inheritance

In Punjab, the Mitakshara school of law is prevalent. In addition to being governed by the Hindu Personal Law, people are also governed by customary law. Since the passing of the Hindu Marriage Act of 1955, the Hindu Succession Act of 1956, Hindu Minority and Guardianship Act of 1956, also apply to Punjab.

With the introduction of the Hindu Succession Act 1956, the customary practice of inheritance has undergone a change. In accordance with the provisions of this act the property of the deceased is distributed equally among sons and daughters, widow and mother. But it has not been accepted by the people and therefore in actuality the Act is found to be not implemented at all. Even the Punjab Legislative Assembly made an endeavour to exclude the daughters from the right of inheriting the family land. In 1960, a corresponding bill was placed before the Punjab Assembly. It was accepted by the Cabinet in 1968, but fell through in the Punjab Assembly the following year (Mies 1980). Sibia's (1985) study reveals that women are rarely given a share in the father's property. The level of awareness regarding the Act was found to be very high in both the states but at the opinion level there was very little approval of it. The main argument of men against the Act was that giving a share to a daughter in the father's property would create many problems. It would lead to fragmentation and subdivision of the family land. It would also lead to the sale of ancestral property because of the exogamous nature of marriage, and since in Punjab there existed a right to pre-emption on the sale of ancestral property it would give rise to many problems. Moreover, it was said that the daughters did get a share of the family property at the time of marriage in the form of dowry and therefore, had no right to a share in the family land.

POLITICAL STATUS

The political status of women can be judged from their political awareness, voting behaviour and freedom enjoyed by them in shaping or sharing power.

In both these states, as far as Assembly seats are concerned, women's participation is very low. In Punjab since 1965 the percentage of women in the Assembly has not been more than 2 to 3 except in 1977 (5 per cent) and in 1985 (6 per cent). In Haryana the highest percentage was in 1968 when women had 9 per cent seats in the Assembly whereas in 1982 they had 6 per cent seats.

Women's position in various political parties including the ruling party is also not very impressive. Also, there are no women trade union leaders.

The report of the National Committee on the Status of Women (1974) reported that in Punjab women voters in urban areas had outstripped the men but not in Haryana. A study conducted in Haryana (Mittal) shows that there is no correlation between the level of literacy in the district and the level of female participation in politics.

HEALTH, FERTILITY AND FAMILY PLANNING

The health status of women is one of the major concerns of society. The health status of women and children, particularly of mothers, is the concern of the government in both these states and the state health services are organized at the district level.

Women in these states have benefited from the general decline in mortality. Their sex ratio has been improving, maternal mortality and female infant mortality rate has come down and there is an increase in their life expectation. In Punjab, in 1901 the sex ratio was 120 whereas in 1981 it became 114 per 100 females while in Haryana it was 116 in 1901 and it came down to 114 in 1981. Similarly female infant mortality in Punjab and Haryana was found to be 110 and 113 respectively in 1981 as against 135 for the country as a whole. Female life expectancy was 56.8 years for Punjab and 55.6 years for Haryana in 1981 and the corresponding figure for India was 49 years.

In spite of these improvements, female infant mortality is still higher than male infant mortality, and life expectancy is lower than that of males.

Fertility level in Punjab and Haryana

The two important indicators of fertility, namely child-woman ratio and total fertility, show declining trends. The table below shows the total fertility and child-woman ratio in both the states (see Table 6).

TABLE 6
Total Fertility and Child-woman Ratio in Punjab and Haryana in 1971 and 1981

State	Total Fertility		CWR	
	1971	1981	1971	1981
Punjab	6.32	5.28	6.11	5.12
Haryana	6.68	6.21	7.81	6.20
India	5.78	4.99	6.55	5.46

Source: *Family Planning Year Book 1983–84.*

Although the data show a declining trend in fertility still it is higher than the national level. The birth rate was 30.3 and 36.5 for Punjab and Haryana respectively in 1981 and the corresponding rate for the country was 33.9. All these data show that fertility is declining in both the states and the decline is more in Punjab than Haryana.

The fertility level in a given region depends upon the number of women in the reproductive age group and the acceptance of family planning. The data indicate that in 1981 the proportion of females in the reproductive age group of 15–44 years for Punjab and Haryana was 80.64 and 69.39 per cent respectively while the corresponding percentage for the country as a whole was 83.90.

A close look at the acceptance of family planning reveals that the percentage of couples effectively protected by all methods is fairly high in Punjab and Haryana: it is 42.9 and 40.2 per cent respectively in Punjab and Haryana as against 29.2 per cent at the national level. In fact Punjab and Haryana occupy the second (Maharashtra being first) and third position in this respect.

Thus on the whole health services have improved and fertility has been declining in both the states, the decline being comparatively higher in Punjab. The greater decline in Punjab may be attributed to higher age at marriage, higher literacy rates, lower proportion of women in the reproductive age and greater acceptance of family planning.

REFERENCES

Chandana, R.C., 1967. 'Female Working Force of Rural Punjab,' *Manpower Journal*, Vol. 2, No. 4.

Darling, M., 1934. *Wisdom and Waste in Punjab Villages* (Humphrey, Milford: Oxford University Press).

D'Souza, V.S., 1975. 'Family Status and Female Work Participation,' in Alfred de Souza (ed.) *Women in Contemporary India* (New Delhi: Manpower).

Garewal, D.S., 1980. *Agricultural Labour in Rural India*, Panjab University (unpublished dissertation).

Government of India, 1983–84. *Family Welfare Programme in India, Year Book*.

Griffin, L.H., 1909. *Chiefs and Families of Note in Punjab* (Lahore: Minerva).

ICSSR, 1974. *Status of Women in India, the Report of the National Committee on the Status of Women*.

Kapor, R., 1986. *Sikh Separatism—the Politics of Faith*. (London: Allen and Unwin).

Karve, Irawati, 1968. *Kinship Organization in India* (Bombay: Asia).

Leaf, M.J., 1972. *Information and Behaviour in a Sikh Village: Social Organization Reconsidered* (New Delhi: Oxford University Press).

Mies, Maria, 1980. *Indian Women and Patriarchy* (New Delhi: Concept).

Minkler, M., 1970. 'Fertility and Labour Force Participation,' in *Journal of Family Welfare*, Vol. XVII, No. 1.

Randhawa, M.S., 1960. *Out of Ashes* (New Delhi: Oxford University Press).

Rees, J.D., 1908. *The Real India*.

Saini, B.S., 1977. *The Social and Economic History of the Punjab 1901–1939* (Delhi: Ess Ess).

Sethi, R.M., 1984. 'Changing Pattern of Female Labour in Agriculture: the Case of Punjab,' in *Social Action*, Vol. 34, October-December.

Sibia, Kiran, 1985. *Hindu Personal Laws Pertaining to a Study of Their Perception by Rural Women*, Panjab University (unpublished M. Phil dissertation).

Singh, Harbans, 1983. 'Status of Women in Sikhism,' in Yash Kohli (ed.), *The Women of Punjab* (Bombay: Chic).

Singh, K.P., 1980. 'Economic Development and Female Labour Force Participation: The case of Punjab,' *Social Action*, Vol. 30, April-June.

Singh, K.P., 1976. 'Polyandry among the Jat Sikhs of Punjab,' paper presented at the *Thirteenth All India Sociological Conference*.

Singh, Yogindra, 1973. *Modernization of Indian Traditions* (Faridabad: Thomson Press).

Westermarck, E., 1926. *The History of Human Marriage*, Vol. III, (London: Macmillan).

Wyon, J.B. and J.E. Gordon, 1971. *The Khanna Study* (New York: Harvard University Press).

Virk, K.S., 1983. 'Sandu's Punjab,' in Marcus Franda (ed.), *Punjabis, War and Women*.

Status of Women in Western India

MALINI KARKAL

Issues with respect to the status of women in India are distinctly different from those of the women in the now industrialized countries. The history of women's status in India has to be traced from its very source in order to get at the right psychological background. The issues connected with the status of women in India therefore are different from those that are discussed in the context of women in the West. Man has not questioned woman's right to enter any field of activity, or any profession, although he has held complete sway everywhere for many years now, keeping the women out and restricting their influence and scope of work by rigid rules and customs. The movement for bringing about an awakening among women is thus not a rebellion or a revolt against men; it is rather an attempt to regain lost ground. Women in India have to fight more against unjust customs than against unfair laws.

WOMEN IN WESTERN INDIA: IN RETROSPECT

Many of the changes in the life of women in Western India can be traced to the British rule. The British conquered Western India in two main stages in the nineteenth century. Gujarat fell to them in 1803, and the greater part of the erstwhile Bombay Presidency in 1818. Sind was annexed in 1843 and North Canara was transferred to Bombay from the Madras Presidency in 1862. Before the conquest of this region by the British, the family, caste and the village community were the three basic social institutions (Sovani 1965). The chief means of living of the people was agriculture. During the Maratha rule agriculture flourished. Divekar writes:

> their system of granting liberally hereditary, rent-free 'inams' and 'vatans' supported the growth of agriculture and expansion of tillage area. Special revenue concessions were given for reclamation

of waste lands, for undertaking irrigational work etc. This helped in the expansion of tillage area, continuous rise in the number of landlords and increase in the village revenue collection.

Birthshere introduced the Raitwari system in the Bombay Presidency which undermined the position of the village headman and also weakened the solidarity of the village. It set aside the joint responsibility of the village and the joint estates of the Mirasdars and the British measured individual family holding separately. The British made rules which made it more easy to alienate and transfer land.

Elphinstone's report in 1819 and Chaplin's reports of 1821 and 1822 categorically mentioned that under the British the existence of well-knit village communities under a recognized village head and the prevalence of heritable land rights among cultivators, paying a fixed land tax to the government, was threatened. The Raitwari system introduced by the British generated as much upward mobility as downward mobility—it made the rich peasants richer and poor peasants poorer. Some of them lost their land, which increased stratification, and led to the pauperization of small peasants. They often resigned themselves to the status of tenant cultivators as landless labourers. These poorer sections of the society were unable to cope with the market-oriented cash economy and on the other hand there was the rise of the prosperous peasant class of a few within the framework of a market economy (Kumar 1983).

During this period of the early nineteenth century the agriculturists supplemented their incomes through several cottage industries. Among these were oil pressing, pottery, and textiles. Since most of the work was done in the homes, women played an important productive role. In the Raitwari system introduced by the British in which individual ownership of the land was established, usually the allotment was made in the name of the male head of the household which undermined the land rights of women. Traditions of joint ownership were eroded undermining women's control over resources, increasing the power of the male heads of households. Rogers (1980) has noted that

the western concept of outright ownership by a single individual as the basis for land tenure has had the effect of suppressing the practice of joint ownership, or qualified rights to land and other resources in which women participate. The right to land and control over its use were almost invariably ascribed to men.

This situation was worsened by more and more land coming under cultivation and denying women access to wasteland and communal land of the village for gathering fuel, fodder and some forest products for sale. Thus lack of control over resources, loss of land rights and restricted use of waste and communal land made women more subordinate and marginalized.

A most important consequence of the British impact on the Indian social structure was the increase in the strength and importance of the middle class. There was an expansion of trading and merchant communities and of government service as well as liberal professions. Over the years the size of the middle class continued to increase (Martin 1837). Under these circumstances, women lost their active participation in social development.

The main items of export from India in the eighteenth century were cotton textiles, sugar, coffee, spices and saltpetre. The East India Company in its initial stages was making money by exporting Indian silk, muslin and other luxury goods to England. The money earned in this trade was sent to England and many economic historians believe that the capital for industrial revolution in England came from overseas, especially from India. The development of industries in Britain was supported by capturing vast Indian markets for their products. The worst effect of this development was on Bombay. Manufactured British goods were imported in return for Indian raw material, thus destroying the well-established native weaving industry. Indian cotton fabrics were prohibited and replaced by cheap cotton fabrics produced on the machines in Lancashire. Wilson wrote (in 1813) that the cotton and silk goods of India could be sold at a profit in the British market at a price from 50 to 60 per cent lower than those fabricated in England. The English products were therefore protected by duties of 70 to 80 per cent on the Indian goods. British goods were forced upon India without paying any duty and the foreign manufacturer employed the arm of political injustice to keep down and ultimately strangle a competitor with whom he would not have contended on equal terms (Dutt Ramesh 1882, *Economic History of British India*, Reprinted in 1960 by Govt. of India, Ministry of Information and Broadcasting, New Delhi, pp. 262–63).

In the seventeenth and eighteenth centuries Britain was able to supply very few commodities that were acceptable to India but in the nineteenth century the pattern of Indian economic life was drastically changed and the home-based handloom cotton industry was under-mined. The Governor General reported in 1834–35: 'the misery hardly finds a parallel in the history of commerce. The bones of cotton weavers are bleaching the plains of India' (Sen 1979).

Women's Movements

The divisiveness of social reform and the rediscovery of India's past led to the Hindu elite to seek a religious foundation for reform movements during the second half of the nineteenth century. Maharashtrian Brahmins founded the Prarthana Samaj, a religious association, after a visit from the Brahmo leader Keshab Chandra Sen in 1867. Its leaders included Sanskrit Professor R.G. Bhandarkar and judges M.G. Ranade and N.G. Chandravarkar. The activities of the Brahmo Samaj encouraged participation of women through the for-mation of Arya Mahila Samaj in 1882 under the leadership of Pandita Ramabai. M.G. Ranade spearheaded the movement asking for government funds for a girls' high school (1882) and legal authority to discourage child marriage (the Age of Consent Act of 1891). The National Social Conference (NSC) was formed in 1887 to discuss social reforms. During the early years the NSC worked with the National Congress. B.G. Tilak bitterly opposed the girls' school, the NSC and the Age of Consent legislation on the grounds that Hindus were sufficiently confident to govern themselves. He argued that Hindus should voluntarily pledge not to marry their daughters until they were of age (Dobbin 1972).

According to Heimsath (1964), even the NSC replaced western values with Indian sources of inspiration. In 1904, its leadership organized a women's section which held annual conference during the NSC sessions. The conference, the Bharat Mahila Parishad (BMP) organized educational and inspirational programmes.

A set of women's institutions, which reflected revivalist values, was founded by D.K. Karve, who was a Professor at Fergusson College. Karve had married a widow in 1893, and had established a widows' home in 1896 where child widows could be educated to become self-supporting. The latter might have been an attempt to compete with Pandita Ramabai's widows' home where child widows were converted to Christianity. In 1907, Karve opened a girls' school and in 1916, he founded the SNDT Indian Women's University. In each of these institutions Karve put into practice his ideas on women's education. He was opposed to offering a British-style education to women and believed that men and women should be educated for their very different roles in life (Jana 1978).

The Bombay Presidency Women's Council (BPWC) was founded in 1918 by Lady Tata and others. This association co-ordinated the activities of women's association in the Bombay Presidency and later joined the National Council of Women in India (NCWI) founded in 1925 by Lady Aberdeen of the International Council of Women. At the National Conferences of these organizations the issues discussed were women's education and the social customs which obstructed access to education.

The All India Women's Conference (AIWC), established in 1927, was primarily concerned with influencing government policy on women in the fields of education, social service, personal law, suffrage, employment and health. The AIWC leaders used various strategies to influence government policy: (*a*) presenting views to government officials at all levels; (*b*) forming committees to investigate conditions and to increase public support for the AIWC demands; and (*c*) demanding that women be selected to sit on official bodies. The AIWC was also involved in other activities. A women's educational fund was established to raise money for the Lady Irwin College, founded in 1932 to offer courses in home economics for women. In the 1930s the AIWC began to support the idea of contraception and advocated birth control instruction in recognized clinics. The constituent conferences of the AIWC debated the policy issues of the central organization and engaged in social service activities, such as raising money for causes, holding adult education classes, establishing rescue homes, and training nurses (Jana 1978).

Like other parts of the country, Western India was influenced by Gandhiji from 1920 onwards. His ideology was very respectful to women and supportive to their upliftment and his leadership encouraged the growth of the women's movement. Gandhiji's ideology and techniques inspired women to participate in public activities and broke down opposition to their entry into social service and nationalist association. His campaign served as a training ground for many women's movement leaders—Hansa Mehta, Durgabai, Kamala Devi Chattopadhyaya and Jaishri Raiji (Mothan 1929).

Industrialization and Women

The rise of powerlooms in cities established under the British destroyed handweaving of certain kinds produced earlier in many parts of the Bombay Presidency. Among the well known were the handlooms from Sind, Karnataka, Surat, Navsari, Baroda etc. The bulk of the outward trade was to Persian Gulf and South East Asia (Enthoven 1986). Thus ended the trade of Surat brocade and Kirkhabs, calico cloth and other such specially woven textiles and the skills that women had developed in these weavings.

In the initial stages, the influence of the British trade was largely confined to urban areas. The demand for goods was much larger in rural areas which had larger populations, but because of bad transportation British goods could not reach the rural areas. This need was met by laying railway lines in 1856. With a well-laid railway network there was considerable expansion in demand for imported goods.

This development was followed by the establishment of powerlooms in many cities. Joshi (1936) says:

> There was a gradual rise in the number of looms in large centres. Smaller centres which were less organised were gradually decaying. The opening of the railways had made the competition of imported and Indian piece goods more intense and the sphere of the handloom was restricted to low count production. In plain clothing and medium counts, the handlooms were yielding place to their machine rivals. At the same time mills had begun to provide coarse yarn to the industry in large quantities.

With the establishment of cotton mills in Bombay, Ahmedabad, Nadiad, Surat, Kaira etc., the handloom industry which gave productive occupation to the men and women in their homes was shifted to organized city centres. Many employment opportunities were available to men and some to women in these mills. Some of the women who opted for these jobs were engaged in occupations which were of lower status than those for men. Also these jobs caused considerable strain on the health of the women and disrupted their family life affecting the upbringing of children and general housekeeping.

By the end of the nineteenth century, such flourishing crafts as handlooms, pottery, brass and ball metalware, Jari goods, were seriously affected by the goods imported from Britain as well as the products of organized industries. The craftsmen who earlier had a comfortable life were driven to a hand-to-mouth existence. Women on the one hand were removed from their earlier productive role and on the other hand had to face the consequences of growing impoverishment. Of course, skilled workmen in larger towns found employment. However, a majority of the rural households were resigned to poverty and crushed under growing indebtedness.

Women in Agriculture

In the pre-British period farmers grew food crops and women played an important role in their cultivation and they were in possession of enough grains for family consumption. With the advent of the British, the cultivators were forced to grow cash crops, instead of food crops, so that there was an increase in the cash revenue to the British. With the cash economy, women lost access to the food grains as well as to the cash. This increased the problems of women in meeting the needs of the family. Many cash crops were labour-intensive and women had to contribute to the land agricultural work whereas the cash obtained through the sale of the produce reached men.

Monetization of the rural agricultural economy affected women's position in the family as control of production and women's labour shifted to the male members of the family. Thus the second half of the nineteenth century saw great changes in the economic role of women. The separation of home from the business premises also ended the active share of women in their husbands' work. This in turn led to the loss of the experience which women had in particular crafts. Except by becoming wage earners outside the home, women could not contribute to the family resources and thus became financially dependent on their husbands. In a social system where women were not encouraged to participate in activities outside home employment, opportunities generated by industrialization were not freely available to them. Thus women who were driven out of home-based industries had no avenues open for paid jobs.

With reduction in their productive capacity women came to be seen as burdens on the family. Further, with no alternatives to keep them gainfully engaged the employed or occupied girls were given away in marriage at very young ages. Early marriage and child bearing made women less desirable as employees and their family responsibility restricted the women's occupational mobility. The decline of the handicraft industry also brought about an increase in male unemployment which further restricted employment opportunities for women. The family land could not support the increased population and men migrated on a large scale to industrial areas such as Bombay, in search of employment, leaving women and children without family support and protection.

Morris (1966) observes:

> The women typically remained behind to be taken care of by the corporate group. The joint family tended to restrict the migration of women, it would seem that typically women migrated only when whole families moved. The limited movement of women is suggested by the fact that unlike the British and New England textile towns, Bombay was a very heavily masculine centre. It was not the individual but the family, even though based in countryside, that became the factory proletariate.

He felt that, apart from jointness, shortage of housing and instability of employment, made a complete severance of rural ties unwise if not impossible.

After the Industrial Revolution, England gained the industrial leadership of the world. As a highly industrialized country, England's interests were mainly confined to the development of industries and mining in India, foreign trade, exchange, currency, banking, British investments, development of railways and roads, shipping, political reforms, defence, recruitment to the Indian army and the covenanted services etc.

Macaulay in 1835 laid the policy of English education in India. In 1844 the government declared that in government services preference would be given to those who had English education. In the kinds of employment mentioned above women had practically no role. They were therefore ignored in planning education, and kept out of developments in the field of education.

The British administrative system pressed itself heavily on the Indian people by its sheer weight and efficiency and the Indian people progressively lost their initiative and self-reliance. The village Panchayats suffered an eclipse simply because all decision-making power became concentrated in the hands of the all-powerful bureaucracy. Self-rule in the villages progressively ceased. As the new law courts and the new system of justice became popular, the judicial function of the village Panchayats fell into disuse. The autonomous character of the village was gradually lost. It became a cog in the administrative wheel (Sovani 1965).

EDUCATION

Literacy, which is defined by the census as the ability to read and write with understanding in any language, is the lowest measure for the development in education that has been achieved. The overall literacy rate in the population of Maharashtra showed an increase from 39.18 (1971) to 47.18 (1981). However, there were wide disparities between the rates for the males and the females. The literacy rates for males showed an increase from 51.04 (1971) to 58.79 (1981), whereas the rates for females were 26.43 (1971) and 34.79 (1981).

Again differences are observed in the urban and rural population. Literacy rate for the urban males increased from 66.88 to 71.80 whereas that for females showed a rise from 47.33 to 54.65. The rates for the rural males were 43.22 and 51.25 respectively whereas those for the females were 17.84 and 24.88 respectively. These figures indicate that among rural women who constitute almost two out of three women in Maharashtra, only one in every four women is literate. Among the urban women every second one is illiterate.

The literacy rate for Gujarat is slightly lower than that in Maharashtra. The rate shows an increase from 35.79 (1971) to 43.70 (1981). For the males, the rate has increased from 46.11 (1971) to 54.44 (1981) and for females it has risen from 24.75 (1971) to 32.30 (1981).

As in Maharashtra, in Gujarat too the literacy rates show wide differences for rural and urban population. The literacy rate for urban males was 63.96 (1971) and it showed an increase to 68.62 (1981) whereas amongst the urban females the rate was 44.77 (1971) and it increased to 51.13 (1981). The literacy level of rural males was 38.92 (1971) and it increased to 47.85 (1981) and for rural females the figures were 17.19 (1971) and 24.08 (1981). The above figures show larger gains in the literacy levels of females, yet their overall level of literacy is much lower than that of males. A look at the data at higher ages and for higher educational levels shows that the dropout rate amongst females shows a rising trend both in itself and also when compared with that for the males.

LABOUR FORCE PARTICIPATION

The census defines work as participation in economically productive activity. For the state of Maharashtra the work participation rate for males showed an increase from 52.09 per cent (1971) to 52.51 per cent (1981) and for the females from 19.07 per cent (1971) to 23.98 per cent (1981). Participation rates for the males increased only in the age group 15–19 and declined in all other age groups. In contrast, for the females participation rate increased in all the age groups between 15 and 59 years, varying from three to seven points. Also, while an increase in female work participation is shown both in the rural and urban areas, the rural participation rate was more than three times the urban participation rate.

In contrast to the males, among the females the share of cultivators has gone up but the share of agricultural labourers has gone down. The share of female workers in household industry shows a decline. However, the share in other than household industrial sector has increased. The work participation rates for males in Gujarat show an increase from 51.24 per cent (1971) to 52.19 per cent (1981) whereas those for females increased from 10.86 per cent (1971) to 11.03 per cent (1981). For Gujarat the age-specific participation rate for the males for 1981 is lower than that for 1971 in all the age groups. In contrast, female participation rate increased in all ages groups. Both in 1971 and 1981, rural female participation rate was more than double the urban female participation rate.

One of the most difficult problems is the measurement of the status of an individual in society. Since the origin of the feminist movement in the 1960s, in the absence of other indices, the status of women is measured by the demographic indicators such as sex ratio of the population, age at marriage of the females, their level of literacy and work participation rates.

Assuming that differential mortality conditions influence the sex ratio of the population, a lower proportion of females in the population is taken as a measure of their health. It is indicated that marriage influences the life of the female considerably and age at marriage is used as an index to understand the opportunities the females have in personal development, before they get married. Literacy level and work participation rates are similarly discussed while considering the status of the females as indicators of social development. Data for these indices are derived from censuses.

POPULATION PROFILE

The census of 1901 showed the Bombay Presidency to contain 331 towns, 40,694 villages and 5,004,095 houses, with a population of 25,468,209. Of these, 18,515,587 were in British territory, 6,908,448 in the Native states, and 43,974 in the outlying settlement of Aden. The density for the Presidency as a whole was 135 persons per square mile (Imperial Gazetteer 1909:36). With the neglect of subsistence farming under the British policy, as explained earlier, the population faced famines. Famine and plague took a toll of roughly 300,000 between 1891 and 1901, one-third of them in the British territory and two-thirds in the Native states. In the districts which were severely affected by the famine, the proportion of the population in the age groups 0–5 and 60-plus was markedly less, which indicated that the greatest sufferers in the famine were young children and old people.

The sex ratio in the 1901 census was 964 females to 1000 males. The Imperial Gazetteer (1909:39) mentions that there was the custom of female infanticide taken from the Rajputs and Kunbis of Gujarat, 'the cause of this barbarous practice' being 'the difficulty of securing bridegrooms from the sections of these castes with whom custom prescribed that intermarriage should take place.'

Females married in the age group 0–10 were three times as numerous as males. The proportion of widowed females was also high (2741 females per 1000 males). The plague in Bombay city to which the male population had migrated, caused deaths of many husbands, widowing their wives.

By 1911, the population of the presidency increased to 27,084,317 of whom 19,626,477 were in the British territory and the remaining 7,411,675 in the Native states. The sex ratio was 954 females per 1000 males. The deficiency of females in the population especially in the ages below 20 is explained by the census (1911) as being due to:

1. Female infanticide, which has been alleged to exist to this day, but only to a very small extent, and that only among certain Rajput clans.
2. Neglect of female infants.
3. Infant marriage and early child-bearing.
4. Unskilful midwifery and in the case of Pardah women the difficulty of securing treatment for female complaints.
5. Abortions in the case of pregnant widows.

6. The brutality of confinement ceremonies and regulations.
7. The hard life of widows and short supply of food to them, and the hard life of women of the lower classes.

In 1911, of the 1,000 males under age ten, 975 reported as not married, 24 as married and 2 as widowed. For the women the figures were 904, 94 and 3 respectively, showing that married females were almost four times as numerous as the males. Similarly the number of widowed females was much larger than that of widowed males.

The ratio of employed females according to the 1911 census was 453 to 1,000 males. Nearly all the economically active women were in occupations that had lower status such as rice husking, flour grinding, fish dealing, silk spinning and weaving, agricultural labour, basket making, wool carding, firewood collection etc.

The census of 1941, which was the last census taken before the country got its independence, showed that the proportion of females to males which had declined from 964 in 1901 to 909 by 1931, rose upward to 941 though the sex ratio of 1941 was lesser than that for 1901.

The 1961 census presented the data by zones, the western zone comprising the states of Gujarat, Maharashtra and the Union Territory of Dadra and Nagar Haveli. The total population in this zone was 60,245,031 and had a sex ratio of 938. As in the earlier censuses, never married males, especially in the younger ages, were more than the females. Widowed, divorced and separated females far outnumbered males. Significantly, the population under age 10 is all reported to be never married. But the number of married males and females in the ages 10–14 showed wide disparities. The same was true for the widowed, divorced and separated.

The data from the censuses consistently reveal that women's problems centred around early marriage, poor education, inadequate opportunities for participation in economic activity etc. In the mid-nineteenth century in the Bombay Presidency, the reform oriented among the elite of the three communities—Parsee, Maharashtrian and Gujarati Brahmins—participated in the activities of the students' literary and scientific society where they discussed the position of women in society. These discussions inspired efforts to educate women in the three communities. Reformist Parsee leaders made headway in their community, starting girls' schools and publishing a women's magazine, *Stri Bodh*. The Alexandra Institution was a girls' high school with an English educational curriculum. The reformists of both Gujarati and Maharashtrian Brahmins however encountered stiff opposition from orthodox leaders.

Sex Ratio

The sex ratio of the areas now comprising Maharashtra and Gujarat has been adverse to females from the beginning of the century. In both states the ratio had been deteriorating up to 1971. However, the figures of 1981 have shown a minor rise. Maharashtra had a higher ratio than Gujarat in the pre-independence period, the respective figures for the two states being 978 and 954 (1901), 966 and 946 (1911), 950 and 944 (1921), 947 and 945 (1931), 949 and 941 (1941). The order was reversed in the post-independence censuses, Gujarat showing a higher ratio than Maharashtra, the figures respectively being 952 and 941 (1951), 940 and 936 (1961), 934 and 930 (1971) and 942 and 937 (1982).

The child-woman ratios for the states of Maharashtra and Gujarat showed a decline in fertility, the ratios for Maharashtra being lower than those for Gujarat. The ratio of children 0 to 4 to women 15 to 49 was 699 for Gujarat in 1961 and 651 for Maharashtra. By 1971 the ratio for Maharashtra declined by 1.2 per cent and was 643; the decline for Gujarat was 6.87 per cent to reach a ratio of 651. For the decade 1971–81 the child-woman ratio for Gujarat declined by 20.43 per cent to reach 518; the figure for Maharashtra was 513, a decline of 20.2 per cent. A similar pattern was observed in the two states for the ratio of children in ages 5–9 to the women 20–54. Maharashtra had ratios of 696 (1961), 728 (1971) and 641 (1981); those for Gujarat were 748 (1961), 787 (1971) and 648 (1981).

Nuptiality

Many major problems of women are linked with marriage. Various issues like age at marriage, procedures for negotiating and executing marriage, customs of dowry and bride wealth, patterns of presentation between the wife's and husband's kin group, multiplicity of spouses, divorce and separation, widowhood and remarriage, are vitally relevant for assessing women's status* (GoI 1974).

* Since 1961, those under age 10 are reported as never married. So though there is enough evidence to believe that marriages take place below age 10, no data can be given.

Although the mean age at marriage for women in Maharashtra and Gujarat has shown a distinct rise, one still notices girls in the age group 10–14 and 15–19 as married. For Maharashtra the percentages of married girls in ages 10–14 were 22.39 (1961), 8.69 (1971) and 3.94 (1981) for rural areas, and 5.65 (1961), 2.30 (1971) and 1.62 (1981) for urban areas. The corresponding figures for Gujarat were 8.88 (1961), 4.44 (1971), and 2.38 (1981) for rural areas and 3.17 (1961), 1.30 (1971) and 1.05 (1981) for urban areas.

In the next age group of 15–19 the percentages of married girls in rural Maharashtra were 81.05 (1961), 63.52 (1972) and 45.49 (1981) and 49.06 (1961), 33.46 (1971) and 25.38 (1981) in urban areas. In Gujarat the corresponding figures were 61.78 (1961), 44.41 (1971) and 29.74 (1981) in rural areas and 42.88 (1961), 27.94 (1971) and 20.70 (1981) in urban areas. The above figures clearly indicate that many girls under 20 get married, though there is a considerable decline in their number over the decades. Also, in every instance, the proportion of married women is much lesser in Gujarat than in Maharashtra.

The Reform Movement of the nineteenth century sought to bring an aversion in the social consciousness against polygyny as being an indignity and offence to the status of women. The demand for legislative action against polygyny gained momentum under the influence of Gandhiji and made women's organizations increasingly vocal, and the result was the passing of an Act in the Bombay Presidency in 1946 banning polygyny. The Hindu Marriage Act introduced the principle of monogamy in 1955. Muslim law however, still permits plurality of wives. The census of 1961 found polygyny to be prevalent among most communities, though the incidence has declined. The percentages of such marriages to the total were 7.96 (1931–40), 8.35 (1941–50), and 9.43 (1951–60) in Maharashtra and 2.59 (1931–40), 3.31 (1941–50) and 1.11 (1951–60) in Gujarat.

The prevalence of dowry is often reported in the press. However, no data are available for either Maharashtra or Gujarat. The Dowry Prohibition Act was passed in 1961. From the general information one is led to the conclusion that the Act has failed to achieve its purpose.

Mortality

Data on medically certified causes of death are available for the urban population. From these data it is observed that 8.1 per cent of total deaths of women are due to accidents and 80.3 per cent of them were of women in the age group 15–44. Considering the mortality of only women in the age group 15–44, it is seen that 24.7 per cent or almost one in four of these deaths were due to accidents and one in five deaths were due to burns.

Of the total deaths in the age group 15–19, 36.4 per cent were due to accidents and 29.0 per cent were due to burns. In the next age group of 20 to 24 the percentages were 31.5 and 26.9 respectively. Interestingly, 61.3 per cent of the burn cases in the age group 15–19 were reported as never married; the percentages of such girls for the following two age groups were 12.7 and 7.6 respectively. Such a high incidence of deaths due to accidents in these age groups has to be related to the social problems linked with marriage (Karkal 1985).

EDUCATION

Education imbues people with the knowledge, the sense of purpose and the confidence essential for building a dynamic, vibrant personality and provides the wherewithal for creating a better, fuller and purposeful life (GOI 1985).

In using the indices for literacy as measures of the status of women one has to be extremely cautious, since the census data are very deceptive for this purpose. For example, the sex ratio of a population can be made favourable to females by cutting down on maternity through forced contraception and overall improvement in public health situation. Females may not have any voice in the decisions and still may show better survival. Hajnal's method, which is used for calculating age at marriage, gives an over-estimation of the age since the data used are the distribution of the never married. The method does not include the effect of mortality, which is significant in India and especially for females. Lastly, since 1981, the census reports all population under age 10 as non-married (Karkal 1985).

There is also reason to believe that in reporting a literate status, a large number of people who have not used the knowledge of reading and writing and therefore are functionally illiterate, also get included in this group, thus giving a higher estimate. Besides, among the cases of rape and bride burning, there are several who are graduates, indicating that education does not necessarily give a woman the power to assert her rights.

Finally, the data on work participation rate for women suffer from serious social biases towards their status. At the national level, the work participation rate has shown a decline from 525 females to 1000 males in 1911 to 210 in 1971 and 253 in 1981. If these figures are taken to indicate that comparatively larger numbers of females are, in the recent times, free of the burden of having to work outside the home, the conclusion is completely wrong. There is abundant evidence that due to social biases women are not recognized as heads of household and/or main earners even when in reality they are the sole support to the family. Secondly, in a patriarchal society the labour of women and children is considered to be the property of the head of the household and therefore a large number of women who are working in agriculture and in small-scale industries are not recognized as contributing to work. These conditions have seriously affected the figures of work participation of females mainly with the development of the capitalist economy in which man has benefited considerably (Karkal 1986).

While judging the status of women on the basis of their engagement in work outside the home it must be noticed that it has essentially meant a burden on them in addition to their reproductive role. In the light of this it is very important that the role of home-making gets its due importance. One may conclude that the status of women in Western India is better than in many northern parts of the country but it is much lower than that of men. There is an urgent need for the education of society to accept all sections of the population as equal.

REFERENCES

Chattopadhyaya, Kamaladevi, 1929. *The Status of Women in Modern India*, ed. by George Eviyns and Choksi Mothan, D.B. Taraporewala Sons and Company, Bombay.

Census of India, 1911, Vol. VII, Bombay, Part I Report, p. 101.

Census of India, 1961. Incidence of Polygynous Marriages in India (mimeo), Reported in 'Towards Equality', p. 66.

Divekar, V.D. (1982), 'Western India's Economy' in *Cambridge Economic History of India*, pp. 332–333.

Dobbin, Christina, 1972. *Urban Leadership in Western India* (London: Oxford University Press) pp. 53–77, 249–253.

Dutt, Ramesh, *Economic History of British India*, pp. 262–263.

Enthoven, R.E. 1986. *The Cotton Fabrics of the Bombay Presidency.*

Everett, Matson Jana, 1978. *Women and Social Change in India*, p. 61.

Government of India (GOI) (1974). *Towards Equality: Report of the Committee on the Status of Women in India*, p. 62.

Government of India, Ministry of Education, 1985. *Challenge of Education—Policy Perspective*, p. 1.

Heimsath, Charles H., 1964. *Indian Nationalism and Hindu Social Reform*. Princeton University Press, p. 337.

Imperial Gazetteer of India, 1909. Provincial Series, Bombay Presidency, Vol. I (Calcutta: Superintendent of Government Printing).

Joshi, N.M., 1936. *Urban Handicrafts of the Bombay Deccan*, Gokhale Institute, pp. 48–49.

Karkal, Malini, 1985. 'How the Other Half Dies in Bombay?' *Economic and Political Weekly*, Vol. 20, No. 34, August 24, p. 1424.

Karkal, Malini, 1986. 'Discrimination — Women in Employment' in *Social Intervention for Social Justice*, R.K. Hebner (ed.) Golden Jubilee Publication of Tata Institute of Social Sciences, Bombay.

Karkal, Malini and Irudaya Rajans, 1985. 'Age at Marriage in India: Has it shown an increase?' paper presented at the Seminar on Demographic and Socio-economic Aspects of Nuptiality in India, jointly organised by the Population Research Centre, JSS Institute of Economic Research, Dharwad and Population Centre, Bangalore from 1–3 February 1985 at Dharwad, Karnataka.

Kumar, Ravindra, 1983. *Essays in Social History of Modern India* (Delhi: Oxford University Press), pp. 6–7.

Morris, Morris D., 1966. 'The Recruitment of an Industrial Labour Force in India, with British and American Comparisons' in *Comparative Studies in Society and History*, Vol. II, No. 3, p. 321.

Montgomery, R. Martin, 1837. *History of the Possessions of the Honourable East India Company* (London: Whittaker) Vol. I, pp. 354–355.

Rogers, B., 1980. *The Domestication of Women in Developing Societies* (London: Tavistock) p. 125.

Sen, S.N., 1979. *History of Modern India 1765–1950* (New Delhi: Wiley Eastern), p. 101.

Sovani, N.V., 1965. 'British Impact on India' in Metraux Guy S. and Crouzet Francois (ed.) *Studies in Cultural History of India*, UNESCO, pp. 296–297, 324–325.

Status of Women in Madhya Pradesh

D. RADHA DEVI

Neither man nor woman can by themselves have a complete life. Together they can perform what is ordained of them by nature. It should follow that they are equal and complementary to each other with their differing attributes. Woman is by nature delicate whereas man is physically strong. The physical strength is often misinterpreted as 'superiority' giving woman an inferior status. Woman's delicate nature has also been misconstrued as submissiveness and taken advantage of. As a consequence women were denied freedom to make their own decisions even in personal matters. Interestingly, it was men who noted the discrepancy in status and advocated a change. Plato, the Greek philosopher, for example, pleaded for the free admission of women to all duties and rights of man and pointed out the loss to the State as a result of their restricted sphere of activity (Stern 1959: 443). The nineteenth century saw the greatest advocate for women's cause in John Stuart Mill, the renowned political economist and philosopher of his time.[1] But the fervour did not catch up, for the majority of men believed like Aristotle that men are by nature superior and therefore fit to rule and women should be ruled (ibid.).

Status is a very complex phenomenon to study. There can be self-perceived status, group-perceived status or objective status (Mukherjee 1975). A person who is very high up in one type of status can be very low in another reflecting status inconsistency. The problem has to be unambiguously clear if a viable solution is to be found. The several ways by which the status of women has been defined have generated more confusion than clarity. For example, women's status has been defined as the extent of their access to social and material resources within the family, society and community (Dixon 1978); as the authority and power she holds within the family/community and the prestige she commands from other members of the family and community (Mukherjee 1975); as a position in the social system distinguishable yet related to other positions (Committee on the Status of Women in

India 1974), as the extent to which women have access to knowledge, to economic resources and to political power and the degree of autonomy they have in decision making and choice at crucial points in life cycle (United Nations, 1975). The concept *status*, therefore, cannot be precisely measured. There can only be pointers to the general status women enjoy in a given society. The actual status any woman enjoys depends upon the treatment she gets from the persons she interacts with.

The status of women in a society has to be viewed in the context of the historical conditions and current social, economic, political and cultural forces in it (United Nations, 1975: 5). What is true elsewhere in the world need not necessarily be true in India.

In the Vedic period women held equal status with men (Kuppuswamy 1975: 239). Jayaswal contends that society in the Rigvedic period being predominantly nomadic, it did not produce enough supplies to allow any section of society to be completely subordinated or withdrawn from the process of production. This perhaps explains the comparatively better position of women in those days (Quoted in Desai and Krishnaraj 1987: 33).

Women's degradation started with the great social reforms that took place after 300 B.C. (Kuppuswamy 1975: 242). In the words of Neera Desai,

> ideologically woman was considered a completely inferior species, inferior to the male, having no significance, no personality; socially, she was kept in a state of utter subjection, denied any right, suppressed and oppressed; she was further branded as basically lacking the ethical fibre. The patriarchal joint family, the customs of polygamy, the purda, the property structure, early marriage, self-immolation of widows (sati) or a state of permanent widowhood, all these contributed to the smothering of the free development of women (Quoted in Kuppuswamy 1975: 243).

This was the situation upto the late nineteenth or early twentieth centuries. Since then several reformists like Rammohun Roy, Ishwar Chandra Vidyasagar, Dayananda Saraswati, K.C. Sen and later Mahatma Gandhi took up the cudgels against female oppression.

Slowly but surely women woke up to their position in society and in 1926, the All India Women's Conference was established. The AIWC plays a major role even today in improving the lot of women in India.

Mahatma Gandhi asserted: 'I am uncompromising in the matters of women's rights. In my opinion she should labour under no legal dissatisfaction not suffered by man' (Quoted in Kuppuswamy, 1975: 252). Independent India made several rules and regulations to protect the rights of women and establish equality of status.[2]

STATUS OF WOMEN IN MADHYA PRADESH

The present study[3] focuses on the objective status of women in Madhya Pradesh, a state of India, using data on mortality, education, employment and marriage obtained mainly from census publications. This study will not examine self-perceived or group-perceived status as that would require data on perceived status at home and community, on perceived social and economic freedom, on decision-making power, on perceived power and autonomy, on degree of perceived privileges, on group-accorded prestige, etc. (Mukherjee 1975).

Sex Ratio and Mortality Indices

Sex ratio (defined as the number of males per 100 females) at birth is around 105 in all human populations, and being biologically so determined, generally will not vary much with differentials in time and space. The preponderance of males in the younger ages will be reduced in later age groups by the higher mortality rate among males. Generally a balance in sex will be achieved in the middle age and then the sex ratio will turn in favour of females. If this general pattern is not found in the observed population there is reason to suspect that the death rate of females is comparatively high resulting from neglect due to their 'low' status.

In Madhya Pradesh the sex ratio at birth is around 104.2 (Saxena 1982). The sex ratio for five broad age groups is provided in Table 1. The data show that the sex ratio has been continuously increasing up to age 60, declining thereafter. The reason could be a differential sex ratio of the deceased being unfavourable to women.

As mortality indices, age-specific death rates (Table 2) and expectation of life at birth are considered. Table 2 shows that death rates among females were higher than those of males till age 44 in 1971 and till age 34 in 1981. This is mainly due to differences in the sex ratio at death. It is common knowledge that in Indian society, the female child is often neglected in terms of general nurture, nutrition and health

TABLE 1
Sex Ratio by Age Group

Age group (in years)	Sex Ratio		
	1961	1971	1981
0-24	104.0	105.9	106.3
25-49	109.6	108.3	107.5
50-59	110.3	111.4	113.8
60-69	90.8	98.7	97.7
70+	72.6	86.3	90.1
Total	105.0	106.2	106.3

Sources: Computed from *Census of India 1961, 1971* and *1981*, Madhya Pradesh, *Social and Cultural Tables*, 1961 Part II C(i) 1971 and Part II C(ii) and 1981 Part IV-A.

TABLE 2
Age Specific Death Rates by Sex, 1971 and 1981

Age group (in years)	Death Rate			
	1971		1981	
	Male	Female	Male	Female
0-4	48.6	51.2	58.2	63.1
5-9	5.3	4.6	5.2	7.5
10-14	2.6	3.9	2.4	2.8
15-19	2.2	6.5	1.6	2.6
20-24	3.9	3.2	1.8	4.9
25-29	3.0	5.1	3.0	5.0
30-34	2.6	6.2	3.6	3.9
35-39	6.0	8.3	5.3	4.9
40-44	6.2	6.8	6.4	4.0
45-49	14.1	8.4	8.1	7.2
50-54	19.8	15.6	13.5	12.4
55-59	19.4	15.4	31.6	25.0
60-64	35.2	27.2	48.0	38.1
65-69	29.4	51.4	70.8	33.3
70+	109.8	92.2	124.2	124.9
All ages	15.3	16.5	16.1	17.1

Source: Office of the Registrar General, Vital Statistics Division, *Sample Registration System*, 1970–75 and 1981.

care. The female child in India is a non-person or non-being (Gnanadason 1986). The causes of sex disparity in death rates are loss of life in early age for girls because of female infanticide, lesser attention at times of illness, lesser share of good and nourishing food, high maternal mortality due to early marriage[4] and consequent early and repeated pregnancies (Dandekar 1975; Gnanadason 1986).

Life expectancy at birth for males and females during 1971–1980 was 48.5 years and 47.5 years respectively. In societies where women get a fair treatment, if not equal treatment, women live longer than men as they are a biologically superior group (Thomlinson 1965).

Educational Indices

In the modern world, education makes a substantial contribution to a person's status. Considering also that education makes a beneficial impact on the type of job accessible, which in turn determines the level of income, it is easy to understand the role of education in determining a person's status.

Looking at the sex ratio of all women by educational enrolment and by level of education and the sex ratio of literates by age, one arrives at the following conclusions (Table 3). There is a wide gap between male and female enrolment and it is closing only slowly. Women account for 55 to 56 per cent of total illiterates. The sex ratio increases with the level of education indicating that women are not equal to men in education. The sex ratio of those with education, matriculation or above has more than halved during the 1961–1981 period. For the illiterates the sex ratio did not register much difference and for the literates without formal education, its decline is not considerable.

The sex ratio of literates by age shows that the education of girls is a comparatively recent phenomenon. In all the three periods of time the sex ratio of the literates is the lowest for the youngest age group and it consistently increased as the age increased. In 1981, there were five literate men for every literate woman, as against eight for one in 1961. In sum, females are still a disadvantaged group compared to males.

Employment Indices

Remunerative employment is one of the important status deciding factors. The common belief is that man's higher status within the family emanated from his earning the means of livelihood. If women's

TABLE 3

Sex Ratio and Femininity Proportion by Educational Indices

Educational Indices	Sex Ratio			Femininity Proportion		
	1959–60	1970–71	1982–83	1959–60	1970–71	1982–83
1. Enrolment in						
Primary school	405	253	195	19.4	28.3	33.9
Middle school	483	327	284	17.1	23.4	26.0
High school +	599	342	226	14.3	22.6	30.7
	1961	1971	1981	1961	1971	1981
2. Level of education						
Illiterate	82	80	80	54.9	55.5	55.6
Literate without formal education	387	270	252	20.5	27.0	28.4
Primary and middle school	507	344	271	16.5	22.5	26.9
Matriculation +	684	446	330	12.8	18.3	23.3
3. Literate by age-group (in years)						
5-14	288	221	196	25.8	31.2	33.7
15-24	393	290	242	20.3	25.7	29.2
25-34	527	392	309	16.0	20.3	24.5
35 +	781	608	493	11.4	14.1	16.9
Total	421	318	215	19.2	23.9	27.0

Sources: Government of India, *Education in the States—1959–60*; Government of India, Ministry of Education and Social Welfare, *Selected Educational Statistics—1982–83*, 1983; Government of India, Ministry of Education and Culture, *A Handbook of Educational and Allied Statistics*, 1980; Computed from *Census of India 1961, 1971, 1981*, Madhya Pradesh, *Social and Cultural Tables*. 1961—Part II-C(i), 1971—Part II-C(ii), 1981—Part IV-A.

economic dependence can be reduced by women's own monetary income they would enjoy a better status. Employment being a major determinant of the level of monetary income, employment-related aspects namely, work participation rate, and sex ratio of agricultural and non-agricultural workers will be discussed here. Wage differentials will also be looked into in brief.

Table 4 indicates that there is a wide gap between male and female work participation rate.[5] It is obvious that if women in Madhya Pradesh are to obtain equal status through employment, they have a long way to go.

TABLE 4
Work Participation by Sex 1961–1981

Sex	Work Participation Rate (Total Population)			Work Participation Rate (10+ Population)		
	1961	1971	1981	1961	1971	1981
Male	60.21	53.74	53.52	86.31	78.23	74.06
Female	43.99	18.65	22.35	63.91	27.58	31.35

Source: Computed from *Census of India*, 1961, 1971, 1981, Madhya Pradesh, *General Economic Tables*, 1961—Part II-B(i); 1971—Part II-B(i), 1981—Part III-A & B(i).

Table 5 presents percentage distribution of workers and non-workers for males and females by level of education and age group. Male-female disparity in work participation rate is indicated for each age group for all levels of education. Looking at female participation rates for the same age group by level of education, it is seen that from age group 20–24 onwards participation consistently increases. Clearly, level of employment is related to education. For each educational level also, female work participation increases with age, indicating that those with education are able to shed their inhibitions with advancing age and take up jobs. However, in the traditional society of Madhya Pradesh, higher level education does not always meet the social or individual demand. Hence it appears that among those who are not working (particularly those with higher education) a majority could be discouraged workers[6] and unemployed women.

Since employment is examined in the context of ability to provide monetary income and a better economic status, the type of employment assumes importance. Table 6 shows that agriculture absorbs the largest

TABLE 5

Percentage Distribution of Workers and Non-workers by Age Groups, Level of Education and Sex, 1981

Age/Group (years)	Sex	Middle School		Matriculation and above but below graduation		Graduation and above	
		Workers	Non-workers	Workers	Non-workers	Workers	Non-workers
15-19	Male	17.09	82.91	10.62	89.38	10.36	89.64
	Female	2.92	97.08	1.47	98.53	2.96	97.04
20-24	Male	76.75	23.25	50.22	49.78	39.38	60.62
	Female	6.07	93.93	7.94	92.06	12.57	87.43
25-29	Male	93.78	6.22	88.14	11.86	80.62	19.38
	Female	7.42	92.58	13.89	86.11	24.47	75.53
30-34	Male	96.61	3.39	96.11	3.89	95.52	4.48
	Female	8.13	91.87	19.86	80.14	35.03	64.97
35+	Male	90.88	9.12	92.07	7.93	95.01	4.99
	Female	11.10	88.90	26.09	73.91	51.48	48.52

Sources: Computed from *Census of India* 1981, Madhya Pradesh, Part III-A & B(ii) General Economic Tables; Part IV-A *Social and Cultural Tables.*

Note: The illiterates, literates without formal education, and those with only primary level education are not considered in this table as education is not expected to play any major role in their level of participation because at least a few years of schooling is essential to have any effect on employment.

number of labour, both male and female, but the concentration of women workers in agriculture is overwhelming. Combining this with the fact that sex discrimination prevails in wage rate (see below) the presumption that the employment of women by itself would raise their status perceptibly seems to be wide off the mark.

TABLE 6

Percentage Distribution of Male and Female Workers by Agricultural and Non-agricultural Sectors, 1961–71

Sector	Males			Females		
	1961	1971	1981	1961	1971	1981
Agricultural	73.44	76.03	71.61	87.75	89.79	87.89
Non-agricultural	26.56	23.97	28.39	12.25	10.21	12.11

Source: Same as Table 3.

Still more revealing are the data on non-agricultural workers (Table 7). About two-thirds of the female workers in the non-agricultural sector are in the category which includes labourers. Further, the occupations of the majority of non-agricultural women workers are of low status, monotonous, time-consuming and tedious. Earnings in these occupations are low. Any substantial upliftment of status cannot be expected through such employment.

TABLE 7

Percentage Distribution of Non-agricultural Women Workers by Occupation, Sex Ratio and Femininity Proportion, 1981

Occupational group	Occupational family	Per cent of women workers	Ratio	Femininity proportion
1	2	3	4	5
1. Professional	All	11.04	528	15.92
Technical and	Nurses	1.76	5	95.18
Related	Midwives and Health visitors	0.15	70	58.69
	Middle school teachers	1.42	416	19.37
	High school teachers	0.98	362	21.62
	Primary school teachers	3.32	465	17.60
	Pre-primary school teachers	0.32	43	70.08
	Others	3.09	—	—

Table 7 (Contd.)

1	2	3	4	5
2. Administrative executive and managerial	All	0.48	4167	2.34
Clerical	All	2.41	2418	3.97
	Clerks—general	1.15	1290	7.19
	Others	1.26	—	—
3. Sales	All	7.46	958	9.45
	Retail trade	4.68	1022	8.91
	Street vendors	2.16	373	—
	Others	0.62	—	—
4. Service	All	8.88	576	14.78
	Ayah, nurse maids	0.15	28	78.42
	Domestic servants	3.40	61	62.10
	Sweepers, cleaners and related workers	3.05	170	7.43
	Others	2.28	—	—
5. Farmers, Fishermen, Hunters, Loggers etc.	All	5.42	755	11.70
	Cultivators	1.17	226	30.63
	Others	4.25	—	—
6. Production and related; transport equipment operation, labour	All	60.96	4ɔ8	17.91
	Quarry workers	0.97	271	26.92
	Weavers and related workers	1.31	740	11.90
	Grain millers and related workers	1.65	307	24.54
	Bidi makers	18.59	106	48.49
	Tailors and dress makers	1.45	1078	8.49
	Potters and related clay workers	4.82	222	31.07
	Basketry weavers and brush makers	5.12	139	41.93
	Construction workers	2.78	268	27.14
	Labourers	12.55	268	27.15
	Others	11.72	—	—
7. Unclassified	All	3.35	519	16.15

Note: 1. Only those occupations where at least about 1 per cent of female non-agricultural workers are found and those occupations with more females than males are given separately.

2. For 'Others' the sex ratio and femininity proportion are not given as they are a conglomeration of several occupations.

Source: Computed from Census of India 1981, Madhya Pradesh, Part III-A & B(v), General Economic Tables.

Wage discrimination based on sex prevails in Madhya Pradesh also. For example in districts like Nimar, Raipur, Ujjain, Mand etc., a male sower gets Rs 5 a day as against Rs 4 a day for a woman sower (Government of India 1982). The same kind of differences are observed for agricultural labourer, reaper, harvester etc.

Marital Status

Marital status is often used as an index of women's status. The contention seems to be that marital status, particularly the proportion never married at the younger ages, is an important indicator of possible access to options other than marriage and the relative acceptability of remaining single for each sex and age group (United Nations 1984: 30).

Table 8 shows that in all age groups a considerably higher proportion of males are never married. But in a society where marriage is universal, the very small proportion of never married women would include, besides those who do not want to get married, those who cannot get married at the 'right' age due to financial problems and therefore will have to accept it as fate and those who are mentally or physically disabled. In other words, the explanation given by the

TABLE 8
Mean Age at Marriage and Marital Status Distribution by Sex 1961–81

	1961		1971		1981	
	Male	Female	Male	Female	Male	Female
Mean age at marriage (in years)	18.4	13.9	19.3	15.0	20.6	16.5
Marital status distribution of 10+ population (per cent)						
Never married	24.98	10.66	28.37	15.46	33.28	21.00
Current Married	68.38	72.54	66.33.	70.97	62.26	67.35
Widowed	5.62	15.99	4.68	13.03	3.77	10.89
Divorced/separated	1.02	0.81	0.49	0.45	0.65	0.72
Percent never married in age group						
10-19	71.90	40.21	78.05	53.40	85.93	66.13
20-49	9.07	0.77	9.09	1.10	11.05	1.92
50+	2.78	0.28	2.21	0.14	1.83	0.15

Source: Same as Table 1.

United Nations that it is suggestive of alternatives available and acceptance of single status as normal, may not be applicable. Further, the larger proportion of unmarried males is to be expected in a society having more males than females.

In Madhya Pradesh, the proportion of widows is several times more than that of widowers. Again if this is considered along with the fact that a larger proportion of unmarried men exist in society, one wonders whether it could be due to social pressures against widow remarriage. If this presumption is true it indicates a low status for women.

CONCLUDING COMMENTS

Using education, employment, marriage and mortality variables the objective status of women in Madhya Pradesh has been examined. All the indices point out that women are at a disadvantage compared to men. The share of women is very low at all levels of education except the zero level, the illiterates. Their work participation rate is low and an overwhelming proportion of workers are in agriculture. The non-agricultural work of women is also such that it cannot improve their status. Girls are married at a very early age and widow marriage seems to be less acceptable than widower marriages. Females, who are biologically superior to men, have high death rate and lower expectation of life at birth.

There are still 'dowry deaths', suicides, physical ill treatment of women by husbands or the latter's immediate relatives etc. in a society where laws and regulations are aplenty for the protection of women's rights. It appears that laws are made only to be violated. A new threat is the medical technology which makes it possible to know the sex of the foetus and these tests 'are increasingly used to discern the sex of the unborn foetus, with a view to abort female children' (Gnanadason 1986: 1631). One is not sure how far this technological threat has reached the masses of Madhya Pradesh.

The solution to all this lies in a change of *attitude*—a realization that man and woman together form a whole. If this can be achieved, the rest will automatically follow. Marx's words seem apt even after a century: 'The social progress (of a society) can be measured with precision by the social position of the female sex' (Quoted in Stern 1959: 446).

NOTES

1. It is said that what *The Wealth of Nations* is for Classical Liberalism and *Das Kapital* for Socialism, *The Subjection of Women* (J.S. Mill 1869) is for the century-old agitation for women's rights.

2. The Fundamental Rights incorporated in the Indian constitution embody several favourable provisions. For example, Article 14 assures equal protection, Article 15 ensures equal accessibility to public places like shops, restaurants, wells, tanks etc., Article 16 guarantees equal opportunity in matters of public employment, whereas Article 39 talks about equal pay for equal work irrespective of sex. Article 51-A deals with the preservation of the dignity of women.

   Besides there are statutory enactments which are exclusively for women. For instance, the Equal Remuneration Act of 1976 (on 18 September 1982 the Supreme Court of India gave the rights to all labourers (especially women) to approach the Supreme Court directly for the violation of Equal Remuneration Act (Data India 1982)) or the Maternity Benefit Act of 1961. The Factory Act of 1948 lays down that women should not be employed in hazardous and dangerous assignments. Setting up of creches was made compulsory in establishments employing more than fifty women workers through Plantations Labour Act of 1951.

   Other related legislations of interest are: Hindu Marriage Act of 1955 which made monogamy the rule for both men and women of Hindu religion. The Hindu Succession Act of 1965 which conferred the rights of inheritance and property on Hindu women. Hindu Adoption and Maintenance Act of 1956 which made it possible for unmarried, widowed and divorced women to adopt children (including female children which was not permitted till then). The Dowry Prohibition Act of 1961 prohibits by law giving or taking dowry. This law was amended in 1984 elaborating the provisions. The Child Marriage Act of 1929 which fixed the age at marriage for girls to be 14 years and for boys to be 18 years was amended in 1978 raising the female age at marriage to 18 and that of males to be 21. The Medical Termination of Pregnancy Act of 1971 made legal the termination of pregnancies if the pregnancy involves risk to the life of child/mother, if the child is likely to be deformed, and if it is the result of rape, contraceptive failure, etc. According to the Criminal Law (Second Amendment) Act of 1983, cruelty in terms of mental and physical torture, abetment to suicide of a woman by her husband or her husband's relatives can be punished and a thorough enquiry by a police officer of a death of a woman within seven years of marriage can also be made.

3. Madhya Pradesh is situated in the central region of the country accommodating 7.6 per cent of the Indian population in 13.5 per cent of the total Indian territory. This population is distributed in 9.32 million households giving an average household size of 5.6 persons. An overwhelming majority of it adheres to Hindu religion, four-fifths of the people live in rural areas and the average village size is 583 persons. Twenty-three per cent of the population belongs to scheduled tribes. The 1971–1981 population growth rate was 25.15 per cent. According to the projections of Expert Committee on Population, the population of Madhya Pradesh will be 751 million by A.D. 2001. The population of the state in 1981 was 26.89 million males and 25.29 million females.

4. The mean age at marriage (in years) for girls and boys is as follows:

	1961	1971	1981
Males	18.4	19.3	20.6
Females	13.9	15.0	16.5

5. The readers are cautioned that the 1961 census definition of workers is not in consonance with that of 1971 and 1981 and as such the rates by themselves are not comparable between 1961 and that in other censuses.
6. Discouraged workers are those who are not actively seeking job due to the difficulty of getting a job but are available for work.

REFERENCES

Committee on the Status of Women in India , 1974. *Towards Equality: Report of the Committee on the Status of Women in India* (New Delhi: Government of India).

Dandekar, Kumudini, 1975. 'Why has the Proportion of Women in India's Population been Declining,' *Economic and Political Weekly*, Vol. X, No. 42, pp. 1663–1667.

Data India, 1982. 13–19 September.

Desai, Neera and Maithreyi Krishnaraj, 1987. *Women and Society in India* (Delhi: Ajanta).

Dixon, Ruth, 1987. *Rural Women at Work* (Baltimore: Johns Hopkins University Press).

Gnanadason, Aruna, 1986. 'Women's Health: Plea for a New Approach',' *Economic and Political Weekly*, Vol. XXI, No 37, pp. 1630–32.

Government of India: Directorate of Economics and Statistics, *Agricultural Wages in India*, 1980–81, 1982.

Kuppuswamy, B., 1975. *Social Change in India*, 2nd edition (Delhi: Vikas).

Mill, John Stuart, 1970. *The Subjection of Women* (Longmans, Green, Reader and Dyer, London, 1869) (Cambridge: M.I.T. Press).

Mukherjee, B.N., 1975. 'Multi-dimensional Conceptualisation of Status of Women,' *Social Change*, Vol. 5, No. 1 & 2, pp. 27–44.

Saxena, P.C., 1982. 'Basic Composition of the Population' in United Nations, *Population of India*, Country Monograph Series No. 10 (New york).

Stern, Bernhard J., 1959. 'Women, Position in Society' in E.A.R. Seligman, *Encyclopaedia of Social Sciences* (New York: Macmillan), pp. 442–450.

Thomlinson, Ralf, 1965. *Population Dynamics* (New York: Random House).

United Nations, Department of Economic and Social Affairs, 1975. *Status of Women and Family Planning* (New York).

United Nations, 1984. *Compiling Social Indicators on the Situation of Women* (New York).

Differential Status of Women and Population Dynamics in Andhra Pradesh

P.J. REDDY

Andhra Pradesh, with an area of 2.75 lakh sq km and a population of 53.5 million (1981), is the fifth largest state in India both in terms of area and population. The state was formed in 1953 with eleven districts of coastal Andhra and Rayalaseema which were then part of the erstwhile composite Madras state together with nine districts of Telengana from the former princely state of Hyderabad. Andhra Pradesh comprises three fairly distinct regions Rayalaseema, coastal Andhra and Telengana which differ geographically and economically. Rayalaseema and Telengana are part of the arid Deccan plateau, while coastal Andhra forms a segment of the fertile but narrow strip of the subcontinent along the coast of the Bay of Bengal.[1] The regional disparities are reflected in the pace of their socio-economic development. While coastal Andhra has emerged as the most prosperous area, Rayalaseema and Telengana have remained backward.

In ancient India, women were highly respected. 'Shakti', symbolizing woman, is believed to be the supreme power from which Brahma, Vishnu and Maheswara have emerged. Saraswati is the goddess of education, Lakshmi of wealth and Parvathi of energy; their blessings are essential to achieve success. Also the men were addressed respectfully by adding as prefix the names of their wives/mothers. For instance, Sri Rama is called as 'Seetapati' (husband of Seeta) and 'Kausalyasuta' (Son of Kausalya). Similarly, Shiva is called 'Girijapati' (husband of Girija).

But the respect given to women rapidly deteriorated. Although all the values promoting the status of women are fostered in society through the formal and non-formal education system as well as the mass media, they are treated only as ideals. In reality, women are not shown much regard. They are treated mostly as procreators and unpaid family workers with no freedom to express their opinion even in such matters as family size. Sons are preferred over daughters as deteriorating economic conditions necessitate hard work outside the home. The need for security in old age in the absence of any social security measures and the high cost of marriage expenses and/or dowry of daughters also explain son preference.

Women in Andhra Pradesh enjoy all the legal rights and privileges as in the rest of India. However, disparities exist in the status of women among the three regions. Women in coastal Andhra have a much higher status than those in Rayalaseema and Telengana. The females in Telengana and Rayalaseema, being socio-economically backward, are generally submissive and dependent while women in coastal Andhra are more individualistic and independent since they are socially and economically better off. The status of women is examined here focussing on several dimensions such as sex ratio, literacy and educational attainment, child marriages, age at marriage, fertility, child labour, work participation rates, political involvement, property ownership, female offerings to the Goddess and birth control. The analysis is based mostly on the 1981 census data. The distinguishing features of the women in these contrasting regions of Andhra Pradesh are outlined in the subsequent sections. In making this comparison among the three regions, Hyderabad, being the capital and metropolitan city, is excluded from Telengana.

The sex ratio, at 975 females per 1000 males, favours men in Andhra Pradesh, less so in coastal Andhra (at a ratio of 986) than Rayalaseema (958) and Telengana (971). The significantly higher sex ratio in coastal Andhra is due to the better nutritional and health care of females in the region than in the more backward Telengana and Rayalaseema.

Women and Education

Education is a crucial determinant of the status of women as it promotes knowledge and also self-confidence. It enables them to think and act rationally on all matters including marriage and family size. It also facilitates participation in gainful employment which can further depress fertility and accelerate their emancipation through greater economic freedom. Article 45 of the Constitution of India provided that 'the state shall endeavour to provide within a period of ten years from the commencement of this constitution for free and compulsory education for all children until they complete the age of 14 years.' However, not much progress has been made in education, particularly female education, even nearly four decades after the Constitution was promulgated.

Only 32 per cent of the female children in the age group 5–14 years in Andhra Pradesh were attending school in 1981. The proportion of female children attending school is the highest in coastal Andhra (37.33 per cent) followed by Rayalaseema (29.77 per cent) and Telengana (excluding Hyderabad) trailing the list at 22.95 per cent. Female pupils are most numerous in Krishna, West Godavari, East Godavari, Guntur and Nellore districts of coastal Andhra while the lowest number is observed in Adilabad, Mahaboobnagar, Karimnagar, Nizamabad, Medak, Warangal and Nalgonda districts of Telengana. Eight of the ten districts in Telengana had a percentage of female pupils which was significantly lower than the state average as against only two of the nine districts in coastal Andhra. The low percentages in Telengana and Rayalaseema speak of the neglect of female education due to poverty and the low status of women.

Female Literacy Rate

The literacy rate in Andhra Pradesh for females aged 5-plus years was 23.26 per cent in 1981, the highest being in coastal Andhra (27.68 per cent) and the lowest in Telengana (14.73 per cent) while Rayalaseema (20.47 per cent) stands in between. (see Table 1). The highest female literacy rates are recorded in Krishna, West Godavari, East Godavari and Guntur districts of coastal Andhra and the lowest in the Adilabad, Mahaboobnagar, Medak, Karimnagar and Nizamabad districts of Telengana. All districts in Telengana except Hyderabad had female literacy rates significantly lower than the state average whereas five of the nine districts in coastal Andhra had literacy rates much higher than the state average.

Educational Attainment of Females

The educational attainment of females in Andhra Pradesh is low. Over one quarter of the literate females (6.43 per cent of the total) in 1981 had not attained even primary level of education. Females educated to graduate level and above were an infinitesimal 0.46 per cent of the total females. Those who completed higher secondary/intermediate/pre-university course were few (0.63 per cent). On the other hand, four out of seven educated females in Andhra Pradesh had primary

Table 1
Literacy and Educational Attainment of Females by Districts and Regions in A.P., 1981

District	Literacy rate	Primary	Middle	Matriculation/ secondary	Higher secondary/ Inter/ PUC	Non-technical dip./ certi. not equal to degree	Technical dip. or cert. not equal to degree	Graduate and above
Srikakulam	14.82	6.54	2.76	0.80	0.20	0.01	0.01	0.07
Vizianagaram	14.19	7.56	2.70	0.93	0.25	0.002	0.02	0.13
Visakhapatnam	21.55	8.62	4.05	2.24	0.78	0.01	0.04	0.63
East Godavari	32.89	16.79	4.83	2.00	0.56	0.02	0.04	0.31
West Godavari	35.88	18.07	5.70	2.31	0.64	0.01	0.08	0.34
Krishna	39.15	16.15	7.37	3.34	1.02	0.02	0.12	0.66
Guntur	30.00	13.76	5.12	2.35	0.76	0.02	0.12	0.53
Prakasam	20.55	9.25	2.95	1.37	0.42	0.01	0.06	0.17
Nellore	26.08	11.18	4.28	2.27	0.82	0.01	0.06	0.46
Coastal Andhra	27.68	12.76	4.65	2.06	0.64	0.01	0.06	0.39
Chittoor	22.90	9.91	4.30	1.91	0.51	0.01	0.04	0.33
Cuddapah	20.10	9.34	2.79	1.36	0.45	0.03	0.05	0.22
Anantapur	18.98	7.92	3.09	1.53	0.45	0.01	0.02	0.23
Kurnool	19.55	8.38	3.06	1.56	0.48	0.02	0.03	0.30
Rayalaseema	20.47	8.89	3.37	1.61	0.47	0.02	0.03	0.27

Table 1 continued

District	Literacy rate	Primary	Middle	Matricula-tion/ secondary	Higher secondary/ Inter/ PUC	Non-technical dip./ certi. not equal to degree	Technical dip. or cert. not equal to degree	Graduate and above
Mahaboobnagar	12.26	4.40	2.29	0.88	0.23	0.01	0.04	0.11
Rangareddy	22.32	7.01	4.29	2.53	0.71	0.02	0.07	0.79
Hyderabad	56.47	14.52	12.46	8.79	3.76	0.08	0.25	4.04
Medak	12.45	4.41	2.21	0.85	0.21	0.002	0.03	0.13
Nizamabad	13.34	4.88	2.64	1.09	0.29	0.005	0.02	0.16
Adilabad	11.01	3.74	2.04	0.83	0.27	0.01	0.01	0.14
Karimnagar	12.50	4.10	2.37	0.83	0.25	0.01	0.02	0.11
Warangal	15.66	5.07	3.20	1.25	0.42	0.01	0.03	0.25
Khammam	20.38	7.25	4.00	1.54	0.48	0.01	0.04	0.25
Nalgonda	14.94	5.29	3.07	0.82	0.21	0.01	0.02	0.10
Telengana	**19.28**	6.07	3.90	1.97	0.70	0.02	0.05	0.63
ANDHRA PRADESH	23.26	9.59	4.14	1.95	0.63	0.01	0.05	0.46

Source: Computed from C-2 Age, Sex and Level of Education—All Areas, Series-2, A.P. Part IV-A, Social and Cultural Tables, *Census of India*, 1981.

education. Only one quarter of the educated females (4.14 per cent of the total) had middle school education. Those who completed matriculation/secondary education were only 1.95 per cent of the total. The proportion of females possessing a technical or non-technical diploma or certificate, not regarded as equivalent to a degree, was negligible (0.06 per cent). It will be observed that the low female literacy rate in Andhra Pradesh is compounded by the fact that the majority of the educated females had attained only primary level of education which hardly improved their status as it did not qualify them for skilled jobs.

Significant differences in the educational attainment of females are observed among the three regions in Andhra Pradesh (see Table 1). The proportion of educated females was 20.57 per cent in coastal Andhra as against 14.66 per cent in Rayalaseema and only 9.60 per cent in Telengana excluding Hyderabad. Coastal Andhra had more than twice the proportion of educated females in all categories than Telengana excluding Hyderabad and significantly higher than Rayalaseema. Five of the nine districts in coastal Andhra had a much higher proportion of educated women in each of the educational categories than the state average in contrast to only one out of nine districts in Telengana excluding Hyderabad.

Urban Female Literacy Rate

The urban women in Andhra Pradesh have a much higher literacy rate (47.23 per cent) than their rural counterparts (see Table 2). In coastal Andhra the urban literacy rate was 48.98 per cent compared to 42 per cent in Rayalaseema and 40.57 per cent in Telengana barring Hyderabad. Krishna district in coastal Andhra ranked first in the state in literacy rate for urban females, scoring even higher than Hyderabad. More than one-half of the urban women were literate in Krishna, Nellore, West Godavari and East Godavari districts of coastal Andhra. In contrast, only Hyderabad in Telengana and Chittoor in Rayalaseema had over one-half literate females in urban areas.

Educational Attainment of Urban Women

A great proportion of the urban women in coastal Andhra have attained higher levels of education (39.20 per cent) than in

Telengana (29.39 per cent) and Rayalaseema (31.76 per cent). The capital city of Hyderabad had 43.91 per cent of educated women (see Table 2). The differences in educational attainment among the three regions narrowed with increase in the level of education. The proportion of primary educated urban females in coastal Andhra was higher by 7 per cent than in Telengana and 3.18 per cent higher than in Rayalaseema. The primary educated females account for one-half of the educated urban women in each of the three regions. Urban females possessing middle school education were 10.46 per cent in coastal Andhra, 9.41 per cent in Telengana (excluding Hyderabad) and 8.42 per cent in Rayalaseema. Those who had completed primary and middle school education together comprised two-thirds of the educated urban females in each of the three regions (29.81 per cent of the total in coastal Andhra, 24.59 per cent in Rayalaseema and 21.83 per cent in Telengana barring Hyderabad). Matriculates were 5.74 per cent in coastal Andhra as against 4.96 per cent in Rayalaseema and 4.78 per cent in Telengana. The higher secondary/intermediate/pre-university passed females represented 2.07 per cent in coastal Andhra, 1.73 per cent in Rayalaseema and 1.57 per cent in Telengana.

Degree Holders and Technical Personnel

In Andhra Pradesh, 1.56 per cent of the urban females held general degrees and technical diplomas or certificates in 1981. Women having a university degree in general subjects were 0.87 per cent of the urban women in coastal Andhra, 0.71 per cent in Rayalaseema. 0.70 per cent in Telengana. Hyderabad had 2.67 per cent female degree holders. The post-graduate degree holders in general subjects were 0.22 per cent of the urban women in coastal Andhra compared to 0.16 per cent in Rayalaseema and 0.14 per cent in Telengana. Hyderabad had 0.70 per cent post-graduate females. Technical diploma or certificate holders, not equivalent to a degree, were 0.16 per cent of the urban women in coastal Andhra as against 0.09 per cent in Rayalaseema and 0.12 per cent in Telengana.

Professional Personnel

Females holding professional degrees in engineering, technology, medicine, agriculture, dairying, veterinary science and teaching,

TABLE 2

Literacy and Educational Attainment of Urban Females by Districts and Regions in A.P. 1981

District	Literacy rate	Primary	Middle	Matricu-lation/secon-dary	Higher secon-dary/inter/P.U.C.	Non-tech. dip. or cert. not equal to degree	Techni-cal dip. or cert. not equal to degree	Graduate degree other than tech. degree	Post-graduate degree other than tech. degree	Engi-neering and tech-nology	Medicine	Agri-culture & dairy-ing	Veteri-nary	Teach-ing	Others
Srikakulam	41.22	15.66	10.31	4.21	1.31	0.01	0.02	0.32	0.09	—	0.01	0.01	—	0.08	—
Vizianagaram	39.03	17.33	9.06	4.03	1.24	0.01	0.06	0.46	0.10	0.003	0.03	—	—	0.14	—
Visakhapatnam	48.15	17.48	10.56	6.26	2.29	0.03	0.10	1.16	0.39	0.01	0.10	0.002	—	0.19	—
East Godavari	50.05	21.86	10.54	5.31	1.81	0.06	0.11	0.66	0.17	0.01	0.08	—	0.002	0.20	—
West Godavari	50.18	21.95	10.86	5.56	1.94	0.03	0.19	0.82	0.17	0.01	0.03	—	—	0.19	0.002
Krishna	56.53	21.12	12.50	6.79	2.41	0.05	0.20	1.08	0.23	0.01	0.07	0.002	—	0.27	—
Guntur	45.21	17.94	9.14	5.25	1.91	0.06	0.23	0.93	0.26	0.01	0.09	0.003	0.001	0.24	—
Prakasam	45.96	17.03	8.20	4.97	1.78	0.02	0.19	0.40	0.12	0.003	0.05	—	—	0.15	—
Nellore	50.87	18.46	10.66	7.08	3.09	0.04	0.17	1.16	0.18	0.003	0.09	0.002	—	0.28	—
Coastal Andhra	48.98	19.35	10.46	5.74	2.07	0.04	0.16	0.87	0.22	0.01	0.07	0.002	0.001	0.21	0.002
Chittoor	50.27	19.21	11.17	6.25	2.05	0.04	0.15	0.95	0.22	0.003	0.09	0.003	—	0.17	—
Cuddapah	40.24	17.11	7.00	4.22	1.67	0.12	0.11	0.56	0.12	0.006	0.05	—	—	0.10	—
Anantapur	41.05	15.70	8.30	5.02	1.74	0.07	0.05	0.66	0.14	0.002	0.04	—	—	0.11	—
Kurnool	37.44	13.58	7.25	4.36	1.50	0.07	0.06	0.66	0.16	0.02	0.08	—	—	0.14	—
Rayalaseema	42.01	16.17	8.42	4.96	1.73	0.06	0.09	0.71	0.16	0.003	0.06	0.001	—	0.13	—

Table 2 continued

District	Literacy rate	Primary	Middle	Matriculation/ secondary	Higher secondary/ inter/ P.U.C.	Non-tech. dip. or cert. not equal to degree	Technical dip. or cert. not equal to degree	Graduate degree other than tech. degree	Post-graduate degree other than tech. degree	Engineering and technology	Medicine	Agriculture & dairying	Veterinary	Teaching	Others
Mahaboobnagar	38.63	12.39	8.74	4.78	1.42	0.01	0.15	0.52	0.07	—	0.04	—	—	0.15	—
Rangareddy	47.39	13.24	10.56	7.58	2.24	0.08	0.22	1.75	0.37	0.03	0.07	0.003	—	0.38	—
Hyderabad	56.47	14.52	12.46	8.79	3.76	0.08	0.25	2.67	0.70	0.03	0.24	0.01	0.002	0.40	0.001
Medak	41.33	13.68	9.20	4.56	1.30	0.01	0.19	0.60	0.08	0.02	0.05	—	—	0.18	—
Nizamabad	35.41	11.46	8.42	4.01	1.24	0.01	0.07	0.43	0.08	—	0.01	—	0.003	0.16	—
Adilabad	31.47	9.74	7.05	3.22	1.15	0.02	0.02	0.37	0.06	0.02	0.03	—	—	0.05	0.004
Karimnagar	36.13	10.87	8.05	3.52	1.20	0.03	0.08	0.42	0.05	0.02	0.03	0.002	—	0.05	—
Warangal	43.51	12.36	10.48	5.18	2.04	0.03	0.15	0.84	0.16	—	0.07	—	—	0.25	0.003
Khammam	46.70	14.93	10.83	5.22	1.99	0.01	0.13	0.62	0.23	0.01	0.03	—	—	0.16	—
Nalgonda	44.75	14.15	11.59	4.50	1.38	0.06	0.07	0.52	0.07	—	0.02	—	—	0.13	—
Telengana	47.61	13.35	10.76	6.55	2.54	0.05	0.18	1.57	0.38	0.02	0.13	0.003	0.001	0.27	0.001
ANDHRA PRADESH	47.23	16.46	10.27	5.94	2.20	0.05	0.15	1.13	0.28	0.01	0.09	0.002	0.001	0.22	0.001

Source: Computed from C-2 part A, Age, Sex and Level of Education—Urban; Series-2, A.P.; Part-IV-A Social and Cultural Tables, *Census of India*, 1981.

together comprised 0.323 per cent of the total urban women in Andhra Pradesh in 1981. Teaching is the most favoured profession of educated females, accounting for two-thirds of the women holding professional degrees. The remaining one-third were physicians. Engineering, technology, agriculture, dairying and veterinary science are the least popular professions for women. A similar trend is observed in all the three regions, with coastal Andhra showing a significantly higher proportion of female urban professionals. In this region, 0.293 per cent of the urban women were professional degree holders compared to 0.194 per cent in Rayalaseema and 0.224 per cent in Telengana excepting Hyderabad which has 0.683 per cent. Nellore, Krishna, Guntur, Visakhapatnam and East Godavari in coastal Andhra have the highest proportion of female professionals. In Telengana, the lowest proportion of professional women are found in the districts of Adilabad, Karimnagar, Nalgonda, Nizamabad, Mahaboobnagar, and Khammam. In Rayalaseema, Chittoor has a relatively high proportion of females holding professional degrees. The higher educational attainment of women in coastal Andhra is a crucial determinant of their greater participation in the non-agricultural sector and the consequent enhancement in their status through increased freedom in financial and familial matters.

For the commendable achievement in female literacy in Telengana, the credit goes to the late Durgabai Deshmukh, a well-known social worker and founder of the Andhra Mahilasabha. Mrs Deshmukh had undertaken several formal and non-formal literacy and vocational programmes for the welfare of women in this region. The Andhra Mahilasabha is also running educational institutions offering degree and BEd courses exclusively for women besides several other extension programmes planned from time to time. Recognizing the importance of women's education for social development, the present Telugu Desam Government has also started the Sri Padmavathi Mahila Viswavidhyalayam which is the first of its kind in the country offering applied vocational courses. The Ministry of Social Welfare, Government of Andhra Pradesh, has also opened several hostels for the education of backward and scheduled caste females. Great strides in the educational attainment of women are expected in the years to come on account of these measures and also because of the increased demand for educated brides in the marriage market.

WOMEN AND MARRIAGE

Early and universal marriage has been traditionally favoured for women in Andhra Pradesh. According to the 1981 census 28.3 per cent of the total females were married by age 19 and 46.8 per cent by age 24 years. The figures for urban females were 21.3 per cent and 40.3 per cent respectively while for rural females the corresponding figures were higher by 9 per cent for both the age groups. The marriage pattern differed significantly among the three regions in Andhra Pradesh.

Child Marriages

The Child Marriage Restraint Acts could not completely deter child marriage in Andhra Pradesh, and 6.7 per cent of girls married in the age group 10–14 years. Female child marriages were almost triple in rural areas (7.9 per cent) compared to urban areas (2.8 per cent). Telengana had an alarming incidence of 12.3 per cent child marriages as against only 3.5 per cent in coastal Andhra and 2.6 per cent in Rayalaseema. All districts in Telengana except Hyderabad and Khammam recorded child marriage rates two to three and a half times higher than the state average (6.7 per cent) ranging from 8.4 per cent in Rangareddy to 22.8 per cent in Nizamabad district. Female child marriages are common among the scheduled castes and scheduled tribes as they prefer immediate marriage of daughters after menarche. The parents fear that delayed marriage will bring a bad name to the family and have difficulty in arranging marriages at a later stage.

Rayalaseema, despite its lower socio-economic profile, registered a significantly lower proportion of female child marriages (2.6 per cent) than coastal Andhra (3.5 per cent), due to the presence of larger number of scheduled castes and scheduled tribes and other backward class people in the latter. This is confirmed by the relatively higher incidence of child marriage in each of the districts in the three regions that have greater proportion of scheduled castes, scheduled tribes and backward classes. The disproportionately high incidence of female child marriages in Telengana (12.3 per cent) is a clear indication of the lower status of females in that region than in coastal Andhra and Rayalaseema.

Age at Marriage

In Andhra Pradesh, 57.5 per cent of the females aged 15–19 and 92.5 per cent in the age group 20–24 were married. The trend in female marriages in the age group 15–19 in the three regions is similar to the pattern of child marriages but with narrower differences, being two-thirds in Telengana (66.0 per cent), more than one-half in coastal Andhra (53.3 per cent) and just half in Rayalaseema (50.0 per cent). The differences in the marriage pattern among the three regions were greatly reduced in the age group 20–24 on account of the universality of marriage. By and large, over 90 per cent of the women in the age group 20–24 were married in all the three regions. However, a reverse trend is noticed with coastal Andhra registering a slightly lower proportion of female marriages (92.18 per cent) in the age group 20–24 than in Rayalaseema (92.31 per cent) and Telengana (93.17 per cent).

Marriages in Andhra Pradesh are generally arranged by parents. Illiterate and non-matriculate females comprise the bulk (93.0 per cent) of the female population. They are seldom consulted by parents even in such crucial matters as age at marriage and selection of bridegroom. The traditional view is that parents are the best judges in such matters and not the prospective brides who are too young to make such critical decisions.

The mean age at marriage for females in Andhra Pradesh was 17.24 years in 1981. The urban females married two years later (18.73 years) than the rural females (16.70 years). As seen in Table 3, the mean age at marriage is the lowest for the total and rural females of Telengana region. The women in rural Telengana married 1.7 to 1.9 years earlier than their counterparts in coastal Andhra and Rayalaseema. All the districts in Telengana except Khammam had much lower mean ages at marriage than the state average for rural women with Nizamabad district having the lowest mean age at marriage (14.72 years) in the entire state. Rayalaseema recorded a higher mean age at marriage than coastal Andhra in respect of both total and rural women on account of the higher proportion of scheduled castes, scheduled tribes and other backward classes in coastal Andhra who, by and large, favour early marriage.

An equally high mean age at marriage for urban women is observed in both Rayalaseema (18.79 years) and Telengana (18.78 years) while it is slightly lower in coastal Andhra (18.67 years). Nevertheless, the coastal districts had the first and second highest mean ages for the

TABLE 3
Mean Age at Marriage of Females by Districts and Regions in A.P., 1981

Districts	Total	Rural	Urban
Srikakulam	18.05	17.89	19.15
Vizianagaram	18.05	17.84	18.92
Visakhapatnam	17.76	17.19	18.71
East Godavari	17.50	17.09	18.61
West Godavari	17.72	17.41	18.69
Krishna	18.05	17.31	18.86
Guntur	17.56	16.77	18.24
Prakasam	16.98	16.73	18.14
Nellore	17.99	17.59	19.15
Coastal Andhra	17.64	17.28	18.67
Chittoor	18.04	17.80	19.02
Cuddapah	17.79	17.56	18.57
Anantapur	18.07	17.70	19.19
Kurnool	17.37	16.96	18.43
Rayalaseema	17.82	17.53	18.79
Mahaboobnagar	15.60	15.30	17.70
Rangareddy	16.82	16.14	18.64
Hyderabad	20.10	—	20.10
Medak	15.82	15.53	17.79
Nizamabad	15.33	14.72	17.66
Adilabad	16.07	15.73	17.38
Karimnagar	15.34	15.03	16.84
Warangal	15.97	15.43	18.18
Khammam	17.44	17.35	17.85
Nalgonda	15.92	15.70	17.40
Telengana	16.50	15.61	18.78
ANDHRA PRADESH	17.24	16.70	18.73

Source: Computed from C-1 Age, Sex and Marital Status, Series-2, A.P., Part IV-A Social & Cultural Tables, *Census of India*, 1981.

marriage of rural women and the second and third highest for urban women in Andhra Pradesh. The high mean age at marriage for urban females in Telengana is due to the location of Hyderabad district in this region which is exclusively urban. Keeping Hyderabad out, the mean age at marriage in Telengana would be 17.7 years for urban females and 16 years for the total, which are much lower than the corresponding figures in Rayalaseema and coastal Andhra. The greater prevalence of child marriage and very early age at marriage in Telengana are indicative of the social backwardness of the women in that region while their counterparts in Rayalaseema and coastal Andhra are relatively better off.

WOMEN AND FERTILITY

Childbirth, according to tradition, is a blessing for females while sterility is a curse. Women having children, especially sons, enjoy a higher social status in the family as well as in society. Infertile women are looked down upon by fellow women, particularly their mothers-in-law. This is the common cause for the remarriage of their spouses. Motherhood is considered by traditional society to be the most crucial of all roles for women. According to the 1981 census, there were 9.68 million married females in Andhra Pradesh in the reproductive age group 15–44 as against 7.85 million in 1971. The growth rate of married females in the reproductive ages (15–44 years) during the decade 1971–81 was 22.3 per cent.

For the analysis of fertility, children ever born are not considered due to high under-reporting in rural areas. This is confirmed by their lower averages for married females in rural areas as compared to urban areas of most of the districts. Hence, the number of live births during the year preceding the 1981 census are analysed here. The total marital fertility rate for Andhra Pradesh was 3.8, 3.88 for rural women and 3.56 for urban women. The figures for rural and urban women in 1971 were 4.6 and 4.1 respectively. This indicates a decline in fertility for both groups, the quantum of decline being higher in rural areas.

Table 4 shows both the general marital fertility rate (GMFR) and total marital fertility rate (TMFR) to be the lowest in Telengana for total, rural and urban females. This is questionable. How can Telengana have the lowest fertility in Andhra Pradesh when the mean age at marriage of females and contraceptive prevalence rates were the lowest in the state? This may largely be due to under-reporting of live births, particularly in rural areas, because of the greater incidence of infant mortality. This is evident from the fact that five of the ten districts in Telengana viz., Medak, Nizamabad, Karimnagar, Warangal, and Nalgonda had lower fertility in rural areas than in urban areas although the rural married females in these five districts had not only

TABLE 4
GMFR and TMFR by Districts and Regions in A.P. 1981

District	General marital fertility rate			Total marital fertility rate		
	Total	Rural	Urban	Total	Rural	Urban
Srikakulam	115	115	107	3.69	3.72	3.35
Vizianagaram	112	111	115	3.69	3.70	3.56
Visakhapatnam	123	123	122	3.88	3.97	3.66
East Godavari	125	127	121	3.95	4.03	3.66
West Godavari	117	118	114	3.74	3.80	3.46
Krishna	127	123	136	3.99	3.90	4.17
Guntur	116	117	113	3.57	3.65	3.35
Prakasam	127	130	109	4.00	4.14	3.24
Nellore	123	124	119	3.87	3.95	3.52
Coastal Andhra	121	121	120	3.83	3.89	3.62
Chittoor	113	112	120	3.56	3.57	3.75
Cuddapah	123	124	116	3.83	3.89	3.56
Anantapur	141	148	115	4.43	4.66	3.55
Kurnool	143	149	124	4.43	4.65	3.76
Rayalaseema	130	132	119	4.05	4.17	3.63
Mahaboobnagar	130	130	131	4.07	4.08	3.97
Rangareddy	131	133	125	3.96	4.07	3.63
Hyderabad	99	—	99	3.00	—	3.00
Medak	120	120	123	3.69	3.69	3.82
Nizamabad	108	105	121	3.34	3.27	3.66
Adilabad	119	121	110	3.74	3.85	3.28
Karimnagar	98	95	111	3.09	3.06	3.20
Warangal	124	121	142	3.93	3.82	4.46
Khammam	135	135	137	4.24	4.26	4.15
Nalgonda	122	120	133	3.80	3.78	3.90
Telengana	117	117	114	3.66	3.73	3.44
ANDHRA PRADESH	121	122	118	3.80	3.88	3.56

Source: Computed from F-20 currently married women by present age and births to them during last year by birth order Series-2, A.P., Part VI-A & B, Fertility Tables, *Census of India, 1981*.

lower mean ages at marriage and lower rates of contraceptive prevalence than their counterparts in the urban areas but also the lowest in this region (see Tables 3 and 5). Hence, caution is to be observed in comparing the fertility of Telengana with that of coastal Andhra and Rayalaseema. The greater reliability of fertility data in coastal Andhra and Rayalaseema is evident from the observation that only one each of the districts in these regions had fertility lower in rural areas than in urban areas. Coastal Andhra showed significantly lower fertility than Rayalaseema for both the total and rural females while it is almost equal in respect of urban women. Urban fertility would be the highest in Telengana (3.77) if Hyderabad is excluded from this region.

The child-woman ratio (CWR), which is a more reliable measure of fertility than the reporting of live births in areas of high infant mortality, showed conspicuous differences among the three regions, in sharp contrast to the observed fertility differentials based on live births. CWR was the lowest in coastal Andhra while the GMFR and ASMFR were the lowest in Telengana even after the exclusion of Hyderabad. Compared with Telengana, the CWRs in coastal Andhra were less by 68 for total, 59 for rural and 98 for urban reproductive (15–49 years) women, respectively. These figures, on the exclusion of Hyderabad from Telengana, would be 74 for total and 117 for urban females. Nine of the eleven districts in Telengana had CWRs much higher than the state average in contrast to only one out of nine districts in coastal Andhra. The CWRs for Rayalaseema are intermediate to coastal Andhra and Telengana. When compared with coastal Andhra, the CWRs in Rayalaseema were higher by 35 for total, 31 for rural and 37 for urban women whereas in Telengana these figures were respectively 33, 28 and 61. Lower fertility in coastal Andhra is a clear indication of the high status of its females compared to Rayalaseema and Telengana as a greater proportion of the women in coastal Andhra are making decisions jointly with the spouse on matters of family size (see Table 5).

Work Participation Rates

Female Child Labour

Female child labour is yet another sensitive indicator of the status of women, the prevalence of female child labour indicating the low status of women. Despite the existence of several Child Labour Acts the

TABLE 5
Child-woman Ratio by Districts and Regions in A.P., 1981

Districts	Child-woman ratio (0-4 age group)		
	Total	Rural	Urban
Srikakulam	509	518	432
Vizianagaram	464	467	448
Visakhapatnam	479	496	442
East Godavari	495	516	429
West Godavari	490	502	416
Krishna	471	487	441
Guntur	463	472	439
Prakasam	523	551	435
Nellore	461	483	385
Coastal Andhra	483	500	431
Chittoor	475	485	425
Cuddapah	486	495	450
Anantapur	557	585	459
Kurnool	555	565	524
Rayalaseema	518	531	468
Mahaboobnagar	597	601	567
Rangareddy	596	620	527
Hyderabad	506	—	506
Medak	546	545	556
Nizamabad	513	561	569
Adilabad	552	555	538
Karimnagar	483	469	556
Warangal	561	566	538
Khammam	570	584	510
Nalgonda	561	557	586
Telengana	551	559	529
ANDHRA PRADESH	514	527	475

Source: Computed from C-6 population by five year age group and sex, Series-2, A.P., Part IV-A Social and Cultural Tables, *Census of India, 1981*.

magnitude of child labour is the highest in Andhra Pradesh, particularly in the rural areas. According to the 1981 census, 10.58 per cent of the total female children in Andhra Pradesh in the age group 5–14 years were main workers, the percentage in rural areas being 12.92 as against 2.62 in urban areas. The marginal workers among female children, although smaller in proportion, were nine times higher in rural (2.78 per cent) than in urban areas (0.32 per cent).

Marked differences in the prevalence of female child labour are observed among the three regions of Andhra Pradesh (Table 6). It is the highest in Telengana, the most backward region, and the lowest in coastal Andhra. The main workers among female children in Telengana excluding Hyderabad were 12.66 per cent, in coastal Andhra 9.31 per cent and in Rayalaseema 11.80 per cent. In urban areas, the percentage was 3.66 in Telengana (excluding Hyderabad), 2.51 in coastal Andhra and 3.33 in Rayalaseema. These figures for rural areas were 14.34 per cent in Telengana, 13.91 per cent in Rayalaseema and 11.24 per cent in coastal Andhra. Interestingly, the proportion of marginal workers among female children was almost equal among the three regions both in the rural and urban (excluding Hyderabad) areas. Five of the nine districts in coastal Andhra had the lowest female child labour rates in the entire state. Among these, East Godavari, West Godavari and Krishna districts have the highest female literacy and educational levels, age at marriage, contraceptive prevalence rate and the lowest fertility in the state. In contrast, seven of the ten districts in Telengana had female child labour rates much higher than the state average. Karimnagar, Nizamabad, Mahaboobnagar and Khammam districts from Telengana which had the highest rate of female child labour had the lowest female literacy and educational levels, age at marriage, family planning adoption rate and the highest fertility in the state. Thus, the lower incidence of female child labour in coastal Andhra is a clear evidence of the higher status of females in that region in comparison to Telengana and Rayalaseema.

Female Work Participation Rates

In Andhra Pradesh, 7.379 million or 27.87 per cent of the total females were main workers in 1981 as against 24.16 per cent in 1971. Thus, the work participation rate for females had increased by 3.71 per cent during 1971–1981 while males experienced a decline in work participation rate of 2.05 per cent.[4] The female main workers showed

increase in work participation rate in all the age groups. Work participation rate of females in rural areas was triple that of urban areas as
the primary sector, particularly cultivation and agricultural labour,
demands less skills and can easily absorb all rural females including
children and aged persons.

There is considerable variation in the work participation rates for
female main workers among the three regions in Andhra Pradesh
(Table 7), with Telengana recording the highest rate for both total and
rural areas, and also for urban areas, if Hyderabad is excluded. The
overall work participation rate for females in Telengana was higher by
2.15 per cent than Rayalaseema and 5.51 per cent than coastal Andhra.
The differences would be sharper on exclusion of Hyderabad from
Telengana, rising to 4.87 per cent and 8.23 per cent respectively. All
the nine districts in Telengana (except Hyderabad) had female work
participation rates much higher than the state average. The female
work participation rate in rural Telengana was 4.54 per cent higher
than in Rayalaseema and 7.76 per cent more than in coastal Andhra.
With respect to urban areas, the work participation rate of 10.91 per
cent for Telengana ranking second would become 12.98 per cent by
exclusion of Hyderabad giving the region the first place in the state.
Seven of the ten districts in Telengana showed female participation
rates higher than the state average.

Coastal Andhra had the lowest work participation rates in both
rural and urban areas, six of its nine districts recording rates much
lower than the state average. East Godavari district in fact registered a
decline during 1971–1981. Rayalaseema ranks first in urban areas and
second in respect of both total amd rural areas. Two of its four
districts had female work participation rates much higher than the
state average.

The female main workers in Telengana show a high participation
rate because of their utter poverty. A large proportion of the households have only small holdings which are mostly barren and depend
exclusively on rainfall. Forty per cent of the holdings in Telengana
were below one hectare and 60 per cent below two hectares. They are
neither economical for cultivation nor can they provide work to all the
working members in the household. The meagre income from the
small holdings is not sufficient for meeting the bare necessities of the
household. Hence, the women members must toil equally with the
men to make both ends meet, often with little success because of their
large family size.

TABLE 6

Percentage Distribution of Female Child Labour (5-14 yrs.) in the Districts and Regions of Andhra Pradesh, 1981

District	Female child labour					
	Total		Rural		Urban	
	Main workers	Marginal workers	Main workers	Marginal workers	Main workers	Marginal workers
Srikakulam	11.36	3.59	12.43	3.98	2.89	0.42
Vizianagaram	10.97	2.51	12.59	2.89	2.16	0.48
Visakhapatnam	8.76	3.00	12.07	4.23	1.06	0.12
East Godavari	4.30	1.14	5.07	1.35	1.48	0.38
West Godavari	8.12	1.17	9.50	1.40	2.60	0.25
Krishna	8.63	2.03	11.38	2.76	2.55	0.42
Guntur	12.49	2.22	16.05	2.90	3.31	0.48
Prakasam	13.11	2.79	14.39	3.15	5.45	0.63
Nellore	8.91	2.57	10.33	3.11	2.93	0.35
Coastal Andhra	9.31	2.20	11.24	2.72	2.51	0.37
Chittoor	9.87	2.30	11.45	2.70	2.12	0.32
Cuddapah	10.84	2.74	12.47	3.16	3.60	0.86
Anantapur	11.39	2.21	13.57	2.74	2.66	0.13
Kurnool	14.90	1.86	18.18	2.34	4.61	0.34
Rayalaseema	11.80	2.25	13.91	2.72	3.33	0.37
Mahaboobnagar	13.56	3.56	14.66	3.91	4.94	0.73
Rangareddy	9.28	2.26	11.58	2.89	1.31	0.08
Hyderabad	0.81	0.04	—	—	0.81	0.04
Medak	10.76	2.91	11.94	3.26	2.96	0.53
Nizamabad	16.45	1.50	19.04	1.70	5.47	0.62
Adilabad	11.87	2.58	14.07	3.06	2.28	0.45
Karimnagar	17.44	1.87	19.42	2.14	7.01	0.42
Warangal	11.26	2.73	12.66	3.22	4.18	0.24
Khammam	11.89	1.94	13.88	2.30	1.49	0.07
Nalgonda	10.36	2.80	11.41	3.12	2.48	0.44
Telengana	11.43	2.24	14.34	2.90	2.45	0.24
ANDHRA PRADESH	10.58	2.22	12.92	2.78	2.62	0.32

Source: Computed from C-4 children (5-14 yrs.) by simple years of age, school attendance and economic activity, Series-2, A.P., Part IV-A, Social and Cultural Tables, *Census of India*, 1981.

TABLE 7
**Work Participation Rate for Female Main Workers by Districts and
Regions in Andhra Pradesh, 1981**

District	Total	Rural	Urban
Srikakulam	27.17	28.84	13.91
Vizianagaram	29.20	32.77	10.40
Visakhapatnam	22.33	28.94	7.44
East Godavari	17.75	20.20	9.14
West Godavari	23.69	26.81	11.81
Krishna	22.86	29.49	9.14
Guntur	30.30	36.81	13.15
Prakasam	31.24	33.73	15.93
Nellore	26.67	30.27	12.78
Coastal Andhra	25.20	29.40	10.86
Chittoor	26.13	29.18	10.79
Cuddapah	25.53	28.22	14.27
Anantapur	29.10	34.02	9.70
Kurnool	33.19	39.14	14.64
Rayalaseema	28.56	32.62	12.33
Mahaboobnagar	36.46	38.85	16.28
Rangareddy	30.60	36.48	11.36
Hyderabad	8.26	—	8.26
Medak	32.35	34.87	12.99
Nizamabad	39.99	44.72	19.30
Adilabad	30.40	35.62	9.20
Karimnagar	38.54	42.38	17.36
Warangal	30.29	34.12	11.55
Khammam	28.46	32.78	6.98
Nalgonda	31.63	34.16	11.14
Telengana	30.71	37.16	10.91
ANDHRA PRADESH	27.87	32.85	11.11

Source: Computed from primary census abstract, Series-2, A.P., Part I of 1981 Supplement, Provisional Population Totals, *Census of India*, 1981.

The situation in Rayalaseema was somewhat better but is deteriorating. Thirty six per cent of the holdings were below one hectare and 58.7 per cent below two hectares consisting largely of dry land.[3] Both Rayalaseema and Telengana have been ravaged by famine in the past several years. The majority of the Taluks in Rayalaseema and several in Telengana are drought-prone most of the time.[3] Consequently, the economy of several families has been shattered reducing middle-class families to marginal farmers and marginal farmers to agricultural labourers. This compels the middle-class females to work on their farm as the family can no longer afford to hire agricultural labourers, and forces those from marginal families to work as agricultural labourers.

Coastal Andhra on the other hand has a prosperous people who have fertile delta land, with perennial irrigation. The land is more fairly distributed. Though 56 per cent of the holdings are below one hectare and 73.7 per cent below two hectares, the land being fertile and largely wet can support all the family members. The family size is low. Being the most prosperous region in the state and the rice bowl of Andhra Pradesh, a low status is ascribed to the females in the agricultural sector, including those who work on their own farms. Hence, the female work participation rate is low. This is clearly evident from the distribution of female main workers into broad industrial categories (see Table 7).

Distribution of Female Main Workers

Female main workers are broadly divided into four categories, namely, cultivators, agricultural labourers, household industry and 'other workers' in various fields such as livestock, forestry, fishing, mining and quarrying; other than household industry; construction; trade and commerce; transport, storage and communications; and other services. Of the total female main workers in the state 81.7 per cent were cultivators and agricultural labourers, 6 per cent in household industry while 'other workers' represented 12.3 per cent. During the decade 1971–1981, the proportion of female workers in the categories of cultivators and household industry had gone up while the proportion of agricultural labourers and 'other workers' had fallen.[5] The increase was 4.77 per cent for cultivators and 1.81 per cent for workers in household industry while the decline in agricultural labourers and 'other workers' was of the order of 5.62 per cent and 0.96 per cent, respectively.

Coastal Andhra is in sharp contrast to Rayalaseema and Telengana, in the distribution of female main workers (Table 7). It had the lowest number of cultivators but the largest number of 'other workers', whether in respect of total, rural or urban areas. In household industry also, coastal Andhra registered a higher proportion of workers than Rayalaseema but not Telengana. Despite assured irrigational facilities, coastal Andhra has a low proportion of cultivators to total female main workers because of the perceived low status for female cultivators and their prosperity which allows many to employ agricultural labourers. On the other hand, the higher proportion of 'other workers' in coastal Andhra is indicative of a higher status for female workers in the tertiary sector due to their higher educational level and greater earning power. Six of the nine districts in coastal Andhra had 'other workers' higher than the state average as against one out of four districts in Rayalaseema and two of the ten districts in Telengana.

To give a new impetus to female work participation and thereby to raise the status of women, the present Telugu Desam government has reserved 30 per cent jobs for women in public employment.[6]

WOMEN AND RIGHT TO PROPERTY

In Andhra Pradesh till recently women had no right to property, and only men used to inherit ancestral property. Parents had the liberty to share their personal property with their daughters also, and in coastal Andhra (but not in Rayalaseema or Telengana) it was customary among upper and middle-class families to present landed property to daughters at the time of their marriage. This gift of landed property would in turn be passed on only to the daughters of the daughter. The Telugu Desam government has passed an Act providing equal rights to women in ancestral property.[6] The effective implementation of this Act would raise the status of females.

WOMEN AND POLITICS

Participation of women in politics shows their emancipation. It also helps to represent their problems and protect their interests. In Andhra Pradesh, female members of the Legislative Assembly (MLAs) were ten in 1981, fifteen in 1983 and thirteen in 1985.[7] Significant differences are also observed among the three regions with regard to the involvement of females in politics. Participation is conspicuously higher in coastal Andhra than in Telengana and Rayalaseema, due to greater political awareness in the former. In 1981, the female MLAs from coastal Andhra constituted 60 per cent of the total as against 20 per cent each from Rayalaseema and Telengana. These figures in 1983 were 53, 20 and 27 per cent respectively. At present, 62 per cent of the female MLAs are from coastal Andhra, 15 per cent from Rayalaseema and 23 per cent from Telengana. There is only one female Member of Parliament, from Hyderabad. The Minister for Women and Child Welfare is from coastal Andhra.

FEMALE OFFERINGS TO GODDESS

Female offerings to goddesses is a sensitive indicator of the low status of women. When a daughter is seriously ill, instead of taking her to the doctor, the poor parents leave the child before the goddess with the promise that the child would be offered to her if it survives. If by chance the child survives, they keep their promise due to fear of being cursed by the goddess. This practice is observed among the scheduled castes, scheduled tribes and Dommara, who are illiterate, ignorant, superstitious and poverty-stricken. Soon after attainment of puberty, the girl will be dedicated to the goddess and named after her. Such women are called Jogins in Telengana and Devadasis/Basivis in Rayalaseema. They are married to the goddesses Yellamma and Matamma. Custom bars them from marriage and normal family life and they become the common property of the community to satisfy the lust of the males. They have to beg for survival. People cannot volunteer to marry them for fear of a curse from the goddess. If they reach old age they will die destitute. This system is widely prevalent in the rural areas of Nizamabad, Mahaboobnagar districts in Telengana[8] and Kurnool and Chittoor districts in Rayalaseema.[9] According to a survey by SALT, a voluntary organization, Jogins are found even in Hyderabad city.[8] The present Governor, Kumudben Joshi, has not only advocated abolition of this evil practice but has also arranged marriages for Jogins in the Raj Bhavan. The State Government has decided to pass an Act and also to initiate several social and economic measures to curb this practice.

WOMEN AND BIRTH CONTROL

Family limitation which helps in alleviating the heavy burden of natural fertility on women also reflects the status enjoyed by them. Differentials in achievement of family welfare targets in respect of the most effective methods, particularly sterilization and IUDs, speak of the differential status of women among the three regions in Andhra Pradesh.

Sterilization

Up to November 1987, 85.60 per cent of the seasonal target set for sterilization was achieved in Andhra Pradesh (see Table 8). Coastal Andhra achieved 102.30 per cent sterilizations, Telengana 75.43 per cent and Rayalaseema 68.09 per cent.[10] Four of the nine districts in coastal Andhra achieved more than 100 per cent of the seasonal target compared to three out of ten districts in Telengana and none in Rayalaseema. In contrast, the achievement was below 50 per cent in two of the nine districts in Telengana as against none in coastal Andhra and Rayalaseema. The top three ranks were achieved by Krishna, West Godavari and East Godavari districts from coastal Andhra with an aggregate achievement of 121 per cent while the bottom three ranks went to Adilabad, Medak and Mahaboobnagar districts in Telengana having an aggregate performance of 47.48 per cent of the target.

Vasectomy Vs. Tubectomy

The adoption of tubectomy, whether voluntary or not, reflects the status enjoyed by women. In male-dominated communities tubectomy is generally thrust upon women though vasectomy is simple and easy. This is indicative of their lower status. Tubectomy is the most widely adopted method of sterilization in Andhra Pradesh. Nearly 90 per cent of the sterilizations in the state during 1986–87 were tubectomies revealing an indirect compulsion from the husband in the majority of the cases. Although vasectomies constituted only 10 per cent of the sterilizations, sharp differences are noticed among the three regions. Vasectomies are the highest in coastal Andhra (13.89 per cent) and the lowest in Rayalaseema (1.42 per cent) with Telengana registering 7.79 per cent (see Table 8).

Intra-uterine Device

Andhra Pradesh achieved 71.28 per cent of the target in the implantation of intra-uterine devices (IUD). The achievement was the highest in coastal Andhra (83.53 per cent) while Telengana recorded the

TABLE 8
**Percentage Distribution of Sterilisations in the Districts and Regions
in A.P. during 1986–87**

District	Percentage	
	Vasectomy	Tubectomy
Srikakulam	21.48	78.52
Vizianagaram	22.96	77.04
Visakhapatnam	42.63	57.37
East Godavari	7.74	92.26
West Godavari	7.93	92.07
Krishna	6.52	93.48
Guntur	1.52	98.48
Prakasam	2.82	97.18
Nellore	4.43	95.57
Coastal Andhra	13.89	86.11
Chittoor	2.73	97.27
Cuddapah	0.51	99.49
Anantapur	1.08	98.92
Kurnool	0.63	99.37
Rayalaseema	1.42	98.58
Mahaboobnagar	0.36	99.64
Rangareddy	0.78	99.22
Hyderabad	2.18	97.82
Medak	2.54	97.46
Nizamabad	2.57	97.43
Adilabad	16.91	83.09
Karimnagar	15.64	84.36
Warangal	26.23	73.77
Khammam	4.79	95.21
Nalgonda	5.12	94.88
Telengana	7.79	92.21
ANDHRA PRADESH	10.29	89.71

Source: Computed from unpublished statistics of State Family Welfare Bureau. Directorate of Medical & Health Sciences, A.P.

lowest performance (58.60 per cent), and Rayalaseema achieved 67.99 per cent. The second, third and fourth ranks in IUD performance were taken by the coastal Andhra districts while the last six ranks (18–23) went to Telengana districts despite the fact that the first rank was held by Rangareddy district in Telengana.[8] Thus, the desire to maintain spacing between subsequent births is greater among the females in coastal Andhra. This also promotes emancipation of women through greater leisure time which facilitates participation in other activities outside the home and strengthens their status.

WOMEN AND ABORTIONS

On the recommendations of the Shantilal Shah Committee, the Medical Termination of Pregnancy (MTP) Act was enacted in 1972. It liberalized the earlier grounds for abortion. The MTP Act was enacted for health and family planning reasons which would raise the status of women.[11] Consequently, MTP services are made available free of cost to the needy even in primary health centres. This is to reduce the incidence of illegal abortions which are very dangerous for the women.

According to available statistics, 994 abortions were legally performed in Andhra Pradesh during 1986–87. Of them, 6,501 MTPs or 48.49 per cent were conducted in Telengana. The largest number of MTPs had taken place in Hyderabad accounting for 40 per cent of the total MTPs in the state of Andhra Pradesh during 1986–87. If Hyderabad is excluded from the total, the proportion of legal abortions in Telengana would fall to the lowest level of 15 per cent ranking it third among the three regions. In coastal Andhra, 2,894 MTPs, were performed constituting 30 per cent of the total MTPs, ranking it second in the state. The performance of MTPs in coastal Andhra would rise to 49.47 per cent if abortions in Hyderabad are excluded from the total, giving it the first place in the state. Rayalaseema ranked third performing 2,799 MTPs or 21.54 per cent of the total abortions which would rise to 35.56 per cent by exclusion from the total of Hyderabad, thus ranking it second among the three regions. A similar trend is observed with respect to MTPs performed up to December 1987. However, the proportion of MTPs to total performed in the state up to November 1987 was higher by 3.67 per cent in coastal Andhra, when compared with the achievement during 1986–87, while Rayalaseema and Telengana registered a decline of 2.79 per cent and 0.88 per cent respectively, in the performance of MTPs during the same period. The higher proportion of MTPs in coastal Andhra (excluding Hyderabad) would reveal the greater freedom of women in coastal Andhra even in matters of family size.

The preceding findings reveal disparity in the status of women among the three regions. Coastal Andhra is distinctly superior to Rayalaseema and Telengana in the status of women. Females in Rayalaseema are somewhat better off than those of Telengana. The females in coastal Andhra are assertive and individualistic while they are generally submissive and dependent in Rayalaseema and more so in Telengana. The distinct personality characteristics of females in coastal Andhra may be due to their better educational status, higher age at marriage and resultant mental maturity. Further they enjoy greater economic freedom because of their absolute power on income from land presented at the time of marriage and also the huge dowry given. Setting up of a separate family is also encouraged among the newly weds which enables them to have equal or greater say in family affairs. On the other hand, the joint family system is encouraged in Rayalaseema and Telengana which does not permit much freedom for females. Their low educational status, early age of marriage, wide gap between spouses in age and mental maturity, no/poor earning power, traditional subordination make them depend very much on male members, thereby, according low status to females in Rayalaseema and Telengana. Special efforts for strengthening female education and effective implementation of the Acts passed reserving 30 per cent jobs for women in the public sector and providing equal rights to women in ancestral property would go a long way in raising the status of women in the future, narrowing the disparity among the three regions in Andhra Pradesh.

REFERENCES

1. Institute of Applied Manpower Research, 1976. *Change in the Working Force Structure in A.P. at the District Level, 1951–71*, New Delhi, p. 3.

2. Premi, M.K. 1982., Population Growth and Economic Development. In: *Population of India*, Series No. 10, New York: United Nations, pp. 312–313.

3. Bureau of Economics and Statistics, 1982. *Statistical Abstract of A.P.*, Hyderabad: Govt. of A.P. pp. 42–43, 104–105.

4. Registrar General of India, 1981. Part-II, *Special Report and Tables based on 5 per cent sample data*, Series-2, A.P. pp. 17, 48–49.

5. Registrar General of India, 1981. *Paper 1 of 1981 Supplement Provisional Population Tables*, Series-2, A.P., p. 43.

6. Govt. of A.P., *New Era in Development*, Hyderabad: Commissioner, Information and Public Relations.

7. A.P. Legislative Secretariat, 1981, 1983, 1985. *List of Members of A.P. Legislative Assembly*, Hyderabad.

8. *Andhra Prabha Daily*, 'Jogins in Hyderabad,' 1st Feb. 1988.

9. *Eenadu Daily*, 'Jogins in Chittoor,' 14th Feb. 1988.

10. State Family Welfare Bureau, 1987. *Monthly Statistics on Family Welfare, A.P.*, Hyderabad: Directorate of Medical & Health Services.

11. Lotika Sarkar, 1982. Law and Population. In: *Population of India*, Series No. 10, New York: United Nations, p. 355.

Status of Women and Population Dynamics in Tamil Nadu

R. Jayasree, N. Audinarayana, G.S. Moni and K. Mahadevan

Tamil Nadu, comprising twenty districts of varying sizes, has a geographical area of 130,058 square kilometres and, according to the census of 1981, a population of 48,408,077, out of whom 32,456,202 live in rural areas. Population density (372) is higher in Tamil Nadu than the all-India average (216). The population is mostly Hindu (88.9 per cent) followed by Christians (5.8 per cent) and Muslims (5.2 per cent). Among the Hindus, 19.4 per cent belong to the scheduled castes and scheduled tribes, the scheduled tribes constituting 1.07 per cent of the total population. Tamil Nadu has 23.9 million women, accounting for a fourteenth of the total female population of India of 330 million, and one-third that of southern India. Next to Kerala's density of female population (333), Tamil Nadu has the highest density of 184 women per square kilometre, which is twice the national average (101) and higher than that of the other two southern states of Karnataka (95) and Andhra Pradesh (95) (Census 1981 and Dew 1986).

Culturally, Tamil Nadu is in the forefront of most of the states in India. The Tamil language spoken in this state is the second ancient language of India, next to Sanskrit, and formed the root of most of the other Dravidian languages—Kannada, Malayalam and Telugu—spoken in the southern India. A major classical work of Tamil literature, the *Tirukural*, is a treasure-house of knowledge, philosophy, culture and the history of Tamil tradition itself. Tamil culture promoted the great Carnatic music of southern India. Most of the present-day maestros of classical music of India, of whom M.S. Subbulakshmi is the most famous, hail from Tamil Nadu. A variety of musical instruments add richness and depth to the music itself. The Veena, the most popular instrument of Carnatic music is of local origin, and is normally studied by many women in Tamil Nadu and in the rest of southern India.

Associated with Carnatic music is another famous art, that of Bharata-natyam (dance), which grew and flourished in Tamil Nadu. These arts were patronized and passionately promoted by princes of the past and the politicians of today. In the past, the famous dynasties of Chera, Chola and Pandyan kingdoms of Tamil Nadu promoted music, dance, drama, temple festivals and other forms of art. On their initiative several architecturally famous and massive temples and centres of cultural activities grew and flourished all over Tamil Nadu. In the sculptures that adorn the towers and walls of temples, female figures received prominence. This indicates the importance given to them in the remote past. Many such institutions exist not only in Tamil Nadu but also in several other parts of southern India. In the cultural activities of many South Indian institutions women predominate.

Tamil culture has a rich variety of famous festivals, functions and feasts. Most of the great temples spread all over the state celebrate several complex festivals in which both men and women participate. In such festivals along with gods, goddesses are worshipped, which testifies to the importance given to women in social life. These festivals are accompanied by performances of fine arts such as music, dance, drama, and other traditional varieties of entertainment like instrumental music (Villupattu) acrobatics, games, sports and display of physical strength of animals (cock fights, bull fights). In a non-formal way these centres disseminate and perpetuate the rich cultural tradition of Tamil Nadu.

These items were generally performed soon after harvest at the Pongal festival or on religiously important days like the birthday of Rama (Ramanavami), the festival of lights (Deepavali) and so on. The festive meal presented a variety of delicious food items. Several varieties of South Indian food, with certain exceptions seen in Kerala, are the contribution of Tamil Nadu. They include several varieties of fermented and fried foods besides sweets. Tamil cuisine developed through the efforts of Tamil women. The cultural diversity, complexity and growth of Tamil Nadu owe a great deal to Tamil women. In the sphere of culture, women enjoyed a high status with men.

However, the Devadasi system (female servant of temples), prevalent in most parts of the state, manifested a mixed position of women in the religious-cum-social life of upper caste Hindu society. The traditional dancers and entertainers of temples promoted and perpetuated the rich dance tradition for the benefit of society in general. Though they had the status of artists they were exploited by the priests, local leaders and managers of temples for their sexual gratification. The illegitimate children born of them had a low status in society (with the exception of a popular leader, who was widely respected during the 1960s through 1970s). Today dance is no longer the prerogative of the Devadasis. It has been formally institutionalized as a fine art. Dancers enjoy a high status in society, the profession being attractive in many ways. Tamilians remember with reverence the legend of Bharatanatyam, the late Rukmini Arundale of the Theosophical Society in Adayar. A legend in her lifetime, she founded the Kalakshetra, which enhanced the prestige and popularity of dance and Carnatic music. She declined to be a candidate for the Presidentship of India, in order to be able to devote the rest of her life to the cause of arts and to serve the Theosophical Society.

The women's complex life style and mode of dress indicate that their position is not much inferior to that of men in the family, and to a certain extent in other fields of social life. The saree is the common dress of women in the Indian subcontinent. A famous and costly variety of saree, the Kanchipuram saree, is manufactured in Tamil Nadu and worn by the middle and upper strata of Tamil women and in many other parts of South Asia. The expense incurred in buying these sarees is much more than that on men's dress. The higher investment made for dress and other accessories for women is a clue that importance is given to women at least in this aspect. But the same pattern does not exist in all other fields of life. For instance, at meal times women in general ate after the men had finished their meals, and got only what remained. The right to inherit property was denied to daughters among most communities in Tamil Nadu till recently. Although at present they have the legal right to parental property, most communities give only dowry to daughters and leave the property to sons. The cost of dowry provided in the form of cash, vessels, furniture and ornaments is less than what the sons inherit.

In many communities, women enjoy a differential status on the family front. Among most of the forward castes, namely, Brahmins, Mudaliars, Vellalas, Gounders and Chettiars, women participate in family decision-making on several issues and in the management of family affairs. But the control of finance mostly remains with men. Selection of brides and grooms is made jointly by elderly men and women but property transactions and management remain mostly with men. Women's privileges are much less among several socially backward communities like the scheduled castes and tribes, with the exception of the Thevars. Among the Thevars, women take decisions in several aspects of family affairs. But among the Chakiliars, the Pallars and the Parayars (scheduled castes), men dominate.

Most communities with the exception of certain scheduled castes and tribes respect elderly women. Among the upper castes there are instances of women, even mothers, being tortured by men. Nevertheless, respect for the mother is almost universal in Tamil Nadu. The word 'Thai' denoting mother is a venerable term. Even Tamil is very often referred to as 'Tamil Thai' meaning that the language is revered like the great mother. But women as wives and daughters are not respected as much. More than one daughter in a family is unwelcome in most communities. Tamil society being universally patrilineal, sons are in greater demand. The increasing cost of marriage of daughters also makes parents nervous over the birth of daughters. Consequently, neglect and even female infanticide are common among certain communities.

Avvaiyyar: A Woman Saint

Avvaiyyar, a great woman saint and composer, continues to inspire the women in Tamil Nadu and awaken their aspiration to move up in the social hierarchy. She was identified as a symbol of the Muruga cult, which is a general feature in all Tamil homes. Her image spread far and wide when a film was produced highlighting her life and work. The term Avvaiyyar is also used to connote an elderly and motherly old woman and to refer to a few poetesses. The Sangam literature refers to 'Avvaiyyars in thirty contexts.' But the Avvaiyyar who lives in the minds of the Tamil people as an old grandmother is the one who is said to have lived during the period of Ottakkuttar (twelfth century A.D.). She lived in the court of the Cholas as well as in the courts of smaller feudal lords. A great wanderer, she mingled with the rural masses eating with them and singing for them. Poets of this kind are celebrated in Tamil literature as 'poets who sang for food.' Avvaiyyar's works included the *Attichudi* and *Kondraivendan* composed for children. Her other famous works, *Mudurai* and *Nalvazhi* are almost like textbooks for school children. Avvaiyyar's influence on later writers and poets can be seen by the fact that Subramania Bharati composed the *Pudiya Attichudi* (the new Attichudi) on the lines of Avvaiyyar in the present century. The other works of Avvaiyyar are *Kalviyolukkam, Namurkovai, Pandanandadi* and *Asadikkovai*. In addition to this

Avvaiyyar of the classical period, there are also references to three more such Avvaiyyars in the history of Tamil literature. They demonstrated the equality of women through their life and works (Sourirajan 1988). Through her songs Avvaiyyar contributed greatly to the popular awakening in Tamil Nadu in general and of women in particular (Ramakrishna et al. 1983).

Thiruvalluvar, the author of *Thirukural*, and Ilanko Adigal, a Chera king who was the author of *Cilapatikaram*, two major classics of Tamil literature, portrayed women with high esteem and status. Both of them decried prostitution which existed perhaps widely in the past and undermined the status of women. The heroine, Kannagi, of *Cilapatikaram*, burnt the ancient city of Madurai, the then capital of the Pandyan kingdom, as a symbol of destroying the prostitution prevalent in Madurai. Another major character in this classical work, Madhavi, abdicated her Devadasi role and became a Buddhist nun along with her beautiful daughter. Thiruvalluvar decried prostitution and advocated monogamous marriage. He said (1976: 1046): 'A husband with one wife should be adored as in the case of a chaste woman.' Both these authors consistently depicted their women characters as free from any degradation and gave them equal status with men to play their manifold roles in Tamil society. One-fourth of the fifty-three poets of the Sangam period were women, which showed the freedom of education, importance and encouragement they received in the past. In thousands of songs of Sangam literature, nowhere mention is made of more than two living children in a family. Thus, in the ancient Tamil Nadu women perhaps had a small family and relatively better status.

WOMEN IN POLITICS AND SOCIAL LIFE

The contribution of the women of Tamil Nadu towards India's freedom struggle was commendable. Women in the state had organized youngsters into a Vanar Sena (monkey army) like the legendary monkey army of Lord Rama. This organization instilled patriotism among young boys and girls for fighting against the British. Women acted as volunteers and leaders besides joining and assisting in Satyagraha (Peaceful Resistance) and Civil Disobedience movements. The most prominent among the women leaders was Annie Besant, who contributed to the momentum for freedom and emancipation of women. Though a foreigner, she dedicated her entire life for Indians. As early as in 1917 she established the pioneering Indian Association for Women at Adyar near Madras City. It grew from strength to strength and enrolled 2,300 active members under forty-three branches all over India. Their activities were welfare-oriented namely education, skill development and recreation among women during leisure. Annie Besant fearlessly spoke against untouchability, and championed the cause of women's education and welfare. The other leaders who worked for the same cause at that time included Margaret Cousins who promoted western education among women. They also fought for the women's right to vote (Rajalakshmi 1985: 19).

Many women leaders also courted arrest for the cause of the freedom of India and underwent many jail terms. In this, Rukmini Lakshmipathi was the pioneer. She was arrested for joining the Vedaranyam salt satyagraha along with several men like Rajagopalachari and Ramachandran. Women leaders like Ammu Swaminathan, Captain Lakshmi and Valleammal were able to show that women, like men, could face boldly the challenges posed by the British. Other women leaders who actively championed the cause of women for their education and participation in public life included Mrs Appasamy and Muthulakshmi. Along with several women many men in Madras Presidency also championed the cause of women during the British rule. The most prominent among them was Diwan Bahadur Krishnan Nayar who condemned the disqualification of women prescribed in the electoral rule in Madras according to which women had the right only to vote and not to contest election as candidates for the council because supposedly women were incapable of and disinterested in public life. Krishnan Nayar's retort was that 'some women are more capable of forming sound judgements than some men' (ibid: 42).

A few women members occupied important positions in the Municipal Corporation of Madras, the Treasury Benches and Opposition parties before and after independence. In Madras Muthulakshmi Reddy, Mrs. Lakshmipathi, R.V. Shastri and Ammu Swaminathan were elected to the municipal corporation, even defeating their male counterparts during the pre-independence period. Muthulakshmi Reddy was also elected to the Madras Legislative Council. Her pioneering services for the abolition of the Devadasi system and child marriage, and for the introduction of medical examination in schools, reduction of fees for poor girl students in schools and colleges to encourage education, and allocation of grants for promotion of job-oriented training for adult women were commendable. As the first woman medical graduate and also an active social worker, Muthu-lakshmi Reddy was a popular and powerful agent for the progress of women in general during her time. On her initiative a resolution was moved in the Madras Legislative Council for raising the age of marriage of girls and was unanimously accepted by the Council. Commenting on her resolution on girls' age at marriage Gandhiji said, 'I am strongly in favour of raising the age at marriage of consent not merely to 14 but even to 16. Therefore, I should heartily endorse any movement, whose object is to save innocent girls under age from man's lust' (Rajalakshmi, 1985: 125). Reddy indeed was a legendary figure having been the first woman in the world to be elected to a legislative body in British India.

After independence a few women leaders served on several councils and bodies in Tamil Nadu. Jothi Venkatachalam, Palaniammal, Anandanayaki and Sathyavani Muthu were elected for more than two terms from one constituency which revealed that people reposed confidence in them and valued their services. Similarly, Soundaram Ramachandran served as Deputy Minister of Education in the Central Government during the prime ministership of Pandit Jawaharlal Nehru. She was a revolutionary woman leader who served the poor, women and children through the pioneering Gandhigram Rural In-stitute that she herself had founded along with her husband who was a great freedom fighter, educationist and social worker and was estab-lished near Dindigal in Anna district. Her services to the cause of public health and family planning are equally commendable. Her marriage itself was a revolutionary event. G. Ramachandran, a Nayar (non-Brahmin) from Kerala married her in the presence of Gandhiji, ignoring the objections of her illustrious father, T.V. Sundaram Aiyangar, who belonged to a prominent and prosperous Brahmin family of Madurai. Thus, she demonstrated the liberation of women from the stranglehold of traditional and conservative principles of the past.

In the field of education, culture and social services, a number of women made their mark in Madras City. Among them the late Mary Clubwala Jadav was an eminent social worker, who established the Guild of Service and Madras School of Social Work for the cause of children, poor people, slum dwellers, destitute women, and old and disabled persons. On her initiative, in 1958, the Madras Legislative Council introduced a bill to prevent children from begging and from indulging in anti-social and immoral ways of life (TLC 1959: 391). Similarly, Jothi Venkatachalam piloted a number of bills in the Madras State Assembly to introduce several measures to prevent the outbreak of epidemics like cholera and smallpox. She was also instrumental in expanding the primary health centres in several districts of the state. She has the distinction of serving not only as a minister for a long period but also as a governor for a term in Kerala state. For the welfare of Harijans, Sathyavani Muthu rendered valuable service, when she was the minister of social welfare under the leadership of Annadurai.

Women secured the pride of place in Tamil Nadu in a big way when M.G. Ramachandran became Chief Minister in 1977. During his tenure more than one woman minister adorned the cabinet for the first time in the history of Tamil Nadu. A number of them had been elected to the Assembly or Parliament and also nominated to Parliament. They also had the opportunity to become chairpersons of several public sector corporations. Sulochana Sampath, wife of the late E.V.K. Sampath, who was a political figure in Tamil Nadu, was the chairperson of a corporation. Till recently, Mrs Sathyavani Muthu and Miss Jayalalitha were Members of Parliament, though they belong to the two splinter groups of the same Dravidian Party.

M.G. Ramachandran also made history by appointing the largest number of widows (over 20,000) and destitute women under the massive Child Welfare programme of noon meal scheme that he introduced for the benefit of poor and school-going children. This scheme, for the first time, rapidly and extensively increased school enrolment and reduced the dropout of children, particularly that of girls from the schools. This will, in course of time, improve the health of poor children, make them literates and reduce the neglect and even homicide and infanticide of girls in Tamil Nadu. It has already reduced childhood mortality considerably, leading to the acceptance of the small family norm and ultimately the principle of family planning by the parents of these children. M.G. Ramachandran also established a premier women's university at Kodaikanal in the name of a great woman social worker, Mother Teresa, in order to promote higher education of women and to strengthen research for several women-oriented welfare programmes. After the sudden demise of M.G. Ramachandran, women also got the opportunity to assume political leadership in the two factions of his former political party, the All India Anna Dravida Munnetra Kazhagam. His wife Janaki and his film heroine Jayalalitha led the two rival political parties in Tamil Nadu for some time and then united. Ms Jayalalitha is now the leader of the opposition in the State Assembly.

In the field of education a few women have become pioneers. Today four women hold the coveted position of vice-chancellor. They are Dr Radha Thyagarajan of Alagappa University, Dr Kothai Pillai of Mother Teresa Women's University, Dr Lalitha Kameswaran of M.G.R. Medical University and Dr Rajammal Devadas of Avinashilingam Deemed University. Three of them are founder vice-chancellors. The first vice-chancellor of Mother Teresa Women's University was Mrs K. Vasanthi Devi, who was a former principal of Ethiraj College for Women in Madras City. Lalitha Kameswaran has promoted maternal and child health programmes in the state, and Rajammal Devadas has strengthened Home Science education in Tamil Nadu and in other parts of the country for the betterment of women. Tamil Nadu may be the only state in the developing regions, where out of the twelve university vice-chancellors in a province/state, four are women. In the whole of India, in 158 universities there are only nine women vice-chancellors, four of them in Tamil Nadu. Women's numbers in university syndicates and academic bodies are fast increasing. Particularly in the field of teaching and career in medical colleges it is almost the same as that of men.

EDUCATIONAL STATUS

In the field of education, Tamil Nadu ranks next only to Kerala in India. The overall literacy rates in Tamil Nadu and in India in 1981 were 46.76 and 36.23 respectively. The respective literacy rates for women are 35 and 25. There is a wide variation in the urban female literacy rate (54 per cent) and that of rural areas (26 per cent), which is almost the same in the country as a whole. During the last three decades, female literacy has almost doubled in the state especially in the rural areas. The literacy rate of women, both in rural and urban areas, remained much lower than that of men during the last three to four decades, which confirms that less importance was given to the education of girls (see Table 1).

School enrolment of girls in Tamil Nadu significantly rose between 1971 to 1981 at the primary and middle level. At the national level, the improvement in higher education is better than in Tamil Nadu but less at the primary and the middle school level (see Table 2).

The distribution of literate women according to their educational level showed a negative association both in Tamil Nadu as well as in India. The percentages of literates at different levels of education more or less remain the same, with only slight differences noticed at different

	Tamil Nadu			India		
	1961	1971	1981	1961	1971	1981
Total	18.17	26.86	34.99	12.96	18.70	24.82
Rural	11.57	18.98	25.80	8.55	13.08	17.96
Urban	36.67	45.42	53.99	34.51	42.05	47.82

Sources: Calculated from Socio-cultural tables of *Census of India 1961*, Vol. I Part II C(i), India; *Census of India 1971* Series I, India Part II (ii); and *Census of India 1981* Series I, India Part IV.A.

TABLE 2
Gross Enrolment Ratios

Levels of Education	Tamil Nadu		India	
	1971	1981	1971	1981
Primary Classes I-V (6-11 years)	83.7	103.3	59.1	64.1
Middle Classes VI-VIII (11-14 years)	32.6	42.9	20.8	28.6
High/Higher Secondary Classes X-XI/XII (14-17 years)	17.4	17.9	10.2	15.4

Source: Ministry of Human Resources Development, Government of India, 1987. *A Hand Book of Educational and Allied Statistics.*

levels. In the period from 1971 to 1981 there was a significant improvement at the high school level, but not at the lower levels. However, the proportion of literates without formal educational level significantly declined in Tamil Nadu (from 40 to 33 per cent). The drop at the all-India level was from 37 to 33 per cent (see Table 3).

When the education of girls of different levels is considered it is the highest at the primary education level followed by middle school both in Tamil Nadu and national level. While the proportion of primary educated girls increased during the last one census decade in Tamil Nadu, it surprisingly decreased at the national level. But a reverse situation is noticed with regard to middle school level of education of girls. However, at the level of matriculation increase in the proportion of school going girls is visible both in Tamil Nadu and India but the increase is slightly more in Tamil Nadu than at the national level. Another noteworthy feature is that the college going girls constitute a higher proportion at the national level than in Tamil Nadu.

TABLE 3

Percentage Distribution of Female Literates by Their Educational Levels in Tamil Nadu and India

Educational Level	Tamil Nadu		India	
	1971	1981	1971	1981
Literate without educational levels	40.44	32.90	36.55	33.42
Primary	35.84	36.08	38.22	33.98
Middle	15.43	14.36	15.58	16.78
Matriculation/High secondary	7.64	14.68	7.93	12.48
Non-technical diploma or Certificate not equal to degree	0.02	0.08	0.21	0.09
Technical diploma or Certificate not equal to degree	0.01	0.14	0.16	0.29
Graduate and above	0.62	1.76	1.35	2.96

Sources: *Census of India 1981* Series I, India Part II Special and ibid. Series 20, Tamil Nadu Part II Special.

EMPLOYMENT STATUS

The employment status of women is one of the major indicators of the status of women in society. In Indian census the employment status of women has been calculated on the basis of work participation rate. In general, female work participation is lower than male work participation rate. These rates were slightly higher in Tamil Nadu during 1961 and 1971 (31.3 and 15.1) than the all-India level (28 and 11.9). During 1981 this rate was significantly higher in Tamil Nadu (22.4) than in India (14.0). The findings were more or less the same in rural and urban areas. Female work participation rates are much higher in rural areas than in urban areas. Mainly because of the changes in the definition of 'worker' adopted in 1971 census, all the rates for female work participation show a decline in the 1971 census both in Tamil Nadu and India. In 1981, an increase is seen in Tamil Nadu as compared to the all-India level (see Table 4). Evidently, in Tamil Nadu more women are participating in economic activities and this exhibits a higher status of women than at the national level.

TABLE 4
Work Participation Rate and Age

	Tamil Nadu			India		
	1961	1971	1981	1961	1971	1981
Work Participation Rate:						
Total	31.28	15.09	22.36	27.96	11.87	13.99
Rural	37.11	17.62	27.85	31.42	13.10	16.00
Urban	14.95	9.14	11.01	11.09	6.61	7.28
Age Group wise:						
5-14	10.64	4.47	6.64	10.58	3.97	3.98
15-59	47.97	23.43	33.57	45.17	19.60	22.61
60+	25.79	13.27	16.47	22.38	10.50	10.15

Sources: Calculated from the General Economic Tables of *Census of India 1961* Vol. I, India Part II B(i); *Census of India 1971* Series I, India Part II B(i); and *Census of India 1981* Series I, India Part III A(i).

Across different age cohorts female work participation rate varies considerably. In general, it is higher among the adult females (15–59 age group), followed by old women (60-plus years) and the female children (5–14 age group). All these rates except for child workers are significantly higher in Tamil Nadu than at the national level.

Sector-wise labour force participation of women in Tamil Nadu remained stagnant during the last two decades. Most of them (78.8 per cent) were engaged in agricultural activities (81.5 per cent at the all-India level). A slightly greater proportion (12.2 per cent) in Tamil Nadu are employed in the secondary sector than at the national level (9.1 per cent) and the same proportion in the tertiary sector (9 per cent; see Table 5). About 14 per cent of the non-agricultural workers are professionals, 11 per cent work in the service sector, 7 per cent as salespersons and another 5 per cent as office assistants. This pattern of employment remained more or less the same during the earlier decade also. It also conforms with the all-India pattern.

The sex ratio of the non-agricultural workers in different occupational groups reveals certain improvements in Tamil Nadu as against the national pattern in most of the categories. The sex ratio of the female professional workers was as high as 410 by 1981 in Tamil Nadu as against only 258 at the all-India level. A similar trend was also noticed during the earlier decades (352) for Tamil Nadu and (220) for India. Among women workers engaged in farming and industrial

TABLE 5
Percentage Distribution of Female Workers by Industrial Categories

Industrial Category	Tamil Nadu		India	
	1971	1981	1971	1981
Cultivators	18.9	22.8	29.7	33.2
Agricultural Labourers	54.4	53.4	50.4	46.1
Livestock, forestry, fishing, mining and quarrying etc.	3.7	2.6	2.9	2.2
Primary sector	77.0	78.8	83.0	81.5
Manufacturing, processing, servicing and repairs:				
Household industry	6.0	6.3	4.2	4.6
Other than household industry	4.4	5.2	2.8	3.6
Construction	0.9	0.7	0.6	0.9
Secondary sector	11.3	12.2	7.6	9.1
Trade and Commerce	2.8	2.6	1.8	2.0
Transport, storage and communication	0.7	0.3	0.5	0.4
Other services	8.2	6.1	7.1	7.0
Tertiary sector	11.7	9.0	9.4	9.4
Total	100.0	100.0	100.0	100.0

Source: Same as Table 4.

productions, while the sex ratio was 335 and 229 respectively in Tamil Nadu by 1981, the figures for all-India were 205 and 147 respectively. Significantly more women are therefore engaged in modern sectors of employment in Tamil Nadu than at the National level.

Employment and Wages

Significant differences in wages exist between adult females and males across most of the communities in Tamil Nadu (Table 6). A similar trend is noticed at the national level except in the case of scheduled tribes. The figures refer to wages during 1977–78 (NSS 1987). For all categories of agricultural jobs, women in different communities earned higher rate of daily wages in Tamil Nadu than at the all-India level. Nevertheless, certain variations in daily wages have been noticed for

TABLE 6
Average Daily Earnings of Adult Males and Adult Females of Rural Households and Household Groups

Households and Communities	Tamil Nadu				All India			
	Adult Males		Adult Females		Adult Males		Adult Females	
	Cash	Kind	Cash	Kind	Cash	Kind	Cash	Kind
Scheduled caste households	2.93	1.02	1.71	0.73	2.89	1.33	1.60	1.17
Scheduled tribe households	5.15	0.32	2.31	0.49	2.48	0.96	1.79	0.90
Other households	4.46	0.60	2.01	0.41	3.64	0.94	1.88	0.81
All households	3.81	0.78	1.88	0.60	3.25	1.07	1.77	0.95

Source: Government of India, 1987. *Sarvekshana: Journal of N.S.S.O.*, Vol. X, No. 4.

different agricultural activities carried out by different communities. All these confirm the need for revising the present meagre wages given to women, particularly in the primary Sector.

Unemployment Status

Unemployment of women has been computed on the basis of their daily as well as weekly activities. The percentage of unemployed adult women by their ages (15–59) to the total female population was much higher in Tamil Nadu than in India both in rural and urban areas during 1972–73 (NSS 29th) and 1977–78 period (NSS 32nd Round). On the basis of daily activity status, the percentages of unemployed female were 9.75 and 8.49 in rural areas of Tamil Nadu during 1972–73 and 1977–78 respectively, whereas the corresponding figures for rural India were only 4.94 and 2.93 respectively. For urban areas these figures were 4.05 and 6.73 in Tamil Nadu and 3.29 and 3.15 at the all-India level. A trend more or less similar was noticed on the basis of weekly activities as the status of women also (see Table 7).

A major part of women's time cannot be used for productive purposes, for want of suitable employment opportunities. Therefore, urgent attention may have to be given for involving women in one or another field of production for the overall development of the economy of the state and the country. Under- and unemployment may only

TABLE 7

Percentage of Persons 'Unemployed' to Total Population by their Ages (15–59)

Unemployment Status	Tamil Nadu				India			
	Rural		Urban		Rural		Urban	
	72–73	77–78	72–73	77–78	72–73	77–78	72–73	77–78
On the basis of daily activity	9.75	8.49	4.05	6.73	4.94	2.93	3.29	3.15
On the basis of weekly activity	3.89	2.94	2.70	4.92	2.80	1.73	2.21	2.66

Source: Government of India, 1980. *Sarvekshana: Journal of N.S.S.O.*, Vol. III, No. 3.

influence women to indulge more in family formation leading to the procreation of unwanted children and problems for the parents.

POPULATION PROFILE

The major parameters considered in this section include the growth of population of women over thirty years, their distribution by age, sex ratio, nuptiality, including age at marriage, fertility behaviour, mortality patterns (including infanticide) and family planning behaviour. Most of these factors have been discussed comparative to the all-India pattern and have also been considered on a historical perspective during the last three decades. Where necessary they have been compared with their male counterparts as well.

The decadal growth of population of women for the last 30 years has revealed that their population continue to grow differentially. While the decennial growth rate of women was very low during 1951–61 (11 per cent) it almost doubled during 1961–71 (21.4 per cent). But it declined during 1971–81 (17.4 per cent) as compared to the preceding decade but grew more compared to 1951–61 period. The same trend continued at the national level also. Comparing the decennial growth rate of females in Tamil Nadu with the country as a whole, the female population grew significantly more at the national level. During all the last three decades, a comparison of the growth rate of the female population as against males in Tamil Nadu showed a declining trend. However, at the national level the male population grew slightly more during 1951–71 but surprisingly the females grew slightly more than males exclusively during 1971–81 period (see Table 8).

TABLE 8
Decadal Growth Rates of Males and Females for 1951–1981

State/India	1951–61		1961–71		1971–81	
	Males	*Females*	*Males*	*Females*	*Males*	*Females*
Tamil Nadu	12.7	11.0	23.2	21.4	17.6	17.4
India	22.0	21.3	25.5	24.0	21.1	21.7

Source: Dew, 1986, *Women in Tamil Nadu: A Profile* (Madras: Tamil Nadu Corporation for Development of Women).

Population growth, both male and female, was significantly lower in Tamil Nadu during the last three decades than at the all-India level. It appears from the table that maternal mortality would have declined considerably during the last one decade on account of the impact of MCH (Maternal and Child Health) programmes. While computing the index of growth rate of female population in Tamil Nadu taking 1901 as base line period (1901=100), their population grew from 154 to 260 during the last four decades (1951 to 1981). The corresponding growth of female population at the all-India level was significantly more and thus it increased from 150 to 274 during the same period (Table not given).

Distribution of female population by their broader age categories (0–14, 15–59 and 60-plus) during the last three decades showed a marginal increase of old age population (5.6 to 6.3 per cent) and adult women population (56.9 to 59 per cent) but the child population declined from 37.5 in 1961 to 34.9 per cent by 1981. A comparison with the national level, shows a difference in the proportion of young and adult population but not old women. While the population of girls in Tamil Nadu constituted 34.9 per cent, their counterparts in India were significantly more—39.6 per cent (1981). On the other hand, during the same period the population of adult women in Tamil Nadu was significantly more (59.0 per cent) than at the national level (53.8 per cent; see Table 9).

The sex ratio in Tamil Nadu, which had been in favour of males throughout the last three decades shows a continuing decline. The female sex ratio at the national level has throughout been much lower than in Tamil Nadu, but in the decade 1971–1981 showed a reversal of decline. Both rural and urban female sex ratio in Tamil Nadu was consistently higher than the national level, though at both state and

TABLE 9
Population of Women by Age

Age groups/State/India	1961	1971	1981
Tamil Nadu			
0-14	37.5	37.8	34.9
15-59	56.9	56.5	59.0
60+	5.6	5.7	6.3
India			
0-14	41.2	42.1	39.6
15-59	53.0	51.8	53.8
60+	5.8	6.0	6.6

Source: Same as Table 1.

national level the urban ratio is lower than the rural. The lower urban sex ratio for women may be due to the migration of more men from rural to urban areas (see Table 10).

TABLE 10
Sex Ratio of Population in Rural and Urban Areas in Tamil Nadu and India

State/India	1961			1971			1981		
	Rural	Urban	All	Rural	Urban	All	Rural	Urban	All
Tamil Nadu	1003	963	992	990	951	978	987	956	977
India	963	845	941	949	858	930	952	880	933

Sources: Dew, 1986; Census of India 1961, Vol. I India, Part II C(i) and Women in Tamil Nadu—A Profile (Madras: The Tamil Nadu Corporation for Development of Women).

Nuptiality

Marriage is universal in Tamil Nadu. By 1981, 44 per cent of the total female population was married; 45 per cent was not yet married, 10 per cent was widowed and 0.7 per cent became divorced or separated. A similar trend was noticed during the preceding two decades. At the national level a slightly lower proportion became widows (8 per cent) and separated or divorced (0.4 per cent). The proportion of married and never married remain more or less the same at the national and Tamil Nadu level (Table not given).

The mean age at marriage of females in Tamil Nadu increased from

18.4 to 20.2 from 1961 to 1981. The corresponding figure for India was 16.1 to 18.3. The increase in age at marriage may have an impact on the future fertility of the state, reducing family size. The age at marriage for men in the state also increased from 24.8 by 1961 to 26 by 1981. The corresponding increase at the national level was from 21.1 to 23.3. The people of Tamil Nadu have exceeded the legal minimum age at marriage prescribed by law whereas at the national level only the age at marriage of girls has come up to the prescribed minimum age. Only a small proportion of girls in Tamil Nadu (less than 1 per cent) got married at 14 or younger as against 6.5 per cent at the national level (7.7 per cent in rural areas and 2.4 per cent in urban areas). In the age group 15–19, less than one-fourth got married by 1981 in Tamil Nadu. The proportion at the national level by 1981 was similar to the situation in Tamil Nadu about two decades earlier (see Table 11).

TABLE 11
Nuptiality Indicators

	Tamil Nadu			India		
	1961	1971	1981	1961	1971	1981
Singulate Mean Age at Marriage						
Females	18.4	19.6	20.2	16.1	17.2	18.3
Males	24.8	25.9	26.0	21.1	22.4	23.3
Per cent Females Married by						
0-14 years						
Total	2.42	0.55	0.36	19.22	11.53	6.48
Rural	2.80	0.63	0.39	22.00	13.47	7.70
Urban	1.43	0.55	0.29	6.79	3.73	2.35
15–19 years						
Total	43.24	26.77	22.81	70.61	55.41	43.44
Rural	43.85	27.97	24.19	73.65	61.03	48.80
Urban	41.69	24.44	20.24	51.60	35.91	28.08

Sources: Agarwala, S.N., 1972, *India's Population Problem; Census of India 1981* Series I, India, Part II Special, and ibid., Series 20, Tamil Nadu, Part II, Special.

Fertility

The fertility measures considered here are the child-woman ratio (CWR), i.e., number of children in 0–4 age per female population aged 15–44, and the crude birth rate (CBR). CWR declined in Tamil Nadu from 547 in 1961 to 435 during 1981 (Table 12). A similar trend was also noticed at the national level (659 in 1961 to 546 in 1981), but the decrease in CWR in Tamil Nadu was higher. Obviously, the decline of fertility registered in Tamil Nadu is higher than at the national level.

TABLE 12
Fertility Measures in Tamil Nadu and India

State/India	Fertility Measures			Percentage Decrease	
	1961	1971	1981	1961–71	1971–81
Child Woman Ratio					
Tamil Nadu	547	531	435	3.01	22.07
India	659	655	546	0.61	16.64
Crude Birth Rate					
Tamil Nadu	34.9	31.2	28.0	11.86	11.43
India	41.7	37.2	33.9	12.10	9.73

Sources: *Census of India 1981*, Series 20, Tamil Nadu Part II Special; *Family Welfare Year Book*, 1972–73 and 1982–83.

According to SRS estimates, CBR of Tamil Nadu was 28.0 by 1981 as against 33.9 at the national level. Historically, CBR in Tamil Nadu showed a drop of 7 points as against 7.8 points during the same period in India, showing an affinity in the trend of decline. However, the reduction from 1971 to 1981 was slightly more in Tamil Nadu than at the national level (see Table 12). .

Health and Mortality Pattern

The health and mortality measures discussed here are the expectation of life at birth, infant mortality and crude death rates. According to Table 13, the expectation of life at birth of women in Tamil Nadu during 1981 was 52.3 years, slightly more than that of men as against only 50.0 years at the national level where the men had a slightly higher expectation of life at birth. Historically, the expectation of life at birth increased considerably more for women (38.8 to 52.3 years) than for men (40.7 to 51.9) during the last two decades in Tamil Nadu. Such increase and differentials are not seen particularly for women at the national level, which may confirm the importance given by the state government for the welfare measures for women in general during the last decade, under the leadership of the late M.G. Ramachandran.

TABLE 13
Health and Mortality Measures for Tamil Nadu and India

Mortality Indices	Tamil Nadu			India		
	1961	1971	1981	1961	1971	1981
Expectation of life at birth:						
Males	40.7	43.9	₃1.9	41.9	46.4	50.9
Females	38.8	42.8	52.3	40.6	44.7	50.0
I.M.R.*						
Males	—	122	107	—	132	120
Females	—	121	99	—	148	131
CDR	22.5	14.2	11.8	22.8	15.1	12.5

Note: * Data refers to 1972 and 1978. Sex-wise data not available after 1978.
Sources: *Family Planning Year Book*, 1972–1973 and 1982–1983; *Family Planning Programme, Gujarat Fact Book*, 1972; *Census of India 1971*. India Series I, Paper I of 1979; and *Census of India 1981*. Series I, India, Paper I of 1985.

The infant mortality rate of girls was only 99 during 1978, which was significantly lower than that of boys (107). The corresponding figures for the girls (131) and boys (120) at the national level were significantly higher. The figures for the preceding decade (1972) also were lower in Tamil Nadu and the actual decline during the last one decade (1971–1981) much greater for girls in Tamil Nadu than at the national level (see Table 13). The general mortality of the population in Tamil Nadu was almost similar to that at the national level during 1981 (11.8 vs. 12.5) and also in the two preceding decades.

Infanticide

Prevalence of infanticide is an indication of the poor status of women. In Tamil Nadu this practice is reported to be common among the Gounders, a forward and well-to-do community and the Thevars, a backward one. The Gounders mostly live in Coimbatore, Periyar, Salem, Dharamapuri and Nilagiri districts. The Thevars are spread over several districts but are more concentrated in the Madurai and Anna districts. The first baby girl is tolerated by the parents but subsequent daughters are often killed. The Gounders feed the new-born girls with honey and chaff normally within a week after birth. The chaff with its thorny edge sticks to the throat of the infant leading to slow internal haemorrhage and subsequent death. The Thevars drown their female infants in water mixed with cowdung. The infanticide is done secretively. The neighbours know it, but keep silent to avoid trouble. Except these two communities, no other group is reported to be committing infanticide in Tamil Nadu, though neglect of females is common among the middle class and poorer sections of society. These pieces of evidence confirm the poor status suffered by women in these communities. Despite such inhuman practices, mothers command respect even among these communities.

Family Planning Behaviour

The family planning behaviour of women by way of couple protection rate and adoption of female sterilization has been analysed in Table 14. Acceptance of family planning by women also indicates their social status. Significantly more women/couples (42.2 per cent) in Tamil Nadu than at the national level (38.7 per cent) have been protected by one or the other contraceptives by 1986. Historically too, the pattern of increase in couple protection rate was more during different periods in Tamil Nadu than at the national level. This trend confirms the acceptability of family planning innovations by more women in Tamil Nadu than at the national level. Considering female sterilization in relation to the total number of sterilizations, during 1985–86, 89.3 per

TABLE 14
Indicators of Family Planning Performance in Tamil Nadu and India during the Last Three Decades

Family Planning Indices	Tamil Nadu %	India %
Percentage of couples currently protected		
Upto March 1973	17.7	15.0
Upto March 1982	28.1	25.7
Upto March 1986	42.2	38.7
Percentage share of Tubectomies to total number of sterilizations		
1961	11.51	38.92
1970–1971	27.47	33.92
1980–1981	93.58	78.62
1985–1986	89.27	80.98

Sources: *Family Welfare Year Book* 1972–73, 1980–81, 1981–82 and 1985–86 and Government of India, 1987 *Pocket Book on Family Welfare Information*.

cent of the women got sterilized in Tamil Nadu as against only 81 per cent at the all-India level. The trend is similar since 1980 both in Tamil Nadu and India. A reverse trend used to be noticed prior to 1980. These findings confirm the changing positive awareness and attitude of women on contraception and the importance they give to family planning, which is a favourable sign of their enhanced status.

IMPLICATIONS FOR DEVELOPMENT

Although several dimensions of the status of women among a few communities in Tamil Nadu have improved considerably during the recent past, most women continue to remain backward in several aspects. Historically and culturally, Tamil Nadu produced magnificent models of women with better status such as saints, social workers, politicians, artists, administrators and educationists, but they were in a minority, though of course, their examples may motivate many women in future to emancipate themselves. The revolutionary Chief Minister M.G. Ramachandran also gave extensive encouragement for women in politics and social life. This may have to be continued in the future. Further, special programmes may have to be identified on the basis of geographical areas and communities to promote modernization of traditional and backward populations in Tamil Nadu. Since the literacy level remains low among the adult women population, and the dropout of girls from schools continues in a big way, effective non-formal education should be expanded. Similarly the age at marriage of girls may have to be further raised. Since most people have very low wages, particularly in the unorganized sector, and they depend mostly on agriculture for employment, increase in their wages and diversification of the employment of women deserve special consideration. As the value of a son is very high and neglect and infanticide of girls exist among certain communities, suitable policy and programme interventions may have to be implemented expeditiously. This may reduce the cost of marriages and thus promote equal liking for girls and may also eliminate the inhuman practice of female infanticide. To improve the health of mothers and children and also to reduce mortality, better facilities may be provided to them in their vicinity at reasonable expense. For conserving the meagre resources, and also for retaining their youthfulness fertility control programmes may be accelerated throughout the state. These are not the only priority areas of their development but many other important aspects can be identified through future studies and experiences, which may be promoted through academic institutions. Unless future developmental programmes take care of these priorities, the women in Tamil Nadu cannot be brought on par with the people of the developed and developing countries in the world. Thus, improvement in the status of women, through all possible means may be considered to improve their overall quality of life in general.

REFERENCES

Census of India, 1981 Series 20, Part II, Tamil Nadu.

Dew, 1986. *Women in Tamil Nadu: A Profile* (Madras: Tamil Nadu Corporation for Development of Women), pp. 1–375.

Ilanko Adigal, 1968. *Cilappatikaram* (Section Madurai kandam), U.V. Swaminatha Aiyar (ed.) 8th edition (Madras: Sri Thyagarajavilasam).

Rajalakshmi, V., 1985. *The Political Behaviour of Women in Tamil Nadu* (New Delhi: Inter-India Publications) pp. 1–140.

Madras Legislative Council Proceedings, Vol. III, 1928, p. 60 cited in Rajalakshmi, 1985, p. 125.

Muthulakshmi Reddy, 1964. *Autobiography—A Pioneer Woman Legislator*, (Madras: MIJ Press (Chapter 15), pp. 59–60.

The National Sample Survey, 1987 (NSS). *Sarvekshana: Journal of N.S.S.O.* (New Delhi: Government of India, Ministry of Planning), Vol. X, No. 4, pp. S-54 and S-94.

Ramakrishna, G. et al., 1983. *An Encyclopaedia of South Indian Culture* (Calcutta: K.P. Bagchi), pp. 33–34.

Sourirajan, P., 1988. 'The Position and Status of Women in Tamil Nadu during Sangam Age (C 300 BC to C 200 AD),' in *Position and Status of Women in Ancient India*, L.K. Tripathi (ed.) (Varanasi: Banaras Hindu University), Vol. 1, pp. 151–163.

Tamil Nadu Legislative Council Debates, 1959, Vol. XXXIV, p. 391.

Thiruvalluvar, 1976. *Thirukural*, K. Vadivel Chettiar (ed.) (Madurai: Madurai University), p. 1046.

III

A CONCEPTUAL MODEL: FUTURE PERSPECTIVES

Status of Women and Population Dynamics: A Conceptual Model

K. MAHADEVAN, AKBAR AGHAJANIAN, R. JAYASREE AND G.S. MONI

The concept of the status of women in society assumed importance at the international level after the first major UN Conference on Women held in 1975, and the subsequent efforts made by the world body during the decade that followed. It took stock of the reality of women's dependence, development and problems in several countries, and devised certain measures to ameliorate their conditions and to enable them to build a proper future. Historically the main aspect did not get the attention it deserves in all the fields including academics, presumably because women have a low profile in the family as subordinates and supporting hands to their husbands on whom they depend for most of their needs. Their dependence shifts, initially from father to husband, and finally to son throughout their life cycle. Their all round dependence on men in the family for physical, economic and other social support has made their role only secondary in society. It is obviously on the basis of this assumption that an ancient Hindu philosopher, Manu, defined the status of women as being permanently subordinate to men at every stage of their lives. A similar code of ethics has been in existence in feudal China also according to Mao (Tuan 1989).

Historically also women's status in Europe was not much better than we see today in developing countries. Women in European countries including England did not have equal rights or opportunities. They did not have even voting rights. The suffragette movement in England spearheaded by Bernard Shaw, John Stuart Mill and others urged women's rights to the suffrage. Mrs Emmeline Pankhurst's

suffrage movement, which came into being in 1905, was militant in its methods; . . . the suffragettes were often imprisoned. The

National Union of Suffrage Societies, inaugurated in 1913, was more pacific in its methods and achieved a measure of success. In the same year twenty-nine countries sent delegates to the Congress of the International Women's Suffrage Alliance in Budapest. In course of time in Britain, the franchise underwent progressive changes in the 19th century. Until then it had been a privilege based upon property . . . Such qualification was reduced in 1867 and in 1884, the franchise was extended to all adult male households and lodgers. In 1918 (The 1918 Reform Act) male franchise at the age of 21 was made universal and women were, however, given right to vote only at 30. Later on in 1928, the voting right of the women was further reduced to 21. The concept of feminism started growing progressively from 1985 onwards and several people advocated the legitimate rights of women and their claims. Even earlier to this in 1870 another claim of women was conceded by passing the Married Women's Property Act, which was introduced in the House of Commons by Russel Gurney.

During the same century, the wind of change for emancipation of women was blowing in the whole of Europe. For instance, in Norway the concept of the new woman spread largely through the writings of Ibsen (1828–1909). He became the spokesman of women who have been subjected to political, social, moral and domestic suppression. His highly sensational and controversial plays, 'A Doll's House' (1879) and 'Ghosts' (1881) shocked the smugly complacent Victorian society into an awareness of the treatment being meted out to women. They were dolls, serving only ornamental purposes. Ignorance of political, religious, scientific and even biological facts was considered as 'innocence' adding to their feminine charm. It was this myth which was exploded by Ibsen. In Ibsen's time, women in Norway did not have the right to inherit property. Nor was a woman's signature valid in a legal document unless it was countersigned by her father or husband. Ibsen influenced Bernard Shaw, who later on founded the Fabian Society in Britain which also championed the cause of women. Shaw's *An Intelligent Woman's Guide to Socialism, Capitalism, Sovietism and Fascism* (1948) was a powerful book for awakening women and emancipating them to the world outside the domestic confines.

However, when we examine this position continent-wise irrespective of religious factors both historically and contemporarily it becomes evident that woman enjoyed better status in several European countries,

North America and places where they constitute the major segment of the population (Australia) and also in Japan (Boserup 1970). Though China is not a fully developed country, its women have a better status than their counterparts in the other Third World countries. In the rest of the world, women in Latin America followed by Asia, and lastly Africa have status ranging from moderate to the lowest. The various dimensions of status are not manifested uniformly in the order mentioned above, but the overall status can be estimated in this order.

The importance of the concept of the status of women is bound to grow when the realization grows on society that the pace of its development will be affected as long as half of the human race, women, remains backward. In addition, the quality of the human race and of posterity in particular, cannot improve beyond a level through the exclusive improvement in the status of men. This reality surfaced through several studies conducted mostly during the twentieth century, when population studies primarily confirmed it. Population scientists could identify that infant mortality, maternal mortality, high fertility and low acceptance of family planning cannot be manipulated only through the improvement in the status of men and increasing the per capita income of the family. These efforts also demand long-drawn-out and expensive programmes. Therefore, alternate strategies had been thought of at the national and international levels. Such efforts culminated in a worldwide action during 1974 when the UN organized its first comprehensive Conference on Population at Bucharest where the world body adopted the slogan, 'Development is the best contraceptive.' Further thinking and operationalization of this theoretical formulation led to the identification of the hitherto neglected area of development, namely, the development of women as a means to realize the goal set at Bucharest. Though 1975 was declared by the UN as the International Year for Women, they could achieve very little within a year. Having realized at the first World Conference on Women that a year-long celebration will not suffice even to discover and highlight their problems, a UN decade for the development of women was accepted subsequently. Eventually, even the decade-long efforts, celebrations and plans of action passed off without making much headway in the amelioration of the status of women. All the same, a certain degree of world-wide awareness for giving priority to the development of women and establishment of a machinery for it were accomplished through these efforts. What the next step should be is the urgent need to make rapid changes and improvements in the overall status of women. Therefore, we have first to clarify the conceptual aspects of the problem and then to identify the priority areas of the probable causal factors affecting this problem. This will deepen the future studies for the benefit of policy formulation and action programmes for the total development of women in an expeditious manner.

Under the legal systems of most countries, except in certain Muslim countries, women enjoy relative freedom, and face less discrimination in political, economic, developmental and cultural fields. But in rights and duties including property rights, discrimination against women exists in most countries. Even in social and economic development absolute equality is not found. There is still discrimination in wages and voting rights. But the discrimination against women has been highlighted and certain policy measures and reforms suggested as a result of the momentum created by the UN efforts. In many countries, an apex body for women's development was formed, several committees at national and regional levels followed, conferences, seminars and symposia were organized and centres and departments were established to study the problems of women and to identify solutions. Many resolutions were passed for taking up follow-up actions for specific areas of life. Depending upon the political support available and the policies followed by the different governments, follow-up actions were carried out in different ways for the welfare of women. But in reality, many of these resolutions could not be implemented effectively in time for one reason or another. The problem is common to many countries. Therefore, specific time-bound policies with appropriate strategies for implementing them may have to be evolved to translate the policies into reality.

THE CONCEPT OF STATUS

Status is a complex, dynamic and relative concept, encompassing certain powers derived either from one's own achievements and/or from ancestors. The power is manifested in prestige and privileges along with rights, roles and autonomy for independent action. Status generally grows periodically and also fluctuates. It normally exists among members of a society irrespective of age and sex, but varies on the basis of class, caste and several other positions and achievements.

Status has been conceived differently by different authors. Linton (1936: 113) defined status as the place of an individual in society, the collection of rights and duties, with certain roles to put the rights and duties into action. In modern social science,

> status denotes (*a*) position in a social system, involving reciprocal expectation of action with respect to occupants of other positions in the same structure; (*b*) place with respect to the distribution of prestige within a social system, and sometimes, by implication, with respect to the distribution of rights, obligations, power and authority within the same system as in the phrases, 'high status', and 'low status'; (*c*) high place with respect to the distribution of prestige within a social system—as in the phrase 'status keeper'. (*Encyclopaedia of Social Sciences* 1934: 373).

The status of women in the real and complete sense is a recent and emerging concept, though women in general enjoyed certain privileges, positions, rights, duties, roles, power and authority in varying degrees in different societies. However, they did not enjoy equal and extensive status in society as did men. The status of women has been defined by a few scholars giving different emphasis to its specific dimensions. The term status is used, first, as an access to resources such as education, gainful employment, and health services and, second, the position (power, prestige, authority) that a woman has in various situations. The term 'role' refers to the various activities that a woman performs in relation to her status in a given situation (Oppong 1980; Dixon 1978). Safilios-Rothschild (1982: 117) differentiates between power and the status of women. While defining their status, Dixon (1978) states

> women's power can be distinguished from women's status, in that status refers to women's overall position in the society; while power refers to women's ability to influence and control at the interpersonal level... Thus, female power can be defined as women's ability to control or change other women's or men's behaviour and the ability to determine important events in their lives, even when men and older women are opposed to them.

Thus, the status of women, like the general concept of status, is a multi-dimensional and dynamic concept which is considered on a relative basis. It comprises several dimensions like one's own legacy and achievements including money, materials, merits, life styles, privileges, and the autonomy to take one's own decisions. Along with these characteristic roles, progressive characteristics of modernization and achievements go together to manifest status. All these dimensions of status may have value over a particular period of time, with reference to a situation, and may be able to function on their own lines.

This evidence confirms that differences and gaps of understanding still exist on many facets of the status of women, which could not be discovered so far in the absence of a comprehensive analytical framework and a conceptual model. Hence effort is made here to discuss these theoretical-cum-methodological issues largely for future studies and policy formulations. The coverage of various concepts related to the status of women that have been presented in the preceding sections reveals the paucity of data and other limitations in the light of this model.

AN ANALYTICAL FRAMEWORK ON THE STATUS OF WOMEN

The status of women may be affected by several factors right from the foetal stage of an individual through the different stages of life cycle. It affects the future health of a girl if there is any complication during pregnancy, delivery and the subsequent period of child rearing. Since a healthy woman may have greater opportunity to grow, educate herself, acquire skills, get suitable employment and lead an independent life with optimum emancipation without becoming a perennial dependent and a problem on society, optimum health is needed for the essential growth of brain and for future development. The health of a woman grows out of several antecedent factors in the environment, family and the mother herself. The healthy growth of the mother and the baby together influences the physical health and the intellectual development in time. In the absence of an adequate level, the future status of women will be affected.

A newborn female baby who should be affectionately reared is, on account of wrong cultural influence, killed in cold blood in several developing countries of Asia, Africa and Latin America (Pakrasi, 1970; Miller, 1981; Tuan, 1989). Female infanticide is widespread in countries where the status of women is relatively low. Incidence of female infanticide affects the status of women.

Several other factors born out of culture, family and the environment itself affect the socialization of the growing female child including dropping out of education and jobs. When she reaches the stage of marriage, the system of dowry through the institution of marriage further affects her status. A most retrograde custom, dowry continue to retard the improvement in the status of women. Even after marriage, male domination and the pernicious custom of Sati make women non-entities in the family. Subsequently during the child rearing process they become unpaid household labour without leisure or opportunity for development. During old age, in the absence of economic independence, they suffer even if they do not become totally destitute. Thus, all these sequential events throughout the life cycle of a woman's status affect her in different ways and in different degrees. These events may not affect her so adversely when society has changed and developed. But even in a developed society, certain negative forces like divorce and prejudices operate against the better status of women.

The list of factors categorized and classified in the analytical framework given below may cover factors that affect the status of women right from birth to death. However, certain factors are relatively more important in certain situations than others. Most of these factors have been gleaned from the existing empirical literature. They may show different types and degrees of relationship in different stages of the development of women in diverse contexts of the culture even in the same country. It is the ingenuity of the researcher, the population under study, and the problem faced in the population related to the status which may guide the selection of one or more groups of factors outlined in the analytical framework. Nevertheless, the list of factors covered under the analytical framework may directly, indirectly, individually and collectively affect the status of women in different ways.

The various dimensions and specific factors involved under each dimension of society have been considered under this section. This has become necessary in the absence of a comprehensive analytical framework on 'status of women' till today. This gap of knowledge has so far been affecting the quality of research, policy formulations and theoretical understanding of this theme. No doubt, certain dimensions and their specific factors may have greater or negligible influence, but they differ across different countries and also in different regions within the same country. On the basis of the cultural patterns and differential developments, the factors may manifest different degrees of influence and types of relationships in affecting the status of women.

In the light of present knowledge, the factors that influence the concept of the status of women have been classified under eighteen major categories. Under each, specific factors have been further identified. Admittedly, gaps still exist in several areas that might affect the status of women and the list of factors outlined here cannot be claimed as complete. Nevertheless, it forms a basis for a systematic approach to the problem of examining the factors that are unknown, to initiate suitable policies and the programmes for the benefit of women and also for scientifically and holistically understanding these problems in their proper perspective.

STATUS AFFECTING VARIABLES (SAVs)

I. **Polity and Policy**
   a. *Policy*
      Public policies and programmes
      Identification of areas for development
      Religious codes and civil laws
      Land and other social reforms
      Wage equality
      Priority in development
      Preference for development of women
      Social justice
   b. *National and international efforts*
      Women's liberation movements
      Suffrage movement
      National and international efforts
      Availability of resources
      Administrative facility and actions
      Opportunities for female entrepreneurship
   c. *Strategies for development*
      Identification and fulfilment of needs
      Management
      Planned development
      Maternal and child welfare schemes
      Direct and indirect benefits of development
      Adoption of science and technology

II. **Voluntary Efforts**
   a. *Reform movements*
      Radical feminists
      Leaders' efforts
      Writers
      Other change agents
      Organizational efforts
      Movements for prohibition, against dowry, deforestation etc.
   b. *Action programmes*
      Identification of schemes
      Mobilization of resources
      Welfare programmes

Rehabilitation of destitute women
Skill development programmes
Employment generation
Recreation activities

III. **Cultural Variables**

a. *Patterns of culture*
Institutional differences
Cultural complexities
Purdah
Fasting
Avoidance
Fads and fallacies
Value of sons
Ethical codes
Bondage
Customs

b. *Life cycle*
Stages in life cycle
Differential responsibilities
Changes in positions
Assignment of privileges
Activities

c. *Culture and behaviour*
Mythological idealism
Neglect of females
Female infanticide
Sex segregation
Preferential treatment
Restrictions in interaction
Sex bias
Modesty
Rights and rituals
Predetermining sex
Child adoption

IV. **Familial Variables**

a. *Family structure*
Joint family/nuclear family
Primogeniture/ultimogeniture
Residential pattern

b. *Home management and chores*
Household leadership
Supervision
Coordination
Child rearing
Housekeeping

c. *Food and nutrition*
Food choice

Food processing
Food distribution
Storage and preservation
Sharing of food
Nutrition consciousness
Growth/retardation

d. *Ascribed status*
Generational factors
Family status
Inheritance of property
Lineage
Reputation

V. **Marital Variables**
a. *Marriage patterns*
Freedom to choose life partner
Endogamy/exogamy
Celibacy
Monogamy/polygyny/polyandry
Patrilocal/uxorilocal/virilocal
Matriliny/patriliny
Sale of girls/traffic in girls
Levirate

b. *Marriage solemnization*
Belief in horoscope
Age at marriage
Beauty consciousness
Ceremonies at puberty
Age difference between spouses/child marriage
Duration of married life
Dowry and presents/other costs of marriage
Marital rituals
Menopause
Philosophy of married life

c. *Marital interaction*
Intraspouse communication
Husband-wife adjustment
Dominance, equality and subordination
Abuse
Love and affection
Esteem

d. *Divorce*
Right to divorce
Conciliatory gift/maintenance allowance
Scope for remarriage
Separation
Alimony
Custody of children
Discrimination of divorces

e. *Widowhood deprivation*
Widow agamy
Widow remarriage
Sati
Deprivation of privileges
Preference in jobs
Avoidance
Taboo in functions
Changes in roles
Widow rehabilitation
Financial assistance for education and marriage of their children

f. *Sexual life*
Customs on sex roles
Sexual rights
Sexual adjustment
Chastity and loyalty
Sex traps
Adultery
Sex prejudices
Permissiveness
Rape
Prostitution
Promiscuity
Concubinage
Extramarital sex

VI. **Structural Changes**
a. *Environmental facilities*
Transport and communication
Drudgery reduction
Space for relaxation

b. *Mechanization*
Electrification
Mechanization of kitchen
Facility for water collection
Fuel availability
Energy saving device/technological innovation/smokeless choola

c. *Service and supplies*
Fuel fetching and use
Water drawing and use
Manual assistance

d. *Institutional and cultural change*
Social institutions/cultural organizations
Duties and taboos

VII. **Socio-Economic Development**
a. *Education*
Denial and neglect
Segregation in education

    Proximity and transport facilities
    Residential facilities
    Scholarships
    Parents resources and encouragement
    Job-oriented courses
    Ignorance
    Mass education

  b. Labour force
    Career goals
    Employment availability
    Equality in employment/universal employment
    Division of labour
    Unemployment allowance
    Productivity
    Occupational mobility
    Age at employment/age at retirement
    Differential wages
    Self employment
    Loan facilities

  c. Job satisfaction
    Convenience in work
    Recognition
    Rewards
    Taboo for jobs
    Loss of face
    Problems in working (Night duty and co-working)
    Physical facilities
    Strain in work
    Leave and permissions
    Sexual harassment
    Maternity leave and benefit

  d. Economic position
    Property right
    Freedom to use money
    Ability to save and invest money
    Cost-benefit considerations
    Insurance and pension
    Equality of wages
    Exploitation

  e. Facilities and Encouragement
    Institutions for training
    Encouragement
    Resources

VIII. ***Urbanization and Migration***
  a. Urban life
    Urbanism

Urban amenities
Knowledge and skill
Entertainments

b. *Social change*
Orientations in life
Individualism
Social control
Tastes
Goals & priorities
Behavioural patterns

c. *Migration*
World view
Freedom of action
Self-confidence
Mobility

IX. **Mortality and Unwanted Children**
a. *Mortality*
Infant mortality
Infanticide
Female child mortality/female adult mortality
Suicide

b. *Unwanted children*
Child abuse
Neglect
Sale of children
Bonded labour/child labour

X. **Norms and Values**
a. *Norms*
Ideal family size
Additional expected children/maximum expected children
Norms on other social life

b. *Values*
Sex preference
Values in personal matters
Values in social aspects

XI. **Attitude**
a. *Attitude change*
Attitude to sex and life
Pessimism/optimism
Fatalism
Motivation
Perception

b. *Behavioural attributes*
Tolerance
Equality

Tact and temper
Discrimination
Prejudice

XII. *Modernization*
a. *Life style*
Liberal feminism
Clothing
Adoption of fashions
Model and sex appeal
Media listening
Reading literature
Smoking/drinking

b. *Innovativeness and planning*
Consumer durables
Planning
Entrepreneurship
Risk taking
Acceptance of innovations
Rationalism

c. *Media and Communication*
Formal communication/non-formal communication
Mass-media facility
Library facilities
Utilisation of media

d. *Social participation*
Awareness of rights and privileges
Political consciousness
Right to vote
Holding offices
Environmental protection
Membership in organizations

(**Certain aspects of modernization are covered under Urbanization, Health and Structural Change**).

XIII. *Autonomy and Decision*
a. *Personality*
Motherhood instinct
Leadership
Male domination/female subordination
Introvert/extrovert
Complexity

b. *Dependency*
Nature of dependency
Financial dependence
Right to perform duties
Subordination

    c. Decision-making
        Women's power
        Authority
        Sharing of power
        Democratic functioning
        Participation in decision making

XIV. *Maternal and Child Health*

    a. Maternal health
        Pregnancy care
        Weight and height
        Periodic medical attention
        Hospital delivery
        Post delivery care
        Preventive care
        Maternity benefits
        Morbidity of mother

    b. Child care
        Crèche
        Pre school education
        Baby care
        Intelligent quotient
        Birth weight
        Immunizations
        Breastfeeding
        Supplementary food
        Child rearing

    c. Health facilities
        Infrastructure
        Sanitation
        Health insurance
        Pollution/infection
        Preventive measures
        Promotive measures
        Health education

XV. *Family Planning*

    a. Contraceptive behaviour
        Timing of contraception
        Freedom to use contraception
        Spacing children
        Limiting children
        Types of contraception
        Complications
        Follow up
        Privacy in service

XVI. **Role Performance**
   a. Roles
      Conjugal role
      Management
      Socialization
      Work-participation
      Social service
      Counselling
      Helping dependents
   b. Work participation
      Agriculture and industries
      Cottage industries
      Activities in service sectors
      Other productive work
   c. Creative work
      Appreciation of Art
      Literary work
      Handicrafts
      Hobbies
   d. Division of labour
      Sharing of responsibilities
      Kinship participation
      Rights and privileges
      Recognition of household work
      Active/passive life
      Female activity rate
      Production and consumption
      Domestic servants
      Availability of parental support
   e. Time and activities
      Budgeting
      Time and different activities
      Time saving devices
      Rest and leisure
      Work load
   f. Conflict
      Role conflict
      Needs and problems
      Neglect
      Role incompatibility
      Wife beating
      Mothers-in-law feud
      Changing responsibility
      Sharing finance and property

XVII. **Fertility**
  a. Fertility problems
    Adolescent pregnancy
    Illegitimate conception
    Second marriage
    Abortion

  b. Fecundity and fertility
    Sterility
    Foetal wastages
    Number of live births
    Number of living children
    Sex ratio

XVIII. **Overall Status of Women**
  a. Quality of life
    Longevity
    Physical fitness and charm
    Planning
    Efficiency in work
    Enlightenment
    Scientific orientation
    Preventive care
    Appropriate life style
    Overall position

  b. Emancipation
    Freedom of action
    Self affirmation
    Relief from over work
    Self/ascribed image

  c. Problems
    Adjustability
    Suspicion
    Misunderstanding
    Disharmony
    Incompatibility

CONCEPTUAL MODEL

A conceptual model is important for operationalizing the problem and scientifically understanding the causal relationship which exists either directly and/or indirectly between the dependent variable and the several independent/or intervening variables. Normally, in the absence of a comprehensive analytical framework, the conceptual model cannot be evolved in a realistic, precise and holistic manner. Though literature available on this theme may have given a hidden or partially visible, conceptual basis, an explicit and broad based model is lacking today for the understanding of the status of women in relation to population dynamics. Even in the existing conceptual model in fertility behaviour, this factor has not been given due importance. For example, the Davis and Blake (1956) framework on intermediate variables discussed certain dimensions of the status of women in relation to fertility behaviour without mentioning it under the theme 'status of women.' Explicit statements and diagrammatic presentation of the various components of the concept of status of women are overdue requirements. The present conceptual model, therefore, may fill this void.

This conceptual model is based on the list of several factors mentioned under the preceding analytical framework of status affecting variables (SAVs). The first five variables namely polity and policy; voluntary efforts; culture and ecology; familial and marital variables constitute the societal foundation of the model. Many of them need changes to facilitate the improvement of status in several societies. Based on the political ideology, commitment and different types of policies pursued by the government, different appropriate or non-appropriate developmental programmes may be formulated which may contribute to subsequent changes on different dimensions of society, which are portrayed in this model. Efforts other than governmental like the participation of voluntary agencies in developmental activities also contribute changes in a parallel manner in the status of women either directly or indirectly. But the speed with which changes take place in the status of women depends upon the cultural and ecological scenario of a given society. They also influence the familial and marital institutions. These societal factors may undergo change on the basis of the policies and programmes followed by government and voluntary agencies. Followed by these developments, urbanization, industrialization and migration etc. may also contribute to progress in a society. These macro-situational and structural variables may promote manifold changes in many facets of life. They may affect or prolong life itself and affect the health and family size formation. All these changes may be based on the concurrent and preceding changes taking place in society and in norms and values, attitude, modernization, autonomy and decision making patterns, and personality. They may all affect the type of roles that a woman would play in society. These factors individually and/or together may influence the fertility pattern of women leading to changes in their overall status. Even independent of fertility behaviour, these preceding factors may also directly influence the status of women under different situations, when women are financially better off, socially developed and hold higher positions in the social hierarchy.

The present model shows the macro-dimension of society and the micro factors of the various dimensions which are offshoots of the former. An attempt is also made to synchronize the related factors under the overall category for the convenience of classifying and presenting them suitably in the model. Here the status of women is considered as the major dependent variable along with fertility behaviour. Both influence each other. Such a reciprocal relationship is very uncommon in empirical studies. Nevertheless, most of the preceding factors influence status either directly or through its fertility behaviour. The factors immediately preceding the dependent variables are the primary factors, which individually and directly influence the status of women. In fact, some of them could be an integral part of the status of women. However, for the analytical understanding they have been presented as specific causal factors that affect status. Depending upon the situation, some of these immediate factors of determinants of the status of women can be considered together as a composite index to measure the status of women per se. An alternative may be to consider a few crucial attributes of the status of women as a dependent variable which may cover the overall quality of life of women, the emancipation they attain in various facets of life including the power they enjoy, the problems they confront and the level of overall status they manifest in the hierarchy of society.

STATUS OF WOMEN AND DEMOGRAPHIC LINKAGES

A number of demographic factors like low age at marriage, prejudice against widows, poor maternal care, high maternal mortality, high fertility, short/closed birth interval, adverse sex ratio, negligible women migration, illegal abortion, non-contraception etc., are inimical to the status of women in developing countries. Early age at marriage forms the major demographic variable that affects the status of women. One of the factors contributing to the higher status of women in Kerala state in India and in Sri Lanka is their higher age at marriage. Early age at marriage prevents girls from acquiring higher education and thereby perpetuates social backwardness among them. After marriage, high fertility further prevents them from getting even the opportunity for non-formal education. It weakens their personal health and efficiency

STATUS OF WOMEN AND POPULATION DYNAMICS: A CONCEPTUAL MODEL.

K Mahadevan, R Jayasree, Akbar Aghajanian, G.S. Moni

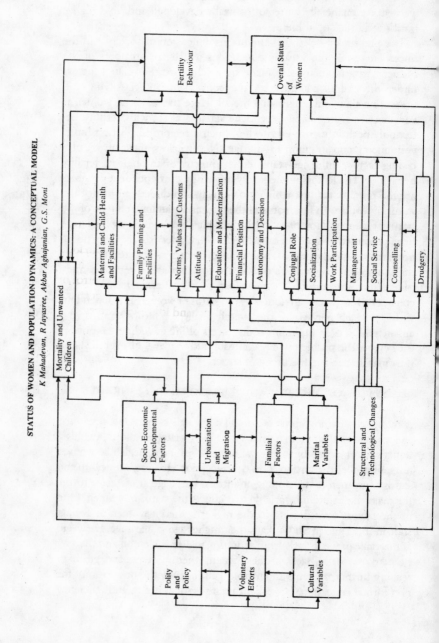

and enhances maternal mortality which leads to an adverse sex ratio for women. A major factor affecting sex ratio is maternal mortality during the reproductive period. Closely spaced deliveries erode health and efficiency, besides not allowing the women time for doing other roles. Thus, all these demographic factors cumulatively affect the status of women to a large extent.

Mortality

Improvement in the social status of women can control infant and childhood mortality. This has been confirmed by several studies and historical experience (Omran 1976; Schultz 1980; Smucker et al. 1980; Palloni 1981; Caldwell 1979–81; Kurup 1982; Mahadevan et al. 1985). But to raise the living standard of people to an optimum level to bring down the level of infant and childhood mortality is a long-term and excessively costly endeavour. The developed countries have achieved it in a century or a longer period, and it is not feasible for the immediate benefit of society in a developing country. We have to look at what is immediately feasible; policies which incur manageable financial investment and get greater returns in terms of the control of infant and childhood mortality in the foreseeable future. Enhancement of the status of women through short-term and long-term strategies is possible as seen from the successful experience of Kerala state in India and in Sri Lanka.

Improvement in the status of women will go a long way in drastically minimizing neonatal, infant and early childhood mortality because mothers are primarily responsible for child rearing during this vulnerable period of life. To achieve this, different strategies for the development of single and married women may have to be considered. All married women in the reproductive group and their birth attendants together may be given education in small group meetings on all major aspects of modern child-rearing practices. Healthy living habits can be taught by trained peripheral workers using audio-visual materials. Detailed exposure to various causes of tetanus neonatorum, diarrhoea, anaemia, aspiration syndromes, bacterial infections particularly TB, respiratory infections and major vitamin deficiency diseases and communicable diseases may be covered during this education. Such discussion may be made more attractive to women by sandwiching the programme with imparting skills in embroidery work, handicrafts, preparation of novel food items and periodic medical check-ups. The programme can be organized once in three months in every village or continuously for a week in a year. It can also be integrated with any other suitable ongoing social welfare schemes like adult education programmes.

For the unmarried girls, a week-long institutionalized training course in handicrafts, cottage industries, family life education, sex education, child rearing practices, education on nutrition and control of communicable diseases can be provided during the summer vacations by the staff of health education, social welfare and small-scale industry. The same programme may be introduced from middle school level onwards for school-going girls. At least one session per week may be devoted to health and social education. Health staff working at the primary health centre level and regional health and family welfare training centres can be given this responsibility. Thus, coverage of drop-out girls during vacation, school-going girls through regular curriculum and adult women through small groups in the community can extend this programme to all women in the society. This may improve their overall status. However, it should become a regular feature for several years and may be repeated on several occasions to get the maximum benefits.

Education of women is the most important long-term factor in reducing infant and childhood mortality in most developing countries. An analysis carried out in ten countries of the four continents using WFS data (Caldwell and McDonald 1982) confirms this. The analysis further confirms that the influence of maternal education on child survival is usually greater than that of parental education. When maternal education was controlled even rural/urban residence showed very little difference on mortality. In another study in Nigeria, Caldwell (1979) confirmed the importance of parental education, in general, as a major determinant of reducing child mortality. The achievements of Kerala in reducing mortality to the level of a developed country with low per capita income are largely through the education of women and other factors of social development (Zachariah 1983; Mahadevan 1986).

FAMILY PLANNING

Family planning behaviour in terms of the acceptance of family planning is generally associated with the higher status of women, and non-contraception results out of their lower status. Women are conditioned by the autonomy they enjoy in the family. As long as most decisions in the family are made by the men, the status of women alone cannot influence the contraceptive behaviour (Mahadevan 1984). Nevertheless, improvement of the status of women through education has directly and indirectly contributed to the development of the small-family norm leading to the acceptance of family planning and sometimes even goes beyond leading to the adoption of family planning measures with a limited number of children (Hull 1977; Oppong 1980; Kupinsky 1977; WFS 1980). Early acceptance of family planning leads to a low fertility. Further, family planning for spacing as well as for limitation improves the health of mothers and children and reduces the risk involved in maternal and childhood mortality.

Family planning with limited numbers of children directly provides opportunity for women for development in several ways. It indirectly benefits the status of women through maternal health, improvement in longevity and reduction in fertility, besides giving women the opportunity for education, modernization and alleviation of drudgery. Family planning may also provide scope for women to assume other than traditional roles in society. Assumption of new roles by women will speed up their participation and development and improve their status.

Fertility Behaviour

The level of fertility and the status of women are co-related. This reciprocal relationship stems out of the common determinants of these two factors and their complementary influence. Here fertility is conceived as a parallel dependent variable along with the status of women because of their reciprocal relationship. Nevertheless, in demographic literature, the status of women in terms of education, labour force participation outside the home, occupational mobility etc., is found to have strong association with fertility behaviour in developed and developing countries in all the continents (UN 1961; Driver 1963; Boserup 1970; Mandelbaum 1974; Rothschild 1977; Hull 1977; Oppong 1977; Kupinsky 1977; Caldwell 1979; Anker 1982). However, efforts made to go deeper into the specific determinants of education and occupation that contribute to the changes in fertility behaviour have been negligible. Education and labour force participation may bring about several qualitative changes in the behaviour of women. They may include changes in life styles, norms, and values, level of aspiration, motivation and modernization, changes in role and so on. In this context it is worth examining the ideas given by Mandelbaum to probe further into the specific causal mechanism of education and labour force participation of women. Mandelbaum (1974: 54–55) wrote:

> An educated woman is usually less closely confined, physically and psychologically, with her husband's family and its narrow familial concerns than is the woman who is brought into their home as an uneducated girl... She is more likely to feel that she can do something about the conditions of her life, including the condition of pregnancies in close succession or conceiving during her later reproductive years. Her horizons of information are wider, if only by being able to read a newspaper; her network of communication is likely to be broader, if only to school friends beyond the confines of household and kin. These differences are not, of course, direct results of her having studied algebra or learned to read another language, but they are potent consequences that help to shape her life and are (more) likely to induce her to limit her fertility.

Caldwell (1979) maintains that there is an essential link between education and declining fertility through the reversal of 'wealth flows' within the family. More studies on this issue are needed to discover all the shades of influence of education and labour force participation in improving the status of women and fertility behaviour.

Mortality-Fertility Interaction

During the last two decades there has been more claim and less disclaim regarding the relationship between mortality and fertility. Historical data from several European countries show a certain relationship between real fertility and mortality (Preston 1975). Several others, examining the relationship between mortality and fertility in developed and developing countries, showed significant association between the two (CICRED and ESCAP 1975). There are three main explanations for the existing link between infant mortality and fertility. The death of a child shortens the amenorrhoea associated with lactation and thereby may increase fecundity and shorten the interval between two successive births. According to Preston (1978) this effect is not largely based on empirical evidence. A second explanation is that parents are motivated to have additional babies to replace the loss. This is called the replacement effect. A third and more extensively held view is that parents do not limit their children until they are reasonably sure that a sufficient number of children will survive to adulthood ('insurance effect').

The same problem has also a reciprocal relationship through nutritional status. While discussing the relationships between fertility, child mortality and nutrition in Africa, Jacqueline (1977) observed that malnutrition is largely responsible for excess mortality among children. This results in a certain increase in fertility which is linked not only with the discontinuance of breast feeding, but also with the parents' desire to replace the deceased child with another. A similar view has been expressed by Lichting et al. (1978): 'The report available and our own data support the hypothesis that short and long term nutritional status of the mother are causally related to infant mortality and are in part responsible for the association between socio-economic status and infant mortality.' The preceding conclusions lead to another probability i.e., most people who suffer from normal nutritional deficiency are poor people, who have generally more children. There are other causes for nutritional deficiency. Therefore, higher fertility coupled with deprivation of adequate food particularly for girls, may cause nutritional deficiency leading to mortality. Hence there is a link between fertility and mortality through the customs of food distribution and nutritional status.

All this evidence confirms that social change in the institution of marriage, family formation and society in general is needed to emancipate women from their present poor levels of social status. On a reciprocal basis, improvement of the social status of women can considerably reduce infant and childhood mortality, reduce fertility, increase the level of acceptance of contraception, enhance the chances of female migration, increase the longevity of women and ultimately improve the overall quality of life of women in particular and the population in general.

DRUDGERY AND STATUS

Minimizing the time-consuming household drudgery will be a boon for women to enable them to spare more time for effective childcare and for finding time for themselves to learn from adult education centres and through mass media. Today, most of the landless and poor women spend the major part of their time in fetching water and firewood, and in cooking besides relaxing or sleeping out of excessive fatigue. Unless a partial relief in these aspects is given to women, they will not be free to learn anything or do justice to child-rearing. Freeing the mother's time at least partially from these traditional roles may enable her to render effective care to the children, who are weak and in need of such services. Action research can be planned for every community and region to study the activities carried out and the time spent for different avocations by women. Suitable remedial programmes can be planned to save women from the present drudgery. A beginning has been made in this direction by a few anthropologists (Dixon 1976; Nag et al. 1977; Anker 1981; Mahadevan et al. 1983). On the basis of the findings of such studies, suitable interventions can be introduced for enhancing the status of women. A few such schemes may include: (a) production of cheap and efficient cooking vessels on a massive scale, (b) development of social forestry at close quarters in private and government lands; (c) marketing of processed food at reasonable prices; and (d) developing devices to relieve women from time-consuming kitchen work viz., grinding and pounding which can be replaced by producing less costly autogrinders on a large scale. Such measures will, in addition, minimize the need for getting many children. Today at least one daughter is required by parents to share household work such as baby-sitting. A long-term remedy lies with at least in the quasi-mechanization of kitchen work with electricity. When parental activities are simplified by technological and other innovations, value for daughters/children will also become less and this in turn will minimize fertility and mortality. All these efforts will also improve the prospects for girls taking up education in large numbers and reducing cases of drop-outs.

Institutionalization of child rearing practices from age two onwards through the creche leads to several benefits for women and children. For parents, it is an opportunity to get time for learning and engaging themselves in other useful activities during their leisure thus improving their health, knowledge, and happiness, leading to a positive attitude and higher status. Creation of such creches provides employment to several women in rural areas. It minimizes the need for additional children for baby-sitting or helping mothers which is a pronatalist force. Children, reared by trained teachers in the creches will grow up in a healthy atmosphere, if the creches are well maintained. Effective training can be given to the teachers of the creches to look after the babies properly. A hygienic environment can be created at the creches at reasonable cost which may not be available in every house. Through these creches complete coverage of immunization can be achieved, if all the poor and middle-class children are reared there. It is these people who need education to improve community health and emancipation of women in general. However the creches should be within a reasonable distance of every family and the teacher must be acceptable to most parents. Periodic medical check-up can also be successfully completed at the creches. Several attractive educational programmes, incentives etc., may have to be created for the successful functioning of creches. Above all, the sanitation and hygienic conditions of creches must be at an optimum level to make such experiments successful. Another opportunity to enhance the status of women is through the establishment of women's organizations in rural areas. Imparting informal training and skills at women's clubs on several aspects may attract them to these clubs regularly. Interaction among women of the same area from different backgrounds and experiences itself will be an opportunity for education for the less privileged.

STATUS AND FAMILY PROBLEMS

Though a panacea for several social problems, an improvement in the status of women has certain adverse consequences on family harmony. Attainment of higher status makes women freer in social life which husbands may find undesirable; they may even doubt their fidelity, leading to conflict. Such problems are greater when the status of women changes drastically during a lifetime in the family, perhaps under different environmental situations. When the status of women improves, their life style, autonomy and behaviour in general may change, and may become incongruous with the husbands' demands in the family. Such incongruity may lead to conflict in the family and even to divorce. Such factors are responsible for large-scale divorces in several developed countries. In the event, the children are the worst affected.

With status change even conjugal autonomy may change, though this is rare among developing countries. However, conjugal autonomy is reported in Africa even without improvement in the status of women (Oppong, 1970). The conjugal autonomy assumed by women as a result of their new status may very often lead to marital conflict. Wife-beating can be explained on the basis of this factor alone in the rural areas of UP state in northern India (Observation by the first author).

When concomitant social changes do not accompany corresponding changes in the status of women, the latter may cause more harm than good. When the status of women improves in a patrilineal society, without corresponding changes among the husbands and the families, problems may arise. But improvement in the status of women in a matrilineal society may not lead to serious problems because of the greater autonomy and privileges that already exist among such women (Bleek 1975; Oppong 1978). Matriliny is a rare occurrence now, and patriliny being the general pattern, appropriate social change in the family and society may have to be explored and promoted to avoid future problems in a society as a result of an improvement in the status of women. While attempting to improve the status of women, corresponding changes among men are equally needed to minimize possible problems in the family in future. For improvement in the status of women should ultimately promote all-round harmony and happiness in the family.

METHOD OF MEASUREMENT

Generally measurement of the status of women is based on limited major dimensions of their status namely, educational attainment and occupational categories in a broad sense. This undermines the real influence of status differences per se on population parameters. In certain studies, educational categories of women are grouped into illiterates and literates. Sometimes the literates are expanded into a few more categories. It is fairly well known that the differentials in fertility behaviour on account of educational status are not very great, when the women studied only up to class five or below. Therefore, further analysis and identification of the changes, benefits, limitations etc., that accompany different levels of education and types of education may also be considered to know the real factors contributing to differential influence of education on fertility behaviour. Similarly, classifying women into two groups, namely housewives and working women cannot make any distinction between different work cultures and their influence on fertility behaviour. Working women in different sectors of employment may have different motivations and inhibitions to have a definite number of children. How is it relevant methodologically to group together working women in administration with teaching or agricultural labourers? As in the case of education, the grouping of different occupational categories may have to be reconsidered on a definite criterion like the inconvenience of children on work, health hazards, discomforts, and day-to-day child rearing problems which are incongruous with changing life style and behaviour.

Intervening factors should also be given due consideration in the analysis to avoid their influence through work on fertility behaviour. For example, in the case of an administrative assistant, who lives in a joint family, where certain elderly women relatives are available to look after the children and if they have enough wealth, work per se may not depress fertility. Such intervening factors also may be considered. Therefore, the measurement of variables in a discrete manner and the selection of appropriate control variables are highly essential. Suitable statistical procedures to pinpoint the direct and indirect influence of most of these causal factors are to be considered in this context. For instance the age of women, education and even work experience could be controlled in different ways to focus on the real influence of certain other factors. There may also be dual contribution of achieved and ascribed status variables, which individually and collectively, affect the overall status of the women differentially. If they are complementary to each other, their joint influence may emerge in a pronounced manner and if it is otherwise, one source of status may nullify the effect of the other and the real status situation may be vitiated at the final stage of assessment.

Status index or even scales comprising suitable and selected dimensions could be constructed to make these variables more sensitive, and quantifiable besides condensing the data for deriving meaningful generalizations. While certain factors are considered for the development of index, selection of items may include not only the respondents' psychological characteristics but familial, environmental and community characteristics as well. This is necessary because the status of a person is in relation to the total environment and it is a diverse and changing concept. In this context, care has to be taken to project the status free from the intervening influence of other related factors. For instance, a woman may be endowed with certain crucial dimensions of status like higher education, and better occupation and yet she may not manifest the real influence of these dimensions of status when she has less personal autonomy in decision-making. If she is married to a more prosperous husband who is an alcoholic with idiosyncrasies, the woman cannot freely manifest her real status in day-to-day behaviour and even in family formation patterns without the sanction of the husband. Similarly, when a wife subscribes to certain Hindu and Islamic value systems concerning the superiority of the husband i.e., the husband should be treated as next to God, she may not apply her autonomy in decision-making, even if she has better status in terms of education and occupation. Therefore, the measurement of the auto-nomy of women, along with other dimensions of the status should go together for the measurement of real and complete manifestation of their emancipation in life.

The inequality of women to men can be measured at least in three broad areas as discussed earlier, namely (i) ability to control important events in life or relative freedom from control of others; (ii) access to valued resources in the context of community and household and (iii) wealth, prestige and autonomy. Various aspects and details of each broad area could be considered in different studies but within a holistic perspective on the lines of analytical framework suggested in this paper. For example relative freedom could be considered in terms of mate selection and timing of marriage; access to health resources is an example of the second broad category; and relative ability to acquire and maintain property is related to the third category.

Measurement of the relative position of women could be done at micro-family level and macro-societal level. How does the relative position of women vary across families (micro) and across commu-nities (macro)? While some aspects of the relative status of women could be measured both at macro and micro levels, relative access to health resources and similar other aspects are more meaningful to be measured at macro community level. A good example of the latter is prestige which is conceived in the context of the community. Another issue is that some aspects of the relative status could be measured as factual characteristics such as relative educational attainment. Others are more attitudinal and perceptive, namely relative prestige.

In dealing with access to valued resources and wealth across com-munities, one way is to calculate a series of ratio variables by utilizing a division of measured characteristics for women to the same measured characteristics for men. An example of this is the ratio of contribution of female education rate to male education-continuation-rate. These ratio variables could be constructed and used for cross-country com-parison-creation of a data set with one record for each country as the unit of analysis. But they are more appropriate for within-the country analysis by measuring these across communities. These communities could be geographic entities (districts) or cultural-social entities (racial and ethnic communities).

Relative freedom and autonomy should be studied by considering cultural patterns such as the existence of polygyny in social practice. However, such social practices and customs should be viewed and attached to its 'status load' within its own social context. For example, Iranian and Bangladeshi women dread the possibility of their husband taking a second wife. But in Ivory Coast they look forward to this possibility (Mason, 1984). Hence, in utilizing cultural pattern and ethics as measures of relative status of women, one should note that a particular social practice for females could vary from one context to another in meaning and interpretation. The implication of a social practice might be unique to a particular society. Therefore an in-depth micro-level analysis should provide a more comprehensive view and a better picture of the issue of relative power and autonomy.

At the micro-level, a survey of families could provide a good data set for understanding the relative status of women within the context of the family. Such survey will not only include the actual roles of women but also their views of the reciprocal roles played by men. In this way, we can measure the position of women vis-a-vis men. Hence, the tool may cover questions about familial roles, conjugal decision making, husband-wife communication, division of labour in the family and use of woman's time, employment and income earning capacity; wealth and control over the family resources; social and political participation; awareness and concern over familial and non-familial issues. Background information about the family and also the extended family and individual characteristics of husband and wife should be measured for inter-family comparison.

Study Design

A two-stage study design commencing with an exploratory study followed by survey, and other types of studies may be the most feasible method of studying this problem. No doubt, for wider generalization, a study on the status of women can be undertaken through large-scale surveys, provided the complete conceptual issues involved in the study of this factor are fairly known. But the method of survey need not be like other general study, because even a case study of limited sample of women may be appropriate, when the population characteristics are generally homogeneous, and developmental differences are not very great in the population under study. When many such issues and uncertainties exist, a safe approach would be to proceed with a two-stage study design. In the first exploratory phase, a limited number of cases of diverse nature can be studied in-depth to generate new variables, hypotheses and to finalize the instrument itself besides conceptually restricting the scope of the study to choose suitable and relevant variables. Other types of studies, either individually or in combination, can also be tried out to evolve a suitable methodology for the study on the status of women and population dynamics in society.

APPLICATION OF THIS MODEL

Since the papers presented in the preceding two parts could not cover all the salient factors affecting the status of women in the absence of a conceptual model in the past and paucity of data, it became necessary to develop a comprehensive conceptual model for strengthening research in this field. No doubt most of the papers can be linked to this model in a limited way on aspects related to policy of government, social and political participation, cultural background, educational status, labour force participation, value of sons, neglect of girls, sex ratio, child-woman ratio, fertility, mortality, female infanticide, family planning etc. Most of the papers presented here can also partially fit in with this model. In fact any model can be tested fully or a part of it based on data, resources and other feasibility. But many other aspects of the framework and model could not be covered in the absence of this model at the time of writing these papers and also due to paucity of data on most of these aspects. Therefore, this model should be viewed not for linking the papers now with it but may be considered for future use to locate the existing gap of knowledge and themes of research in different countries. It may help future research to produce comprehensive data base on the status of women and population dynamics in developed and developing countries alike.

REFERENCES

Ali, Abdullah Yusuf (undated). *The meaning of Glorious Quran* (Cairo: Dar Al-Kitab Al-Masri).

Anker, Richard, 1982. *Research on Women's Roles and Demographic Change*: Survey questionnaire for household women, men and communities with background explanations, ILO.

————, 1981. 'Demographic Change and the Role of Women: A Research Programme in Developing Countries' in Anker Richard et al. (ed.), *Women's Roles and Population Trends in the Third World* (London: Croom Helm) pp. 29–47.

Bleek, W. 1975. 'Appearance and Reality: The Ambiguous Position of Women in Kwahu, Ghana in P. Kloos and K.W. Van der Voen (eds.) *Rule and Reality: Essays in Honour of Andre J.F. Kobben* (Amsterdam: University of Amsterdam) pp. 50–65.

Boserup, Ester, 1970. *Women's Role in Economic Development* (London: George Allen and Unwin) pp. 37–51, 119–139.

Caldwell, John and Peter McDonald, 1982. 'Influence of Maternal Education on Infant and Child Mortality: Levels and Causes,' *Health Policy and Education*, 2, pp. 251–267.

Caldwell, J.C. 1979. 'Education as a Factor in Mortality Decline: An Examination of Nigerian Data,' *Population Studies*, Vol. 33, pp. 395–413.

Davis, Kingsley and Judith Blake, 1956. 'Social Structure and Fertility: An Analytical Framework' in Charles B. Nam (ed.), *Population and Society*, 1968, pp. 196–215.

Dixon, B. Ruth, 1976. 'The Roles of Rural Women: Female Seclusion, Economic Production and Reproductive Choice' in *Population and Development*, Ronald G. Ridker (ed.) (Baltimore: The Johns Hopkins University Press).

Dixon, Ruth, 1978. *Rural Women at Work* (Baltimore: The Johns Hopkins University Press).

Driver, Edwin, D. 1963. *Differential Fertility in Central India* (Princeton: Princeton University Press).

Hull, Valerie J., 1977. 'Fertility, Women's work and Economic Class: A Case Study for Southeast Asia' in Stanley Kupinsky (ed.), *The Fertility of Working Women* (New York: Praeger).

Ibsen, Henrik, 1881. *Ghosts*.

————, 1879. *The Doll's House*.

Jacqueline, M.M.B., 1977. *Relationships between Fertility, Child Mortality and Nutrition in Africa*, Technical Papers (Paris: OECD).

Kane, P.V., 1974. *History of Dharma Sastra*, Vol. II, Part I, Bhandarkar Oriental Research Institute, Poona, Chapter, VII to IX.

Klein, Viola, 1949, *The Feminine Character* (New York: International Universities Press), p. 18.

Kupinsky, Stanley, 1977. *The Fertility of Working Women* (New York: Praeger) pp. 36–78.

Kurup, R.S., 1984. *Demographic Transition in Kerala* (mimeo).

Lechtig, Aaron; Hernan Delgado; Reynaldo Martorell; Douglas Richardson; Charles Yarbrough; Robert E. Klein (1978). Effect of Maternal Nutrition on Infant Mortality see Nutrition and Human Reproduction (ed.) by Mosley Henry W. Plenum Press. New York and London, pp. 147.

Mahadevan, K., 1989. *Population Dynamics in the Indian States* (Delhi: Mittal).

————, 1986. *Fertility and Mortality: Theory, Methodology and Empirical Issues* (New Delhi: Sage).

————, 1986. *Culture, Nutrition and Infant and Childhood Mortality* (Delhi: Mittal).

————, 1984a. *Decision-making and Diffusion in Family Planning* (Tirupati: S.V. University).

————, 1984b. *Strategies for Population Control: Essays in Applied Anthropology and Sociology* (Tirupati: S.V. University).

Mahadevan, K. and M. Sumangala 1987. *Social Development, Cultural Change and Fertility Decline: Study on Fertility Decline in Kerala*, New Delhi: Sage.

Mason, Karen, 1974. *Women's Labour Force Participation and Fertility*, Research Triangle Park, N.C. Research Triangle Institute.

Miller, Barbera, D., 1981. *The Endangered Sex: Neglect of Female Children in Rural North India* (Ithaca: Cornell University Press).

Mandelbaum, D., 1974. *Human Fertility in India* (Berkeley: University of California Press).

Nag, Moni, 1977. 'Economic Value of Children in two Peasant Societies,' *International Population Conference*, Mexico, 1977, Liege, IUSSP, Vol. I, pp. 123–39.

Nayar, P.K.B., 1984. Kerala Women in Historical and Contemporary Perspective, *Kerala Women*. Second National Conference on Women's Studies, Dept. of Sociology, University of Kerala.

Omran, A.R. et al. (ed.), 1976. *Family Formation Patterns and Health* (Geneva: WHO).

Oppong, Christine M., 1982. *A Synopsis of Seven Roles and Status of Women: An Outline of a Conceptual and Methodological Approach*. World Employment Programme working paper No. 94 (Geneva: ILO).

————, 1982. 'Family Structure and Women's Reproduction and Productive Roles: Some Conceptual and Methodological Issues' in Anker Richard et al. (ed.), *Women's Roles and Population Trends in the Third World*.

————, 1978. 'Modernization and Aspects of Family Change in Ghana: With Particular Reference to the Effects of Work,' paper presented at the Asian Institute, Iran Workshop, Gajenesh, Iran, 27 May to 2 June.

————, 1970. Conjugal Power and Resources: An Urban African Example, *Journal of Marriage and the Family*, Vol. 32, No. 4, pp. 676–80.

Pakrasi, Kanti, B. 1970. *Female Infanticide in India* (Calcutta: ISI).

Pakrasi, Kanti, B. (date not known). *The Genesis of Female Infanticide*, pp. 255–281.

Palloni, Albert, 1981. 'Mortality in Latin America: Emerging Patterns,' *Population and Development Review*, Vol. 7, No. 4, pp. 623–629.

Preston, S.H., 1978. 'Mortality, Morbidity and Development,' paper presented at a *Seminar on Population and Development in the ECWA Region* (mimeo).

————, 1975. *The Changing Relation between Mortality and Fertility Trends*, Public Health Reports, No. 831.

Radin, M., 1934. *On status in Encyclopaedia of Social Sciences*, E.R.A. Seligman (ed.) (New York: The Million Company) Vol. 14, p. 374.

Schultz, T.P., 1976. 'Inter-relationships between Mortality and Fertility' in *Population and Development*, Ronald G. Ridker (ed.) (Baltimore: Johns Hopkins University Press).

Smucker, C.M., G.B. Simmons, Bernsteins, B.D. Mishra, 1980. 'Neonatal Mortality in South Asia, The Special Role of Tetanus', *Population Studies*, Vol. 34, No. 2.

Safilios-Rothschild, Constantina, 1982. 'Female Power, Autonomy and Demographic Change in the Third World' in Anker Richard et al. (ed.), *Women's Roles and Population Trends in the Third World* (London: Croom Helm), pp. 117–130

Safilos-Rothschild, Constantina, 1977. 'The Relationship between Women's Work and Fertility: Some Methodology and Theoretical Issues' in Stanley Kupinsky (ed.) *The Fertility of Working Women* (New York: Praeger), pp. 355–367.

Shah, Nasra M. 1986. *Pakistani Women: A Socio-economic and Demographic Profile* (Honolulu: East-West Population Institute).

—————, 1981. 'Redefinition of Female Roles and Status in Pakistan: Issues and Suggestions,' paper contributed to Session F. 29, *Demographic Consequence of Change in the Roles of Women*, XIX, General Conference of the IUSSP, Manila, 9–16 December 1981. p. 3.

Shah, Makhdoom A., 1981. 'Role and Status of Women in Pakistan: Prescription and Reality' in Nasra M. Shah (ed.), *Pakistani Women: A Socio-economic and Demographic Profile* op. cit.

Shaw, Bernard, 1948. *The Intelligent Woman's Guide to Socialism, Capitalism, Sovietism and Fascism* (London: Constable).

Srinivas, M.N., 1978 *The Changing Position of Indian Women* (Delhi: Oxford University Press).

Srinivas, M.N., 1974. *Some Reflections on Dowry* (Delhi: Oxford University Press).

The New University Library. 1968. Vol. V, VI, XIII (London: Coxton), p. 155

Tuan, Chi-hsien, 1989. *Women in China To-day* (mimeo).

UN, 1984. *Report of the International Conference on Population*, Mexico City, New York, 6–14 August, 1984.

—————, 1961. *Mysore Population Study, Report of a Field Survey Carried out in Selected Areas of Mysore State, India*, (New York: United Nations).

Zachariah, K.C., 1983. *Anomaly of Fertility in Kerala* (New York: World Bank).

About the Contributors

Akbar Aghajanian is Professor of Sociology-Demography at Shiraz University, Iran. Prior to this, he was Visiting Scholar at the International Population Programme, Cornell University, USA. Prof. Aghajanian has to his credit several publications in reputed journals in the field.

Mohammed A. Al-Sharnoubi is Professor of Geography at the Kuwaiti University, Kuwait. His areas of interest include Population Geography, Labour and Women's Problems.

Hamid Arshat is Director-General, National Population and Family Development Board, Malaysia. Prior to this he was Professor, Universiti Kebangsaan, Malaysia, and is a Member, Royal College of Obstetricians and Gynaecologists, England. Professor Arshat is the editor of numerous publications serving medical professionals and is actively involved in programmes related to contraception and reproduction research.

N. Audinarayana is a Lecturer in the Department of Population Studies, Bharatiar University, Coimbatore, Tamil Nadu. His interests are Nuptiality, Fertility and Women's Problems.

Dominic E. Azuh is a Research Scholar at the Department of Population Studies, S.V. University, Tirupati. He is working on his doctoral thesis under the guidance of Prof. Mahadevan. He has specialized in Mortality and Women's Studies.

Chi-hsien Tuan is Research Associate at the East-West Population Institute, USA. Dr. Chi-hsien has a special interest in China's population and development, and worked in Beijing for several years before taking up his present post. He is the author of *Population Control in China: Theory and Applications*.

D. Radha Devi is currently Associate Professor at the International Institute for Population Studies, Bombay. She is an Economist interested in Labour and Women Studies.

Pranati Datta is a demographer working at the Population Research Centre of Indian Statistical Institute, Calcutta. Her interests relate to Demography and Women's Studies.

Asfia Duza is a Faculty Member in the Department of Sociology, University of Dacca, Bangladesh. Her major academic interests include Population and Women's Problems.

Sabita Guha is a Senior Officer in the Planning Commission of the Government of West Bengal. She is interested in Economic Planning and Development besides Population and Women's Studies.

R. Jayasree is a Demographer in the Human Reproduction Unit of the Jawaharlal Institute of Post-graduate Medical Education and Research (JIPMER), at Pondicherry. She is a Sociologist and has specialized in Fertility and Women Studies. She is also associated with the Social Obstetrics Programme of the same Institute.

Malini Karkal is currently Professor and Head of the Department of Public Health and Mortality Studies at the International Institute for Population Studies, Bombay. Her areas of interest are Public Health, Mortality and Women's Problems.

Lan-hung Nora Chiang is currently Professor of Geography and Co-ordinator of the Women's Research Program of the Population Studies Centre at the National University of Taiwan.

K. Mahadevan is Professor of Population Studies and Dean, Faculty of Arts, Sri Venkateswara University, Tirupati. In 1988, he received the Best University Teacher Award from the Government of Andhra Pradesh. Professor Mahadevan has to his credit several publications which include *Social Development, Cultural Change and Fertility Decline* (co-author), *Fertility and Mortality: Theory, Methodology and Empirical Issues* (edited) and *Fertility Policies of Asian Countries* (edited). Prof. K. Mahadevan has delivered lectures at several universities in India and abroad as Visiting Professor. Recently he was a Distinguished Visiting Professor at the University of Alberta, Canada.

G.S. Moni is on the faculty of Social and Preventive Medicine at JIPMER, Pondicherry. He is a Sociologist and Health Educator. He has specialized in health education, post-partum programme and mortality studies as well as the status of women.

P.K.B. Nayar is presently Professor and Head of the Department of Sociology and Women's Studies Centre at Kerala University. His areas of specialization and interest include Sociology of Development, Population and Women's Studies.

Suchart Prasith-rathsint is currently Professor of Sociology and Director, Research Centre, National Institute of Development Administration, Thailand. Dr. Prasith-rathsint has been a Consultant to several UN organizations and has to his credit numerous publications in the field of fertility, urbanization, development and methodology.

G. Radhamani is a Senior Faculty Member in the Department of English Literature and Fine Arts at S.V. University, Tirupati. She has specialized in Commonwealth Literature and particularly, 'Black Literature'.

P.J. Reddy is a Reader in the Department of Population Studies, S.V. University, Tirupati. He is a Psychologist and has specialized in Fertility and Population Psychology. He is also interested in Women's Studies.

Nasra M. Shah is currently a Consultant to the Ministry of Public Health in Kuwait. She has earlier worked in the East-West Population Institute, USA and the Pakistan Institute of Development Economics. A Sociologist, she is interested in Population and Women's Studies.

K.P. Singh is currently Director of the Population Research Centre and Head of the Department of Sociology, Panjab University, Chandigarh.

Masitah Mohd. Yatim is on the Faculty of the National Population and Family Development Board of Malaysia. He has specialized on Fertility, Family Planning and Women's Studies.